Health Communication
in the 21st Century

Health Communication in the 21st Century

Kevin Bradley Wright,
Lisa Sparks, and H. Dan O'Hair

WILEY-BLACKWELL

A John Wiley & Sons, Ltd., Publication

This second edition first published 2013
© 2013 John Wiley & Sons, Inc

Edition History: Blackwell Publishing Ltd (1e, 2008)

Wiley-Blackwell is an imprint of John Wiley & Sons, formed by the merger of Wiley's global Scientific, Technical and Medical business with Blackwell Publishing.

Registered Office
John Wiley & Sons Ltd, The Atrium, Southern Gate, Chichester, West Sussex, PO19 8SQ, UK

Editorial Offices
350 Main Street, Malden, MA 02148-5020, USA
9600 Garsington Road, Oxford, OX4 2DQ, UK
The Atrium, Southern Gate, Chichester, West Sussex, PO19 8SQ, UK

For details of our global editorial offices, for customer services, and for information about how to apply for permission to reuse the copyright material in this book please see our website at www.wiley.com/ wiley-blackwell.

The right of Kevin Bradley Wright, Lisa Sparks, and H. Dan O'Hair to be identified as the authors of this work has been asserted in accordance with the UK Copyright, Designs and Patents Act 1988.

Wiley also publishes its books in a variety of electronic formats. Some content that appears in print may not be available in electronic books.

Designations used by companies to distinguish their products are often claimed as trademarks. All brand names and product names used in this book are trade names, service marks, trademarks or registered trademarks of their respective owners. The publisher is not associated with any product or vendor mentioned in this book. This publication is designed to provide accurate and authoritative information in regard to the subject matter covered. It is sold on the understanding that the publisher is not engaged in rendering professional services. If professional advice or other expert assistance is required, the services of a competent professional should be sought.

Library of Congress Cataloging-in-Publication Data

Wright, Kevin B.
  Health communication in the 21st century / Kevin Bradley Wright, Lisa Sparks, and H. Dan O'Hair. – 2nd ed.
       p. ; cm.
  Health communication in the twenty-first century
  Includes bibliographical references and index.
  ISBN 978-0-470-67272-3 (pbk. : alk. paper)
  I. Sparks, Lisa. II. O'Hair, Dan. III. Title. IV. Title: Health communication in the twenty-first century.
  [DNLM: 1. Health Communication. 2. Communications Media. 3. Professional-Patient Relations. WA 590]
  610.69'6–dc23

2012037008

A catalogue record for this book is available from the British Library.

Cover image: Doctor with high-tech computer screen viewing patient data. © Luis Louro / Prisma.
Cover design by RBDA

Set in 10.5/12.5 pt Dante by Toppan Best-set Premedia Limited
Printed and bound in Malaysia by Vivar Printing Sdn Bhd

4   2014

Contents

Part I

Introduction

Chapter 1

Overview of Communication and Health

This second edition of *Health Communication in the 21st Century* provides an in-depth look at one of the fastest growing and pragmatic areas of research in the communication discipline: health communication. Most people would agree that our health and our ability to communicate are two central and very important aspects of human life. Yet, at some point in your study of communication, you may be asked the same thing that family members and friends frequently ask us: *What exactly is health communication?* Many people do not understand how the concept of health is related in any way to the term communication. For most people, the term *health* conjures up images that seem to have little or nothing to do with communication, including doctors, laboratory tests, waiting rooms, dieting, and exercise regimes. Moreover, the term *communication* is usually associated with things like interpersonal relationships, the Internet, and radio and television.

However, as we will see throughout this book, many different aspects of health and a variety of communication processes are intertwined in complex and interesting ways. We will examine many contexts of communication and communication-oriented topics, including communication and perceptions of health, provider–patient relationships, everyday relationships and physical health, communication networks within health organizations, intercultural communication and health beliefs, health risk messages, health campaign message design and dissemination, health information and images in the mass media, and the use of new communication technologies in healthcare. We hope that as you read this book you will be excited and intrigued by the rich perspective the study of health communication can bring to our everyday understanding of health and healthcare.

Arguments for the Need to Study Health Communication

Despite vast improvements in public health and healthcare in the US and worldwide over the last century, we still have a long way to go in terms of making our society

Health Communication in the 21st Century, Second Edition. Kevin Bradley Wright, Lisa Sparks, and H. Dan O'Hair.

and the world a healthier place. Within the US, we currently spend over one trillion dollars a year on healthcare services, making it the leading sector of the US economy (US Census Bureau, 2005). However, a wide variety of problems still exist in terms of our nation's ability to provide adequate care for everyone and in terms of maximizing efforts to prevent and control diseases and other health problems. It appears that the severity of many of these problems could potentially be reduced by improving communication among providers, between providers and patients, between health researchers, and between public health leaders and the public.

One-half of all deaths in the US can be attributed to preventable behavioral and social factors, such as unhealthy diets, smoking, alcohol use, and inadequate exercise (Neuhauser & Kreps, 2003). Over 60 percent of Americans are overweight and only 24 percent engage in moderate physical exercise on a regular basis (Neuhauser & Kreps, 2003). Current disease screening is inadequate. Cancer mortality rates alone could be reduced by 60 percent if people were to follow early detection recommendations (Willett, Colditz, & Mueller, 1996). Cancer is still one of the most significant health challenges facing society, and the second leading cause of death in the US (American Cancer Society, 2006). A lack of health maintenance behaviors among people who are currently living with a disease has been found to be significantly related to mortality rate. For example, one study found that only 30 percent of hypertensive men act to control their high blood pressure (US Department of Health and Human Services (USDHHS), 1999). In addition, there have been relatively few studies of how to improve the quality of life among people living with disease, such as cancer and HIV survivors, especially the ways in which communication processes and practices may help people to cope with living with disease (Kreps, 2003a).

In terms of health promotion, a large portion of health campaigns have not led to substantial health behavior change among members of the US population (Snyder & Hamilton, 2002). For example, health campaign designers spent millions of dollars on California's 5-a-day campaign, which was designed to raise people's awareness of the benefits of eating more fruits and vegetables. While the campaign was successful at raising people's awareness of the issue, researchers found that relatively few people actually increased their consumption of fruits and vegetables following the campaign (Foerster & Hudes, 1994).

Worldwide, we see a number of health issues that are directly and indirectly related to communication. Global issues such as lack of access to adequate healthcare, war, poverty, hunger, environmental injustice, and lack of education about health issues continue to pose problems for people around the world. Unfortunately, many of these issues have had the greatest impact in underdeveloped countries and among the underserved populations. In Africa, for example, over nearly 25 million people are living with HIV/AIDS, and over 6 million are living in Asian countries (Joint United Nations Program on HIV/AIDS, 2004). More recent issues, such as avian flu and terrorism, present health communication researchers with numerous challenges in terms of finding ways to best communicate information about health risks and in terms of coordinating efforts to cope with these types of crises after they occur.

Health communication researchers are currently working to better understand these issues so that they can offer suggestions for improvement. While communication issues may not account for all of the problems mentioned above, it is clear that communication is an important underlying factor for most of them. A better understanding of how communication is related to these and other health problems may ultimately help to reduce incidents of disease, human suffering, and mortality rates while increasing physical and psychological well-being and satisfaction with healthcare among members of society. The chapters in this book examine multiple ways in which a better understanding of health communication in a variety of contexts, including relationships, organizations, and the mass media, can improve health outcomes.

Defining Health Communication

Despite the fact that we all have ideas about what it means to be healthy or ill, the term health is a complicated concept to define, due to multiple interpretations based on individual experience and culture. The World Health Organization (WHO) defines health as a "state of complete physical, mental and social well-being" (cited in Costello, 1977, p. 558). Moreover, the WHO definition conceptualizes health and disease as dynamic processes as opposed to stable entities. In other words, both health and disease are seen as being in a constant state of change. This definition also recognizes that health goes beyond physical and psychological health to include aspects such as a person's quality of life. As we will see in this book, a variety of communication problems can occur in healthcare settings due to different conceptions of health and disease.

Defining communication presents similar challenges. Most definitions of communication view it as a process that involves a sender, a receiver, a message, and a channel. However, a variety of issues, such as the ability of multiple messages to be communicated simultaneously through both verbal and nonverbal channels, the transactional nature of communication (when sender and receiver mutually influence one another), physical and psychological noise in the channel, channel limitations on multiple senders and receivers, and many other facets of the communication process, make it difficult to define.

If you are a communication major, then you may have noticed that communication courses typically focus on one context of communication (e.g. interpersonal or mass communication). Health communication research encompasses many different contexts of communication. For example, researchers who study health communication from an intrapersonal communication perspective tend to focus on people's attitudes, beliefs, values, and feelings about health-related concepts and messages. Interpersonal health communication scholars tend to focus on relationships, such as those between providers and patients, or they study how everyday relationships (i.e. family members, co-workers, and friends) impact our health.

Other health communication scholars examine health from an organizational standpoint, and they tend to focus on features of the health organizations such as hierarchies, information flow in organizations, and employee–management relationships. Intercultural health communication scholars tend to focus on the unique role that culture plays in terms of how people understand health and illness as well as how intercultural differences affect healthcare relationships. A large number of health communication scholars focus on social influence and they devote their efforts to understanding how health messages and campaigns can be improved in terms of leading to health behavior changes for large groups of people. Many health communication researchers are interested in the role of the mass media in helping to shape our understanding of specific health-related issues and our more general conceptions of health and illness. Finally, a growing number of health communication researchers are interested in the role that new technologies play in disseminating health information, facilitating relationships among people who share similar health conditions, and improving communication between providers and patients and within health organizations.

A Brief History of Health Communication Research

Although the term health communication has only been around since the mid-1970s (Atkin & Marshall, 1996; Rogers, 1996), communication scholars have taken a scientific approach to studying communication within health contexts for decades. Prior to the formation of the communication discipline in the 20th century, the US has had a rich history of communication campaigns addressing a variety of health issues, such as alcohol abuse, smallpox, improper handling and storage of food, and inadequate healthcare for underserved populations (Paisley, 2001). According to Thompson, Robinson, Anderson, and Federowicz (2005), research in the area of health communication has grown exponentially over the last 30 years. This growth has not only occurred in the US, but can also be seen in the work of scholars from around the world, including researchers from the eastern European/Scandinavian countries, Australia/New Zealand, Asia, and the UK. Organizations such as the European Association for Communication and Healthcare now publish the journal *Patient Education and Counseling*, and it sponsors a conference every two years that attracts interdisciplinary health communication researchers from all over the world.

Scholars in the social sciences who were interested in the study of communication began to examine the healthcare system in the late 1960s, which encouraged communication scholars to follow. Korsch and Negrete's (1972) "Doctor–Patient Communication," published in *Scientific American*, is still regarded as a foundation of the field (Thompson *et al.*, 2005). Much other work came from medical researchers, influencing the study of provider–patient interactions in particular. In 1972 a group of scholars with backgrounds in communication formed the Therapeutic Communication interest group of the International Communication Association (ICA), which was renamed the Health Communication Division in 1975 (Thompson *et al.*, 2005).

The formation of this area provided the earliest forum for the presentation of research on health communication. When ICA began publishing annual reviews in *Communication Yearbook*, there were many chapters on health communication that began defining and showcasing the field. The Commission on Health Communication of the Speech Communication Association (later renamed the National Communication Association) was formed in 1985, further indicating the growth of work in this area. These developments were followed by numerous conferences and mini-conferences focusing on health communication, including those held at the University of Kentucky.

This widespread interest in health communication led to the creation of two important publication outlets for health communication researchers. The first issue of the journal *Health Communication* appeared in early 1989. This was followed in 1996 by the *Journal of Health Communication*. These publications played an instrumental role in helping to spur the growth of health communication as an area by disseminating health communication research to a wider audience within and outside of the communication discipline.

At the same time that these developments were taking place, important curricular growth was being observed in health communication courses at universities around the world. Many universities now offer programs focusing primarily on health communication and others have strengthened and expanded their health communication offerings. Funding opportunities have increased. Health communication scholars have moved into important policy and administrative positions within the Centers for Disease Control, the National Cancer Institute, and the National Institute for Drug Abuse.

The area of health communication is now widely recognized as vibrant, theoretically driven, pragmatic, and a key contributor in shaping national health policies (Kreps, 2003b). The research in health communication has always focused on real-world, significant problems, not "ivory tower" concerns that are sometimes seen in academia, and this is still the case today. According to Atkin and Marshall (1996):

> This specialization has grown rapidly in response to growing pragmatic policy interests, particularly in the public health agencies of the federal government and among private sector healthcare providers. Pressing needs to address alarming problems such as smoking, substance abuse, poor nutritional habits, and AIDS have given a strong impetus (and expanded funding) to the systematic study of communication processes and effects. (p. 479)

The many opportunities for researchers to address real-world health concerns make health communication an exciting area to study. Health communication scholars have had a rich history of conducting research outside of the academic setting. In fact, many of the health communication research studies you will read about in this book were interventions designed to improve physical and mental health outcomes in a number of contexts, such as health campaigns, provider–patient relationships, organizations, and the use of new technologies in healthcare.

The area of health communication continues to grow and diversify. New areas of research have expanded health communication into health domains that many people in the communication discipline probably did not consider 30 years ago, such as hospice and palliative care, spirituality and health, on-line support groups, and telemedicine. However, a number of health communication topics have remained as prominent themes in the health communication literature over the past 30 years. According to Thompson *et al.* (2005), in an analysis of the topics that appeared in the journal *Health Communication* between 1989 and 2003, over 20 percent of the articles have dealt with provider–patient interaction, followed by health campaigns (13.4%), risk communication (11.8%), health and aging (8.4%), language and health (7%), media (5.9%), and social support and health (4.3%).

Many of the prominent theories that are still used in the area of health communication have their origins in communication, social psychology, and anthropology (Atkin & Marshall, 1996). This reflects the ways in which theory has developed in the various contexts of health communication research. For example, several theories of provider–patient interaction have their roots in interpersonal communication research, a number of the theories used to understand intercultural health issues have their origins in anthropology, and many of the theories of social influence that are associated with health campaigns have been borrowed from social psychology. As we will see, communication scholars are continuing to refine these earlier theories as well as developing new health communication theories.

Current Challenges to the Healthcare System and the Role of Health Communication Research

There are a number of other current issues that may challenge the US healthcare system in the future. This section presents a brief overview of some of the most prominent issues affecting healthcare within the US, and some of the ways in which health communication research can make a difference.

Aging population

The next several decades will witness a substantial increase in older adults within the US. As we will see, while age by itself is not necessarily predictive of illness, health problems do tend to occur more frequently as we age. Unfortunately, our healthcare system still suffers from a number of communication-related problems when it comes to providing care to older patients. In terms of physician training, geriatrics is still a subspeciality of family medicine, and other issues, such as negative stereotypes of older patients, misunderstandings about the aging process, and health insurance needs of older people, will likely present numerous challenges to the healthcare system. There is a substantial need for health communication researchers to gain a better understanding of health issues associated with our aging population and for the development of interventions that can make a positive impact on this situation.

Cultural diversity and healthcare

Cultural diversity will continue to have a major influence on our healthcare system as people from cultures that have very different perceptions of illness, health, and healthcare immigrate to the US. As we will see, some cultural belief systems regarding health can be at odds with more mainstream conceptions of health, causing problems for both patients and providers. In addition, within the US, there are many different co-cultures based on ethnicity, region, and socioeconomic status. Culture is often related to health disparities, access to healthcare services, and health literacy, which puts many groups within the US at greater risk for health problems. Health communication scholars are attempting to gain a better understanding of how intercultural differences impact health and healthcare. In addition, many health communication scholars are researching ways that health communication problems based on intercultural differences can be improved as well as ways in which health disparities can be reduced.

Tension between traditional and new approaches to healthcare

Healthcare providers have followed a number of traditional approaches to healthcare that have been challenged in recent years, and the tension between advocates of these approaches and people who favor new ways of thinking about healthcare will likely continue in the future. For example, physicians and other healthcare providers have traditionally been trained to follow the *biomedical model of medicine* (Schreiber, 2005; Tyreman, 2006). This is an evidence-based (and largely physical health-oriented) approach to medicine that relies on scientific methods and procedures for verifying disease, such as laboratory tests (Tyreman, 2006). While the strength of this approach lies in its ability to accurately pinpoint causes of symptoms (which also aids in selecting the appropriate treatment), it is not without its limitations. By focusing primarily on physical causes of illness, the biomedical approach does not always take into account *psychosocial* aspects of illness, such as cultural norms, coping abilities, and life events that may interact with physical health problems. Allegiance to this approach may result in a number of problems, including failure to recognize how features of a patient's day-to-day world (such as cultural beliefs, support networks, and financial status) may lead to their inability to comply with recommended treatments. In addition, conditions that do not necessarily have a clear biological cause (e.g. chronic fatigue syndrome) may be dismissed by providers who follow this approach.

Other traditional approaches to healthcare include a *curative* approach to fighting disease. While most people would agree that using available medications and procedures that can save a person from suffering or death are beneficial, the nature of illness makes this a more complicated issue. With many diseases, such as cancer, chemotherapy and other curative treatments may only temporarily fight the disease. Moreover, these approaches have negative implications for a patient's quality of life (e.g. sickness from chemotherapy, loss of hair from radiation treatment, time spent in the hospital while recovering from surgery). In many cases, a person who does not have long to live due to a terminal illness may spend his or her days in the hospital, sick, embarrassed, or in pain rather than spending quality time with family and friends. As a result, in recent years, we have seen a greater interest in homeopathic and other alternative treatments to fighting disease that have fewer side effects than traditional medications. In addition, there has been a rising interest in *palliative care*, or an approach to medicine that emphasizes reducing pain and suffering among terminally ill patients as opposed to prolonging life at the expense of sickness, pain, embarrassment, and time away from loved ones. As you can imagine, there are many differences of opinion on what is best for the patient when dealing with these issues, and these debates are likely to continue in the future. Health communication researchers will continue to play an important role in examining how people often view illness and treatment differently, in providing evidence for the benefits of alternative approaches to medicine, and as advocates for alternative ways of understanding illness and treatment.

Funding for health research

Since September 11, 2001 and the continued threat of terrorist attacks, funding for a variety of healthcare initiatives has been reallocated to the War on Terror. While curtailing terrorist threats is certainly related to our physical and psychological health, the costs of fighting terrorism are substantial. As a result, money that was once allocated to government agencies such as the Department of Health and Human Services, which provides money for research to such organizations as the National Institutes of Health and the Centers for Disease Control and Prevention, has been diverted to the Department of Homeland Security. This funding is important in order to gain a better understanding of health problems and develop healthcare interventions for important underserved populations within the US. The threat of terrorism will likely continue to impact funding for healthcare research in the future. Health communication scholars play an important role as advocates for health research funding and in providing scientific evidence for the key role of communication in improving health outcomes. Such efforts are needed to insure that government funding of research in this area continues.

Changes to health insurance and managed care

The rising cost of health insurance and health services will likely continue to have a substantial impact on consumers in the coming years. Healthcare organizations are always trying to find innovative ways to reduce the cost of healthcare services (which ultimately influences the cost of healthcare insurance). Health communication researchers have discovered that many costly problems, such as high provider turnover rates, are often related to communication problems. As a result, health communication researchers have developed interventions designed to ameliorate these problems and reduce costs that are ultimately passed along to consumers. However, much more research is needed to discover how communication interventions can be used to make healthcare organizations more efficient, helpful, and satisfying for patients.

The impact of new technologies on healthcare

In recent years, the widespread adoption of computers, new software programs, the Internet, and other new technologies (e.g. cellular technology, global satellite positioning chips) has led to a variety of changes in communication within the healthcare system, the ways in which people obtain health information, and the ways in which they communicate about health in daily life. Communication technologies will likely continue to develop and significantly impact the ways in which we communicate about health. At no other time has health information been more accessible to people due to the advent of the Internet. However, not all people have access to this technology, the skills to use it, or the ability to interpret the available health information. The Internet has also become an important channel for providers to communicate with other providers, as a source of social support for patients, and as a means for health campaign designers to reach large numbers of individuals with unique health-oriented messages due to the features of this new medium (e.g. interactivity, multimedia, and the ability to use the computer to tailor health messages). Health communication researchers will continue to play a crucial role in examining the benefits and limitations of these technologies.

Overview of the Book

This second edition of the book provides expanded coverage of issues in all of the chapters based on recent developments in the growing body of health communication research. In addition to this expanded coverage, we also added an additional chapter (Chapter 12) on political issues and health communication. The following section provides a description of each chapter and it highlights new areas of research that we cover in this edition.

Chapter 2 examines key issues and theories related to provider–patient interaction, including patient information and affective needs, communication skills training for providers, patient/provider differences in perspective of health, barriers to effective provider–patient communication, communication issues related to medical malpractice and dissatisfaction, and privacy issues in provider–patient communication.

Chapter 3 explores a number of communication issues and theories related to caregiving, including communication needs of patients and caregivers, hospice and palliative care, and communication issues related to end-of-life decision-making, death, and dying.

Chapter 4 provides an in-depth look at social support theories and processes as they relate to health. It examines dilemmas of social support and the relationship between support and health outcomes, and it takes an in-depth look at research on support groups for people coping with various types of health issues.

Chapter 5 examines cultural differences in beliefs about health and healthcare and different cultural healthcare practices within the USA, integrating intercultural communication theories and intergroup theories. The chapter also examines topics such as homeopathic approaches to healthcare and spirituality and health.

Chapter 6 explores health organizations from the standpoint of organizational communication theory. The chapter focuses on issues such as the flow of information in organizations, the history and influence of managed care, the interrelationships of multiple organizations in the allied health professions, and current issues facing healthcare organizations.

Chapter 7 looks at the growth and application of new communication technologies in healthcare settings. It examines a variety of topics, such as telemedicine, provider and patient use of the Internet for health information, electronic records, computer-mediated support groups, and the use of new technologies to tailor and disseminate health campaign messages.

Chapter 8 focuses on the role of the mass media in influencing our health beliefs, attitudes, and behaviors. It discusses theories about the influence and uses of mass media. It explores topics such as the relationship between mass media messages and lifestyle choices, the mass media and health policy, and direct-to-consumer advertising.

Chapter 9 provides an introduction to theory/research in the area of risk communication. In addition, the chapter discusses current issues such as responding to terrorism and natural disasters, and various approaches to campaigns designed to target at-risk populations.

Chapter 10 examines health communication campaigns. It introduces a number of social influence theories related to the design and implementation of health campaigns. In addition, it focuses on mediated and interpersonal approaches to health campaigns, message design issues, and campaign evaluation.

Chapter 11 looks at theories of teamwork and group communication as they relate to healthcare teams. In addition, it focuses on interdisciplinary healthcare teams, leadership, and problems that can occur in healthcare group decision-making.

Chapter 12 examines the growing area of political issues and health communication. It provides an overview of recent health-related issues that have appeared in the political arena, including the healthcare reform debate, stem cell research, right to life issues, factory farming and nutrition, medical marijuana, and a host of other issues. Specifically, the chapter explores the role of media in political discussions and focuses on framing theory. In addition, it examines health disparities and access to healthcare issues, health-related stigma and discrimination, and the politics of global health problems.

Chapter 13 highlights a number of promising areas of health communication research that will likely be research trends in the future. Specifically, it focuses on a variety of topics, such as media convergence and self-care, mental health issues, emerging trends in intercultural health communication, research, and developments in risk/crisis communication research. Moreover, the chapter will briefly discuss some of the limitations to current health communication research.

Summary

Health communication is a vibrant and growing area of the communication discipline. In addition, researchers from other disciplines, such as medicine, public health, psychology, and business, are making significant contributions to our knowledge of this area. While health communication has been a defined area of academic research for only about 30 years, the US has had a rich history of addressing public health issues. However, statistics dealing with disease incident rates, patient dissatisfaction with healthcare, and the failure of many health campaigns to significantly impact health outcomes point to the need for health communication research in the future. People who are interested in a variety of contexts of communication are attracted to the area of health communication, particularly because of the ability to address significant real-world problems. Despite advances in health communication over the last three decades, there are a number of current issues that will likely pose problems for the healthcare system in the future. Health communication researchers are in a unique position to find ways to confront these issues and ultimately make improvements to the healthcare system and health outcomes.

References

American Cancer Society (2006). *Cancer statistics*. Retrieved January 23, 2006, from www.cancer.org.

Atkin, C., & Marshall, A. (1996). Health communication. In M. B. Salwen & D. W. Stacks (Eds), *An integrated approach to communication theory and research* (pp. 93–110). Mahwah, NJ: Lawrence Erlbaum.

Costello, D. E. (1977). Health communication theory and research: An overview. In B. D. Ruben (Ed.), *Communication yearbook I* (pp. 557–568). New Brunswick, NJ: Transaction Books.

Foerster, S. B., & Hudes, M. (1994). *California dietary practices survey: Focus on fruits and vegetables, trends among adults, 1989–1993, topline report*. Sacramento, CA: California Department of Health Services and California Public Health Foundation.

Joint United Nations Program on HIV/AIDS. (July, 2004). 2004 report on the global AIDS epidemic. Retrieved August 28, 2004, from www.unaids.org/.

Korsch, B., & Negrete, F. (1972). Doctor–patient communication. *Scientific American, 227*, 66–74.

Kreps, G. L. (2003a). The impact of communication on cancer risk, incidence, morbidity, mortality, and quality of life. *Health Communication, 15*, 161–169.

Kreps, G. L. (2003b). Opportunities for health communication scholarship to shape public health policy and practice: Examples from the National Cancer Institute. In T. L. Thompson, A. M. Dorsey, K. I. Miller, & R. Parrott (Eds), *Handbook of health communication* (pp. 609–624). Mahwah, NJ: Lawrence Erlbaum.

Neuhauser, L., & Kreps, G. L. (2003). Rethinking communication in the e-health era. *Journal of Health Psychology, 8*, 7–23.

Paisley, W. J. (2001). Public communication campaigns: The American experience. In R. E. Rice & C. K. Atkin (Eds), *Public communication campaigns* (3rd ed., pp. 3–21). Thousand Oaks, CA: Sage.

Rogers, E. M. (1996). The field of health communication today: An up-to-date report. *Journal of Health Communication, 1*, 15–23.

Schreiber, L. (2005). The importance of precision in language: Communication research and (so-called) alternative medicine. *Health Communication, 17*, 173–190.

Snyder, L. B., & Hamilton, M. A. (2002). A meta-analysis of US health campaign effects on behavior: Emphasize enforcement, exposure, and new information, and beware the secular trend. In R. C. Hornik (Ed.), *Public health communication: Evidence for behavior change* (pp. 357–383). Mahwah, NJ: Lawrence Erlbaum.

Thompson, T. L., Robinson, J. D., Anderson, D. J., & Federowicz, M. (2005). Where have we been and where can we go? In K. B. Wright & S. C. Moore (Eds), *Applied health communication: A sourcebook*. Cresskill, NJ: Hampton Press.

Tyreman, S. (2006). Causes of illness in clinical practice: A conceptual exploration. *Medicine, Health Care and Philosophy, 9*, 285–291.

US Census Bureau. (2005). Healthcare and social assistance industry data. Retrieved July 23, 2012, from www.census.gov/econ/www/servmenu.html.

US Department of Health and Human Services (USDHHS) (1999). *Health people 2000, progress review: Heart disease and stroke*. Bethesda, MD: Department of Health and Human Services.

Willett, W., Colditz, G., & Mueller, N. (1996). Strategies for minimizing cancer risk. *Scientific American, 275*, 325–333.

Part II

Interpersonal Perspectives

Chapter 2

Provider–Patient Communication

Chances are you have had an experience similar to the following when visiting the doctor. You arrive 30 minutes early for your appointment for a persistent cough, and fatigue, and find that you have to wait 30 minutes in the waiting area for a nurse to bring you into an examination room where you have to wait another 10 minutes for the doctor to arrive. Finally, the doctor arrives, briefly listens to your lungs, and asks you only a few questions before calling in the nurse to give you a prescription for some antibiotics. You might feel that the doctor did not spend as much time as you would have liked him or her to spend with you, or perhaps you had questions about whether or not you were contagious, questions about the prescription, or how long your symptoms might last. Maybe you did not get the opportunity to voice your concerns about how frequently you have been sick lately, or you never got an opportunity to ask the doctor for a note for your boss verifying that you are sick. You may have left the doctor's office feeling unsatisfied with the visit because you were still uncertain about what caused you to be sick, what to expect in terms of getting better, or because he or she did not meet your other needs. Research indicates that communication interventions to improve quality of care should target both providers and patient communicative behaviors (see e.g. Epstein *et al.*, 2007; Sparks, 2007, 2008; Sparks & Villagran, 2010). Research reveals physicians who are more patient-centered are perceived as better communicators, resulting in more satisfied and compliant patients (Street, Gordon, & Haidet, 2007).

The reality for most doctors and patients is that the fear, dread, and terror that can accompany certain diagnoses (such as cancer or HIV) require a greater emphasis on communication processes to combat the uncertainty and negativity greatly affecting an individual's cognitive and emotional capacity in ways never before experienced (Sparks & Villagran, 2010). Open, honest, communication between providers and patients can be a valuable weapon against the assault on self-identity that often accompanies a negative diagnosis. Communication becomes more important as cognitive, affective, and

Health Communication in the 21st Century, Second Edition. Kevin Bradley Wright, Lisa Sparks, and H. Dan O'Hair.
© 2013 John Wiley & Sons, Inc. Published 2013 by John Wiley & Sons, Inc.

behavioral responses to illness intersect with biological problems that patients must face and overcome (Villagran & Sparks, 2010). Negative experiences such as these that you may have had with your doctor or other healthcare providers are often due to a variety of communication problems that commonly occur within healthcare settings. While it might be easy to blame providers in these cases, it is important to remember that communication problems are rarely one-sided, and there may have been a variety of reasons for them. Communication between providers and patients can potentially lead to successful health outcomes and improved quality of life, or it can create major problems for both providers and patients depending upon how it is handled. Many patients feel that their doctors do not listen to them, they are controlling, or they are not sensitive to many of their concerns. However, people often do not recognize that they play an important role as patients in the provider–patient relationship, and the way they communicate with their physician and other providers is important in terms of receiving the care they need in a satisfying manner. Providers also want their patients to be satisfied with the care they receive. Health communication does not just influence whether or not we are satisfied with our healthcare providers. Scholars within the fields of medicine, nursing, and communication have extensively studied provider–patient communication over the last few decades, and they have found that how providers and patients communicate in healthcare settings can potentially impact physical and psychological health outcomes, and problems such as medical errors and malpractice suits.

This chapter explores many aspects of provider–patient relationships. Specifically, it examines how providers and patients often differ in their perceptions of healthcare and healthcare needs, characteristics of communication between provider and patient, and successful and unsuccessful outcomes of provider–patient interaction.

Provider and Patient Views of Health and Healthcare

Providers and patients often have very different views about health and healthcare. The perspectives of providers are heavily influenced by the specialized training and education they receive in their training and through their day-to-day work in healthcare settings. Most patients typically do not have specialized training in healthcare or related subjects such as biology and anatomy. Instead, everyday people learn about health and the healthcare system largely through the media, interpersonal channels, and their own subjective everyday experiences of health (Cline, 2011). The following sections explore the different perspectives providers and patients have of health and the healthcare system, and how these perceptions can influence provider–patient communication as well as health and quality of life outcomes.

Provider Perspective

Provider training

In many ways, providers learn about many aspects of health in ways that are similar to patients (at least prior to their training). For example, providers learn about a variety of health issues and lifestyle behaviors that affect health from the media, in the same way that patients do. In addition, providers have typically been patients themselves at some point in their lives. Yet, the specialized training most providers receive socializes them in ways that can lead to a much different perspective of health and healthcare than the average patient. The amount, length, and complexity of training, of course, depend upon the type of provider we are talking about. Physicians, physician assistants, nurses, and technicians differ from each other in their education and training, but all of these providers share some commonalities in terms of their socialization into medical and health occupations.

Being a medical doctor is one of the most difficult professions an individual can prepare for in terms of education and skills training, and this is one of the reasons why physicians have such a high status among healthcare professionals. Most physicians begin their college education as pre-medicine majors, and they take an extensive amount of coursework in the physical and biological sciences. Similar to other standardized tests, potential medical students have to take the Medical College Admission Test (MCAT) exam and obtain a high enough score to get into a medical school. Medical school is an arduous process for most medical students, who in addition to hundreds of hours of study and clinical training have to cope with rites of passage such as hazing and often intense criticism from medical faculty and peers.

Medical school is also a socialization process where physicians learn formal medical terminology and informal jargon. In addition, medical students often earn a privileged status due partially to the power and status that society attributes to physicians and the reinforcement of these perceptions during day-to-day activities in medical school (du Pré, 2004), such as when medical students interact with patients and lower-status providers (e.g. technicians) during clinical rounds. While many medical schools now teach students about the importance of communication in healthcare settings, and there are classes that emphasize communication skills, the majority of physician training is focused on aspects of physical health and the development of clinical skills. Following medical school (which typically requires four years of study), most states require an internship period followed by a residency period (time varies depending upon state licensure requirements and specialty) prior to obtaining a license to practice medicine.

Physicians, of course, are among many healthcare professionals who comprise the provider segment of the healthcare system. Physician assistants, nurse practitioners, technicians, pharmacists, occupational therapists, and dieticians are some of the many types of providers that are typically seen in most hospitals and clinics. Like physicians, these occupations vary in terms of amount of education, training, and status. In terms of communication, these providers often interact with patients as frequently (or more often than) physicians and are important contributors to successful patient outcomes.

Other health fields, such as dentistry, also have similar diversity and status differences among providers. Dental school can be similar to medical school in terms of education, training, and stress. Dentists parallel medical doctors in the world of dentistry as regards professional status. Other dental occupations, such as dental hygienists and dental assistants, vary as to level of education and training. In most states, a Bachelor of Science degree is needed to become a dental hygienist whereas only a two-year degree or certificate is required to be a dental assistant. Health organizations also typically have a number of staff positions, such as receptionists, office managers, and individuals who handle insurance claims. While the focus of this chapter is primarily on physician–patient communication, it is important to recognize that patients interact with many other providers when seeking healthcare, and a number of the provider–patient communication issues that are examined in this chapter can be applied to other providers as well. However, given the education and social status of physicians, and their important role in medical decision-making when diagnosing and treating health problems, it is not surprising that most communication research has focused on physician–patient interactions.

Provider communication skills training

As you probably have already observed, healthcare providers spend a great deal of their time communicating with patients. However, it may surprise you to know that until relatively recently most providers have received relatively little training about how to effectively communicate with patients. Over the last several decades, researchers have found that communication skills training may improve provider–patient communication, and effective provider communication skills have been linked to positive health outcomes for patients, such as improved compliance, satisfaction with care, and benefits to physical and psychological health (Aspden, Wolcott, Bootman, & Cronewett, 2007; Kaplan, Greenfield, & Ware, 1989; Stewart, 1995). Perhaps the most emotionally difficult communication providers must master is breaking bad news in an empathetic and comforting manner (Sparks, Villagran, Parker-Raley, & Cunningham, 2007; Sparks & Villagran, 2010). Patients create opportunities for providers to express empathy during medical interactions, even when the patient is relatively unfamiliar with the physician, but physicians most often deal with the opportunity by acknowledging the situation without really sharing their own experiences or feelings (Bylund & MaKoul, 2005). Direct communication of the basic bad news message focuses on the topic itself, as opposed to the social or emotional implications of the message for the patient or provider (Sparks *et al.*, 2007). Empathic communication can bolster patients' views of a provider's communication competence, and most often expresses understanding for the patient's feelings, without actually sharing the patient's emotions (Hemmerdinger, Stoddard, & Lilford, 2007). Beach *et al.* (2004) found that physicians rarely self-disclose anything about themselves in medical encounters, and disclosure of personal feelings is rare. Providers most often use a direct style of delivering bad news.

Most likely because of the rigorous training dealing with physical aspects of health in medical schools, nursing schools, and other health-related occupational training, communication skills training is a relatively underdeveloped part of the medical/ healthcare curriculum at most universities and colleges in the US. While efforts by medical school and health science faculties in recent years have succeeded in adding more content dealing with psychosocial concerns in medical and health-related courses (including communication issues), communication skills training is still typically only a small part of medical and health education. However, the growing evidence from research that suggests communication skills, such as the ability to competently break bad news to patients (Eggly & Tzelepis, 2001; Wakefield, Cooke, & Boggis, 2003), have important health implications for patients has gained the attention of influential organizations such as the American Medical Association (AMA) (Association of American Medical Colleges, 1999). The AMA requires all medical schools to test medical students on their knowledge of communication skills as part of the medical licensing process (van Zanten, Boulet, & McKinley, 2007).

Despite the belief among professional medical organizations, such as the AMA, that communication skills are an important part of quality healthcare, people studying to be healthcare providers often have negative attitudes toward communication skills training (Batenburg & Smal, 1997; Rees, Sheard, & McPherson, 2002) and toward taking communication skills training courses. Medical students often feel that these courses are basically common sense or too easy, or they feel that they already have sufficient communication skills for practicing medicine. Compared to courses in medicine, biology, and other physical sciences, some medical students and other future providers often view communication as a "soft science," or as having less scientific rigor and/or practical value, and this can lead to the perception that communication skills are relatively unimportant, mainly because they may have not had much exposure to the sophisticated research conducted by health communication scholars. For example, for most of these students, few have had training in communication outside of an undergraduate public speaking class. Yet, communication skills are not "soft" when you stop to consider the enormous impact of costly medical errors that are often related to misunderstandings resulting from communication problems (Cohen, 2007; Valente, Antlitz, Boyd, & Troisi, 1988). For example, medical error costs have been estimated at US$887 million (Aspden *et al.*, 2007) and they frequently lead to increased patient suffering and death (Gandhi *et al.*, 2003). Given the number of communication problems that can potentially occur between provider and patients and these and other negative health outcomes related to communication, it appears that physicians and other providers would benefit from communication skills training.

When communication skills are taught in medical education, "many courses do not introduce teaching of communication skills until midway into the medical curriculum, to coincide with the traditional starting point of the clinical component of training" (Humphris & Kaney, 2001, p. 225), and communication skills training has been found to be inconsistent within the curriculum of other providers, such as pharmacology students (Noland & Rickles, 2009). Third- and fourth-year medical student training is much more focused on actual clinical work than the training of first- and second-year students, who primarily deal with classroom lectures about communication or simulated training with standardized patients (people who pretend to be patients). It appears that actual experience with patients is important for learning and practicing medical communication skills. Kaufman, Laidlaw, and Macleod (2000) found that medical students who had performed basic communication skills with patients in a clinical setting had more confidence in their ability to communicate with patients than medical students who lacked this experience. Female medical students also tend to have more positive attitudes toward communication skills learning than male students, and researchers have found that male medical students are slower at learning communication skills than females (Marteau *et al.*, 1991; Wright *et al.*, 2006).

Challenges providers face in healthcare delivery

Rising costs of healthcare and competition Americans spend over $1 trillion on healthcare each year, and this figure is projected to increase substantially over the next decade (US Census Bureau, 2005). Given these costs, providers face a number of challenges in communicating with patients and providing quality care in today's healthcare system. The pressure from health organizations to provide services to a large number of patients while simultaneously cutting costs in order to remain financially viable has influenced provider behaviors in many ways. Increased competition in terms of the number of hospitals and health facilities providing healthcare in most US markets has given consumers many different choices of where to obtain healthcare, and health organizations have become increasingly concerned about losing market share to competitors. In many urban areas, specialized health organizations such as cancer centers, acute care service facilities, and women's health centers are competitors to larger hospitals. While these specialized services give consumers more choices in terms of obtaining services, the increased competition from their presence has augmented economic pressures in these markets, and they have led many organizations to raise provider workloads while also limiting many types of services that providers are allowed to offer patients in an effort to stay competitive financially.

Impact of managed care on provider–patient communication Since the mid-1980s, the rise of managed care has been an important response to rising costs and increased competition. Managed care refers to "a financial and organizational arrangement for the provision of health care services" (Lammers, Barbour, & Duggan, 2003). The term managed care is often perceived negatively because it has become synonymous with the idea of control by big business, loss of autonomy, and limited choices over services. However, most providers would have a difficult time surviving financially without managed care, and most patients would not be able to afford healthcare services if these organizations did not exist. We will examine managed care in greater depth in Chapter 6.

Most managed care plans place financial restrictions on the types of procedures, medications, diagnostic tests, and other treatment recommendations physicians can make to any given patient as a means of controlling costs. This practice is known as *capitation*. Capitation helps to keep the overall costs of managed care plans relatively low for consumers by eliminating costly procedures and service in cases when lower-cost alternatives can be found. However, in cases where the patient would benefit from a more expensive procedure or medication, providers and patients often feel frustrated if the plan will not pay for these services (or only a small portion) and the patient has to cover these costs. The first author's wife recently had to have her physician write to her managed care organization to request increased coverage for a $600 a month medication that is normally not covered by her plan because her physician thought the medication would be helpful for her condition.

Working within a managed care system is often a source of stress for providers who often feel that their ability to provide patients with the best care possible is compromised by the restrictions of the managed care health plan. Providers often feel too constrained by the limitations of plans, and some may resent having plan administrators dictate the course of patient treatment. Physicians often feel pressure to see patients for shorter periods of time, and this may lead to communication behaviors that negatively affect the provider–patient relationship. In addition, because the provider–patient relationship under managed care plans is subject to the conditions of the plan, this relationship can be disrupted when a patient's plan is bought by another managed care organization or if the organization decides to drop a provider from the patient's list of eligible providers.

Privacy and provider–patient relationships

Providers often struggle with managing information about patients as well as information pertaining to patients in healthcare settings. For example, patients are typically asked to reveal significant amounts of private and sensitive information in medical interactions (Duggan & Petronio, 2009; Petronio & Sargent, 2011), such as information about sexual activities, embarrassing information about bodily functions, the truth about diet and exercise practices, fears about illness, and issues such as domestic abuse. At the same time, providers know information about patients, such as how long they will likely live if diagnosed with a terminal illness, the amount of pain or cost involved with certain medical procedures, and issues that could potentially violate patient confidentiality. Nurses in particular often struggle with the need to know certain private things about their patients while simultaneously feeling the need to shield them from certain types of information in their attempts to balance patient care and patient confidentiality.

One theory that is helpful for understanding these types of predicaments for providers is Communication Privacy Management Theory (Petronio, 2002). This theory posits that people believe that they are the owners of their private information and they assume the right to control access to it. However, there are expectations about the responsibility for managing information, and healthcare professionals often assume they are co-owners of patient information (Petronio & Reierson, 2009). Yet, the need to gather private information from patients in healthcare often leads to a one-way street where patients disclose sensitive information while nurses and other practitioners do not share sensitive or private information about their own lives with patients. In addition, as mentioned above, nurses and other healthcare professionals often shield patients from certain types of information, particularly if that information could potentially increase fear, discomfort, or violate patient confidentiality. In an attempt to establish personal and professional boundaries, providers may withhold information from patients, and this can lead to perceived interpersonal distance between providers and patients (Petronio & Sargent, 2011). Communication Privacy Management Theory is often used as a framework for better understanding the strategies people use to manage tensions surrounding the communication of private or sensitive information as well as how the rules for communicating about private information shift depending upon the situation or context.

Provider perceptions of patients and communication

While physicians are trained in medical school to conduct medical interviews, communicating with patients effectively can be an extremely complex process. In a relatively short amount of time, physicians must be able to make one or more diagnoses from hundreds of possible diseases and medical conditions, and patients' self-disclosures about their medical history and their ability to articulate their chief complaint play a crucial role in helping physicians narrow down a wide array of competing possibilities for the causes of their condition or source of concern (Mentzer & Snyder, 1982). Many diseases and conditions can have similar symptoms. For example, chest pain can be associated with something as benign as indigestion or as serious as a myocardial infarction (heart attack).

Because identifying the causes of patient problems is largely a process of elimination, physicians and other providers need specific information from patients to help rule out factors that are not influencing the patient's condition. Gathering this information from a patient is often a difficult task for providers. They will typically ask a number of questions they feel are useful for narrowing down probable causes of the patients' condition while simultaneously steering away from information that they perceive to be irrelevant. Providers rarely rely solely on patient self-disclosures about problems, and the information that a patient provides is corroborated with information from physical exams, diagnostic tests, consultations with peers, and information from medical books and databases. Physicians who adhere to a more biomedical approach to medicine tend to focus specifically on the physical dimension of health, and their communication with patients tends to be very focused and specific, such as gathering information about physical symptoms (Roter *et al.*, 1997).

Problems can occur when information that a provider thinks is irrelevant is perceived by the patient to be relevant, and a patient might feel a provider is being insensitive if one or more of his or her comments are ignored. Complicating the situation further, providers are not always correct when it comes to assessing the causes of a patient's condition initially, and in these cases further information from the patient is often crucial to help establish the right diagnosis. Patients may also withhold sensitive information about their lifestyles, or about body parts or functions they feel uncomfortable talking about, and patients often vary in their ability to accurately disclose information about their health. For example, some patients do not want to disclose information about drinking, eating, and smoking habits because they feel their provider will negatively judge them or because they are afraid that this information might raise their medical insurance premium. It is also difficult for many patients to talk about their sex organs, bowel movements, or other topics they don't perceive to be appropriate or relevant. Talking about these types of issues also violates many ethnic and cultural norms, and this can be problematic in health settings where there is a diverse patient population.

Other factors, such as the age of the patient, are associated with problematic provider–patient communication. Young children often lack the developmental skills to give a provider accurate information about their health history or symptoms, and older adults with cognitive impairment may have a difficult time recalling or communicating health information that might be useful to providers in making a correct diagnosis (Nussbaum, Ragan, & Whaley, 2003). This can create additional challenges for providers when communicating with pediatric or older adult patients.

As you can see, providers must walk a fine line between attempting to obtain the information they need from a patient in order to make a correct diagnosis, assessing what might be irrelevant information and discouraging it, and encouraging the patient to provide information he or she may be reluctant to discuss with the provider but may be relevant to the case.

Assessing patient cues and provider expectations Physicians and other providers are trained to rely on both verbal and nonverbal cues from patients when assessing their health problems. However, preexisting beliefs and attitudes toward patients can influence the ways in which providers communicate with them. Physicians' interpretations of patient cues not only affect their interaction with patients but can also influence their medical decisions when treating patients (Geist & Hardesty, 1990). For example, social cues, such as race, gender, and age, and physical cues, such as if a patient is overweight, have been found to influence the type of information a physician provides to the patient and the type of treatment options he or she discusses. Providers also assess patient attitude cues, such as whether a patient has a "good" attitude or if he or she is seen as a "bad patient" (typically a complainer/arguer, or someone who challenges the doctor's authority). Doctors often try to get rid of "bad patients" more quickly. A problem is that providers' perceptions of patients are often based upon socialization and prior experiences with patients. Providers, like all human beings, may engage in *selective perception*, or the tendency to perceive information in ways that are consistent with past experiences.

Providers' expectations about patients are often based on verbal and nonverbal patient cues, and this may influence their recommendations for treatment and the amount of information they provide patients. For example, provider expectations about patient adherence has been found to influence the degree to which doctors will discuss or advocate colorectal cancer screening with patients (Dulai *et al.*, 2004; Shokar, Carlson, & Shokar, 2006).

Patient Perspective

Patient socialization

Most people learn about the healthcare system from a variety of sources, including the mass media, family members, and friends, and through their experiences interacting with providers when seeking healthcare (Brashers, Goldsmith, & Hsieh, 2002; Cline, 2011). All of us have been patients at one time or another, but few people critically examine how they learn the role of being a patient or their own communication behaviors when interacting with providers. Much of what we know about being a patient comes from what we see and hear in the mass media. Television shows, such as "Grey's Anatomy," give us insight into the world of medicine, and through these types of shows we see examples of how patients interact with providers. These insights can sometimes lead people to develop unrealistic expectations, such as expectations about the friendliness and efficiency of their providers or their ability to effectively diagnose and treat illness. We will examine the relationship between health in the mass media and individual perceptions in Chapter 8.

Most people learn perceptions of health and the healthcare system through everyday language (Cline, 2003, 2011). In other words, our perceptions of reality about health and health situations are shaped by our day-to-day interactions. This perspective is known as the social construction of reality (Berger & Luckman, 1966). Our families and friends play an important role in socializing us when it comes to learning about providers and how to behave as a patient, and over our lifetime the language we encounter involving health each day influences our perceptions over a long period of time. Even our first-hand experiences with providers and healthcare settings are mediated through language, and common perceptions of illness, providers, the healthcare system, and many other aspects of health are shaped by the way in which language about health is used by the people in our social networks.

Language is rarely neutral, and common uses of language, such as metaphors like "doctors are mechanics," convey meanings and understandings about doctors and drug use that imply certain behaviors. For example, if a woman thinks her doctor is essentially a mechanic, then this understanding of a doctor might influence her to think about doctors in very specific ways. Most individuals have relatively little interaction with mechanics other than telling them what needs to be fixed and obtaining an estimate, and mechanics feel little need to convey warmth or empathy to a car when fixing a radiator. Thus, referring the term "doctor" to the term "mechanic" conveys certain expectations for a doctor's behavior, such as the doctor being somewhat impersonal and perfunctory when "repairing" a broken arm.

Other factors, such as health history, gender, socioeconomic status, culture, and age, play an important role in socializing patients. Individuals who have an ongoing health problem are more likely to see providers more frequently than people with fewer health problems and they often develop different perceptions of providers and health settings due to their relational history with providers and their more extensive experience with the healthcare system. Women are more likely to seek healthcare than men in general in the US, they are more likely to make regular visits to providers such as gynecologists for female-specific health concerns, and they often experience more problems with healthcare than men (Beck, 1997). Cultural differences, including ethnic differences, sexual orientation, and religious beliefs, are important factors in patient socialization (see Chapter 5). For example, some immigrants mistrust the US healthcare system or do not follow mainstream cultural conceptions of health. Finally, older adults in our society often have very different views of providers and the healthcare system than younger adults. Many older adults lived the majority of their life in a time when few people questioned a physician's authority and before the advent of managed care, and these experiences often impact perceptions older adults have of healthcare and the way they communicate with providers. Not only do these factors influence patient perceptions of healthcare, but also providers often communicate with patients much differently based upon age, gender, status, and ethnicity.

Patient perceptions and expectations

Think about how you think about health and healthcare. It is likely that the way you see them has been influenced by a variety of sources, such as television and other mass media, our everyday interactions with others, our first-hand experiences with being ill and going to the doctor, or a combination of all of these things. Each of these experiences influences our current perceptions of health and health providers. Over time, these experiences are stored in memory as *schema*, which are mental structures or templates that help guide our behaviors (Reed, 1988; Schank & Abelson, 1977). Schema are useful to us since they help to reduce the amount of thinking, or cognitive effort, we exert when performing daily activities. For example, if we had to process all of the information available to us each time we went to the doctor, such as understanding the role of receptionists, nurses, or the process of the medical interview, as if we had never experienced them in the past, we would probably suffer from what is called cognitive overload, or too much information for our brain to process.

Fortunately, schema give us a mental blueprint that helps to guide our expectations and behaviors in medical settings. However, because schema are based upon previous experiences, they can influence our expectations and communication behaviors during provider–patient interaction (O'Hair, Allman, & Moore, 1996). People may react positively or negatively when their initial expectations for a social situation are violated, and this appears to be true in health settings. For example, if a patient expects her new doctor to be warm and empathetic based upon her previous experiences with other physicians, and the new doctor violates this expectation by communicating in a cold and distant manner, then the patient will probably be unsatisfied with the interaction. However, another patient, such as an elderly male, might expect his doctor to be controlling, and he may be uncomfortable about the interaction if the physician violates this expectation by encouraging him to be more involved in selecting treatment options.

It is important to recognize that patients differ considerably in terms of their perceptions of providers and their expectations for provider–patient interaction. Some patients may not expect their doctor to talk about their lifestyles, feelings, or to have time to answer their questions, while other patients may have high expectations for these behaviors. However, many patients desire both technical and interpersonal competence in providers, although in the case of physicians, technical competence is often one of the most important expectations for patients (Anderson, 2001).

Patient expectations can be influenced by broader perceptions of the provider–patient relationship. For example, patients who have a *paternalistic* view of provider–patient relationships tend to feel that their role as patients is to obey and cooperate, that the provider should take a dominant role during provider–patient interaction, that the provider is more knowledgeable than the patient, and that the provider has their best interest in mind (Beisecker & Beisecker, 1993). Patients who have a paternalistic view of the provider–patient relationship tend to expect and be satisfied with a provider who communicates in ways that are consistent with this view.

Other patients hold a *consumeristic* view of the provider–patient relationship and are more likely to take an active role when communicating with a doctor (e.g. ask questions, communicate concerns), expect the provider to be less dominant during interaction, and place less emphasis on the provider's authority or status (Beisecker & Beisecker, 1993). Patients with a consumeristic view tend to have much different expectations about provider–patient interactions than patients with a paternalistic view. They see the relationship more as an exchange of information between the two parties, similar to a business transaction that would take place among providers and consumers of other types of services. In other words, patients with this view of the provider–patient relationship often feel: "I am paying a lot of money for this visit... I should get what I want!" This need may override perceptions of a physician's social status. For example, think about how much money you pay for college tuition. College students often do not care about how prestigious a professor is if they do not feel they are getting their money's worth from a class (e.g. if they are not learning much or the professor is boring).

Yet, the consumeristic view of medicine is not without its problems. Sometimes we do not know what is best for us as patients. Similarly, college students often do not have the expertise in a class to know what is important to learn about a given subject, and they may object to having to read certain books or participate in some assignments. In much the same way, patients often object to some tests or procedures and may perceive them as unimportant or excessive, while their doctor may view them as a crucial part of treating a patient's health problem.

Health beliefs/attributions and patient behavior Patient beliefs about health and the attributions they make regarding causes of health problems can affect their behaviors in important ways within healthcare settings. Martin (2007) found that people who believed they had a low level of susceptibility to develop carpal tunnel syndrome at their jobs (even if they were engaging in tasks that put them at risk for developing carpal tunnel syndrome) were less likely to engage in help-seeking behavior from providers. Beliefs surrounding the severity of chronic health problems that people are living with have been found to influence how often the visit the doctor, seek information from providers, and how well they adhere to suggested treatments (Cameron & Leventhal, 2003). For example, patients with asthma who believe that the condition in is not serious are less likely to adhere to corticosteroid treatments (Chambers *et al.*, 1999), and patients living with high blood pressure are less likely to see their physician or adhere to medicine if they do not believe that high blood pressure makes a person more susceptible to heart disease or strokes (Kressin *et al.*, 2007).

Patient uncertainty

Think about how worried you might be if you were to suddenly develop a rash that rapidly spreads across your body. Is it poison oak, food poisoning, or something worse? The experience of uncertainty is directly linked to the communication processes of gathering and interpreting information about an illness (Babrow, 2001; Brashers, 2001; Parrott, Stuart, & Cairns, 2000), and it can affect provider–patient communication in a variety of ways. Patients often experience considerable uncertainty in provider–patient interactions because their knowledge level of medicine is typically much less than their physician (Sheer & Cline, 1995). In addition, contradictory information about diseases from the media, family, and friends and uncertainty about the healthcare system are among the many reasons patients feel uncomfortable when talking to healthcare professionals (Shore, 2003).

Sources of uncertainty during times of illness and when visiting the doctor can stem from many sources, such as the technical language and discourse used by physicians, the known potential for mistakes by the healthcare provider, and the stress of gathering accurate information while attempting to stay positive when coping with an illness (Babrow, Kasch, & Ford, 1998). Reducing uncertainty about illness may help patients cope with their health problems better, but this is not always the case (Czaja, Manfredi, & Price, 2003). Sometimes, a diagnosis of a life-threatening illness, such as cancer or HIV, may increase uncertainty rather than reduce it. While the patient may learn that the symptoms he or she is experiencing are due to cancer, the diagnosis may raise a host of uncertainties, such as uncertainty about their prognosis, treatment options, and how the disease will affect his or her relationships.

Austin Babrow (2001) developed *problematic integration theory* in an effort to investigate the communicative processes people facing illness use to manage health information in order to deal with uncertainty. Babrow (2001, 2007) argued that the meaning of uncertainty is largely dependent on the values of the individual who is experiencing an illness, with those values guiding the ways that information is used to manage uncertainty. Problematic integration theory posits that uncertainty is a complex phenomenon, and some people seek to increase uncertain rather than reduce or avoid it (Babrow, 2007). In addition, a person's desire to seek or avoid information influences the ways in which he or she ultimately copes with health issues. For example, a person with cancer may decide to gather certain types of information about the most aggressive forms of chemotherapy if he or she primarily values stopping the progression of cancer, regardless of the side effects of the treatment in an effort to reduce uncertainty about the disease. In addition, if an individual knows he or she has cancer, this may influence the decision to seek support from others (Babrow, 2007). However, a person who suspects he or she has HIV may avoid seeking information (such as an HIV test or information about symptoms) because living with uncertainty may be more comfortable than dealing with knowing that he or she has an HIV positive status. This is especially the case when a person believes that being HIV positive will lead to being negatively stigmatized by others or if the person fears confronting his or her own mortality.

Problematic integration theory has been a helpful framework for understanding patients' experiences with uncertainty surrounding a variety of health-related issues, including pregnancy and birth (Matthias, 2009), breast cancer (Dennis, Kunkel, & Keyton, 2008), and end-of-life decision-making (Hines, Babrow, Badzek, & Moss, 2001). Problematic integration theory will likely continue to be an important framework for understanding patient uncertainty and coping strategies for confronting health concerns in the future.

Patient needs and goals

Have you ever seen a doctor even when you were feeling relatively well so that you could get a note from him or her to help document an absence from work or school? Or perhaps there have been times when you were not really suffering from symptoms, such as a rash or a pain in your stomach, when visiting the doctor, but you were concerned that the symptoms might be a sign of a larger health problem. Patients often have multiple needs and goals when they communicate with physicians and other providers. While many patients go to their doctor to obtain relief from physical symptoms, they also have other needs that they want their providers to meet. These include the need for the provider to validate or legitimize their health concern. For example, after several visits to the emergency room for abdominal pain several years ago, the first author of this book was told on each visit that it was "most likely indigestion," and he was told to take an antacid. At the time, he was working on his doctoral dissertation, and several physicians told him that the indigestion was probably related to stress. However, he felt that the pain might be related to a more serious problem despite the fact that his doctors had dismissed the problem as "nothing serious." He felt angry that nobody seemed to take the problem seriously. Finally, after going to the emergency room one night at 3:00am with severe pain, a doctor decided to run a blood test and a sonogram, and it turned out that he needed emergency gallbladder surgery. As in this case, patients often want physicians to validate their perceived health problem as a legitimate problem.

Even when a patient is experiencing physical symptoms, the need to manage the symptoms is secondary to the patient's need to reduce his or her fear over possible causes of the symptoms. For example, a patient may have an ongoing skin rash that is causing him some discomfort, but due to his past history of unprotected sex with multiple partners, coupled with information from a pamphlet he read about symptoms of HIV that include skin rashes, this patient may be more concerned about whether or not he has HIV than obtaining relief for the rash. Other patients might have a need to confess their medical fears to a provider. Some people suffer from health problems in silence and they are afraid to see a doctor because of the fear that the symptoms might be caused by a serious disease (such as cancer). In this scenario, the physician might be the first person a patient has told about the symptoms after living with the fear of them for weeks, months, or years, and the patient's need to alleviate or understand the symptoms might be secondary to getting the issue out into the open. In addition, patients also have a need for providers to convey concern, emotional support, reassurance, and interpersonal warmth during medical interviews. Having these needs fulfilled by the provider may be just as important as or more important to the patient than the need for medical treatment.

Provider–Patient Interaction

Provider–patient communication has seen many changes in recent years. Until relatively recently, providers and patients were both accustomed to a paternalistic approach toward healthcare where the doctor "knows best" and should not be questioned. Today, healthcare providers are encouraged to focus more on their patients and their needs, while patients are taking more responsibility for their care. Communication scholars and medical researchers have become increasingly interested in provider–patient communication in the past decade, and even the *Journal of the American Medical*

Association (*JAMA*) now devotes a regular section to provider–patient communication issues. The following section explores characteristics of provider–patient communication and their relationship with various outcomes. It begins by exploring *communication accommodation theory* as a conceptual framework for studying provider–patient communication.

Communication accommodation theory as a framework for understanding provider–patient interaction

Communication accommodation theory (CAT) proposes that when speakers from different social groups interact, they adjust or modify their verbal and nonverbal communication in order to accommodate each other (Giles, Coupland, & Coupland, 1991; Giles, Mulac, Bradac, & Johnson, 1987). Although each person is individually unique, we are all members of multiple social groups based on variables such as age, race, ethnicity, socioeconomic background, beliefs, attitudes, values, and interests, and we are constantly in the process of making judgements about other people in terms of whether they are members of in-groups (groups to which we feel we belong) or out-groups (groups to which we feel we don't belong). Providers and patients can be seen as members of different social groups based upon education, training, status (in the case of physicians), and perceptions of health and healthcare. Not only do provider and patients speak different languages, but also these differences often reflect very different perceptions of health and medicine.

CAT predicts that our perceptions of members of out-groups will influence our communication behaviors in a variety of ways. When we adapt our verbal and non-verbal communication in a way in which we emphasize similarities (in terms of speech, gestures, topics, etc.) between ourselves and another person, this is known as *convergence*. Although physicians and patients come from different social groups, a physician can engage in convergence with a patient by explaining his or her problem or the recommended treatment using language that the patient can understand (as opposed to using medical jargon).

Conversely, if we emphasize differences between ourselves and another individual based upon perceived social group differences when communicating, this is known as *divergence*. Providers may engage in divergence when communicating with patients by emphasizing their medical expertise or social status. Providers may use medical jargon or communicate their medical expertise in other ways when attempting to persuade a patient to try a certain treatment option or to get them to comply with a treatment. Providers can engage in *overaccommodation* when communicating with patients if they emphasize expertise or status differences too much. In these cases, patients may feel that their doctor is patronizing them or communicating with them in other conde-scending ways (e.g. talking to the patient as if he or she is a child, chastising the patient for an unhealthy lifestyle or not adhering to a treatment).

As Sparks, Rogers, and Bevan (2012) indicate, all parties involved in the provider and patient relationship must have a good understanding of the socially and contextu-ally determined expectations for appropriate conversational behavior and practice it in their accommodation styles for the interaction to be a successful one. Selection of appropriate accommodation is highly dependent on the context in which the interaction occurs and the caregiving relationship certainly plays an important role when it comes to provider and patient interaction. Sparks, Rogers, and Bevan found support for healthcare accommodation in informal provider relationships. Their study revealed that aspects of perceived accommodation, explained 34.57 percent of the variance and taps into accommodation, respect, politeness, and trust, which seem to indicate these components' increasing level of importance in provider and patient interaction, particularly as pertaining to informal providers in distant caregiving situations. Their validated healthcare communication accommodation scale measured the degree to which the informal providers or caregivers perceive their care recipients to be accommodating, which is the reverse of many previous studies that examined how provider accommodation impacted patient adherence and health outcomes. The perceived accommodation factor, then, suggests that caregiver perceptions of recipient accommodation and trust of the care recipient may play a much larger role than we completely understand (Sparks, Rogers, & Bevan, 2012).

As we discuss examples of both good and bad provider–patient communication below, think of how communication accommodation theory can be used to explain how perceptions of providers and patients from the standpoint of in-group and out-group differences may influence the ways providers and patients interact with each other.

Characteristics of problematic provider–patient communication

Unfortunately, many providers do not thoroughly listen to what a patient has to say, or they interrupt patients, causing them to miss diagnoses or pertinent information. As we saw earlier in this chapter, physicians and other providers spend a great deal of their time with patients attempting to isolate specific causes of their symptoms or complaints. Given the heavy workloads of most physicians and other pressures that limit their time with individual patients (such as managed care pressures), doctors try to assess possible causes of the patient's problems in a time-efficient manner. In an attempt to help the patient in an opportune manner and to systematically rule out factors that are unrelated to the patient's condition, providers often engage in specific communication behaviors that allow them to control the direction of the conversation.

Physicians may attempt to control conversations with patients by using close-ended questions or by providing the patient with directive statements (e.g. "lie down on your side and breathe normally"). Physicians sometimes have an agenda for their conversations with patients based upon information about the patient they view in his or her chart prior to the interaction. In these cases, the chart can give the physician information about the patient's complaint and medical history, and this information may provide the physician with some insight into possible causes of the problem. And while this agenda may help the physician save time, it can cause problems if the patient feels that he or she is not being allowed to give adequate input into the conversation.

Nonverbal communication often plays a problematic role in provider–patient communication. Communication occurs at the *content level*, or what is said verbally, and the *relational level*, which relies heavily on nonverbal cues. Power, status, and control are often communicated at the relational level. We tend to give people with higher status (such as doctors) more physical space, and we often yield the conversation to them. The tone of voice that is used when communicating often reveals more about the relationship between two people than what is actually said. Patients may sound assertive or passive when communicating information to their providers, and this can affect the relationship in a variety of ways. Physicians are allowed to touch patients, but it would be considered inappropriate for a patient to touch his or her doctor. Patients wait for their physicians to see them and not the other way around.

According to O'Hair (1989), physicians and patients attempt to negotiate relational control in medical encounters. Physicians may try to assert control by questioning patients, making assertions, talking over patient responses, or interrupting patients. Patients also attempt to control conversations with their physician by questioning their doctor, asking for certain medications or treatments, or by changing the topic. O'Hair (1989) found that physicians were twice as likely as patients to assume control of the conversation when the patient did not attempt to gain control or responded to the doctor with a neutral message. However, patients were unlikely to attempt to gain control after their physician responded to them with a neutral message. In other words, patients, while attempting to control the conversation at times, often concede control to their physicians.

If patients concede control to the physician (or another provider), then they run the risk of not being able to provide information that could be helpful to the diagnosis or of not having their needs met during the interaction. While asserting control over a conversation may be necessary at times, physician–patient communication can become problematic if a physician uses control strategies to dominate the conversation and does not allow for patient input (Eggly & Tzelepis, 2001). In these cases, the physician runs the risk of not obtaining useful information from the patient or not meeting his or her needs. Moreover, patients who feel their doctor dominated the conversation may feel less satisfied with the encounter, but this depends upon their expectations for the interaction (e.g. whether they have a more paternalistic or consumeristic view of the physician–patient relationship).

Improving Provider–Patient Communication

Although the different backgrounds, perceptions, needs, and expectations of provider and patients make it challenging for successful and satisfying communication to take place in medical encounters, understanding these issues and how they may impact health outcomes is a first step toward improving provider–patient communication. This section explores several ways that communication between providers and patients can be improved so that it is beneficial to both parties.

Addressing patient concerns

Providers can often address psychosocial concerns when communicating with patients without significantly increasing the amount of interaction time, although it can be more time consuming depending upon the specific circumstances (Brown, Stewart, & Ryan, 2003). Addressing patient concerns is important to patient satisfaction and improved health outcomes (see discussion below), so providers and managed care organizations have become increasingly more interested in *patient-centered communication*. Patient-centered communication focuses on the patient as a "whole person" in the context of his or her psychological and social circumstances (Hirsch *et al.*, 2005; Mast, Kindlimann, & Langiwitz, 2005). In other words, a patient-centered perspective promotes healthcare based on individual patients' unique characteristics, conditions, and circumstances (Smith, 2002). Roter and Hall (2004) identified a number of variables that describe patient-centeredness, including allowing the patient to disclose information that he/she believes is meaningful, use of open-ended questions, providing information to patients that addresses both biomedical and psychosocial needs, encouraging patient assertiveness, and a variety of other behaviors that shift the focus of communication to the patient. Patient-centered communication has been associated with higher levels of general satisfaction and improved biomedical and functional outcomes (Smith, 2002; Wanzer, Booth-Butterfield, & Gruber, 2004).

As a result, a growing number of healthcare centers offer relatively "holistic" approaches to better meet the physical and psychosocial needs of individual patients (Lefkowitz, 2006). This includes environmental restructuring of traditional healthcare environments, such as designing them so that they more closely resemble a living room in a private home than an institutional setting (Frey, Adelman, Flint, & Query, 2000; Richardson *et al.*, 2000). Moreover, an increasing number of healthcare centers are offering patients alternative services to traditional healthcare in an effort to meet psychosocial needs, such as relaxation therapies, massage, counseling, and support groups (see Wright & Frey, 2008).

Lambert *et al.* (1996) argue that patient-centered care "requires that patient needs, preferences, and beliefs be respected at all times" (p. 27). Vanderford, Jenks, and Sharf (1997) argue that patients are active interpreters, managers, and creators of the meaning of their health or illness, rather than passive receivers of or reactors to messages. These researchers advocate a patient-centered approach to healthcare that has three assumptions: (i) patients' experiences matter; (ii) patient identity is a central issue in patients' experience of illness; and (iii) patients' experiences must be understood in context. Providers also need to take into account how a patient's age, gender, education, needs, expectations, cultural conceptions, and many other perceptions and experiences of health may influence his or her viewpoint during medical encounters.

Providers should avoid interrupting patients, and they should encourage patient input whenever possible. By being aware of relational communication and their specific communication patterns, providers can alter their communication to be more accommodating to patients. Providers should not assume that patients understand everything that is discussed during medical interviews, and whenever possible the provider should attempt to tailor his or her language to the patient's level of education and background. In addition, providers should try to communicate with patients in ways that do not patronize them, that express respect for their feelings and perspective about health, and that communicate concern for the patient.

Roter and Hall (2011) underscore the need for more provider–patient interaction research that focuses on nonverbal communication. Nonverbal communication is a key component of empathetic listening, expressing emotional concern and positive affect toward patients. Nonverbal communication involves a wide array of cues, such as body language, gestures, facial expressions, eye movement, vocal tone, use of touch, use of time, and body positioning. Providers' nonverbal communication skills are crucial in terms of decoding nonverbal cues from patients, such as confusion, expression of pain, fear, anxiety, physical sensitivity toward touch, and discomfort. Successful decoding of such nonverbal communication cues can help providers better meet patient needs, increase satisfaction with the provider–patient relationship (Griffith, Wilson, Langer, & Haist, 2003), and can reduce the probability of misunderstanding or negative interactions that could potentially lead to treatment adherence problems, loss of business, and malpractice lawsuits. For example, Ambady *et al.* (2002) found that physicians who had been sued for medical malpractice had more negative vocal tone than physicians who had not been sued. Surprisingly, relatively few communication skills training programs offer extensive training in nonverbal communication, although more and more research is underscoring the importance of this type of training (Hall *et al.*, 2009).

Finally, successful patient-centered nonverbal communication typically goes hand and hand with patient-centered verbal communication (Roter & Hall, 2011). Both elements are necessary to convey and decode a sophisticated range of content and relational messages within provider-patient interaction.

Recognizing provider perspectives and needs

In order to improve the dissemination and understanding of health information, Sparks and Villagran (2010) argue that we must first see improvement in provider–patient communication by increasing the health knowledge of the provider. Surprisingly, Frank, Elon, Carrera, and Hertzberg (2007) found that providers, overall, have a limited knowledge of the many health effects impacting patients, including mosquito-borne diseases and infected drinking water (see also Villagran, Weathers, Keefe, & Sparks, 2010). Providers have an array of responsibilities beyond interacting with patients that have little to do with actual diagnosis and treatment of healthcare conditions (Sparks & Villagran, 2010).

However, as the most utilized source of health information (Pecchioni & Sparks, 2007; Pennbridge, Moya, & Rodrigues, 1999), providers are still primarily responsible for disseminating the most relevant and up-to-date health information to patients. Surprisingly, however, healthcare providers and medical establishments are often equally unprepared to provide patients and caregivers with pertinent health related information—information that is necessary for informed medical decision-making (Villagran *et al.*, 2010). Health communication scholars increasingly report that treatment choices are often made in an environment of uncertainty, ambiguity, misinformation, high emotion, and anguish; thus, the outcome ends up being less favorable than recent medical advances could allow (Sparks & Villagran, 2010). Therefore, providers must be savvy as they gather credible health information from a variety of sources, and consider how to best communicate with patients in ways that exemplify, for instance, the four components of health literacy including: (i) cultural and conceptual knowledge; (ii) listening and speaking (oral literacy); (iii) writing and reading (print literacy); and (iv) numeracy (knowledge of statistics and other numeric data) (IOM, 2004).

Successful provider–patient communication, however, is not only the responsibility of providers; patients need to recognize the constraints that providers face and they should take a more active role during medical encounters (Harrington, Noble, & Newman, 2004). Patients need to realize that their providers cannot do everything, and they should be aware of the many pressures providers must cope with in attempting to diagnose and treat illness among multiple patients in today's complex healthcare system. While patients have a right to expect providers to be respectful and provide quality care, they should also realize that providers are only human, and as in any business situation, the occupational pressures providers face can have a negative impact on communication. Patients can also improve provider–patient communication by becoming more knowledgeable about health and being more assertive when talking to providers. Of course, this is no easy task given the diversity of patients' education level, cultural conceptions of health, needs, and perceptions of healthcare. However, health education and patient communication skills training have been found to improve provider–patient communication in terms of increased involvement on the part of the patient (Cegala, McClure, Marinelli, & Post, 2000; Cegala, Post, & McClure, 2001). More recently, Cegala, Street, and Clinch (2007) found that patient participation in the medical interviews significantly influenced the amount and type of information physicians provided patients. In addition, Harrington *et al.* (2007) found that parents of sick children who received communication skills training were more likely to verify information and express their concerns to the physician than parents who did not receive the training. In short, these and other studies demonstrate the importance of increased patient participation within provider–patient interactions during medical encounters.

Outcomes of Provider–Patient Communication

A number of successful and unsuccessful outcomes have been linked to provider–patient communication. While communication is rarely the only influence on outcomes in health settings, it has been shown to have a significant impact on whether or not people feel their encounters with providers were satisfactory and whether or not their needs have been met. This section explores various outcomes of provider–patient interaction for both patients and providers.

Satisfaction with healthcare

Patient satisfaction appears to be one of the key outcomes associated with provider–patient communication. Satisfaction with one's providers may affect other outcomes such as adherence to treatment, and ultimately better physical health outcomes.

Patients who are more satisfied with their provider are more likely to continue seeing him or her, and they may also refer friends and family members. This, of course, is a potentially positive financial outcome of patient satisfaction for providers.

Patient satisfaction with providers is largely associated with a provider's interpersonal communication skills. Studies have found that satisfaction is often linked to a provider's ability to communicate warmth, emotional support, availability, understanding, and caring to the patient (Brown, Stewart, & Ryan, 2003; Kim, Kaplowitz, & Johnston, 2004), and a provider's success at achieving a balance between addressing biomedical and psychosocial concerns when communicating with patients (Roter *et al.*, 1997). Patients are also more satisfied with their providers when they are encouraged to express concerns, raise topics for discussion, and ask questions (Linn, Linn, & Stein, 1982). In addition, patient satisfaction has been linked to factors such as perceptions of technical competence, although this does not appear to be as important as perceptions of a provider's interpersonal skills (Tarrant *et al.*, 2003). Conversely, patient dissatisfaction has been found to be associated with lack of interpersonal warmth or friendliness on the part of a provider, waiting room time, provider failure to acknowledge patient concerns, unclear explanations of medical condition, diagnosis, and treatment, and inappropriate use of medical jargon (Brown, Stewart, & Ryan, 2003).

Adherence to treatment

Successful provider–patient communication is also related to increased patient compliance to treatments and health condition management strategies suggested by their providers (Golin, DiMatteo, & Gelberg, 1996; Kim, Kaplowitz, & Johnston, 2004; Moore *et al.*, 2004). In fact, researchers consider provider–patient communication to be one of the most important variables in terms of predicting patient adherence (Brown, Stewart, & Ryan, 2003; Moore et al., 2004). Nonadherence to prescription medications has been called an "epidemic" (Sherman, 2007) and a "worldwide problem of striking magnitude" (World Health Organization, 2003). For instance, on average, 16.4 percent of chronic disease patients do not fill their prescriptions (Gadkari & McHorney, 2010). Medical adherence in chronic disease populations is primarily driven by perceived need for medications, perceived concerns about medications, and perceived affordability of medications (Gadkari & McHorney, 2010; McHorney, 2009). Among these three predictors, perceived need and perceived concerns are particularly strong drivers of adherence (McHorney, 2009). Good provider–patient communication often leads to more knowledgeable patients, and when patients know more about their condition, symptoms, and treatment options, they are more likely to follow their doctor's suggestions. Communication plays an important role in terms of influencing patient perceptions of provider credibility, which has been found to influence patient adherence to recommended treatments (Avtgis, Brann, & Staggers, 2006; Wrench & Booth-Butterfield, 2003).

Physicians play an important role in educating patients and explaining complex medical information to them in ways that increase understanding (Thompson, Whaley, & Stone, 2011). Physicians and other providers who try to communicate too much information to patients, who use too much medical jargon or do not attempt to explain what it means, or who assume the patient understands his or her medical situation run the risk of not having their patients adhere to their proposed treatment suggestions.

In addition, providers who do not take the time to understand aspects of the patient's life that can inhibit adherence limit the likelihood that patients will successfully adhere to treatment of their condition. For example, suppose a physician prescribes several different medications and a physical therapy regime for an elderly patient who has just had a hip replacement, and the physician fails to ask pertinent questions about the patient's daily life, such as the availability of family members for support, or the patient's understanding of the medications. The patient may not make it to physical therapy sessions if he or she lacks adequate family support or transportation. In terms of medications, the patient may not understand that taking two or three medications at the same time can lead to drug interaction effects such as making the patient drowsy or nauseous, and this might keep the patient from using some or all of the medications.

Finally, successful provider–patient communication has also been linked to a variety of physical and psychological health outcomes, including reduced patient anxiety, psychological distress, reduced reports of pain and symptoms, and increased ability to function normally (Greenfield *et al.*, 1988; Roter *et al.*, 1995).

Communication and Medical Malpractice Lawsuits

Most people do not necessarily think of communication playing a role in medical malpractice suits. As you may be aware, medical malpractice litigation is a serious problem facing the US healthcare system, and many of these lawsuits have been linked to provider–patient communication problems (Hickson *et al.*, 2002; Wofford *et al.*, 2004). Medical malpractice suits are costly to the healthcare system, and that cost is passed on to you in the form of higher health insurance premiums and charges for visiting the doctor. Between 1995 and 2000, medical malpractice awards rose 70 percent to approximately $3.5 million per claim (Freedman, 2002). While most patients do not sue their providers, the amount of money that is awarded to those patients who do win malpractice suits often ranges from hundreds of thousands to millions of dollars. The increase of medical malpractice claims has led to the need among physicians to purchase malpractice insurance, and physicians often cannot afford the insurance or their practices suffer financially due to the additional cost of the insurance.

In order to cover the cost of malpractice insurance and lawsuit awards, managed care organizations have substantially raised patient premiums in recent years. Money for new equipment or other services that could benefit patients is often used to pay for malpractice insurance. Even tax-supported government healthcare agencies such as Medicaid and Medicare have begun to request more federal funding (resulting in the need for higher taxes) as a result of malpractice litigation. Recently, many states have pushed to pass laws that limit the amount of money a person can receive from malpractice lawsuits, but this issue will likely continue to be a problem for the health-care system in the future.

Provider–patient communication problems may increase the risk of malpractice litigation (Hickson *et al.*, 2002; Vincent, Young, & Philips, 1994). It is vitally important that we understand how communicating about specific and delicate health conditions with targeted populations (i.e. cancer diagnoses of older adults) and their family members in appropriate and effective ways can reduce incidence and mortality, under-stand complicated diagnoses, enhance treatment and survivorship, and can even reduce malpractice (Sparks, O'Hair, & Kreps, 2008b). According to Brown *et al.*, (2003), malpractice is best reduced when providers can demonstrate clear evidence that he or she has fully informed the patient about the risks and benefits of intervention and offered the patient the opportunity to make an informed choice. Healthcare providers are negatively evaluated when providers fail to disclose risks and when medicine promises more than can be delivered (O'Hair, Kreps, & Sparks, 2007). Thus, effective communication in the provider–patient relationship is a crucial component of health-care delivery (Sparks & Villagran, 2010).

Hickson *et al.* (2002) found that when patients feel that they have not been treated well by their physician or another member of the medical organization during a medical visit, or if their complaints are not adequately addressed, this can increase the likelihood of the patient suing the provider or the organization. Most patients who are prone to making malpractice claims report communication problems such as their feelings being ignored by their physician, inadequate explanation of the diagnosis or treatment, or feeling hurried by the physician (Hickson *et al.*, 1994). Moreover, patients who feel that their doctor is not empathetic to their situation or needs, if they feel he or she lacks interpersonal warmth, or if they feel he or she is dismissive of their problems or deceptive may be more likely to pursue legal action. Conversely, good provider–patient communication has been linked to fewer malpractice suits (Beckman, Markakis, Suchman, & Frankel, 1994).

Other Challenges of Provider–Patient Communication

In this final section, we discuss two additional provider–patient communication chal-lenges that have received attention from health communication scholars in recent years: breaking bad news to patients/loved ones and provider–patient communication issues when working with older patients.

Breaking bad news

Health communication scholars in recent years have been paying more attention to how healthcare providers break bad news in healthcare settings (Gillotti & Applegate, 1999; Gillotti, Thompson, & McNeilis, 2002; Sparks, Villagran, Parker-Raley, & Cun-ningham, 2007 ; Thompson, 1994). Health information is the critical resource derived from successful health communication (Kreps, 1988a, 1988b, 2003). Effective and timely communication enables patients and their families to gather relevant health information about significant threats to health, and helps them identify strategies for avoiding and responding to these threats (Kreps, 2003). An increasing concern for physicians is how to effectively and appropriately communicate health information that is bad news to patients (Mast, Kindlimann, & Langiwitz, 2005; Ptacek & Eberhardt, 1996).

Although the task of breaking bad news is a fundamentally important part of many healthcare interactions, it can be intimidating to providers (Barnett, 2004). Delivering bad news is difficult for physicians; therefore, phrases like "dropping the bomb" are often used to describe the daunting task (Baile *et al.*, 2000; Mueller, 2002). Although delivering bad news is challenging, it can be done effectively, creating increased patient satisfaction and decreased patient emotional responses (Mast, Kindlimann, & Langiwitz, 2005).

Although physicians have always been the bearers of bad news, the increase in chronic illness and in issues related to quality of life (see Chapter 3) heightens the importance of understanding how the delivery of bad news affects patients and providers. The manner in which this type of communication occurs can significantly impact the patient's level of satisfaction with his or her interaction with hospital staff and overall treatment by the healthcare providers (Whaley, 1999). In addition, the outcome of delivering healthcare information, particularly medical disclosures that result in bad news, has serious implications for the physician–patient interaction and is directly related to important communication variables such as patient satisfaction and compliance (Thompson, 1994). Moreover, recent research indicates that delivering bad news requires complex communicative strategies that tend to differ from other kinds of medical interactions (Gillotti, Thompson, & McNeilis, 2002). Patients, however, increasingly desire to know more about the state of their health and related diagnoses, which indicates that the ability to deliver health information in an appropriate way is now a necessity (Gillotti & Applegate, 1999). Patients want to know the truth about their diagnoses, particularly in acute situations such as cancer (Sparks, 2003a, 2003b).

Defining bad news Bad news has been defined in the medical literature as a multi-step process that creates situations where there is either a feeling of no hope, a threat to a person's mental or physical well-being, a risk of upsetting an established lifestyle, or a message is given which conveys to an individual fewer choices in his or her life (Barnett, 2004; Bor, Miller, Goldman, & Scher, 1993). In other words, bad news in the healthcare context refers to any information that creates a negative view of a person's health (Buckman, 1996). Although most of the medical literature on breaking bad news has focused on conveying diagnoses of objectively serious conditions, especially cancer (Hoy, 1985), bad news can range from a wart, to psoriasis, to pink eye, to infertility.

Regardless of the type of bad news, there are many reasons why physicians have difficulty breaking it. A common concern is how the news will affect the patient, and this is often used to justify withholding bad news. For example, physicians often conceal information from patients because they are afraid that bad news might cause their condition to deteriorate (Mueller, 2002). The American Medical Association's first code of medical ethics advised physicians to be leery of breaking bad news to ill patients (Vanderkieft, 2001).

Demographic effects on bad news delivery

An important component of breaking bad news is that communication from physicians can vary in its subjective and objective severity. When providers deliver bad news, a number of different demographic characteristics potentially influence how the news is delivered. Patients' and providers' sex, age, ethnicity, and education level may modify the message strategy that providers use to deliver bad news.

For example, the sex of provider–patient dyads can alter providers' delivery of bad news. When female providers encounter female patients, they are more likely to communicate about preventive care, such as breast and pelvic exams (Franks & Bertakis, 2003). Same-sex provider–patient dyads experience fewer communication barriers. As such, providers consistently engage in the comforting strategy (Gjerberg, 2002). In addition, the age of providers and patients modifies provider–patient interactions (Eva, 2002). Older providers play a parenting role and tend to comfort patients habitually (Thom, 2001). Regardless of who is older or younger in the provider–patient dyad, research demonstrates that age impacts patients' perceptions of communication satisfaction (Eva, 2002). Finally, the ethnicity of the patient also changes the providers' delivery of bad news. When providers deliver bad news to Caucasian and African American patients, they are direct (Ishikawa, Roter, Yamazaki, & Takayama, 2005; Johnson, Roter, Powe, & Cooper, 2004). Providers who deliver bad news to Latinos and Asians are consistently comforting (Sleath, Rubin, & Huston, 2003; Sung, 1999).

Providers also alter their communication strategies for breaking bad news based on patients' education levels. Patients who are less educated often have a lower socioeconomic status. Due to a common misperception on the part of some providers that more educated patients know more about medical issues in general, patients with higher education tend to receive less information and comfort when receiving bad news from providers (Alshidi, Bener, Brebner, & Dunn, 2001; Duran-Tauleria & Rona, 1999; Gergen, 1996; Mitchell, Stewart, Pattenmore, & Asher, 1989).

Patients' perception of bad news is likely impacted not only by demographic characteristics but also by their individual thoughts and experiences. Patients do not uniformly consider a majority of diagnoses as bad news. An individual's reactions to bad news will vary depending on a host of personal factors, including age, familial obligations, and culture (Davis, 1991). For instance, while the vast majority of patients in English-speaking countries want to know about their diagnosis and treatment, the proportion of individuals who want and receive relatively full disclosure in other countries is much lower (Davis, 1991).

Effective doctor–patient communication can alter patients' behavior both prior to (preventive) and after a diagnosis is received while patients are undergoing treatment (Dearing *et al.*, 1996; Greenfield, Kaplan, & Ware, 1985; Kreps & O'Hair, 1995). Research suggests that many factors influence a patient's satisfaction with the manner in which communication and breaking bad news occurs. For instance, it is well documented that the style of bad news delivery can greatly affect the manner in which the patient reacts to the news (Kreps & O'Hair, 1995; Mast, Kindlimann, & Langiwitz, 2005; Mueller, 2002).

Provider education in breaking bad news Despite the fact that breaking bad news is frequently cited as one of a physician's most difficult duties, medical schools do not typically offer formal training for this complicated undertaking (Vanderkieft, 2001; Yedidia *et al.*, 2003). This void creates a demand for health communication scholars to assist healthcare providers in competently addressing the discomfort and uncertainty associated with breaking bad news (Cegala & Lenzimeir Broz, 2003). When healthcare providers are given the opportunity to practice breaking bad news through skills training and simulated encounters, they feel more confident and less isolated (Eggly & Tzelepis, 2001; Wakefield, Cooke, & Boggis, 2003). Effective training allows providers to become aware of their personal attitudes and emotional reactions when breaking bad news. In addition, it helps skill physicians in crisis intervention and communication techniques (Ungar *et al.*, 2002).

Physicians note the importance of the physical and social settings of bad news interactions. Physicians agree that the news should be delivered in a comfortable location that offers patients privacy and is relatively quiet. The space should be large enough to comfortably accommodate multiple staff and family members (Buckman, 1996; Maynard, 1991). Second, the timing of the news is important, and arrangements should be made to convey the information at a time that is convenient for the patient. If rushed, the physician may be perceived as uninterested in the patient and the process. However, evidence suggests that physicians may delay breaking bad news despite the fact that the majority of patients want to hear it (Blanchard, Labrecque, Ruckdeschel, & Blanchard, 1988; Hopper & Fischbach, 1989) and that some physicians want to avoid situations in which a prognosis is discussed (Seale, 1991), possibly because of the discomfort associated with such interactions.

Whatever the severity of the diagnosis, it is clear that breaking bad news is a frightening and stressful aspect of the healthcare profession. Medical students should be exposed to various communication strategies to employ when breaking bad news. Providers have a substantial amount of power over patient satisfaction and compliance in such situations. More training programs need to be created and implemented, not only for medical students but also for practicing physicians. By using the communication guidelines set forth, formal and informal providers, educators, and trainers can enable their students and employees to have greater confidence during bad news interactions.

Provider communication with older patients

People aged 65 and older spend a significant portion of their time interacting with physicians, and they are more likely to spend time in hospital than younger patients (Thompson, Robinson, & Beisecker, 2004). The number of physician visits by older Americans is expected to increase in the next 20 years as people live longer and medical technologies and new medications allow them to manage health problems for longer periods of time than in previous decades (Thompson, Robinson, & Beisecker, 2004).

Interactions with physicians have important consequences for the quality of life of older patients (Beisecker & Thompson, 1995). Most older individuals report being satisfied with their healthcare providers. However, studies of provider–older patient interaction have demonstrated that many communication problems do occur between providers and older patients and that these can have negative implications for health-care and quality of life for older individuals (Adelman & Greene, 2000; Greene & Adelman, 2001, 2002). These communication issues are discussed in greater detail below.

Adelman, Greene, and Charon (1991) found physicians to be more condescending and indifferent towards older patients compared with younger patients. Physicians are often less likely to share decision-making with older patients (Greene, Adelman, Charon, & Hoffman, 1989), although again this depends upon the training the pro-vider has received in working with older patients. Physicians often initiate more of the topics in conversations with older patients, although patients also initiate a rela-tively high percentage of topics (Thompson, Robinson, & Beisecker, 2004).

In many cases of problematic interaction between providers and older patients, the patient may not have his or needs met. One study found that 27 percent of older diabetic patients' current problems were not addressed during the medical encounter with their physician (Rost & Frankel, 1993). As with other age groups, many physicians avoid addressing older patients' psychosocial concerns. Researchers have found that physicians often focus on medical issues when communicating with older patients and tend to spend relatively little time discussing psychosocial concerns. This is because many of these issues, such as relationship problems and financial difficulties, are uncomfortable topics for many physicians to discuss since they often elicit strong emotions such as embarrassment and fear. Physicians are often reluctant to address psychosocial concerns with older patients. Psychosocially oriented communication during medical encounters may facilitate an exchange of social support between provider and patient, and it could also play an important role in enabling accurate diagnosis of health problems and the prescription of more appropriate treatments. Most studies of providers and older patients have focused on physician–patient rela-tionships, and less is known about older patient interactions with nurses, clinical staff, and other types of providers.

Older patients often have more paternalistic attitudes toward providers, especially physicians, and they may be less likely than younger patients to be assertive with their doctor, initiate a topic change during a medical encounter, or challenge their doctor's decisions. Older patients are often reluctant to express complaints, confusion, disap-pointment, or misunderstandings to physicians, and they ask fewer questions than younger patients when talking to physicians (Adelman *et al.*, 1991). Older patients are often reluctant to communicate their concerns in medical encounters (Adelman *et al.*, 1991), but researchers have argued that if given time to present their concerns and raise issues, older patients may engage in more information-seeking behaviors.

Compliance with medical regimes can be a significant problem for older patients, especially when they have multiple chronic conditions and must follow a number of medication treatments (Coe, 1997; Haug & Ory, 1987). However, lack of compliance does not appear to be due to reluctance to follow instructions on the part of older patients. When providers spend more time explaining medications, interaction effects, and other important aspects of treatment to older adults, this appears to increase compliance with medical regimes (Beisecker & Thompson, 1995).

Stereotypes of older patients Like other individuals in our society (including older adults themselves), many physicians have negative stereotypes of older people, and this can affect their communication and treatment decisions. Older people are often viewed by providers as being too open about negative topics such as bereavement or health problems. Unfortunately, like all stereotypes, stereotypes of older people are often based on misconceptions about older adults and the aging process (Hummert, Shaner, & Garstka, 1995). Providers with negative stereotypes of older patients may attempt to limit their time with them or communicate in ways that are based upon negative stereotypes, such as engaging in patronizing behaviors (e.g. talking to the elderly patient as if he or she is a child). In addition, providers who are less knowledgeable about geriatric medicine may attribute some health problems to age as opposed to illness, and this may influence their medical decision-making. While physicians receive some geriatric medical training in medical school, only a relatively small number specialize in geriatric medicine. Other types of providers who see older patients may be even less knowledgeable about the aging process and older adult health issues.

CAT is a useful framework for understanding the relationship between stereotypes of older people and provider–older patient interaction. CAT proposes that when speakers from different social groups interact, they adjust or modify their verbal and nonverbal communication in order to accommodate each other (Gallois, Ogay, & Giles, 2004; Giles, Coupland, & Coupland, 1991; Giles, Mulac, Bradac, & Johnson, 1987).

Recall that as we make evaluations based upon whether a person is part of one of our in-groups or a member of some out-group, we have a number of choices about how to adapt our communication to that person, including convergence, divergence, overaccommodation, and underaccommodation. One common type of communication behavior that providers engage in with older patients is *overaccommodation*. For example, it is common for younger healthcare providers to raise the volume of their voice or speak more slowly when talking with older people, especially if they perceive the older person to be hard of hearing or cognitively deficient. Moreover, *underaccommodation* can occur when people from different social groups feel that they do not have anything in common to talk about. Providers may stick to "safe" topics, such as talk about the weather, if they perceive they do not have much in common with the older patient. Underaccommodation may deprive an older patient of more meaningful types of talk. In general, overaccommodating behaviors are often perceived as patronizing and underaccommodating behaviors lead to dissatisfying conversations. While healthcare providers often need to *diverge* from patients when interacting with other providers or for other professional reasons, during interactions with elderly patients providers should attempt to *converge* with the older patient's communication style and avoid overaccommodating or underaccommodating communication.

Discourse management is an important communication skill to learn for providers who work with older patients. Discourse management focuses on the receiver's conversational needs and the receptor's ability to attune to those needs, such as topic selection, backchanneling (e.g. noises like "humm" and "uh huh" that people make during conversation), or turn-taking behaviors (Gallois, Ogay, & Giles, 2004; Shepard, Giles, & Le Poire, 2001). Discourse management can be very important during communication to show conversation partners that they are being listened to and that the receptor understands what they are trying to communicate. Behaviors like backchanneling let the speaker know that the listener is still there and paying attention. It is important for healthcare providers communicating with older patients to employ discourse management to ensure that patients feel able to discuss their needs and concerns.

Similar to other age groups, successful communication between physicians and older patients has been linked to higher satisfaction with care, better disclosure of patient problems, improved compliance with physician treatment recommendations, and decreased use of emergency services (Stuart, 2002; Wasson *et al.*, 1984). In addition, Weiss and Blustein (1996) found that older patients in long-term relationships with physicians were less likely to be hospitalized and used fewer costly services than individuals who had shorter relationships with physicians.

Companions and provider-older patient interaction The presence of a companion (typically a spouse or an adult child) can have a significant impact on communication between older patients and healthcare providers (Adelman, Parks, & Albrecht, 1987). Beisecker (1989) found that about half of the older people in her study brought a companion to the medical interview. When a companion is present, older patients tend to raise fewer topics with physicians, tend to be less assertive, and engage in fewer joint decisions with physicians.

Companions often play a variety of roles in interaction during medical visits, including helping older individuals to remember information, providing emotional support and companionship, aiding in decisions, and serving as an advocate or interpreter for the patient. Beisecker and Thompson (1995) identify three distinct roles for companions of older patients during medical visits. According to these researchers, companions who take on the *watchdog* role give information on behalf of the patient, or elaborate upon information provided by the patient, encouraging the provision of precise, complete, and accurate information to the doctor. Those who play the *significant other* role provide feedback to both the patient and the physician about the interview. Finally, the *surrogate patient* role is characterized by the companion taking a more active role in the medical encounter than the actual patient, such as answering questions for the patient or raising concerns. In these cases providers may communicate with the companion more than with the patient.

Managed care influence on provider–older patient interaction Issues related to managed care organizations, health insurance, and Medicare often impact provider–older patient relationships. At age 65, older Americans are eligible for Medicare, and Medicare benefits make it possible for older individuals who are managing ongoing health problems to receive affordable healthcare. Services that are reimbursed by Medicare are often subject to restrictions, such as limited access to certain providers, procedures, and medications. Older adults often receive only minimal reimbursement through Medicare for medications they need for managing ongoing health conditions, and many older people must reduce expenses in other areas of their life in order to fill prescriptions. Many of these same individuals are not able to afford (or obtain) supplementary health insurance to make up the difference between the price of medications and what Medicare will reimburse. Unfortunately, this means that older people with limited financial means may have to give up food or other necessities in order to have medications, or they may decide not to take the medications altogether (which can worsen their health condition).

While managed care helps to make healthcare more affordable, its focus on cost-cutting can negatively affect provider–older patient interactions. According to Crystal (2002), pressure from managed care organization administrators to keep physician visit lengths brief can significantly affect the ability of providers to effectively influence elderly patients' health behaviors. Moreover, the managed care administrative practice of frequently changing the providers who are allowed to participate in managed care networks in an effort to reduce costs can undermine older patients' trust, deny access to physicians and other providers with whom older patients have a history, and lead to greater dissatisfaction with overall healthcare (Crystal, 2002). In addition, both providers and older patients may become frustrated by the limitations of managed care plans (Stuart, 2002).

Summary

Communication between providers and patients can be complex due to the different perceptions of health and healthcare that result from each party's level of education, training, and life experience. Despite the differences between provider and patients, it is possible for competent and satisfying communication to occur in the provider–patient relationship. To achieve this goal, it is important for both providers and patients to recognize important differences between them in terms of perceptions about health and healthcare, needs, goals, and interaction styles. Successful communication between healthcare providers and patients can lead to a number of important outcomes, including greater patient satisfaction, improved health outcomes, and lower healthcare costs.

References

Adelman, R. D., & Greene, M. G. (2000). Communication between older patients and their physicians. *Clinics in Geriatric Medicine*, 16(1), 1–24.

Adelman, R. D., Greene, M. G., & Charon, R. (1991). Issues in physician–elderly patient interaction. *Ageing and Society*, 2, 127–148.

Adelman, M. B., Parks, M. R., & Albrecht, T. L. (1987). Beyond close relationships: Support in weak ties. In T. L. Albrecht & M. B. Adelman (Eds), *Communicating social support* (pp. 126–147). Newbury Park, CA: Sage.

Alshidi, A. M., Bener, A., Brebner, J., & Dunn, E. V. (2001). Asthma diagnosis and management in adults: Is the risk of underdiagnosis and undertreatment related to patients' education levels? *Journal of Asthma, 38,* 121–126.

Ambady, N., LaPlante, D., Nguyen, T., Rosenthal, R., Chaumeton, N., & Levinson, W. (2002). Surgeons' tone of voice: A clue to malpractice history. *Surgery, 132,* 5–9.

Anderson, C. M. (2001). Communication in the medical interview team: An analysis of patients' stories in the United States and Hong Kong. *Howard Journal of Communications, 12,* 61–72.

Aspden, P., Wolcott, J., Bootman, J. L., & Cronewett, L. R. (2007). *Preventing medication errors: Quality chasm series.* National Academy of Sciences Executive Summary. Retrieved February 7, 2007 from http://www.nap.edu, 1–7.

Association of American Medical Colleges (AAMC). (1999, October). Contemporary issues in medicine: Communication in medicine (Report III). Washington, DC.

Avtgis, T. A., Brann, M., & Staggers, S. M. (2006). Perceived information exchange and health control expectancies as influenced by a patient's medical interview situation. *Communication Research Reports, 23,* 231–237.

Babrow, A. S. (2001). Uncertainty, value, communication, and problematic integration. *Journal of Communication, 51,* 553–573.

Babrow, A. S. (2007). Problematic integration theory. In B. B. Whaley & W. Samter (Eds), *Explaining communication: Contemporary theories and exemplars* (pp. 181–200). Hillsdale, NJ: Lawrence Erlbaum Associates.

Babrow, A. S., Kasch, C. R., & Ford, L. A. (1998). The many meanings of uncertainty in illness: Toward a systematic accounting. *Health Communication, 10,* 1–23.

Baile, W. F., Buckman, R., Lenzi, R., Glober, G., Beale, E., & Kudelka, A. P. (2000). SPIKES—A six-step protocol for delivering bad news: Application to the patient with cancer. *Oncologist, 5,* 302–311.

Barnett, M. (2004). A GP guide to breaking bad news. *The Practitioner, 2,* 392–404.

Batenburg, V., & Smal, J. A. (1997). Does a communication skills course influence medical students' attitudes? *Medical Teacher, 19,* 263–269.

Beach, M. C., Roter, D., Larson, S., Levinson, W., Ford, D. and Frankel, R. (2004) What do physicians tell patients about themselves? A qualitative analysis of physician self-disclosure. *Journal of General Internal Medicine, 19,* pp. 911–916.

Beck, C. S. (1997). *Partnership for health: Building relationships between women and health caregivers.* Mahwah, NJ: Lawrence Erlbaum.

Beckman, H. B., Markakis, K. M., Suchman, A. L., & Frankel, R. M. (1994). The doctor–patient relationship and malpractice: Lessons from plaintiff depositions. *Archives of Internal Medicine, 154,* 1365–1370.

Beisecker, A. E. (1989). The influence of a companion on the doctor-elderly patient interaction. *Health Communication, 1,* 55–70.

Beisecker, A. E., & Beisecker, T. D. (1993). Using metaphors to characterize doctor–patient relationships: Paternalism versus consumerism. *Health Communication, 5,* 41–58.

Beisecker, A. E., & Thompson, T. L. (1995). The elderly patient–physician interaction. In J. F. Nussbaum & J. Coupland (Eds), *The handbook of communication and aging research* (pp. 397–416). Mahwah, NJ: Lawrence Erlbaum.

Berger, P. L., & Luckman, T. (1966). *The social construction of reality.* New York: Anchor Books.

Blanchard, C. G., Labrecque, M. S., Ruckdeschel, J. C., & Blanchard, E. B. (1988). Information and decision-making preferences of hospitalized adult cancer patients. *Social Science Medicine, 27,* 1139–1145.

Bor, R., Miller, R., Goldman, E., & Scher, I. (1993). The meaning of bad news in HIV disease: Counseling about dreaded issues revisited. *Counsel Psychological Quarterly, 6,* 69–80.

Brashers, D. E. (2001). Communication and uncertainty management. *Journal of Communication, 51,* 477–497.

Brashers, D. E., Goldsmith, D. J., & Hsieh, E. (2002). Information seeking and avoiding in health contexts. *Human Communication Research, 28,* 258–271.

Brown, J. B., Stewart, M. A., & Ryan, B. L. (2003). Outcomes of patient–provider interaction. In T. L. Thompson, A. M. Dorsey, K. I. Miller, & R. Parrot (Eds), *Handbook of health communication* (pp. 141–161). Mahwah, NJ: Lawrence Erlbaum.

Buckman, R. (1996). Talking to patients about cancer. *British Medical Journal, 31,* 699–700.

Bylund, C., & MaKoul, G. (2005). Examining empathy in medical encounters: An observational study using the empathic communication coding system. *Health Communication, 18,* 123–140.

Cameron, L. D., & Leventhal, H. (2003). *The self-regulation of health and illness behavior.* London: Routledge.

Chambers, C. V., Markson, L., Diamond, J. J., Lasch, L., & Berger, M. (1999). Health beliefs and compliance with inhaled corticosteroids by asthmatic patients in primary care practices. *Respiratory Medicine, 93*, 88–94.

Cegala, D. J., & Lenzimeir Broz, S. (2003). Provider and patient communication skills training. In T. L. Thompson, A. M. Dorsey, K. I. Miller, & R. Parrott (Eds), *Handbook of health communication* (pp. 95–119). Mahwah, NJ: Lawrence Erlbaum.

Cegala, D. J., McClure, L., Marinelli, T. M., & Post, D. M. (2000). The effects of communication skills training on patients' participation during medical interviews. *Patient Education and Counseling, 41*, 209–222.

Cegala, D. J., Post, D., & McClure, L. (2001). The effects of patient communication skills training on the discourse of elderly patients during a primary care interview. *Journal of the American Geriatrics Society, 49*, 1505–1511.

Cegala, D. J., Street, Jr., R. L., & Clinch, C. R. (2007). The impact of patient participation on physicians' information provision during a primary care medical interview. *Health Communication, 2*, 177–185.

Cohen, M. R. (2007). Causes of medication errors. In M. R. Cohen (Ed.), *Medication errors* (pp. 55–66). Washington, DC: American Pharmacist Association.

Cline, R. J. (2003). Everyday interpersonal communication and health. In T. L. Thompson, A. M. Dorsey, K. I. Miller, & R. Parrott (Eds), *Handbook of health communication* (pp. 285–313). Mahwah, NJ: Lawrence Erlbaum.

Cline, R. J. (2011). Everyday interpersonal communication and health. In T. L. Thompson, R. Parrott, & J. F. Nussbaum (Eds), *The Routledge handbook of health communication, 2nd ed.* (pp. 377–396). New York: Routledge.

Coe, R. M. (1987). Communication and medical care outcomes: Analysis of conversations between doctors and elderly patients. In R. A. Ward & S. S. Tobin (Eds), *Health in aging* (pp. 180–193). New York: Springer.

Crystal, S. (2002). Commentary: Health care organizational structure, prevention, and health behavior among the elderly. In K. W. Schaie, H. Leventhal, & S. L. Willis (Eds), *Effective health behavior in older adults* (pp. 287–299). New York: Springer.

Czaja, R., Manfredi, C., & Price, J. (2003). The determinants and consequences of information seeking among cancer patients. *Journal of Health Communication, 8*, 529–562.

Davis, H. (1991). Breaking bad news. *Practitioner, 235*, 522–526.

Dearing, J. W., Rogers, E. M., Meyer, G., Casey, M. K., Rao, N., Campo, S., & Henderson, G. M. (1996). Social marketing and diffusion-based strategies for communicating health with unique populations: HIV prevention in San Francisco. *Journal of Health Communication, 1*, 343–363.

Dennis, M. R., Kunkel, A., & Keyton, J. (2008). Problematic integration theory, appraisal theory, and the Bosom Buddies Breast Cancer Support Group. *Journal of Applied Communication Research, 36*, 415–436.

Duggan, A., & Petronio, S. (2009). When your child is in crisis: Navigating medical needs with issues of privacy management. In T. Socha & G. Stamp (Eds), *Parents, children, and communication II: Interfacing outside of home* (pp. 117–132). Thousand Oaks, CA: Sage.

Dulai, G. S., Farmer, M. M., Ganz, P. A., Bernaards, C. A., Qi, K., Dietrich, A. J., *et al.* (2004). Primary care provider perceptions of barriers to and facilitators of colorectal cancer screening in a managed care setting. *Cancer, 100*, 1843–1852.

du Pré, A. (2004). *Communicating about health: Current issues and perspectives* (2nd ed.). Boston: McGraw-Hill.

Duran-Tauleria, E., & Rona, R. J. (1999). Geographical and socioeconomic variation in the prevalence of asthma symptoms in English and Scottish children. *Thorax, 54*, 476–481.

Eggly, S., & Tzelepis, A. (2001). Relational control in difficult physician–patient encounters: Negotiating treatment for pain. *Journal of Health Communication, 6*, 323–347.

Epstein, R. M., Shields, C. G., Franks, P., Meldrum, S. C., Feldman, M. & Kravitz, R. L. (2007). Exploring and validating patient concerns: Relation to prescribing for depression. *Annals of Family Medicine, 5*, 21–28.

Eva, K. W. (2002). The aging physician: Changes in cognitive processing and their impact on medical practice. *Academic Medicine, 77*, S1–S6.

Frank, E., Elon, E., Carrera, J. S., & Hertzberg, V. S. (2007). Predictors of US medical students' prevention counseling practices. *Preventive Medicine. 44*(1), 76–81.

Franks, P., & Bertakis, K. D. (2003). Physician gender, patient gender, and primary care. *Journal of Women's Health, 12*, 73–80.

Freedman, M. (2002, June). The tort mess. *Forbes*. Retrieved September 29, 2002, from www.forbes.com.

Frey, L. R., Adelman, M. B., Flint, L. J., & Query, J. L., Jr. (2000). Weaving meanings together in an AIDS residence: Communicative practices, perceived health outcomes, and the symbolic construction of community. *Journal of Health Communication, 5,* 53–72.

Gadkari, A., & McHorney, C. A. (2010). Medication nonfulfillment rates and reasons: Narrative systematic review. *Current Medical Research & Opinion, 26,* 683–705.

Gallois, C., Ogay, T., & Giles, H. (2004). Communication accommodation theory: A look back and a look ahead. In W. Gudykunst (Ed.), *Theorizing about intercultural communication* (pp. 121–148). Thousand Oaks, CA: Sage.

Gandhi, T. K., Weingart, S. N., Borus, J., Seger, A. C., Peterson, J., Burdick, E., *et al.* (2003). Adverse drug events in ambulatory care. *New England Journal of Medicine, 348,* 1556–1564.

Giles, H., Coupland, N., & Coupland, J. (1991). Accommodation theory: Communication, context, and consequence. In H. Giles, J. Coupland, & N. Coupland (Eds), *Contexts of accommodation: Developments in applied sociolinguistics* (pp. 1–68). Cambridge: Cambridge University Press.

Giles, H., Mulac, A., Bradac, J. J., & Johnson, P. (1987). Speech accommodation theory: The first decade and beyond. In M. L. McLaughlin (Ed.), *Communication yearbook 10* (pp. 13–48). Beverly Hills, CA: Sage.

Gillotti, C. M., & Applegate, J. L. (1999). Explaining illness as bad news: Individual differences in explaining illness-related information. In B. B. Whaley (Ed.), *Explaining illness: Research, theory, and strategies* (pp. 101–120). Mahwah, NJ: Lawrence Erlbaum.

Gillotti, C. M., Thompson, T., & McNeilis, K. (2002). Communicative competence in the delivery of bad news. *Social Science and Medicine, 54,* 1011–1023.

Geist, P., & Hardesty, M. (1990). Reliable, silent, hysterical, or assured: Physicians assess patient cues in their medical decision making. *Health Communication, 2,* 69–90.

Gergen, P. (1996). Social class and asthma, distinguishing between the disease and the diagnosis. *International Journal of Epidemiology, 25,* 388–393.

Giles, H., Coupland, J., & Coupland, N. (Eds). (1991). *Contexts of accommodation: Developments in applied sociolinguistics.* Cambridge: Cambridge University Press.

Giles, H., Mulac, A., Bradac, J. J., & Johnson, P. (1987). Speech accommodation theory: The next decade and beyond. *Communication Yearbook, 10,* 13–48.

Gjerberg, E. (2002).Gender differences in doctors' preference—and gender differences in final specialization. *Social Science Medicine, 54,* 591–605.

Golin, C. E., DiMatteo, M. R., & Gelberg, L. (1996). The role of patient participation in the doctor visit: Implications for adherence to diabetes care. *Diabetes Care, 19,* 1153–1164.

Greene, M. G., & Adelman, R. D. (2001). Building the physician–older patient relationship. In M. L. Hummert & J. F. Nussbaum (Eds), *Aging, communication, and health: Linking research and practice for successful aging* (pp. 101–120). Mahwah, NJ: Lawrence Erlbaum.

Greene, M., & Adelman, R. (2002, January). Physician–older adult patient communication about cancer. In G. L. Kreps (Chair), *Consumer–Provider Communication Symposium,* Bethesda, MD.

Greene, M. G., Adelman, R., Charon, R., & Hoffman, S. (1989). Concordance between physicians and their older and younger patients in the primary care medical encounter. *Gerontologist, 29,* 808–813.

Greene, M. G., Adelman, R. D., Friedmann, E., & Charon, R. (1994). Older patient satisfaction with communication during an initial medical encounter. *Social Science and Medicine, 38,* 1279–1288.

Greenfield, S., Kaplan, S., & Ware, J. E. (1985). Expanding patient involvement in care: Effects on patient outcomes. *Annals of Internal Medicine, 102,* 520–528.

Greenfield, S., Kaplan, S. H., Ware, J. E., Jr., Yano, E. M., & Frank, H. J. (1988). Patients' participation in medical care: Effects on blood sugar control and quality of life in diabetes. *Journal of General Internal Medicine, 3,* 448–457.

Griffith, C. Wilson, J. F., Langer, S., & Haist, S. A. (2003). House staff nonverbal communication skills and standardized patient satisfaction. *Journal of General Internal Medicine, 18,* 170–174.

Hall, J. A., Roter, D. L., Blanch, D. C., & Frankel, R. M. (2009). Nonverbal sensitivity in medical students: Implications for clinical interactions. *Journal of General Internal Medicine, 24,* 1217–1222.

Harrington, J., Noble, L. M., & Newman, S. P. (2004). Improving patients' communication with doctors: A systematic review of intervention studies. *Patient Education & Counseling, 52,* 7–16.

Harrington, N. G., Norling, G. R., Witte, F. M., Taylor, J., & Andrews, J. E. (2007). The effects of communication skills training on pediatricians' and parents' communication during "sick child" visits. *Health Communication, 2,* 105–114.

Haug, M. R., & Ory, M. G. (1987). Issues in elderly patient–provider relations. *Research on Aging*, 9, 3–44.

Hemmerdinger, J., Stoddard, S, & Lilford, R. (2007). A systematic review of tests of empathy in medicine. *BMC Medical Education*, 24, 1–8.

Hickson, G. B., Wright Clayton, E., Entman, S., Miller, C., Githens, P. B. *et al.* (1994). Obstetricians' prior malpractice experience and patients' satisfaction with care. *Journal of the American Medical Association*, 272, 1583–1587.

Hickson, G. B., Federspiel, C. F., Pichert, J. W., Miller, C. S., Gauld-Jaerger *et al.* (2002). Patient complaints and malpractice risk. *Journal of the American Medical Association*, 287, 2951–2957.

Hines, S. C., Babrow, A. S., Badzek, L., & Moss, A. (2001). From coping with life to coping with death: Problematic integration for the seriously ill elderly. *Health Communication*, 13, 327–342.

Hirsch, A. T., Atchison, J. W., Berger, J. J., Waxenberg, L. B., Lafayette-Lucey, A., Bulcourf, B. B., & Robinson, M. (2005). Patient satisfaction with treatment for chronic pain: Predictors and relationship to compliance. *Clinical Journal of Pain*, 21, 302–310.

Hopper, S. V., & Fischbach, R. L. (1989). Patient–physician communication when blindness threatens. *Patient Education Counsel*, 14, 69–79.

Hoy, A. M. (1985). Breaking bad news to patients. *British Journal of Hospital Medicine*, 34, 96–99.

Hummert, M. L., Shaner, J. L., & Garstka, T. A. (1995). Cognitive processes affecting communication with older adults: The case for stereotypes, attitudes, and beliefs about communication. In J. F. Nussbaum & J. Coupland (Eds), *Handbook of communication and aging research* (pp. 105–131). Mahwah, NJ: Lawrence Erlbaum.

Humphris, G. M., & Kaney, S. (2001). Assessing the development of communication skills in undergraduate medical students. *Medical Education*, 35, 225–231.

Institute of Medicine (IOM) (2004). *Health literacy: A prescription to end confusion*. Washington, DC: National Academy of Sciences Press.

Ishikawa, H., Roter, D. L., Yamazaki, Y., & Takayama, T. (2005). Physician–elderly patient–companion communication and the roles of companions in geriatric encounters. *Social Science Medicine*, 60, 2307–2320.

Johnson, R. L., Roter, D., Powe, N. R., & Cooper, L. A. (2004). Patient race/ethnicity and quality of patient–physician communication during medical visits. *Journal of General Internal Medicine*, 19, 101–110.

Kaplan, S. H., Greenfield, S., & Ware, J. E., Jr. (1989). Assessing the effects of physician–patient interactions on the outcomes of chronic disease. *Medical Care*, 275, S110–S127.

Kaufman, D. M., Laidlaw, T. A., & Macleod, H. (2000). Communication skills in medical school: Exposure, confidence, and performance. *Academic Medicine*, 75, S90–S92.

Kim, S. S., Kaplowitz, S., Johnston, M. V. (2004). The effects of physician empathy on patient satisfaction and compliance. *Evaluation and the Health Professions*, 27, 237–251.

Kreps, G. L. (1988a). Relational communication in health care. *Southern Speech Communication Journal*, 53, 344–359.

Kreps, G. L. (1988b). The pervasive role of information in health and health care: Implications for health communication policy. In J. Anderson (Ed.), *Communication yearbook* (Vol. 11, pp. 238–276). Newbury Park, CA: Sage.

Kreps, G. L. (2003). Impact of communication on cancer risk, incidence, morbidity, and quality of life [Special issue]. *Health Communication*, 15(2), 163–170.

Kreps, G. L., & O'Hair, D. (Eds). (1995). *Communication and health outcomes*. Cresskill, NJ: Hampton Press.

Kressin, N. R., Wang, F., Long, J., Bokhour, B. G., Orner, M. B., Rothendler, J., *et al.* (2007). Hypertensive patients' race, health beliefs, process of care, and medication adherence. *Journal of General Internal Medicine*, 22, 768–774.

Lambert, B. L., Street, R. L., Cegala, D. J., Smith, D. H., Kurtz, S., & Schofield, T. (1996). Provider–patient communication, patient-centered care, and the mangle of practice. *Health Communication*, 9, 27–43.

Lammers, J. C., Barbour, J. B., & Duggan, A. P. (2003). Organizational forms of the provision of health care: An institutional perspective. In T. L. Thompson, A. M. Dorsey, K. I. Miller, & R. Parrott (Eds), *Handbook of health communication* (pp. 319–345). Mahwah, NJ: Lawrence Erlbaum.

Lefkowitz, B. (2006). *Community health centers: A movement and the people who made it happen*. New Brunswick, NJ: Rutgers University Press.

Linn, M. W., Linn, B. S., & Stein, S. R. (1982). Satisfaction with ambulatory care and compliance in older patients. *Medical Care*, 6, 606–614.

Marteau, T. M., Humphrey, C., Matoon, G., Kidd, J., Lloyd, M., & Horder, J. (1991). Factors influencing the communication skills of first-year clinical medical students. *Medical Education, 36*, 127–134.

Mast, M. S., Kindlimann, A., & Langiwitz, W. (2005). Recipients' perspective on breaking bad news: How you put it really makes a difference. *Patient Education and Counseling, 58*, 244–251.

Martin, H. (2007). Patients' health beliefs and adaptation to carpal tunnel syndrome based on duration of symptomatic presentation. *Journal of Hand Therapy, 20*, 29–35.

Matthias, M. S. (2009). Problematic integration in pregnancy and child-birth. Contrasting approaches to uncertainty and desire in obstetric and midwifery care. *Health Communication, 24*, 60–70.

Maynard, D. W. (1991). Bearing bad news in clinical settings. In B. Dervin & M. J. Voigt (Eds), *Progress in communication sciences* (Vol. 10, pp. 143–172). Norwood, NJ: Ablex.

McHorney, C. A. (2009). The adherence estimator: A brief, proximal screener for patient propensity to adhere to prescription medications for chronic diseases. *Current Medical Research and Opinion, 25*, 215–238.

Mentzer, S. J., & Snyder, M. L. (1982). The doctor and the patient: A psychological perspective. In G. S. Sanders & J. Suls (Eds.), *Social psychology of health and illness* (pp. 161–181). Hillsdale, NJ: Lawrence Erlbaum.

Mitchell, E. A., Stewart, A. W., Pattenmore, P. K., & Asher, M. I. (1989). Socioeconomic status in childhood asthma. *International Journal of Epidemiology, 18*, 888–890.

Moore, P. J., Sickel, A. E., Malat, J. Williams, D. Jackson, J., & Adler, N. E. (2004). Psychosocial factors in medical and psychological treatment avoidance: The role of the doctor-patient relationship. *Journal of Health Psychology, 9*, 421–433.

Mueller, P. S. (2002). Breaking bad news to patients. *Postgraduate Medicine, 112*, 3–18.

Noland, C. M., & Rickles, N. M. (2009). Reflection and analysis of how pharmacy students learn to communicate about medication errors. *Health Communication, 24*, 351–360.

Nussbaum, J. F., Ragan, S., & Whaley, B. (2003). Children, older adults, and women: Impact on provider–patient interaction. In T. L. Thompson, A. M. Dorsey, K. I. Miller, & R. Parrott (Eds), *Handbook of health communication* (pp. 183–204). Mahwah, NJ: Lawrence Erlbaum.

O'Hair, H. D. (1989). Dimensions of relational communication and control during physician–patient interactions. *Health Communication, 1*, 97–115.

O'Hair, H. D., Allman, J., & Moore, S. D. (1996). A cognitive-affective model of relational expectations in the provider–patient context. *Journal of Health Psychology, 1*, 307–322.

O'Hair, H. D., Kreps, G. L., & Sparks, L., (2007). Conceptualizing cancer care and communication. In H. D. O'Hair, G. L. Kreps & L. Sparks (Eds), *Handbook of communication and cancer care* (pp. 1–12). Cresskill, NJ: Hampton Press.

Parrott, R., Stuart, T., & Cairns, A. B. (2000). The reduction of uncertainty through communication during adjustment to spinal cord injury. In D. O. Braithwaite & T. L. Thompson (Eds), *Handbook of communication and people with disabilities: Research and application* (pp. 339–352). Hillsdale, NJ: Lawrence Erlbaum.

Pecchioni, L., & Sparks, L. (2007). Health information sources of individuals with cancer and their family members. *Health Communication, 21*, 143–151.

Pennbridge, J., Moya, R., & Rodrigues, L. (1999). Questionnaire survey of California consumers' use and rating of sources of healthcare information including the internet. *Western Journal of Medicine, 171*, 302–305.

Petronio, S. (2002). *Boundaries of privacy: Dialectics of disclosure.* New York: SUNY Press.

Petronio, S., & Reirerson, J. (2009). Privacy of confidentiality: Grasping the complexities through Communication Privacy Management. In T. Afifi & W. Afifi (Eds), *Uncertainty and information regulation in interpersonal contexts: Theories and application* (pp. 365–383). New York: Routledge.

Petronio, S., & Sargent, J. (2011). Disclosure predicaments arising during the course of patient care: Nurses' privacy management. *Health Communication, 26*, 255–266.

Ptacek, J. T., & Eberhardt, T. L. (1996). Breaking bad news: A review of literature. *JAMA, 276*, 496–502.

Reed, S. K. (1988). *Cognition: Theory and applications* (2nd ed.). Pacific Grove, CA: Brooks/Cole.

Rees, C., Sheard, C., & McPherson, A. C. (2002). A qualitative study to explore undergraduate medical students' attitudes towards communication skills learning. *Medical Teacher, 24*, 289–293.

Richardson, M. A., Sanders, T., Palmer, L. J., Greisinger, A., & Singeltary, S. E. (2000). Complementary/

alternative medicine in a comprehensive cancer center and the implications for oncology. *Journal of Clinical Oncology, 18*, 2505–2514.

Roter, D. L., & Hall, J. A. (2004). Physician gender and patient-centered communication: A critical review of empirical research. *Annual Review of Public Health, 25*, 497–519.

Roter, D. L., & Hall, J. A. (2011). How medical interaction shapes and reflects the physician-patient relationship. In T. L. Thompson, R. Parrott, & J. F. Nussbaum (Eds), *The Routledge handbook of health communication, 2nd ed.* (pp. 55–68). New York: Routledge.

Roter, D. L., Hall, J. A., Kern, D. E., Barker, L. R., Cole, K. A., & Roca, R. P. (1995). Improving physicians' interviewing skills and reducing patients' emotional distress: A randomized clinical trial. *Archives of Internal Medicine, 155*, 1877–1884.

Roter, D. L., Stewart, M., Putnam, S. M., Lipkin, M. J., Stiles, W., & Inui, T. S. (1997). Communication patterns of primary care physicians. *Journal of the American Medical Association, 277*(4), 350–356.

Rost, K., & Frankel, R. (1993). The introduction of the older patient's problems in the medical visit. *Journal of Health and Aging, 5*, 387–401.

Schank, R., & Abelson, R. (1977). *Scripts, goals, and understanding.* Hillsdale, NJ: Lawrence Erlbaum.

Seale, C. (1991). Communication and awareness about death: A study of a random sample of dying people. *Social Science Medicine, 32*, 943–952.

Sheer, V. C., & Cline, R. J. (1995). Testing a model of perceived information adequacy and uncertainty reduction in physician–patient interactions. *Journal of Applied Communication Research, 23*, 44–59.

Shepard, C. A., Giles, H., & Le Poire, B. A. (2001). Communication accommodation theory. In W. P. Robinson & H. Giles (Eds), *The new handbook of language and social psychology* (2nd ed.). Chichester: John Wiley.

Sherman, F. (2007). Medication nonadherence: A national epidemic among America's seniors. *Geriatrics, 62*, 5–6.

Shokar, N. K., Carlson, C. A., & Shokar, G. S. (2006). Physician and patient influences on the rate of colorectal cancer screening in a primary care clinic. *Journal of Cancer Education, 21*, 84–88.

Shore, D. A. (2003). Communicating in times of uncertainty: The need for trust. *Journal of Health Communication, 8*, 13–14.

Sleath, B., Rubin, R. H., & Huston, S. A. (2003). Hispanic ethnicity, physician–patient communication, and anti-depressant adherence. *Comprehensive Psychiatry, 44*, 198–204.

Smith, R. C. (2002). *Patient-centered interviewing: An evidence-based method* (2nd ed.). Philadelphia, PA: Lippencott Williams & Wilkins.

Sparks, L. (2003a). An introduction to cancer communication and aging: Theoretical and research insights. *Health Communication, 15*, 123–132.

Sparks, L. (Ed.). (2003b). Cancer communication and aging [Special Issue]. *Health Communication, 15*(2), 123–258.

Sparks, L. (2007). Cancer care and the aging patient: Complexities of age-related communication barriers. In H. D. O'Hair, L. Sparks, & G. L. Kreps (Eds), *Handbook of communication and cancer care* (pp. 233–249). Cresskill, NJ: Hampton Press.

Sparks, L. (2008). Family decision-making. In W. Donsbach (Ed.) *The international encyclopedia of communication, 4*, (pp. 1729–1733). Oxford, UK and Malden, MA: Wiley-Blackwell.

Sparks, L., & Villagran, M. (2008). *La Comunicación en el Cancer: Comunicación y apoyo emocional en el laberinto del cancer. [English translation: Communication and emotional support in the cancer maze.]* Spain: Aresta.

Sparks, L., & Villagran, M. (2010). *Patient and provider interaction: A global health communication perspective.* Cambridge: Polity Press.

Sparks, L., Rogers, K., & Bevan, J. (2012). Factors in distant caregiving relationships: An intergroup communication approach. *Journal of Communication in Healthcare, 5*, 12–22.

Sparks, L., O'Hair, H. D., & Kreps, G. L. (Eds) (2008a). *Cancer communication and aging.* Cresskill, NJ: Hampton Press.

Sparks, L., O'Hair, H. D. & Kreps, G. L. (2008b). Conceptualizing cancer communication and aging: New directions for research. In L. Sparks, H. D. O'Hair, & G. L. Kreps, (Eds), *Cancer communication and aging* (pp. 1–14). Cresskill, NJ: Hampton Press.

Sparks, L., Villagran, M., Parker-Raley, J., & Cunningham, C. (2007). A patient-centered approach to breaking bad news: Communication guidelines for health care providers. *Journal of Applied Communication Research, 35*, 177–196.

Stewart, M. A. (1995). Effective physician–patient communication and health outcomes: A review. *Canadian Medical Association Journal, 152*, 1423–1433.

Street, R. L., Jr., Gordon, H., & Haidet, P. (2007). Physicians' communication and perceptions of patients:

Is it how they look, how they talk, or is it just the doctor? *Social Science Medicine, 65,* 586–598.

Stuart, B. (2002). How provider payment policies affect the health-care-seeking behavior of the elderly. In K. W. Schaie, H. Leventhal, & S. L. Willis (Eds), *Effective health behavior in older adults* (pp. 191–228). New York: Springer.

Sung, C. L. (1999). Asian patients' distrust of western medical care: One perspective. *Mount Sinai Journal of Medicine, 66,* 259–320.

Tarrant, C., Windridge, K., Boulton, M., Baker, R., & Freeman, G. (2003). Qualitative study of the meaning of personal care in general practice. *British Medical Journal, 326,* 1310–1315.

Thom, D. H. (2001). Physician behaviors that predict patient trust. *Journal of Family Practice, 50,* 323–328.

Thompson, T. L. (1994). Interpersonal communication and health care. In M. L. Knapp & G. R. Miller (Eds.), *Handbook of interpersonal communication* (pp. 696–725). Newbury Park, CA: Sage.

Thompson, T. L., Robinson, J. D., & Beisecker, A. E. (2004). The older patient–physician interaction. In J. F. Nussbaum & J. Coupland (Eds.), *Handbook of communication and aging research* (2nd ed., pp. 451–477). Mahwah, NJ: Lawrence Erlbaum.

Thompson, T. L., Whaley, B. B., & Stone, A. M. (2011). Explaining illness: Issues concerning the co-construction of explications. In T. L. Thompson, R. Parrott, & J. F. Nussbaum (Eds), *The Routledge handbook of health communication, 2nd ed.* (pp. 293–305). New York: Routledge.

Ungar, L., Alperin, M., Amiel, G. E., Beharier, Z., & Reis, S. (2002). Breaking bad news: Structured training for family medicine residents. *Patient Education and Counseling, 48,* 63–68.

US Census Bureau. (2005). 2005 service sector annual survey: Health care and social assistance services. RetrievedJuly 23, 2012, from: www.census.gov/svsd/www/services/sas/sas_data/sas62.htm.

Valente, C. M., Antlitz, A. M., Boyd, M. D., & Triosi, A. J. (1988). The importance of physician-patient communication in reducing medical liability. *Maryland Medical Journal, 37,* 75–78.

Vanderford, M. L., Jenks, E. B., & Sharf, B. F. (1997). Exploring patients' experiences as a primary source of meaning. *Health Communication, 9,* 13–26.

Vanderkieft, G. K. (2001). Breaking bad news. *American Family Physician, 64,* 1975–1978.

van Zanten, M., Boulet, J. R., & McKinley, D. (2007). Using standardized patients to assess the interpersonal skills of physicians: Six years' experience with a high-stakes certification examination. *Health Communication, 22,* 195–205.

Villagran, M. M., & Sparks, L. (2010). Social identity and health contexts. In H. Giles, S. Reid, & J. Harwood (Eds), *The dynamics of intergroup communication* (pp. 235–248). New York & Berlin: Peter Lang.

Villagran, M. M., Weathers, M. Keefe, B., & Sparks, L. (2010). Medical providers as global warming and climate change health educators: A health literacy approach. *Communication Education, 59*(3), 312–327.

Vincent, C., Young, M., & Philips, A. (1994). Why do people sue doctors? A study of patients and relatives taking legal action. *Lancet, 343,* 1609–1613.

Wasson, J. H., Sauvigne, A. E., Mogielmicki, R. P., Frey, W. G., Sox, C. H., Gaudette, C., & Rockwell, A. (1984). Continuity of outpatient medical care in elderly men: A randomized trial. *Journal of the American Medical Association, 252,* 2413–2417.

Wakefield, A., Cooke, S., & Boggis, C. (2003). Learning together: Use of simulated patients with nursing and medical students for breaking bad news. *International Journal of Palliative Nursing, 9,* 32–40.

Wanzer, M. B., Booth-Butterfield, M., & Gruber, K. (2004). Perceptions of health care providers' communication: Relationships between patient-centered communication and satisfaction. *Health Communication, 16,* 363–384.

Weiss, L., & Blustein, J. (1996). Faithful patients: The effect of long-term physician–patient relationships on the costs and use of health care by older Americans. *American Journal of Public Health, 86,* 1742–1747.

Whaley, B. B. (Ed.). (1999). *Explaining illness: Research, theory, and strategies.* Mahwah, NJ: Lawrence Erlbaum.

Wofford, M. M., Wofford, J. L., Bothra, J., Kendrick, S. B., Smith, A., & Lichstein, P. R. (2004). Patient complaints about physician behaviors: A qualitative study. *Academic Medicine, 79,* 134–138.

World Health Organization. (2003). *Adherence to long-term therapies.* Geneva: World Health Organization.

Wrench, J. S., & Booth-Butterfield, M. (2003). Increasing patient satisfaction and compliance: An examination of physician humor orientation, compliance-gaining strategies, and perceived credibility. *Communication Quarterly, 51,* 482–503.

Wright, K. B., & Frey, L. R. (2008). Communication and care in an acute cancer center: The effects of patients' willingness to communicate about health, healthcare environment perceptions, and health status on information seeking, participation in care practices, and satisfaction. *Health Communication, 23,* 369–379.

Wright, K. B., Bylund, C., Ware, J., Parker, P., Query, J. L., Jr., & Baile, W. (2006). Medical student attitudes toward communication skills training and knowledge of appropriate provider–patient communication: A comparison of first-year and fourth-year medical students. *Medical Education Online, 11,* Available: http://www.med-ed-online.org.

Yedidia, M. J., Gillespie, C. C., Kachur, E., Schwartz, M. D., Ockene, J. O., Chepatis, A. E., Snyder, C. S., Lazare, A., & Lipkin, M. (2003). Effect of communications training on medical student performance. *JAMA, 290,* 1157–1165.

Chapter 3

Caregiving and Communication

While you may never have had to care for a loved one who is living with an illness, chances are that you will be a caregiver at some point in the future. Most young people do not think about the possibility of becoming a caregiver for someone who is ill. Caregiving is one of the most difficult yet rewarding processes one may experience during one's lifetime. However, when faced with such a daunting prospect, most of us are not prepared for the relatively unknown caregiving challenges that lie ahead. Approximately 65.7 million Americans, or 29 percent of US adults, engage in informal care (National Alliance for Caregiving/American Association for Retired Persons [NAC/AARP], 2009). Of these, five to seven million provide care from a distance, a figure that is expected to double within 15 years (Benefield & Beck, 2007).

According to the National Family Caregivers Association (2005), there are more than 50 million caregivers in the US. These individuals are family members and friends who do not receive payment for the assistance they provide their loved ones. The number of lay caregivers in the US is expected to increase within the next several decades due to factors such as an average increased life span, a growing segment of older adults, and advances in medical technology that can prolong the lives of people with a long-term illness (Stoltz, Uden, & Willman, 2004). It is worth noting, that family caregiving is unpaid, can continue for a lengthy time period, be a nearly constant time commitment (Baillie, 2007), and be a passive decision if the caregiver believes there is no one else or no other alternative (Brereton & Nolan, 2000). As Bevan and Sparks (2010) point out, caregiving experiences are often transitional times for families who must communicatively and behaviorally adapt as they adjust in ways that enable them to manage stressful family changes and emerge resilient and emotionally intact. The ability to communicate competently is thus particularly crucial in the context of distance family caregiving, as research indicates a link among family communication, health, and adjustment to diseases such as cancer (Helgeson & Cohen, 1999).

Health Communication in the 21st Century, Second Edition. Kevin Bradley Wright, Lisa Sparks, and H. Dan O'Hair.
© 2013 John Wiley & Sons, Inc. Published 2013 by John Wiley & Sons, Inc.

Mark Twain once said, "The difference between the right word and the almost right word is the difference between the lightning and the lightning bug." Communication is a central component to a successful and effective caregiving experience for the patient, who will encounter many formal and informal caregivers and medical professionals at any given time from the onset of illness to either recovery or, for many, the process of dying. Unfortunately, most people in our culture do not feel comfortable talking about caregiving and the dying process. As a result, many find themselves unprepared to deal with these issues when they are faced with caring for someone or coping with the death of a loved one. Caring for a loved one who is facing a long-term illness and coping with the process of dying are difficult aspects of life, and the discussion of death and dying is a taboo topic in our culture. Younger individuals often feel that caring for a loved one is something that they will not have to deal with for many years to come. Unfortunately, researchers have found that lay caregivers are often unprepared to deal with the many challenges of caregiving, and they often find it difficult to cope with the demands of providing care for family members and other loved ones (Andrews, 2001; Sarna & McCorkle, 1996).

Researchers have found that the US healthcare system often provides inadequate care for the dying (Field & Cassel, 1997; Foley & Gelband, 2001), and dying individuals frequently experience underdiagnosis and undertreatment for pain and psychosocial concerns (Bernabei *et al.*, 1998; Martin, Emanuel, & Singer, 2000; Reb, 2003). In addition, dying individuals are not always treated with respect, they experience communication problems with providers, and their family members often do not receive adequate social support during the dying process (Lawton, 2000). In the US and other countries, end-of-life care is typically provided by doctors and nurses who have limited training in caring for the dying (Barclay *et al.*, 2003; Rhymes, 1990). Researchers have suggested that we need to learn how to communicate more effectively about these issues and take measures as a society to reform this important aspect of health (e.g. Sparks, 2003; Travis, Sparks-Bethea, & Winn, 2000). This chapter explores communication issues surrounding the caregiving process, end-of-life care, and the dying process.

Caregiving

Characteristics of people requiring long-term care and caregivers

A caregiver is defined as "anybody who provides unpaid help, or arranges for help, to a relative or friend because they have an illness or disability" (Donelan *et al.*, 1998, p. 243). As we mentioned earlier, a growing number of people are becoming caregivers in our society (Sparks, Travis, & Thompson, 2005; Travis & Sparks-Bethea, 2001; Travis, Sparks-Bethea, & Winn, 2000). Many of these individuals, such as middle-aged adults, find themselves simultaneously supporting both their children and parents, a phenomenon known as the "sandwich generation" (Richards, Bengston, & Miller, 1989; Williams & Nussbaum, 2001). Caregiving is a potential public health issue that will challenge society with caregivers who themselves suffer from various medical conditions (Talley & Crews, 2007). Caregiving is correlated with negative caregiver health with 17 percent of US caregivers reporting fair or poor health, compared with 13 percent of the general adult population (NAC/AARP, 2009). As the length of the human life span increases individuals are living longer, and with advances in medicine it is now possible for people with a variety of long-term illnesses to live with their condition for many years. However, despite the ability of medical advances to prolong life, terminally ill people often experience pain and discomfort from the symptoms of their illness, psychological distress from living with their illness and coping with their own mortality, and conditions that may limit their mobility or make them incapable of living on their own.

Getting older does not necessarily mean being unhealthy or requiring care from loved ones. Only about 5 percent of older Americans currently experience institutional long-term care, but this number is projected to grow in the next several decades with the aging of the baby boomer age cohort (Blevins & Deason-Howell, 2002). Most older individuals are healthy, although people over the age of 65 represent the majority of deaths in the US (Blevins & Deason-Howell, 2002). The majority of dependent older adults in the US who require long-term assistance currently receive care from family members (Sparks-Bethea, 2002), and the number of couples in their middle years who will have to care for their parents is expected to increase over the next decade (Moody, 1994).

While most people tend to equate long-term illness with older adults, it is important to remember that a person requiring long-term care may be of any age. Diseases, such as certain types of cancer, affect people of all ages (although older adults tend to be at higher risk for most types of cancer), and other diseases that can create the need for long-term care, such as HIV and AIDS, are more likely to affect younger individuals. The majority of individuals who are dying of long-term illnesses today have conditions such as cardiovascular disease, cancer, and cerebrovascular disease (Centers for Disease Control and Prevention, 2004).

Relatively few people in our society have the financial means to afford a professional caregiver for their loved ones, so they take on the responsibility themselves. As caregivers, marital partners and family members may have to spend an enormous amount of time meeting the physical needs of a parent, and most people do not have the experience, skills, or training that are necessary to handle the immense responsibility of caregiving. Research indicates that as the older adult population continues to expand, extended comprehensive care often becomes the responsibility of the aging adult's family (Miller, Shoemaker, Willyard, & Addison, 2008). Adult children and women are much more likely than men to become caregivers in our society (Fowler & Fisher, 2009; Wolff & Kasper, 2006) because of factors such as women having a longer life span than men and the tendency for men to marry younger women. In addition, women are often stereotyped as more nurturing than men, and these perceptions shape societal expectations that women are better suited as caregivers than men. Unfortunately, these conditions and expectations have led to a situation where women have had to bear the brunt of caregiver responsibilities in our society, and many individuals are largely unprepared for taking on the role of caregiver (Fowler & Fisher, 2009). Many of these female caregivers are older women living on fixed incomes and who may have limited financial and social resources (Williams & Nussbaum, 2001). Further, intergenerational barriers such as stereotyping, memory, and language issues often present multiple communication problems for older adults, which can create conflict and hinder effective healthcare (Sparks & Nussbaum, 2008).

Distance caregiving

Long-distance caregiving is defined by Bevan and Sparks (2011) as individuals who perceive themselves as being geographically distant in a caregiving situation. Long-distance caregiving is becoming more and more common in the US (Bevan & Sparks, 2011) impacting information quality, uncertainty, and quality of care (Bevan, Jupin & Sparks, 2011), increasing topic avoidance and negative health perceptions (Bevan, Rogers, Andrews, & Sparks, in press), as well as increasing interpersonal conflict and health perception, especially in distant caregiving contexts (Bevan, Vreeburg, Verdugo, & Sparks, 2012). As family residential distance increases (e.g. Zechner, 2008), stress is often placed on individuals who provide distant care to an aging adult (Bevan, Vreeburg, Verdugo, & Sparks, in press). Research shows that distance often presents an additional caregiving burden (Kelsey & Laditka, 2009; Mitnick, Leffler, & Hood, 2010). The American College of Physicians recently recommended that doctors "recognize that geographically distant caregivers may face unique challenges" in their ethical guidelines for caregivers (Mitnick, Leffler, & Hood, 2010, p. 257). Further, the various ways by which geographic distance is linked with emotional support is also a relevant aspect of interpersonal and health communication, as it involves messages that are intended to assist another to cope with emotional distress (Burleson, 2003). Research indicates that some distant family caregivers' primary responsibility was providing emotional support (Roff et al., 2007). For sibling caregivers of those with traumatic brain injury, affective support including elements of providing encouragement, general support, and companionship, and finding time to check in on the care recipient, was unrelated to geographic distance (Degeneffe & Burcham, 2008). In addition, expected future provision of emotional support did not differ by geographic distance in adult child–parent caregiving (Baldassar & Baldock, 2000; Baldassar, Wilding, & Baldock, 2007).

Bevan *et al.* (2012) investigated conflict frequency and strategy usage in relation to negative health perceptions in the long-distance caregiving context. Their results indicate that conflict frequency and usage of both distributive and avoidant conflict strategies positively predicted distant caregivers' negative health perceptions. However, collaboration and compromise were not associated with negative health perceptions in the long-distance caregiving environment. Further, Koerner, Shirai, and Kenyon (2010) determined that the more frequent family conflict about care provision, the greater caregivers' experience of physical health symptoms. In addition, lower family relationship quality, including conflict, was linked to increased caregiver health difficulties (Francis, Worthington, Kypriotakis, & Rose, 2010). Although a relatively underresearched area, long-distance caregiving is increasingly becoming a significant public health issue, which should be more thoroughly investigated to better understand the repercussions it has on care providers, care recipients, and the overall healthcare system (Bevan & Sparks, 2011).

Caregiver roles

Caregivers play a vital role in meeting patient needs (Andrews, 2001; Meyers & Gray, 2001; Siegel, Raveis, Houts, & More, 1991; Weitzner, McMillan, & Jacobson, 1999), and they often deal with a variety of communication-related issues that have important implications for the physical and psychological well-being of patients and for the caregivers themselves. According to Allen, Haley, Small, and McMillan (2002), "prior research suggests that the quality of communication among terminally ill individuals, their caregivers, and hospice staff influences patient and caregiver outcomes" (p. 508). Although researchers have identified communication as an important part of the process of providing care (Bakas, Lewis, & Parsons, 2001; Martinez, 1996; Zamborsky, 1996), few studies have actually examined how specific communication variables are related to health outcomes of people with long-term illnesses.

Some of the many responsibilities caregivers must contend with include: (i) providing physical assistance and emotional support to the patient; (ii) being a liaison between the patient and an interdisciplinary team of providers; (iii) handling financial and social affairs for the patient; and (iv) monitoring symptoms and communicating them to providers. These tasks present numerous communicative challenges for caregivers of people with cancer enrolled in hospice programs, and we will examine these in greater detail below.

As we have seen, most primary caregivers for people facing illnesses are family members who are ill-equipped to deal with the physical and emotional stress of caregiving duties (Andrews, 2001; Rusinak & Murphy, 1995; Sarna & McCorkle, 1996). While trained health workers (such as hospice workers, who we will discuss later) provide support in terms of administering medical care and attending to a variety of the patient's physical needs, family caregivers must handle a variety of tasks, including providing emotional support, providing transportation, managing finances, monitoring symptoms, coordinating schedules, coping with increased housework, and running errands, and caregiver burden has been found to increase as patients enter into later stages of the disease (Andrews, 2001; Laizner, Yost, Barg, & McCorkle, 1993). These activities, coupled with the stress of coming to terms with the imminent death of a loved one, can lead to physical and emotional exhaustion for the caregiver. Moreover, caregiver burden has been linked to poorer care in the home, increased risk for institutionalization for the loved one who is being cared for, increased levels of depression, and increases in stress-related diseases for the caregiver (Haley *et al.*, 2003; Skirton & Glendinning, 1997; Turner, Killian, & Cain, 2004).

Caregivers' communication with their social network and providers can have a positive impact on their stress levels, particularly when they are able to use their communication skills to obtain assistance and emotional support. In addition, many caregivers have found the use of humor to be an effective way of coping with the complexities of caregiving as it often provides relief from the stresses involved in the caregiving process (Harzold & Sparks, 2007; Sparks *et al.*, 2005; Sparks-Bethea, Travis, & Pecchioni, 2000). Further, Harzold and Sparks' (2007) finding that a parent's withholding of cancer information from an adult child is dissatisfying also implies that topic avoidance often emerges as a problem in the caregiving relationship. In terms of adult siblings, Willyard *et al.* (2008) found that, though siblings used avoidance to deal with negotiating who would participate in their parent's care, caregivers also perceived that siblings did little or nothing to assist with caring for parents. The stresses involved in caregiving bring about a host of difficulties in communication such as topic avoidance and conflict in the relationship, which are often exacerbated when the caregivers must carry out their role from a distance (Bevan & Sparks, 2011).

Unfortunately, caregivers often lack the diverse communication skills necessary to effectively meet the needs of the patient and their own needs (Andrews, 2001; Bakas, Lewis, & Parsons, 2001). One variable that may influence a caregiver's ability to use communication to mobilize support from his or her social network is *communication competence*. Communication competence refers to the ability to construct and use appropriate and effective messages to meet goals/needs and to successfully create and maintain satisfying relationships (Wiemann, 1977). Query and Wright (2003) found that both older adults with cancer and their caregivers with higher communication competence had lower perceived stress levels and higher satisfaction with their support networks than individuals with lower communication competence.

Caregiving and changes in relationships

Communication between family members may exhibit a number of changes when they take on caregiver roles (Richards, 2004; Sparks-Bethea, 2002; Williams & Nussbaum, 2001). Marital satisfaction can be damaged by the financial cost of providing for children and parents, as well as the emotional costs associated with the caregiving relationship. Married couples caring for a parent who report lower marital satisfaction state that the presence of a parent in the home reduces the amount of overall communication time within the marital dyad, the amount of private time between the couple, and increases certain types of communication between the couple, such as decision-making. These changes in communication appear to affect even long-term marriages, since partners have been found to experience declines in marital satisfaction when they are caring for an aging parent (Sparks-Bethea, 2002).

It is also important for caregivers to understand that patients often experience dramatic shifts in their identities as they move through the stages of being healthy and well to being sick. Identification as someone who was previously healthy shifting to someone who is sick, identification as a patient, and identification as a survivor are all important aspects to consider. Whether we experience a difficult health issue such as cancer through a friend, family member, or personal experience, it is our various relationships and/or conversations about the health experience across the continuum of care from prevention, diagnosis, treatment, survivorship to end of life that continually reinforce, renegotiate, and bring about shifts in our social identities across the life span (Sparks & Harwood, 2008). Another issue here is that particular conceptualizations of self within the health condition(s) have the capacity to change psychological orientation and behaviors related to one's health, and hence to influence concrete outcomes (see, e.g. Harwood & Sparks, 2003; Sparks & Harwood, 2008). For example, cancer patients concerned about the stigma associated with a cancer diagnosis may pursue numerous strategies to avoid such stigma while they are fighting the disease. Such shifts in a patient's social identity may greatly impact the way the patient and the various caregivers involved relate to the patient.

As Harwood and Sparks (2003) further point out, family identity may be crucial among those who have family histories of particular health issues (e.g. cancer or heart disease). Women in a family with a history of breast cancer, for instance, are in a situation where information and awareness about the disease should be heightened, preventive measures should be relatively automatic, and knowledge about treatment options in the case of illness should be readily available (Harwood & Sparks, 2003; Pecchioni & Sparks, 2007). However, the extent to which those women identify with the family may be crucial. People who are less involved and identified with their family may dissociate from the medical history and perhaps perceive themselves as less vulnerable (Harwood & Sparks, 2003; Sparks & Harwood, 2008).

Shifts in one's social identity(ies) from one who is healthy (belonging to group memberships reinforcing this) to one who is not healthy (introduced to new group memberships not previously experienced) is an important component for formal and informal caregivers to consider when communicating with patients. By understanding the complexities involved in patients who were previously vital and energetic, full of life, and so on, but who now exhibit characteristics not demonstrating these strong dimensions, caregivers can use more appropriate, effective, and understanding communication strategies in relating to patients and their strong identity orientations and subsequent shifts in identity.

Communication issues surrounding symptom management

Researchers have found that caregivers and people with a long-term illness mutually influence one another during interactions in ways that can affect both parties psychologically and physically. For example, several researchers have found a relationship between patient symptom distress and caregiver depression and/or perceptions of caregiver burden (Andrews, 2001; Given *et al.*, 1997; Sarna & Brecht, 1997). Increased patient symptom distress can increase the number of tasks in a caregiver's daily schedule as well as add to his or her stress level. People with cancer may experience a number of symptoms associated with the disease and its treatment, including pain (Allen *et al.*, 2002; Donnelly, Walsh, & Rybicki, 1994), fatigue, and dyspnea (Nail, 2002). According to Bakas, Lewis, & Parsons (2001), "family caregivers must be able to not only recognize these symptoms, but also assist patients in managing them" (p. 849).

The need to alleviate pain is a common aspect of caring for individuals with a terminal illness (Brescia *et al.*, 1992). Adequate pain relief among terminally ill patients has been found to be a significant problem across studies (Foley & Gelband, 2001; MacMillan & Small, 2002), and many of the problems related to pain control are associated with communication problems experienced by the patient or between the patient and caregiver (Panke, 2002). Pain is a multifaceted concept and it is experienced differently by different people. For example, people vary in terms of their tolerance of pain and they may react to pain in a variety of ways. Different experiences and perceptions of pain make it difficult for people with cancer and caregivers to assess the degree to which people are in pain and how pain should be treated. Most studies have concluded that self-reports of pain are the most reliable indicator of the pain a terminally ill patient is experiencing, but according to Allen *et al.* (2002), "the presence of cognitive and sensory deficits, however, may hamper an individual's ability to communicate painful experiences" (p. 508).

In situations where a patient cannot communicate the amount of pain they are experiencing due to their illness, caregivers run the risk of under-medicating or over-medicating their loved ones. According to Panke (2002), "patients who aren't able to communicate verbally are at risk for underassessment and inadequate pain relief, those at highest risk being patients with cognitive impairment, intubated patients, infants, and patients older than 85" (p. 28). Family caregivers are important sources of information about patient behaviors, and they are often crucial in communicating information about pain to providers (Pecchioni & Sparks, 2007). Family caregivers commonly typically act as liaisons between patients and providers in terms of reporting pain, but family caregivers may have difficulty accurately assessing the actual amount of pain their loved one is experiencing (Allen *et al.*, 2002; Elliot *et al.*, 1997), and this can lead to a situation where a patient remains in pain due to under-medication but cannot do anything about it.

In cases where people with an illness cannot verbally communicate with their caregivers, a caregiver must rely on nonverbal signs of pain, such as facial expressions and body movements. Nonverbal and behavioral cues indicating pain are often used by caregivers as a sign of whether to increase pain medications. However, it can be difficult for caregivers to "recognize that a particular behavior indicates pain, especially if they are unfamiliar with how the patient usually behaves" (Panke, 2002, p. 28). Effective assessment of pain is important in order to control it, and information about pain needs to be effectively communicated to providers in order to achieve a balance between adequate pain control and over- or under-medication (Panke, 2002; Travis & Sparks-Bethea, 2001; Travis, Sparks-Bethea, & Winn, 2000). Over-medicating a patient can lead to numerous problems, such as the accumulation of toxins associated with pain medications, renal dysfunction, decreased cognitive functioning, and organ failure. Under-medication can lead to inadequate pain control and unnecessary suffering for the patient.

Even in cases where verbal communication between caregivers and patients is possible, patients often remain silent when it comes to making their needs known to the caregiver due to reluctance to talk about terminal illness openly and/or the desire of the person receiving care not to burden the caregiver (Bachner & Carmel, 2009; Zhang & Siminoff, 2003). In some cases, this lack of talk about patient needs may delay recognition and treatment of pain and other symptoms that can even be life-threatening (Hinds, 1992). Studies have found higher levels of psychological and physical problems in families where people are not able to openly discuss terminal illness (Mesters *et al.*, 1997). In situations where there is open communication about death and dying, researchers have found that there are lower levels of feelings that the loved one is a burden among caregivers (Fried, Bradley, O'Leary, & Byers, 2005) and greater emotional acceptance of death (Lepore & Hegelson, 1998).

Communication challenges associated with caregiving

Willingness to communicate concerns Many family caregivers are reluctant to communicate problems they encounter during the caregiving process to the people they are caring for or to others within their social network because they do not want to burden them with the added stress of thinking about these concerns (Bakas, Lewis, & Parsons, 2001; Laizner *et al.*, 1993). This is consistent with other research that has found that family member caregivers often avoid communicating about their problems with others because they do not want to overstep interpersonal boundaries or add stress to the lives of others by raising concerns about caregiving (Chesler & Barbarin, 1984).

However, by not communicating their concerns to others, caregivers do not give themselves the opportunity to vent their frustrations or to receive advice or other offers of assistance from their social network. Caregivers may experience added stress when they do not have the opportunity to express their concerns, and this can lead to depression, burnout, anxiety, social withdrawal, and reduced quality of life (Bakas, Lewis, & Parsons, 2001; Given *et al.*, 1993). In addition, the reluctance of caregivers to communicate their needs and concerns may also affect their ability to provide care (Bakas, Lewis, & Parsons, 2001).

Communication of emotional support Researchers have found that the provision of emotional support is one of the most time-consuming and challenging aspects of caregiving, often requiring more of a caregiver's time and effort than other daily caregiving tasks (Bakas, Lewis, & Parsons, 2001; Egbert & Parrott, 2003; Toseland, Blanchard, & McCallion, 1995). This has been found to be true for both lay and professional caregivers (Travis & Sparks-Bethea, 2001; Travis, Sparks-Bethea, & Winn, 2000). According to Andrews (2001), "because the caregiver is the center of support for the needs of the patient with cancer, if the caregiver fails, the patient suffers" (p. 1469). Given the uncertainty and fear associated with coming to terms with one's own mortality among people with diseases like cancer, it is not surprising that emotional support is a common need among terminally ill patients and other patients requiring long-term care. Listening to patient concerns and providing empathetic responses to patients is an important aspect of providing holistic hospice care. However, it can be very time consuming for caregivers (professional and lay), especially when faced with accomplishing multiple tasks when providing daily care to patients. Patient irritability, confusion, and aggressive behaviors during late-stage cancer may make it even more difficult and exhausting for caregivers to provide emotional support. Moreover, both professional and lay caregivers often have little training regarding the provision of emotional support, and there is a need for education and training about how to deal with these issues and effectively provide emotional support (Bakas, Lewis, & Parsons, 2001).

Hospice and Palliative Care

Over the past two decades, hospice and palliative care have become popular options for people facing terminal illness and their loved ones. It is the desire of most patients with serious, incurable diseases to die at home. Dying at home is associated with greater satisfaction by bereaved family members (Ratner, Norlander, & McSteen, 2001). Lynn (2001) described the importance of dying with dignity: "most people want more than just longer life; they want the end of life to be meaningful, comfortable, and supportive to loved ones" (p. 926). According to the National Hospice and Palliative Care Organization (NHPCO, 2006), over 400 000 hospice volunteers offer services and support to dying people and their caregivers in the US. Over 1.3 million patients and families utilize hospice services in the US (NHPCO, 2007). This section will explore the growth and impact of hospice and palliative care and a variety of communication issues associated with them.

History of hospice and palliative care

The term hospice refers to programs that provide support and care for people in the last phases of an incurable disease, with a focus on maintaining the quality of their remaining life by providing services that both aid physical comfort and address psychological and spiritual needs (NHPCO, 2004). While hospice began as an alternative health movement, the goals of hospice care—to provide a dignified, comfortable death for the terminally ill and to care for the patient and family together—are being given increasing recognition in mainstream medical care (Query, Wright, & Gilchrist, 2006).

The hospice movement originated in England and was largely influenced by the work of Dame Cicely Saunders, an English nurse who promoted the idea that a patient's care should be managed by an interdisciplinary team, that pain and symptom management should be a primary goal of hospice nursing, and that death education and bereavement counseling for family members should be included in hospice care (NHPCO, 2004). Saunders, who originally studied to be a nurse, was motivated by the pain and loneliness of the dying to become a physician. In 1957, she began her first job as a physician investigating terminal pain and its relief. As a result of her ideas, in 1967 St. Christopher's Hospice was opened in Sydenham, London (Howarth & Leaman, 2001). Saunders continued to work full-time as St. Christopher's chair well into the 1980s (Moore, 1998). In addition, hospice programs were influenced by the work of Elizabeth Kubler-Ross, a psychiatrist who brought attention to the taboo topic of death in our culture, and who promoted the idea that the focus of medicine for people facing incurable diseases should be to control pain and symptoms, and to promote quality of remaining life (Query, Wright, & Gilchrist , 2006).

In 1974, hospice arrived in the US with the opening of *Hospice Inc.* in Connecticut. Since that time, we have witnessed the rapid growth of hospice organizations in the US. In 1983, Medicare began offering a hospice option to Medicare Part A insurance to reimburse terminally ill patients who meet certain criteria, and the number of US hospices grew from 516 in 1983 to over 1000 today (Query, Wright, & Gilchrist, 2006). More than 90 percent of hospice care is provided in patients' homes and 78 percent of hospice care is for cancer patients (Moore, 1998).

Hospice services and care

When a candidate for a hospice program is identified, hospice staff members generally hold an initial meeting with the patient's primary physician(s) and a hospice physician to discuss the patient's history, physical symptoms, and life expectancy. Following this initial meeting, hospice staff members meet with both the patient and his or her family to discuss the hospice philosophy, available services, and expectations. In addition, staff and patients discuss pain and comfort levels, support systems, financial and insurance resources, medications, and equipment needs. A plan of care is then developed for the patient, and this plan is regularly reviewed and revised according to the patient's condition.

Most hospice care takes place in the patient's home, although more and more in-patient hospice facilities are becoming available. In-patient hospice facilities are helpful for patients who do not have family members or other loved ones to care for them. In home settings, hospice staff members do not usually serve as primary caregivers for a patient enrolled in a hospice program. A family member is typically the primary caregiver and he or she often helps make decisions for the terminally ill individual (Sparks *et al.*, 2005; Sparks, 2008). Members of the hospice staff support the family caregiver by making regular visits to assess the patient and provide additional care or other services. Hospice staff are usually on-call 24 hours a day, seven days a week.

The hospice physician and/or nurses are usually responsible for making decisions about increases and decreases in pain medication and the treatment of other physical symptoms, although pain and symptoms are usually monitored on a daily basis by the family caregiver (Travis & Sparks-Bethea, 2001; Travis, Sparks-Bethea, & Winn, 2000). Hospice staff members provide family caregivers with training in pain and symptom monitoring as well as a host of other caregiver tasks, and the hospice program provides all medications and supplies needed to care for the patient (NHPCO, 2004). Home care hospice programs sometimes make short-term in-patient care available (usually through an affiliated hospital) when pain or symptoms become too difficult for the family caregiver to manage at home, or the caregiver needs respite time (time to cope with the physical and emotional strain of caregiving). The hospice team also assists the patient with the emotional, psychosocial, and spiritual aspects of dying. Following the death of a hospice patient, bereavement services and counseling are typically available to loved ones for a year (Hospice Foundation of America, n.d.).

Barriers to hospice care

Despite the increased number of hospice organizations in the past 15 years, there are many barriers that may inhibit their growth. In the late 1990s, fewer than 50 percent of patients with terminal illness received the benefit of hospice care (Emanuel & Emanuel, 1998), and the situation has not improved much in recent years. Even among individuals who are admitted to hospice programs, many problems exist that may hinder the quality of care patients receive, such as the lack of continuity of care between hospice team members, the inability of hospice staff to meet the emotional and spiritual needs of patients, and the lack of adequate training among healthcare professionals in taking care of those who are dying (Egbert & Parrott, 2003; Gloth, 1998; Ragan & Goldsmith, 2008). There is currently no mandatory nationwide accreditation for hospice organizations. Many programs are accredited by the Joint Commission on Accreditation of Healthcare Organizations (JCAHO) or by the Community Health Accreditation Program (CHAP).

One reason for the relatively low number of people entering into hospices is the hospice eligibility requirements for Medicare patients (which reimburses older patients and their families for hospice services) that require physicians to certify potential hospice patients have six months or less to live (Foley & Gelband, 2001; Reb, 2003). According to Reb (2003), many hospices are reluctant to accept patients whose conditions might improve over time. Doctors are often reluctant to certify that a person only has six months or less to live because it can be extremely difficult to estimate how long a person will live when he or she has certain types of diseases, such as heart disease or dementia (Zerzan, Stearns, & Hanson, 2000). Complicating this matter are the continuous advances that are being made in medicine that can prolong the lives of individuals with a "terminal" illness. For example, a diagnosis of HIV was once thought to be 100 percent fatal to a patient, but new HIV medications have made it possible for HIV-positive individuals to live for many years. Similar advances (although not always as promising) are being made with Alzheimer's disease and a variety of other diseases and conditions.

In addition, providers may be reluctant to refer individuals to hospice programs because current healthcare insurance options do not provide many financial incentives for doing so (Reb, 2003). Also, according to Walsh and Gordon (2001), physicians are also hesitant to refer people to hospice programs because they fear punitive damages from insurance company oversight committees and organizations such as the Centers for Medicare and Medicaid. In recent years, these organizations have targeted physicians who referred patients to hospice programs who ended up living longer than six months in an effort to investigate insurance fraud. Walsh and Gordon (2001) contend that because of these investigations, physicians may be more conservative when estimating the survival times of patients and cautious about referring people to hospice programs.

Most insurance plans to not adequately cover services needed for quality end-of-life care (Raphael, Ahrens, & Fowler, 2001). Outside of hospice organizations, there are few ways that people can be reimbursed for these types of services. One of the reasons that insurance plans are reluctant to cover end-of-life care is the fact that some diseases, such as cancer, progress to late stages where people experience multiple physical symptoms that can be expensive to treat. Most insurance plans currently do not recognize or provide only limited reimbursement for services that meet the psychosocial needs of patients, such as patient counseling, counseling for family members, or other services that do not deal with physical health (Reb, 2003).

The result of these factors is that most individuals who are referred to hospice programs often do not live long enough to reap the benefits that these programs provide. Thirty percent of hospice patients on Medicare die within one week of admission, and hospice care providers often label this "brink of death" care, as compared to genuine end-of-life care (Nicoll, 2002). Such services are also described as "drive-by hospice care" as hospice team members often move from one patient to the next, rushing to complete visits, documentation, and follow-up only to learn of the death of the patient the next morning, before "care" could be provided (see Nicoll, 2002). One week or less of hospice care does not give hospice staff sufficient time to meet the various physical, psychological, spiritual, and social needs of patients and their families.

There are other barriers to the hospice movement as well. Many physicians and nurses have not been trained in caring for the terminally ill and most feel uncomfortable doing so (Block & Sullivan, 1998; Rhymes, 1990). Also, hospice staff members often have difficulty communicating with other members of the hospice team because hospice teams tend to be interdisciplinary, and members often have limited knowledge of each member's area of expertise (Coopman, 2001; Street & Blackford, 2001). In addition, studies have found that individuals with lower socioeconomic status are less likely to be referred to hospice programs (Grande, McKerral, & Todd, 2002), and Karim, Bailey, and Tunna (2000) found that black/minority ethnic populations are referred to hospice less often than white populations. There are cultural barriers to hospice as well, and despite the inclusion of psychosocial concerns, most hospice organizations have largely adopted a mainstream western perspective of healthcare. Poulson (1998) identified several salient cultural issues to be considered during end-of-life care, including the possible need for translators, varying religious traditions, differing communication patterns, diverse social customs, familial hierarchies, and death rituals.

Additionally, although one of the goals of the hospice movement is to provide end-of-life care to patients at home rather than in hospitals, the majority of individuals in the US still die in hospitals and nursing homes (von Gunten, 2002). Each of these barriers seriously undermines the original goals and ideals of the hospice movement, and they will need to be reexamined in order for the hospice movement to thrive in the future.

Palliative care

Palliative care refers to the comprehensive care of terminally ill individuals and their family members using an interdisciplinary approach. The term *palliation* refers to any treatment, care, or support that relieves symptoms and suffering (Query, Wright, & Gilchrist, 2006). This is in contrast to *curative* care, which has the primary goal of curing disease and prolonging life. In terms of comprehensive care, palliative care includes pain and symptom relief, attention to psychological and spiritual aspects of dying, and involving a patient's family and other support network members in the process of dying (Ragan *et al.*, 2008).

Palliative care approaches accept death as a normal process and focuses on improving the quality of life for terminally ill patients and their families by compassionately helping them to make the transitions that precede the final stages of life (Winker & Flanagin, 1999). As you can see, dealing with all of these facets of health requires an interdisciplinary team of health professionals (see Chapter 11 for a discussion of interdisciplinary teams), and palliative care organizations often include the services of physicians, nurses, counselors, and clergy.

Palliative care is closely associated with the hospice movement. Hospice organizations attempt to provide clients with palliative care. However, while palliative care may include services provided by hospices, palliative care can be offered at any point during an illness while hospice services are usually only provided during the last six months of life due to medical insurance reimbursement requirements (Reb, 2003; Zerzan, Stearns, & Hanson, 2000). Palliative care and hospice care are often used interchangeably because they overlap in many ways. However, palliative care is typically offered simultaneously with curative approaches to relieve suffering from stressful, painful, or debilitating symptoms (Ragan *et al.*, 2008). By contrast, hospice care typically excludes curative treatment of primary illness and is limited to comforting terminally ill patients.

Barriers to palliative care

Much like the barriers to hospice care, quality palliative care in the US has been limited by insurance reimbursement requirements as well as by a shortage of well-trained healthcare providers who are knowledgeable about end-of-life issues. According to Goldsmith, Wittenberg-Lyles, Ragan, & Nussbaum (2011), "on of the primary barriers to the dissemination and utilization of palliative care is the medical community's own ignorance and lack of health literacy regarding palliation and palliative care" (p. 449). Even among cancer centers and other sites that offer palliative care to patients, few organizations have the resources or the trained staff to address the various needs of dying individuals. There is some controversy among healthcare providers as to exactly when palliative care should begin (Goldsmith *et al.*, 2011), and while it is typically reserved for later stages of terminal illness, efforts to relieve pain and suffering should be considered by providers in earlier stages of disease as well. Among those organizations that do provide palliative care, services are severely limited by insurance reimbursement restrictions. Ragan, Wittenberg, and Hall (2003) conclude from their review of palliative care literature:

> The practice of and the research in palliative care in particular need to focus more on patients' psychological, emotional, and spiritual needs rather than on their physical needs alone—this entails the adoption of a holistic perspective that recognizes the inextricable blending of physical, mental, and spiritual health for patients' overall quality of life. (p. 225)

Healthcare professionals who provide palliative care often have limited training in pain control. Physicians and nurses often lack information about the appropriate dosages of narcotics used in pain control, and many providers fear that increased dosages of pain medication will cause addiction or a heightened tolerance for the medication among patients receiving palliative care (Rhymes, 1990). As a result, patients often receive insufficient doses of pain medication and may suffer needlessly. Providers are even less educated in most cases about addressing the psychosocial needs of patients receiving palliative care. This, coupled with few resources within the healthcare system to address psychosocial concerns (due to insurance reimbursement restrictions), is a significant barrier to quality palliative care. For example, managed care organizations can save money by delaying referrals to hospice and palliative care programs—in some cases anywhere from $1700 to $4900 per admission (Morrison *et al.*, 2008), which is one of the major reasons why people are referred to hospice and palliative care programs late in the cycle of terminal illness. More education is needed among providers about end-of-life care, and insurance organizations will need to create new policies for the reimbursement of services in order for palliative care to flourish in the US.

Older Adult Health Concerns and Communication Issues

Given that older adults make up the largest portion of individuals who interact with lay caregivers, this section investigates health issues that many older individuals face and the impact the impact of these issues on health communication. Older adults are the fastest-growing segment of the US population. Individuals aged 85 and older were the fastest-growing segment of the older adult population (US Census Bureau, 2000). The number of individuals aged 65 and older is projected to increase from 35 million (in 2000) to nearly 80 million in 2050 (Federal Interagency Forum on Aging-Related Statistics, 2000).

One reason for the large number of older Americans is that the average life span is increasing. At the beginning of the 20th century, the average life span was around 47 years, but since then life expectancy has increased to an average of 74 years for men and 79 years for women (US Census Bureau, 2000). Infant mortality rates have decreased substantially in the US during the last several decades, and this, coupled with advances in preventive health efforts and healthcare, will likely contribute to further increases in the life span.

Older individuals face a variety of unique health concerns. While the majority of older adults tend to be healthy, the sheer number of people over the age of 65 makes them a large proportion of consumers of the US healthcare system. Many of these individuals are on fixed incomes that may make it difficult to meet all of their healthcare needs. In addition, most healthcare providers in the United States tend to be from younger age cohorts, and many of these individuals have a relatively limited knowledge of aging and health issues. Even worse, some older individuals are negatively stereotyped by healthcare providers and by people in general, and this can often lead to depression and other negative psychological health outcomes for older people. Given the scope and importance of this issue, this section examines many of the unique health concerns and health communication issues related to older adults.

Getting older and experiencing health problems

How do you feel about getting older? If you are like many Americans, you are probably not overly enthusiastic about the idea. In our society, individuals often associate aging with health problems, and this belief is supported by some scientific evidence. People are more likely to develop health problems such as chronic illness and physical/

cognitive impairments as they age (Mosqueda & Burnight, 2000). For example, older adults are diagnosed with cancer more than any other segment of the population (Hewitt, Rowland, & Yancik, 2003), and they have higher incident rates of arthritis and hypertension than other age groups. In addition, individuals 85 and older have higher incidents of memory impairment than younger age cohorts. However, while the elderly often do contract more disease and illness than other groups, many of the conditions are not intrinsic to aging (Nussbaum, Pecchioni, Robinson, & Thompson, 2000; Stahl & Feller, 1990). Instead, other factors such as lifestyle choices and genetic predispositions for disease or negative health conditions are more likely to cause health problems for older people than the process of aging itself.

In terms of mental health, it is a common belief that aging is associated with a decreased ability to function mentally. Yet, cognitive decline is not necessarily related to the aging process, but may be more likely to occur due to conditions such as high blood pressure (Eisdorfer & Cohen, 1980; Sparks, 2008). Unfortunately, it is a common misperception that the majority of older adults are unhealthy or experience major health problems. To make matters worse, many older individuals believe this stereotype about aging, and they may attribute health problems to age as opposed to other variables. Yet, as we will see, aging is not necessarily related to poor health. And while there are some physical aspects of aging that can certainly lead to health problems, the next section will examine how social factors such as communication problems can actually create more difficulties for older adults than physical problems associated with aging.

Age-related issues affecting older adult health and healthcare

Presbycusis Have you ever raised the volume of your voice when talking to a grandparent or another older person you know? It is a common belief that older people have difficulty hearing us. However, as we will see, severe hearing problems among older people are relatively rare. Presbycusis is defined as age-related hearing loss, and hearing problems do tend to increase after the age of 45. However, most people do not realize that older adult deafness is relatively rare. For example, only 15 percent of individuals over the age of 75 are considered to be deaf (Darbyshire, 1984; Verbrugge, 1984). Presbycusis is caused by a number of age-related changes to the ear, including deterioration of parts of the outer ear, hair loss in the cochlea in the inner ear, and nerve damage in the auditory systems within the brain (Villaume, Brown, & Darling, 1994). These changes affect the reception of sound waves and transformation of these sound waves to neural signals to the brain. In addition, according to Villaume, Brown, and Darling (1994), common types of background noise in social situations where older individuals communicate (e.g. simultaneous conversations, street noise, television) can significantly increase hearing problems for older people with presbycusis, even when it is only in mild form.

Presbycusis can make it difficult for older adults to process speech content quickly during conversations. However, many individuals with average hearing loss can usually compensate for this loss by using proactive strategies, such as lipreading, relying on information from the context of the conversation or the environment to interpret meaning, or by requests for clarification from their conversational partners. Presbycusis reduces a person's ability to decipher the content of speech by "detecting, discriminating, and recognizing words, phrases, and sentences" (Villaume, Brown, & Darling, 1994, p. 85). One of the biggest problems associated with presbycusis is the reduced ability to decipher paralinguistic cues (e.g. fluctuations in the voice that convey meaning). Paralinguistic cues are very important in conveying relational messages, or nonverbal messages that convey social cues such as affection, emotion, and power (Villaume *et al.*, 1993). The inability to hear paralinguistic cues can make it difficult for people to understand many of the complex aspects of everyday language, such as assessing whether someone is sad, tired, or being sarcastic in a conversation. However, it is important to point out that while these aspects of presbycusis do present problems for many older adults, the majority of older adults with average levels of presbycusis can compensate for their hearing loss with relatively little trouble (although conversations may be more time consuming and mentally exhausting for them).

Younger people (including many healthcare providers) are often unfamiliar with the characteristics of presbycusis, and they can become frustrated by the increased amount of time it takes some individuals with hearing loss to process information and create a response. They often perceive older individuals with presbycusis as less competent conversational partners than older people without hearing problems, despite the fact that most people with age-related hearing loss are fully competent and able to adapt to their situation (Villaume, Brown, & Darling, 1994). As a result, people often withdraw from conversations with individuals with presbycusis or do not give the individual an adequate amount of time to compensate for their hearing loss during a conversation. Thus, the perception that an older person cannot hear is often more problematic than the hearing loss itself.

Older adults with hearing loss can quickly lose confidence about their hearing abilities when people treat them differently or avoid conversations with them. This phenomenon is known as the *communicative predicament of aging model* (Nussbaum *et al.*, 2000), and the loss of confidence, coupled with the common stereotype that older adults have poor conversational skills, can cause many problems for seniors with presbycusis when others avoid communicating with them. It can lead to a reduction in the size and quality of an older person's social network, diminishing the amount of social support he or she receives. This, in turn, can lead to feelings of inadequacy, loneliness, and depression. In addition, healthcare providers who perceive an older patient's hearing loss to be worse than it actually is may spend less time with the patient or negatively influence the interaction in other ways.

Cognitive decline, Alzheimer's disease, and dementia Another popular stereotype of older people is that many become senile or lose their mental abilities as they age. While Alzheimer's disease and other types of dementia affect older individuals more than any other age group, and the number of people with Alzheimer's disease and other types of dementia is increasing, relatively few older adults experience substantial cognitive declines as they age (Gatz, Kasl-Godley, & Karel, 1996; Kemper & Lyons, 1994).

Alzheimer's disease is a degenerative and fatal disease that is estimated to affect nearly 4.5 million Americans, and the number of Alzheimer's disease cases is expected to increase to between 11 and 16 million by 2050 (Hebert *et al.*, 2003). While people can be diagnosed with Alzheimer's disease at younger ages, risk for the disease increases with age, and it is seen most frequently among people over the age of 85. Alzheimer's disease is named after Dr Alois Alzheimer, a German doctor who lived during the early 1900s and studied changes in the brain tissue of mentally ill patients. In 1906, Alzheimer linked a specific pattern of neurological degeneration with symptoms of dementia, and this later became known as Alzheimer's disease (Kemper & Lyons, 1994).

The disease is characterized in the brain by abnormal clumps (amyloid plaques) and tangled bundles of fibers (neurofibrillary tangles) composed of misplaced proteins (Kemper & Lyons, 1994). The causes of Alzheimer's disease are still unclear, but genetics, diet, exercise, and mental activity throughout the life span are all thought to contribute to risk for the disease.

The symptoms of Alzheimer's disease change as the disease progresses. Early symptoms include short-term memory problems, confusion, and communication impairments, such as failure to take part in family conversations and inability to start and sustain conversations. While these problems are not major threats to an older individual's physical health, they can lead to feelings of frustration and social isolation (Kemper & Lyons, 1994). Later symptoms of the disease may include inability to perform everyday tasks, such as getting dressed and bathing, and changes in mood and behavior, such as increased irritability or aggressiveness. In the late stages of Alzheimer's disease, people typically become dependent on caregivers, they suffer further cognitive decline, and eventually die from the disease. The life expectancy for individuals with Alzheimer's disease ranges from 5 to 20 years, with an average survival rate of 8.5 years from initial diagnosis (Kemper & Lyons, 1994).

Many other types of dementia can be confused with Alzheimer's disease. In addition, healthy older adults often experience short-term memory problems, difficulties remembering names during conversations, slower processing speed when interpreting and recalling information, and mild forms of non-Alzheimer's dementia that may lead people to believe they have Alzheimer's disease (Cohen, 1994; Kemper, 1992; Salthouse, 1992). Unfortunately, when people meet an older individual who exhibits some of these characteristics, they often assume the person is suffering from Alzheimer's disease or is "losing it" mentally, despite the fact that the person is healthy and fully capable of carrying on a conversation.

In terms of the ways in which Alzheimer's disease affects communication, Kemper and Lyons (1994) mention cognitive problems, such as attention deficits, and short- and long-term memory problems, which lead to the disruption of communication within Alzheimer's patients. Specifically, people with Alzheimer's often use vague words or words with nonspecific references during conversations (e.g. words like "stuff" or "things"), and they have difficulty adapting speech to changing situations. In addition, they often have difficulty interpreting complex sentence structures when interacting with others. As a result of these communication problems, "Alzheimer's patients themselves may become socially withdrawn, irritable, and physically agitated as their efforts to communicate or to understand others fail" (Kemper & Lyons, 1994, p. 75).

Communication problems associated with Alzheimer's disease can be challenging and frustrating for people caring for Alzheimer's patients, both healthcare professionals and lay caregivers (e.g. a spouse or family member). Nearly 75 percent of care for people with Alzheimer's disease is provided by family and friends at home (Rice *et al.*, 1993). Caring for these individuals is expensive for most lay caregivers (Ernst & Hay, 1994), and the symptoms of the disease make interaction with the person with Alzheimer's disease difficult (Query & Kreps, 1996).

Physical activity/mobility Physical activity is an important predictor of health status throughout the life span. Most Americans, young and old, do not engage in a sufficient amount of physical activity, despite the fact that insufficient activity has been linked to a host of health problems including obesity, cardiovascular disease, osteoporosis, hypertension, and increased risk of certain types of cancer. Among older adults, increased exercise is associated with reduced risk for these health problems and with many physical and psychological benefits, such as reduced fatigue, anxiety, and depression, and increased mood and emotional well-being. A number of factors associated with aging may limit mobility and subsequently the ability to engage in physical activity among older adults. In addition, decreased mobility among older adults may decrease social contact. This section briefly explores the effects of decreased activity/mobility on physical and psychological health.

According to Burns (2002), after age 65 a large proportion of older women and men report reduced levels of physical activity, and for adults over the age of 75, 34 percent of men and 50 percent of women report no regular physical exercise. There are a number of reasons why older individuals may find it harder to engage in regular physical activity. Nearly 35 percent of individuals over 65 have impaired walking ability (Burns, 2002), 50–60 percent of people of 65 and older have arthritis (Center for Disease Control, 1996), and these conditions can limit mobility. While many of these health conditions may not physically prevent older individuals from engaging in adequate levels of some form of physical activity to keep them healthy, they may experience feelings of discomfort, frustration, and fear that greater physical exertion might lead to larger health problems (e.g. a heart attack). Providers frequently perceive that older patients may be at greater risk for cardiac events due to heavy exertion, and this may make them reluctant to recommend more physical exercise, even among older individuals who may not be at significant risk and may actually benefit from increased activity (Burns, 2002).

In addition to physical problems that limit physical activity, factors such as living on a fixed income, access to transportation, and a declining social network can present barriers to sufficient exercise. Health clubs and access to walking areas can be limited for older people with restricted financial means or those without a vehicle or nearby public transportation. While a person does not need to join a health club in order to be physically active, there may be social reasons why some older people do not engage in inexpensive physical activities such as shopping or taking walks around the neighborhood. Older individuals living alone or those with fewer friends may find it hard to locate companions who are willing to participate in physical activities with them. Some senior centers and other community-based facilities often host activities that may help older individuals get more exercise (e.g. aerobics classes, trips to museums), although these types of services may be far from where many older people live or nonexistent in more rural areas of the country. As the older population increases, greater awareness of the physical activity needs of older adults is needed so that communities can provide resources for seniors.

Polypharmacy Older patients are also more likely than younger patients to experience multiple illnesses (Nussbaum, Ragan, & Whaley, 2004), a situation that can lead to the need to take multiple medications to treat these conditions. Unfortunately, this often leads to *polypharmacy*, or the problems that arise from the prescription of an excessive number of medications and the interactions between them. Polypharmacy is common among older patients, particularly those individuals who are coping with multiple health conditions. Older adults account for almost a third of all prescribed medications and about 40 percent of all over-the-counter medications (Colley & Lucas, 1993; Gandhi *et al.*, 2000).

For example, an older patient who already has hypertension and arthritis may be diagnosed with cancer and require chemotherapy. Her oncologist needs to know what medications she is taking for hypertension and arthritis to assess which types of chemotherapy will not interact with these medications. Because drug interactions can produce a variety of unpleasant and sometimes life-threatening complications (such as fatigue, hallucinations, dizziness, and falls), physicians and other providers need to have a complete list of medications an older patient is taking in order to avoid problems (Colley & Lucas, 1993). However, many older patients do not know all of the medications they are taking, and this situation is complicated by multiple classes of medications, different brand names, and generic versions of medications. In addition, many patients are unaware of how prescription medications interact with over-the-counter medications, vitamins, and herbal supplements, which can also cause drug interaction effects. Our kidneys and liver are important organs for removing toxins from the blood stream, and as we age these organs often work more slowly. This can cause problems for older adults taking multiple medications when medications take hours or days apart to interact with one another.

Other problems can occur when older individuals do not adhere to some or all of the medication protocols (e.g. not taking the proper dosage, irregular use of medications) for reasons such as being unclear about the directions or taking or not taking the drug depending upon how they feel, or if they are not aware of or do not understand the various interaction effects that can occur among their medications (Hanlon *et al.*, 1997). Older people sometimes take medications on an irregular basis, take only half the prescribed amount, or they simply do not refill prescriptions in an effort to help lower the cost of medications. To help prevent polypharmacy, providers often urge older patients to bring their medication bottles or a list of medications with them to healthcare visits, and this helps to circumvent memory problems about which medications a patient is taking. Providers also need to inform older patients about interaction effects prescribed medications can have with over-the-counter drugs, vitamins, alcohol, and other substances an older person might be taking.

Institutionalized older adults

Approximately 25 percent of adults aged 65 and older die in nursing homes and other longer-term care facilities each year in the US (Gabrel, 2000; Happ *et al.*, 2002), although only about 4–5 percent of people over the age of 65 reside in a nursing home at any one point in time (Magaziner, Zimmerman, Fox, & Burns, 1998; Nussbaum, Ragan, & Whaley, 2004). With the increase in the older adult population, particularly in individuals aged 85 and older, it is estimated that the number of seniors requiring long-term institutional care will double by 2040 (Magaziner *et al.*, 1998; Schneider & Guralnik, 1990).

Given the rapid growth of the older adult population, there is a great deal of concern among healthcare professionals about the ability of current long-term care facilities to meet the needs of the increasing number of older Americans who will require such services. Moving an elderly loved one to a nursing home is typically a stressful event for family members, and it can be traumatic for older adults who are being relocated to a nursing home, particularly since few older individuals participate in the decision to relocate and many are in poor physical health at the time of relocation (Nussbaum, Ragan, & Whaley, 2004). Once an elderly person is relocated to a nursing home, many face a variety of undesirable conditions.

Currently, many nursing homes and other long-term care facilities for older adults frequently consist of staff members who have limited knowledge of aging issues or who are unprepared to provide comprehensive end-of-life care (Happ *et al.*, 2002). When nursing home residents need treatment for more severe health problems, they are typically hospitalized outside of the nursing home. Unfortunately, nursing home residents often experience poor continuity of care between the nursing home and hospitalization. This lack of continuity of care often stems from the absence of coordination between hospital staff and nursing home staff, and it can lead to unnecessary suffering for older residents. One quarter of nursing home residents with daily pain report receiving no pain treatment (Won *et al.*, 1999), and many experience unwanted interventions and have little control over end-of-life care decision-making (Happ *et al.*, 2002).

There are many reasons for the poor quality of care within many nursing homes. Nursing home personnel are often poorly paid, they receive inadequate training, there is a high rate of staff turnover, and they must cope with very challenging and stressful work conditions. Approximately 40–50 percent of all older residents in long-term care institutions are diagnosed with some form of dementia, with the highest percentage of individuals with dementia over the age of 85 (Magaziner *et al.*, 1998), and this can lead to numerous problems for nursing home staff when interacting with residents and attempting to meet their needs. Between 45 and 58 percent of nursing home residents require assistance to bathe, about 25 percent suffer from urinary incontinence, and a large proportion of individuals spend the majority of their time in bed or in a wheelchair due to physical disabilities (Morgan *et al.*, 1995). Working with residents who have these conditions requires a great deal of patience and understanding, and it can be difficult for many staff members to consistently provide quality care when they feel overloaded, tired, or emotionally drained from working with residents each day.

As regards staff communication with residents within nursing homes and meeting residents' social needs, several researchers have found nursing homes to be poor communication environments (Grainger, 2004; Nussbaum, 1983). Nussbaum (1983) found that residents in nursing homes often experience "interactive starvation" due to limited (and poor-quality) interaction with other residents and staff members. Grainger (2004) found that older adults in nursing homes often suffer from an absence of talk due to environmental barriers to communication within these facilities, such as loud televisions in sitting areas and placement of chairs that inhibit conversations among residents. In addition, residents are rarely given any incentive to talk to other residents because of activities that do not encourage interaction. Nursing home staff members often complain that their busy schedules do not leave much time for conversing with residents. In addition, the heavy use of medications in many nursing homes can impair the communicative abilities of older residents who would otherwise be able to communicate effectively (Nussbaum, Ragan, & Whaley, 2004).

When communication does occur between staff members and residents, it is often task-oriented talk (Grainger, 2004). Task-oriented talk may consist of brief interactions between staff and residents centered around day-to-day physical care tasks that workers must accomplish, such as feeding residents, bathing, changing bedding, and providing medication. Grainger (2004) contends that the majority of talk between workers and residents is to ensure efficient execution of tasks as opposed to more meaningful conversations (e.g. such as talk about life experiences and feelings). Too much talk that is task-oriented can be dehumanizing to residents, especially if staff members treat interactions as tasks to be accomplished as opposed to real conversations.

Task-oriented talk is also related to busy work schedules, which often leave little time for quality interaction with residents, but Grainger maintains that the preponderance of task-oriented talk is also linked to lack of education and/or inadequate training about such issues among nursing home staff. Finally, Grainger argues that much of the communication between nursing home staff and residents consists of dependency-inducing talk. Researchers have found that nursing home staff members frequently engage in patronizing talk, or "baby talk," with older residents (Caporael, 1981; Caporael & Culbertson, 1986). Baby talk with seniors is a form of speech that is almost indistinguishable from speech addressed to young children, and it includes less complex sentence structures, shorter utterances, and more questions (Grainger, 2004). Nursing home residents often engage in interaction with staff members who use baby talk because many are starved of any type of conversation in what is typically an interaction-deficient environment. Caporael and others (e.g. Ryan, Hummert, & Boich, 1995) have argued that baby talk actually induces dependency by undermining an older person's confidence in his or her own abilities to communicate and to perform ordinary tasks over time. In other words, through repeated statements like

"Let me move that for you, sweety," older individuals actually learn to become dependent on nursing home staff members, believing that they could not perform the task on their own.

The decision to move an older loved one to a nursing home often leads to an increased financial burden for family members (Nussbaum, Ragan, & Whaley, 2004). Long-term institutional care is quite expensive, and unfortunately the nursing homes that provide the best quality of care are also typically the most expensive. In addition, moving a parent or an aging spouse to a nursing home is a stressful event for family members who often do not have the ability to care for them, and yet they simultaneously do not want to make things worse for their loved ones. Given the number of older individuals who are expected to require long-term care over the next several decades, more education about long-term care and current nursing home problems for family members is needed, as well as more counseling and support.

Attitudes Toward Death and Dying

Death and dying are taboo topics that most people avoid talking about in the US and other western cultures (Callahan, 2009; Leichtentritt & Rettig, 2002). According to Martin, Emanuel, and Singer (2000), while death has historically been a central focus of social and religious life, modern society has privatized and secularized death, keeping it hidden behind institutional walls. Most Americans know relatively little about the day-to-day activities of medical examiners or the embalming process, and even fewer individuals feel comfortable discussing these things. The mass media, our families, religious groups with whom we affiliate, and the larger culture and co-culture to which we belong influence our attitudes, beliefs, and values about death and dying. In general, serious discussion of death is largely avoided in our culture, and when it is talked about, people tend to joke about death or talk about it in indirect ways.

Most people spend little time thinking about their own inevitable death or the death of those who are close to them, and this can cause problems when death needs to be discussed with friends, family members, and healthcare providers. People facing life-threatening illnesses often find it frustrating when loved ones or healthcare providers avoid talking about death and dying, especially at a time when they desire validation, empathy, and other types of support from these individuals. Studies have found that people will even distance themselves from individuals who have lost a loved one or negatively view a bereaved person who talks about their loss beyond a certain (and often limited) amount of time (Cluck & Cline, 1989). Moreover, most Americans know very little about end-of-life medical care and have not talked to anyone in their social network about these issues (Scharader, Nelson, & Eidness, 2009). The absence of talk about death and dying and end-of-life care issues in most families often leads to family difficulties, misunderstandings, and rushed decision-making in terms of caring for a terminally ill loved one (Holst, Lundren, Olsen, & Ishoy, 2009).

At some point in the life span, most individuals realize that they are not going to live forever, and they must decide how they will cope with the idea of their mortality and their eventual death. Keith (1979) developed a typology of attitudes that people commonly have towards death and dying. According to Keith, individuals who feel that they have largely achieved the goals they have set for themselves in life and who reflect positively upon their present life are known as *positivists*. *Negativists* are people who reflect negatively upon their lives, especially those individuals who did not have the opportunity to fulfill dreams or who have regrets about their behaviors, and these people may look on death with despair. People who view death as an end to future opportunities for achievement and self-fulfillment but who are largely satisfied with their past are known as *activists*, and those people who see death as an end to life's problems and suffering are called *pacifists*. A person's attitude towards death and dying may influence the way he or she communicates about these topics, or whether or not he or she talks about them at all.

In terms of talking about death with providers, there is a bias among physicians and providers in our culture toward being optimistic when talking to patients about life-threatening illnesses. Many doctors feel that they will be perceived as "giving up" on the patient if they talk about dying, and that this will eliminate the patient's sense of hope and lead to depression (Hines, Moss, & McKenzie, 1997). Hines, Babrow, Badzek, and Moss (1997) found that doctors and patients avoided discussing life-threatening conditions as long as possible and as minimally as possible, which often leads to rushed decision-making about treatment decisions. Although physicians are trained to deliver bad news to patients in medical school, studies have found that medical students feel anxious communicating with dying patients and that they have inadequate training in communicating and caring for dying patients (Fields & Howells, 1985; Sykes, 1989).

Communicating with others about death and dying

While coming to terms with death and dying is largely a process that occurs on the individual level, it is also important to consider the ways in which we communicate with others about death and dying. Most people tend not to think about their own end-of-life care, and healthcare professionals and researchers have paid relatively little attention to this subject until recently. There are a number of communication problems surrounding death and dying. Dying individuals may avoid talking to their loved ones about death due to cultural inhibitions against discussing such topics (Planalp & Trost, 2008). Moreover, this problem is exacerbated by caregivers who often feel uncomfortable talking about death and dying as well, and they may keep silent about these issues even when the person they are caring for may want to talk. When death and dying are not avoided in conversations, they are frequently discussed using sarcasm or black humor (Leichtenritt & Rettig, 2002). As a result, the needs and wishes of dying individuals are often not made known to family members and friends (Planalp & Trost, 2008). Hospice volunteers may play an important role in terms of providing a resource for dying individuals to talk about death and dying. For example, while patients do not want to burden family members with talk about death and dying, they often feel safe discussing these issues with hospice volunteers (Planalp & Trost, 2008). In addition, Egbert and Parrott (2003) found that hospice volunteers were more likely to provide emotional support to dying patients than regular hospital staff.

Given the increase in technological innovations that allow healthcare providers to prolong life, more and more people have become aware that the preservation of life does not necessarily mean quality of life. Many people die in severe pain or with uncontrolled symptoms, and family members and others often shoulder the psychological and financial burden of making and living with decisions about end-of-life care for a loved one (Ramsay, 1999). For example, a person may not want his family to deal with the stress of keeping him alive on a life support machine for months or years after he loses consciousness, so he might include a "do not resuscitate" or DNR order within an *advance care directive*. Advance care directives are legal documents that instruct family members and other loved ones about the wishes of an individual after he or she dies. While these are not easy topics to discuss, individuals may need to express their wishes to family members over what should be done if they should face a terminal illness or impending death.

Advanced care directives give individuals much more control over how they will be treated by healthcare professionals if they should lose their ability to communicate with others. Advanced care planning helps people to determine settings for healthcare and limits for life-sustaining treatments that may lengthen the dying process. Advanced care directives allow people the reassurance that they will be treated in ways that are consistent with their values in situations where others are making decisions about their life and death. For example, some people value life at all costs, and they may specify in an advanced care directive that providers should do anything they can to keep them alive even if they are in a long-term coma. Other individuals are more concerned with quality of life or the needs of their loved ones, and may consider death to be a better alternative to being kept alive by a machine. These kinds of personal and emotional choices are often very difficult to make and certainly involve complexities that vary greatly for each individual as well as family members who may or may not be involved in the decision-making.

Physicians play an important role in discussing the implications of advanced care directives with patients (Martin, Emanuel, & Singer, 2000). There are many types of advanced care directives that people can choose from, and they can be confusing to laypersons due to the legal language and specific goals of different types of advanced care directive documents. For example, one type of advance care directive is an instruction directive, or living will, which describes what type of care a person wants to receive in various situations (does the person want to be resuscitated by providers or should surgery be performed if there is little hope for recovery?). Proxy directives (also known as durable powers of attorney for healthcare) indicate whom a person would want to make treatment decisions on his or her behalf (usually a spouse or family member). Advanced care directives also vary in terms of detail. Non-detailed directives provide basic information about a person's wishes if he or she were to become incapacitated due to a wide range of scenarios, such as ending up in a coma as the result of an automobile accident or facing some other chronic disability. More detailed directives, such as disease-specific directives, can be drafted for individuals who know they are likely to die from a long-term illness, such as HIV or cancer. In these more detailed directives, patients can indicate preferences for treatment options and other important decisions that are directly related to the disease they are facing.

For example, a person with cancer might opt to stop chemotherapy treatment once the cancer has progressed to an advanced stage in order to avoid side effects from chemotherapy (such as nausea, reduced energy, and hair loss) during the last part of his or her life. Less detailed directives may be helpful for individuals who want to be sure their basic end-of-life wishes (such as a "do not resuscitate" order) are taken care of for a variety of unforeseen circumstances (e.g. an accident), while more detailed directives may be more helpful for individuals who have been diagnosed with a life-threatening illness and might have greater ability to predict the course of the disease.

Despite the importance of provider–patient communication in clarifying the details of advanced care directives, both patients and providers often find it difficult to communicate about them. According to Martin, Emanuel, & Singer (2000):

> Unfortunately, many patients consider their physician to be too busy for lengthy discussions about end-of-life issues; other patients consider these issues as private. Physician-identified barriers to communication also exist, including discomfort talking about death and dying, lack of knowledge, difficulty determining appropriateness, and time constraints. (p. 1675)

Physicians often introduce patients to advanced care directives, but they often don't discuss a patient's values concerning life and death. Discussion of these values is important in order to insure that a patient's wishes will ultimately be carried out if they are unable to communicate in a life-threatening situation. According to Martin, Emanuel, & Singer (2000), providers should consider patient goals and values when advising patients about advanced care directives, tailor advanced care directives to a patient's needs (and the needs of his or her family), translate difficult information and terminology contained in advanced care directives in terms that the patient can understand, and approach the topic of advanced care directives in an open, warm, and caring manner. Furthermore, patients should think critically about their values and goals when it comes to end-of-life care and talk to their providers and family members about advanced care directives. As we have seen, this is not an easy subject for most people to talk about given societal norms surrounding the discussion of death and dying. However, given advances in medicine and technology, people are more likely to be faced with end-of-life decision-making than in the past, and these decisions can help ensure that people will die in a way that is consistent with their values and thus minimize stressful decisions for family members and other loved ones.

Coping with the death of a loved one

Coping with the death of a loved one is a very difficult process whether the death is the result of a long-term illness or an unexpected event. This section examines the grieving process and discusses ways in which family members and friends can help each other following the loss of a loved one.

Grief can be defined as the normal process of reacting both internally and externally to the perception of loss (Corr, Nabe, & Corr, 1997). *Bereavement* refers to the period of time in which an individual experiences grief and mourns the death of a loved one.

When a person is dying from a long-term illness, his or her loved ones often experience *anticipatory grief*. This is the normal mourning that occurs when a patient or family is expecting a death, and it may have many of the same symptoms as those experienced after a death has occurred. However, anticipatory grief does not always occur while a loved one is dying, and the grief experienced before a death does not make the grief after the death last a shorter amount of time.

Family members and friends must contend with many issues following the death of a loved one, including making funeral arrangements, writing obituaries, and other important decisions such as whether or not to perform an autopsy or donate organs (discussed below). All of these activities can become overwhelming for individuals coping with grief, and family and friends play an important role in helping the bereaved individual adjust.

Reactions to grief Individuals often experience and express grief in different ways, and the way in which a person will grieve depends on the personality of the grieving individual and his or her relationship with the person who died. People who have unresolved issues with a loved one may experience grief differently than those individuals who do not, and some people may be troubled by unfulfilled wishes or goals they had for the deceased. Some people feel shock, disorientation, disappointment, and separation anxiety following the death of a loved one. Physical reactions can include sleep difficulties, appetite changes, somatic complaints, or illness. In time, people learn to cope with their loss in their own unique ways, but bereaved individuals may vary considerably in terms of the amount of time it takes them to adjust. Members of a bereaved person's social network do not always understand grief or do not know how to communicate appropriately with someone who has experienced the death of a loved one.

For example, Cluck and Cline (1989) found that members of a bereaved person's social network often distance themselves from him or her. In addition, social network members sometimes have unrealistic expectations about the appropriate period of time for grief to take place. In Cluck and Cline's (1989) study, bereaved individuals reported that family members and friends often wanted them to stop grieving after a relatively short period of time, and the bereaved person was seen as not adjusting well if he or she grieved for more than a few weeks or months. It is important to remember that it can take a great deal of time for some people to grieve, and there is no appropriate amount of time for someone to work through the difficulties of experiencing death. In addition, and perhaps most importantly, our relationships with those who have passed away are not gone forever. Instead, our relationship changes form. In other words, we still carry on a different type of relationship when those we are close to die. We continue to think about the times shared together. When a person sees something that reminds him or her of the loved one, aspects of the relationship resurface in their own way, often bringing joy, sometimes bringing sadness, but the relationship continues, changing from the way it was to take on a different form (e.g. through memories).

It is also possible for people to experience grief in unhealthy ways. Some individuals may experience prolonged periods of depression, survivor's guilt, substance abuse, or have suicidal thoughts during the bereavement process. For these people, grief counseling and/or joining a grief support group may be helpful. If you have a friend or family member who is having a difficult time adjusting to loss, be sure to talk with that person when possible so you can be there to help show him or her how to get appropriate help if needed.

Organ donation

Over 96 000 Americans are awaiting a life-saving organ donation (United Network for Organ Sharing, 2007). Unfortunately, many of these people will not receive a life-saving organ because of public resistance to donating organs and tissue after death (Morgan, 2004) and because family members are reluctant to donate organs from their deceased loved ones (Vincent, 2006). The discussion of questions such as autopsies and organ donation with providers is often emotionally charged and difficult for bereaved individuals (Marchand & Kushner, 2004; Morgan & Miller, 2002), and these issues, along with a generally negative perception of organ donation in the US, have led to a severe shortage of available organs for transplant patients.

Individuals can become designated organ donors during life, but they need to remember to carry their organ donor card and discuss their wishes with family members so that their families are aware of their desire to donate organs and feel more comfortable with the idea. It is important to remember that there are different age limits on the donation of some organs and tissue, and a person's age and medical history are taken into consideration when an organ donation is made. However, at least some organs from the majority of individuals who die can be used to prolong or enhance the quality of life of another person. In many ways, knowing that a deceased family member is helping another human being through the donation of an organ can be a comforting thought for bereaved individuals.

There are a variety of reasons why people are reluctant to donate organs and tissue after death, including lack of knowledge about donation, religious and spiritual beliefs, concerns about body mutilation, and the deservingness of potential recipients of organs and tissue, such as criminals (Morgan, 2004; Morgan *et al.*, 2008). Clearly, more education and awareness about organ donation as well as the resistance to organ donation are necessary in order to help people who need organ and tissue transplants. Yet, it appears that frank and open communication about death and dying and the need for organ and tissue donation may facilitate people's willingness to sign an organ donation card.

Summary

A greater number of individuals are finding themselves in the role of caregiver due to factors such as an increased life span and life-prolonging medical and technological advances. Caring for a loved one with a long-term illness is a challenging experience for most people, and communication plays an important role in the caregiving process.

Hospice and palliative care can help people who are dying and their lay caregivers by providing important holistic services, including pain monitoring and control, symptom management, education about the dying process, and psychological and spiritual counseling. However, barriers to hospice and palliative care, such as undertrained providers and insurance eligibility requirements, have limited the use of these services in the US. Coping with the dying process and death are difficult for most individuals to think and talk about, but communication is important in creating advanced care directives, comforting dying individuals and their family members, and in getting through the grieving process following the death of a loved one.

References

Allen, R. S., Haley, W. E., Small, B. J., & McMillan, S. C. (2002). Pain reports by older hospice cancer patients and family caregivers: The role of cognitive functioning. *Gerontologist, 42*, 507–514.

Andrews, S. C. (2001). Caregiver burden and symptom distress in people with cancer receiving hospice care. *Oncology Nursing Forum, 28*, 1469–1474.

Bachner, Y. G., & Carmel, S. (2009). Open communication between caregivers and terminally ill cancer patients: The role of caregivers' characteristics and situational variables. *Health Communication, 24*, 524–531.

Baillie, L. (2007). Family caregiving when relationships are poor. In: I. Paoletti (Ed.), *Family caregiving for older disabled people* (pp. 127–149). New York: Nova Science Publishers.

Baldassar, L., & Baldock, C. V. (2000). Linking migration and family studies: Transnational migrants and the care of ageing parents. In: B. Agozino (Ed.), *Theoretical and methodological issues in migration research: Interdisciplinary, intergenerational and international perspectives* (pp. 61–89). Aldershot: Ashgate.

Baldassar, L., Wilding, R., & Baldock, C. (2007). Long-distance caregiving: Transnational families and the provision of aged care. In: I. Paoletti (Ed.), *Family caregiving for older disabled people* (pp. 201–227). New York: Nova Science Publishers.

Bakas, T., Lewis, R. R., & Parsons, J. (2001). Caregiving tasks among family caregivers of patients with lung cancer. *Oncology Nursing Forum, 28*, 847–854.

Barclay, S., Wyatt, P., Shore, S., Finlay, I., Grande, G., & Todd, C. (2003). Care for the dying: How well prepared are general practitioners? A questionnaire study in Wales. *Palliative Medicine, 17*, 27–39.

Benefield, L. E., & Beck, C. (2007). Reducing the distance in distance-caregiving by technology. *Clinical Interventions in Aging, 2*, 267–272.

Bernabei, R., Gambassi, G., Lapane, K., Landi, F., Gatsonis, C., Dunlop, R., *et al.* (1998). Management of pain in elderly patients with cancer. *Journal of the American Medical Association, 279*, 1877–1882.

Bevan, J., & Sparks, L. (2011). Communication in the context of long-distance family caregiving. An integrated review and practical applications. *Patient Education and Counseling, 85*, 26–30.

Bevan, J., Jupin, A., & Sparks, L. (2011). Information quality, uncertainty, and quality of care in long distance caregiving. *Communication Research Reports, 28*(2), 190–195.

Bevan, J., Rogers, K., Andrews, N., & Sparks, L. (in press). Topic avoidance and negative health perceptions in the distant caregiving context. *Journal of Family Communication.*

Bevan, J., Vreeburg, S. K., Verdugo, S., & Sparks, L. (2012). Interpersonal conflict and health perception in long-distance caregiving relationships. *Journal of Health Communication, 0*, 1-15.

Blevins, D., & Deason-Howell, L. M. (2002). End-of-life care in nursing homes: The interface of policy, research, and practice. *Behavioral Sciences and the Law, 20*, 271–286.

Block, S. D., & Sullivan, A. M. (1998). Attitudes about end-of-life care: A national cross-sectional study. *Journal of Palliative Medicine, 1*, 347–355.

Brereton L, Nolan, M. (2000). "You do know he's had a stroke, don't you?" Preparation for family caregiving—the neglected dimension. *Journal of Clinical Nursing, 9*, 498–506.

Brescia, F. J., Portenoy, R. K., Ryan, M., Krasnoff, L., & Gray, G. (1992). Pain, opioid use, and survival in hospitalized patients with advanced cancer. *Journal of Clinical Oncology, 10,* 149–155.

Burleson, B. R. (2003). Emotional support skill. In: J. O. Greene, & B. R. Burleson (Eds), *Handbook of communication and social interaction skills* (pp. 551–594). Mahwah, NJ: Erlbaum.

Burns, E. A. (2002). Commentary: Challenges to using exercise interventions in older adults. In K. W. Schaie, H. Leventhal, & S. L. Willis (Eds), *Effective health behavior in older adults* (pp. 179–189). New York: Springer.

Callahan, D. (2009). Death, mourning, and medical progress. *Perspectives in Biological Medicine, 52,* 103–115.

Caporael, L. R. (1981). The paralanguage of caregiving: Baby talk to the institutionalized aged. *Journal of Personality and Social Psychology, 40,* 876–884.

Caporael, L. R., & Culbertson, G. H. (1986). Verbal response modes of baby talk and other speech at institutions for the aged. *Language and Communication, 6,* 99–112.

Center for Disease Control (CDC) (1996). *Physical activity and health: A report of the Surgeon General.* Hyattsville, MD: US Public Health Service.

Centers for Disease Control and Prevention. (2004). Vital and health statistics. Retrieved July 23, 2012, from www.cdc.gov/.

Chesler, M. A., & Barbarin, O. A. (1984). Difficulties of providing help in a crisis: Relationships between parents of children with cancer and their friends. *Journal of Social Issues, 40,* 113–134.

Cluck, G. G., & Cline, R. W. (1989). The circle of others: Self-help groups for the bereaved. *Communication Quarterly, 34,* 306–325.

Cohen, G. (1994). Age-related problems in the use of proper names in communication. In M. L. Hummert, J. M. Wiemann, & J. F. Nussbaum (Eds), *Interpersonal communication in older adulthood: Interdisciplinary theory and research* (pp. 40–57). Thousand Oaks, CA: Sage.

Colley, C. E., & Lucas, L. M. (1993). Polypharmacy: The cure becomes the disease. *Journal of General Internal Medicine, 8,* 278–283.

Coopman, S. J. (2001). Democracy, performance, and outcomes in interdisciplinary health care teams. *Journal of Business Communication, 38,* 261–284.

Corr, C. A., Nabe, C. M., & Corr, D. M. (1997). *Death and dying, life and living* (2nd ed.). Pacific Grove, CA: Brooks/Cole.

Darbyshire, J. (1984). The hearing loss epidemic: A challenge to gerontology. *Research on Aging, 6,* 384–394.

Degeneffe, C. E., & Burcham, C. M. (2008). Adult sibling caregiving for persons with traumatic brain injury: Predictors of affective and instrumental support. *Journal of Rehabilitation, 74,* 10–20.

Donelan, K., Hill, C. A., Hoffman, C., Scoles, K., Feidman, P. H., Levine, C., & Gould, D. (1998). Challenged to care: Informal caregivers in a changing health system. *Health Affairs, 21,* 222–231.

Donnelly, S., Walsh, D., & Rybicki, L. (1994). The symptoms of advanced cancer in 1,000 patients. *Journal of Palliative Care, 10,* 57.

Egbert, N., & Parrott, R. (2003). Empathy and social support for the terminally ill: Implications for recruiting and retaining hospice and hospital volunteers. *Communication Studies, 54,* 18–34.

Eisdorfer, C., & Cohen, D. (1980). The issue of biological and psychological deficits. In E. Borgatta & N. McCluskey (Eds), *Aging and society: Current research and policy perspectives* (pp. 49–70). Beverly Hills, CA: Sage.

Elliot, B. A., Elliot, T. E., Murray, D. M., Braun, B. L., & Johnson, K. M. (1997). Patients and family members: The role of knowledge and attitudes in cancer pain. *Journal of Pain and Symptom Management, 12,* 209–220.

Emanuel, D. J., & Emanuel, L. L. (1998). The promise of a good death. *Lancet, 351,* 21–29.

Ernst, R. L., & Hay, J. W. (1994). The US economic and social costs of Alzheimer's disease revisited. *American Journal of Public Health, 84,* 1261–1264.

Federal Interagency Forum on Aging-Related Statistics. (2000). Older Americans 2000: Key indicators of well-being [On-line]. Retrieved August 25, 2004, from www.agingstats.gov.

Field, M. J., & Cassel, C. K. (Eds) (1997). *Approaching death: Improving care at the end of life.* Washington, DC: National Academy Press.

Fields, D., & Howells, K. (1985). Medical students' self-reported worries about aspects of death and dying. *Death Studies, 10,* 147–154.

Foley, K. M., & Gelband, H. (Eds) (2001). *Improving palliative care for cancer.* Washington, DC: National Academy Press.

Fowler, C., & Fisher, C. L. (2009). Attitudes toward decision making and aging, and preparation for future care needs. *Health Communication, 24,* 619–630.

Francis, L. E., Worthington, J., Kypriotakis, G., & Rose, J. H. (2010). Relationship quality and burden among caregivers for late-stage cancer patients. *Supportive Care in Cancer*, DOI: 10.1007/s00520-009-0765-5.

Fried, T. R., Bradley, E. H., O'Leary, J. R., & Byers, A. L. (2005). Unmet desire for caregiver-patient communication and increased caregiver burden. *Journal of American Geriatrics Society, 53*, 59–65.

Gabrel, C. S. (2000). *Characteristics of elderly nursing home residents and discharges: Data from the 1997 National Nursing Home Survey*. Washington, DC: US Department of Health and Human Services, Centers for Disease Control and Prevention.

Gandhi, T. K., Burstin, H. R., Cook, E. F., *et al.* (2000). Drug complications in outpatients. *Journal of General Internal Medicine, 15*, 149–154.

Gatz, M., Kasl-Godley, J. E., & Karel, M. J. (1996). Aging and mental disorders. In J. E. Birren & K. W. Schaie (Eds), *Handbook of psychology and aging* (4th ed., pp. 365–382). San Diego, CA: Academic Press.

Geist-Martin, P., Ray, E. B., & Sharf, B. F. (2003). *Communicating health: Personal, cultural, and political complexities*. Belmont, CA: Wadsworth.

Given, B. A., Given, C. W., Helms, E., Stommel, M., & DeVoss, D. N. (1997). Determinants of family caregiver reaction. New and recurrent cancer. *Cancer Practice, 5*, 17–24.

Given, C. W., Stommel, M., Given, B. A., Osuch, J., Kurtz, M. E., & Kurtz, J. C. (1993). The influence of cancer patients' symptoms and functional states on patients' depression and family caregivers' reaction and depression. *Health Psychology, 12*, 277–285.

Gloth, F. M. (1998). Foreword. *Hospice care: A physician's guide*. Alexandria, VA: National Hospice Organization.

Goldsmith, J., Wittenberg-Lyles, E., Ragan, S., & Nussbaum, J. F. (2011). Life span and end-of-life health communication. In T. L. Thompson, R. Parrott, & J. F. Nussbaum (Eds), *The Routledge handbook of health communication, 2nd ed.* (pp. 441–454). New York: Routledge.

Grainger, K. (2004). Communication and the institutionalized elderly. In J. F. Nussbaum & J. Coupland (Eds), *Handbook of communication and aging research* (2nd ed., pp. 479–497). Mahwah, NJ: Lawrence Erlbaum.

Grande, G. E., McKerral, A., & Todd, C. J. (2002). Which cancer patients are referred to hospital at home for palliative care? *Palliative Medicine, 16*, 115–123.

Haley, W. E., LaMonde, L. A., Han, B., Burton, A. M., & Schonwetter, R. (2003). Predictors of depression and life satisfaction among spousal caregivers in hospice: Application of a stress process model. *Journal of Palliative Medicine, 6*, 215–224.

Hanlon, J. T., Schmader, K. E., Koronkowski, M. J., *et al.* (1997). Adverse drug events in high-risk older patients. *Journal of the American Geriatric Society, 145*, 945–948.

Happ, M., Capezuti, E., Strumpf, N., Wagner, L., Cunningham, S., Evans, L., & Maislin, G. (2002). Advance care planning and end-of-life care for hospitalized nursing home residents. *Journal of the American Geriatrics Society, 50*, 829–835.

Harwood, J., & Sparks, L. (2003). Social identity and health: An intergroup communication approach to cancer. *Health Communication, 15*, 145–170.

Harzold, E., & Sparks, L. (2007). Adult child perceptions of communication and humor when the parent is diagnosed with cancer: A suggestive perspective from communication theory. *Qualitative Research Reports in Communication, 7*, 1–13.

Helgeson VS, Cohen S. (1999). Social support and adjustment to cancer: Reconciling descriptive, correlational, and intervention research. In R. N. Suinn, & G. R. VandenBos (Eds) *Cancer patients and their families: Readings on disease course, coping, and psychological interventions* (pp. 53–79). Washington DC: American Psychological Association.

Hewitt, M., Rowland, J., & Yancik, R. (2003). Cancer survivors in the United States: Age, health, and disability. *Journals of Gerontology, Series A, 58*(1), 82–92.

Hebert, L. E., Scherr, P. A., Bienias, J. L., Bennett, D. A., & Evans, D. A. (2003). Alzheimer's disease in the US population: Prevalence estimates using the 2000 Census. *Archives of Neurology, 60*, 1119–1122.

Hinds, C. (1992). Suffering: A relatively unexplored phenomenon among family caregivers of non-institutionalized patients with cancer. *Journal of Advanced Nursing, 17*, 918–925.

Hines, S. C., Babrow, A. S., Badzek, L., & Moss, A. L. (1997). Communication and problematic integration in end-of-life decisions: Dialysis decisions among the elderly. *Health Communication, 9*, 199–217.

Hines, S. C., Moss, A. H., & McKenzie, J. (1997). Prolonging life or prolonging death: Communication's role in difficult dialysis decisions. *Health Communication, 9*, 369–.

Holst, L., Lundren, M., Olsen, L., & Ishoy, T. (2009). Dire deadlines: Coping with dysfunctional family dynamics in an end-of-life care setting. *International Journal of Palliative Nursing, 15*, 34–41.

Hospice Foundation of America. (n.d.). Caregiver concerns. Retrieved June 14, 2004, from www.hospicefoundation.org/.

Howarth, G., & Leaman, O. (Eds). (2001). *Encyclopedia of death and dying*. London: Routledge.

Karim, K., Bailey, M., & Tunna, K. (2000). Nonwhite ethnicity and the provision of specialist palliative care services: Factors affecting doctors' referral patterns. *Palliative Medicine*, 14, 471–478.

Kemper, S. (1992). Language and aging. In F. M. Craik & T. Salthouse (Eds), *Handbook of aging and cognition* (pp. 213–270). Hillsdale, NJ: Lawrence Erlbaum.

Kemper, S., & Lyons, K. (1994). The effects of Alzheimer's dementia on language and communication. In M. L. Hummert, J. M. Weimann, & J. F. Nussbaum (Eds), *Interpersonal communication in older adulthood: Interdisciplinary theory and research* (pp. 58–82). Thousand Oaks, CA: Sage.

Kelsey, S. G., & Laditka, S. B. (2009). Evaluating the roles of professional geriatric care managers in maintaining the quality of life for older Americans. *Journal of Gerontological Social Work*, 52, 261–276.

Keith, D. M. (1979). Life changes and perceptions of life and death among older men and women. *Journal of Gerontology*, 34, 870–878.

Koerner, S. S., Shirai, Y., & Kenyon, D. B. (2010). Sociocontextual circumstances in daily stress reactivity among caregivers for elderly relatives. *Journal of Gerontology*, DOI: 10.1093/geronb/gbq045.

Laizner, A. M., Yost, L. M., Barg, F. K., & McCorkle, R. (1993). Needs of family caregivers of persons with cancer: A review. *Seminars in Oncology Nursing*, 9, 114–120.

Lawton, J. (2000). *The dying process: Patients' experiences of palliative care*. London: Routledge.

Leichtentritt, R. D., & Rettig, K. D. (2002). Family beliefs about end-of-life decisions: An interpersonal perspective. *Death Studies*, 26, 567–594.

Lepore, S. J., & Hegelson, V. S. (1998). Social constraints, intrusive thoughts, and mental health after prostate cancer. *Journal of Social and Clinical Psychology*, 17, 89–106.

Lynn, J. (2001). Serving patients who may die soon and their families: The role of hospice and other services. *Journal of the American Medical Association*, 285(7), 925–932.

MacMillan, S. C., & Small, B. J. (2002). Symptom distress and quality of life in patients with cancer newly admitted to hospice home care. *Oncology Nursing Forum*, 29, 1421–1428.

Marchand, L., & Kushner, K. (2004). Death pronouncements: Using the teachable moment in end-of-life care residency training. *Journal of Palliative Medicine*, 7, 80–84.

Magaziner, J., Zimmerman, S. I., Fox, K. M., & Burns, B. J. (1998). Dementia in United States nursing homes: Descriptive epidemiology and implications for long-term residential care. *Aging and Mental Health*, 2, 28–35.

Martin, D. K., Emanuel, L. L., & Singer, P. A. (2000). Planning for the end of life. *Lancet*, 356, 1672–1676.

Martinez, J. M. (1996). The interdisciplinary team. In D. C. Sheehan & W. B. Forman (Eds), *Hospice and palliative care: Concepts and practices* (pp. 21–29). Sudbury, MA: Jones and Bartlett.

Masters, I., Van Den Borne, H., McCormick, L., Pruyn, J., Boer, M., & Imbos, T. (1997). Openness to discuss cancer in the nuclear family: Scale, development, and validation. *Psychosomatic Medicine*, 59, 269–279.

Meyers, J. L., & Gray, L. N. (2001). The relationships between family primary caregiver characteristics and satisfaction with hospice care, quality of life, and burden. *Oncology Nursing Forum*, 28, 73–82.

Miller, K. I., Shoemaker, M. M., Willyard, J., & Addison, P. (2008). Providing care for elderly parents: A structurational approach to family caregiver identity. *Journal of Family Communication*, 8, 19–43.

Mitnick, S., Leffler, C., & Hood, V. L. (2010). Family caregivers, patients and physicians: Ethical guidance and optimize relationships. *Journal of General Internal Medicine*, 25, 255–260.

Moody, H. R. (1994). *Aging: Concepts and controversies*. Thousand Oaks, CA: Pine Forge.

Moore, A. (1998). Hospice care hijacked? *Christianity Today*, 42, 38–41.

Morgan, S. E. (2004). The power of talk: African Americans' communication with family members about organ donation and its impact on the willingness to donate organs. *Journal of Personal and Social Relationships*, 21, 112–124.

Morgan, S. E., Harrison, T. R., Afifi, W. A., Long, S. D., & Stephenson, M. T. (2008). In their own words: The reasons why people will (not) sign an organ donation card. *Health Communication*, 14, 121–134.

Morgan, S. E., & Miller, J. K. (2002). Beyond the organ donor card: The effect of knowledge, attitudes, and values on willingness to communicate about organ donation to family members. *Health Communication*, 14, 121–134.

Morrison, R. S., Penrod, J. D., Cassel, J. B., Caust-Ellenbogen, M., Litke, A., Spragens, I., & Meier, D. E.:

Palliative Care Leadership Centers' Outcomes Group. (2008). Cost savings associated with United States hospital palliative care consultation programs. *Archives of Internal Medicine, 168,* 1783–1790.

Mosqueda, L., & Burnight, K. (2000). Multidimensional assessment in the ambulatory clinic. In D. Osterweil, K. Brummel-Smith, & J. C. Beck (Eds), *Comprehensive geriatric assessment* (pp. 187–202). New York: McGraw-Hill.

Nail, L. M. (2002). Fatigue in patients with cancer. *Oncology Nursing Forum, 29,* 537–546.

National Alliance for Caregiving in collaboration with AARP. (2009, December). *Caregiving in the U.S. 2009.* Retrieved July 11, 2012, from http://www.aarp.org/research/surveys/care/ltc/hc/articles/caregiving_09.html

National Family Caregivers Association. (2005). Who are family caregivers? RetrievedJuly 11, 2012, from www.thefamilycaregiver.org/who/.

National Hospice and Palliative Care Organization (NHPCO). (2004). Caregiving issues. Retrieved April 18, 2004, from www.nhpco.org/.

National Hospice and Palliative Care Organization. (2006, November). *NHPCO's facts and figures—2005 findings.* Retrieved December 8, 2006, from http://nhpco.org/

National Hospice and Palliative Care Organization. (2007, November). *NHPCO facts and figures: Hospice care in America.* Retrieved July 11, 2012, from http://www.nhpco.org/research

Nicoll, L. H. (2002). When there's little time left. *Journal of Hospice and Palliative Nursing, 4,* 4–5.

Nussbaum, J. F. (1983). Relational closeness of elderly interaction: Implications for life satisfaction. *Western Journal of Speech, 47,* 229–243.

Nussbaum, J. F., Pecchioni, L., Robinson, J. D., & Thompson, T. (2000). *Communication and aging* (2nd ed.). Mahwah, NJ: Lawrence Erlbaum.

Nussbaum, J. F., Ragan, R., & Whaley, B. (2004). Children, older adults, and women: Impact on provider–patient interaction. In T. L. Thompson, A. M. Dorsey, K. I. Miller, & R. Parrott (Eds), *Handbook of health communication* (pp. 183–204). Mahwah, NJ: Lawrence Erlbaum.

OPTN. (2005). The organ procurement and transplantation network: Waiting list removal reasons by year. Retrieved April 30, 2005, from www.optn.org/.

Panke, J. T. (2002). Difficulties in managing pain at the end of life. *American Journal of Nursing, 102,* 26–33.

Planalp, S., & Trost, M. R. (2008). Communication issues at the end of life: Reports from hospice volunteers. *Health Communication, 23,* 222–233.

Pecchioni, L., & Sparks, L. (2007). Health information sources of individuals with cancer and their family members. *Health Communication, 21,* 143–151..

Poulson, J. (1998). Impact of cultural differences in care of the terminally ill. In N. MacDonald (Ed.), *Palliative medicine: A case-based manual* (pp. 244–252). New York: Oxford University Press.

Query, J. L., Jr., & Kreps, G. L. (1996). Testing a relational model for health communication competence among caregivers for individuals with Alzheimer's disease. *Journal of Health Psychology, 3,* 335–351.

Query, J. L., Jr., & Wright, K. B. (2003). Assessing communication competence in an on-line study: Toward informing subsequent interventions among older adults with cancer, their lay caregivers, and peers. *Health Communication, 15,* 205–219.

Query, J. L., Jr., Wright, K. B., & Gilchrist, E. S. (2006). Communication and cancer hospice care: Towards negotiating attitudinal and research obstacles. In H. D. O'Hair, L. Sparks, & G. L. Kreps (Eds), *Health communication and cancer* (pp. 301–319). Cresskill, NJ: Hampton Press.

Ragan, S. L., & Goldsmith, J. (2008). End-of-life communication: The drama of pretense in the talk of dying patients and their MDs. In K. B. Wright & S. C. Moore (Eds), *Applied health communication: A sourcebook* (pp. 207–227). Boston: Allyn & Bacon.

Ragan, S. L., Wittenberg-Lyles, E. M., Goldsmith, J., & Sanchez-Reilly, S. (2008). *Communication as comfort: Multiple voices in palliative care.* New York: Routledge.

Ragan, S. L., Wittenberg, E., & Hall, H. T. (2003). The communication of palliative care for the elderly cancer patient. *Health Communication, 15,* 219–226.

Ramsay, S. (1999). International research agenda set for end-of-life care. *Lancet, 354,* 1361.

Raphael, C., Ahrens, J., & Fowler, N. (2001). Financing end-of-life care in the USA. *Journal of the Royal Society of Medicine, 94,* 458–461.

Ratner, E., Norlander, L., & McSteen, K. (2001). Death at home following a targeted advanced-care planning process at home: The kitchen table discussion. *Journal of the American Geriatrics Society, 49,* 778–781.

Reb, A. M. (2003). Palliative and end-of-life care: Policy analysis. *Oncology Nursing Forum, 30,* 35–50.

Rhymes, J. (1990). Hospice care in America. *Journal of the American Medical Association, 264,* 369.

Rice, D. P., Fox, P. J., Max, W., Webber, P. A., Lindeman, D. A., Hauck, W. W. *et al.* (1993). The economic burden of Alzheimer's disease. *Health Affairs, 12,* 164–176.

Richards, F. (2004). Couple's experiences of predictive testing and living with the risk or reality of Huntington disease: A qualitative study. *American Journal of Medical Genetics, 126A,* 170-182.

Richards, L., Bengston, V., & Miller, R. (1989). The "generation in the middle": Perceptions of changes in adult intergenerational relationships. In K. Kreppner & R. Lerner (Eds), *Family systems and life span development* (pp. 341–366). Hillsdale, NJ: Lawrence Erlbaum.

Roff, L. L., Martin, S. S., Jennings, L. K., Parker, M. W. and Harmon, D. K. (2007). Long distance parental caregivers' experiences with siblings: A qualitative study. *Qualitative Social Work, 6,* 315–335.

Rusinak, R. L., & Murphy, J. F. (1995). Elderly spousal caregivers: Knowledge of cancer care, perceptions of preparedness, and coping strategies. *Journal of Gerontological Nursing, 21,* 33–41.

Ryan, E. B., Hummert, M. L., & Boich, L. (1995). Communication predicaments of aging: Patronizing behavior towards older adults. *Journal of Language and Social Psychology, 14,* 144–166.

Salthouse, T. A. (1992). *Mechanisms of age–cognition relations in adulthood.* Hillsdale, NJ: Lawrence Erlbaum.

Sarna, L., & Brecht, M. (1997). Dimensions of symptom distress in women with advanced lung cancer: A factor analysis. *Heart and Lung, 26,* 23–30.

Sarna, L., & McCorkle, R. (1996). Burden of care and lung cancer. *Cancer Practice, 4,* 245–251.

Scharader, S., Nelson, M., & Eidsness, L. (2009). Dying to know: A community survey about dying and end-of-life care. *Omega, 60,* 33–50.

Schneider, E. L., & Guralnik, J. M. (1990). The aging of America: Impact on health care costs. *Journal of the American Medical Association, 263,* 2335–2340.

Siegel, K., Raveis, V. H., Houts, P., & More, V. (1991). Caregiver burden and unmet patient needs. *Cancer, 68,* 1131–1140.

Skirton, H., & Glendinning, N. (1997). Using research to develop care for patients with Huntington's disease. *British Journal of Nursing, 6,* 83–90.

Sparks, L. (Ed.) (2003). Cancer communication and aging [Special issue]. *Health Communication, 15*(2).

Sparks, L. (2008). Family decision-making. In W. Donsbach (Ed.) *The international encyclopedia of communication,* 4, (pp. 1729–1733). Oxford, UK and Malden, MA: Wiley-Blackwell.

Sparks, L. (in press). The SMILE health care communication model (SMILE-HCCM): An interpersonal theory-based approach to message framing in health care interventions. In S. S. Travis & R. Talley (Eds), *Caregiving across the professions.* New York: Oxford University Press. Project supported by a grant from Johnson and Johnson and the Rosalynn Carter Institute for Human Development.

Sparks, L., & Harwood, J. (2008). Cancer, aging, and social identity: Development of an integrated model of social identity theory and health communication. In L. Sparks, H. D. O'Hair, & G. L. Kreps, (Eds), *Cancer communication and aging.* Cresskill, NJ: Hampton Press.

Sparks, L., & Nussbaum, J. F. (2008). Health literacy and cancer communication with older adults. *Patient Education and Counseling, 71*(3), 345–350.

Sparks, L., Travis, S., & Thompson, S. (2005). Listening for the communicative signals of humor, narratives, and self-disclosure in the family caregiving interview. *Health and Social Work, 30,* 340–343.

Sparks-Bethea, L. (2002). The impact of an older adult parent on communicative satisfaction and dyadic adjustment in the long-term marital relationship: Adult children and spouses' retrospective accounts. *Journal of Applied Communication Research, 30,* 107–125.

Sparks-Bethea, L., Travis, S. S., & Pecchioni, L. L. (2000). Family caregivers' use of humor in conveying information about caring for dependent older adults. *Health Communication, 12,* 361–376. Project supported by a grant from the Nursing Research Program, Clinical Applications Research, Glaxo-Wellcome, Inc.

Stahl, S. M., & Feller, J. R. (1990). Old equals sick: An ontogenetic fallacy. In S. M. Stahl (Ed.), *The legacy of longevity: Health and health care in later life* (pp. 21–34). Newbury Park, CA: Sage.

Stoltz, P., Uden, G., & Willman, A. (2004). Support for family carers who care for an elderly person at home: A systematic literature review. *Scandinavian Journal of Caring Sciences, 18,* 111–119.

Street, A., & Blackford, J. (2001). Communication issues for the interdisciplinary community palliative care team. *Journal of Clinical Nursing, 10,* 643–650.

Sykes, N. (1989). Medical students' fears about breaking bad news. *Lancet, 2,* 564.

Talley, R. C., & Crews, J. E. (2007). Framing the public health of caregiving. *American Journal of Public Health, 97,* 224–228.

Toseland, R. W., Blanchard, C. G., & McCallion, P. (1995). A problem solving intervention for caregivers of cancer patients. *Social Science in Medicine, 40,* 517–528.

Travis, S. S., & Sparks-Bethea, L. (2001). Medication administration by family members of dependent elders in shared care arrangements. *Journal of Clinical Geropsychology, 7*(3), 231–243. Project supported by a grant from the Nursing Research Program, Clinical Applications Research, Glaxo-Wellcome, Inc.

Travis, S. S., Sparks-Bethea, L., & Winn, P. (2000). Medication hassles reported by family caregivers of dependent elders. *Journals of Gerontology: Medical Sciences, 55A,* 7, M412–M417. Project supported by a grant from the Nursing Research Program, Clinical Applications Research, Glaxo-Wellcome, Inc.

Turner, M. J., Killian, T. S., & Cain, R. (2004). Life course transitions and depressive symptoms among women in midlife. *International Journal of Aging and Human Development, 58,* 241–265.

US Census Bureau. (2000). Keeping up with older adults: Older adults 2000 [On-line]. Retrieved July 11, 2012, from www.census.gov/population/pop-profile/2000/chap18.pdf.

United Network for Organ Sharing. (2007). United Network for Organ Sharing. Retrieved September 4, 2007, from http://www.unos.org/data

Verbrugge, L. (1984). A health profile of older women with comparisons to older men. *Research on Aging, 6,* 291–322.

Villaume, W. A., Brown, M. H., & Darling, R. (1994). Presbycusis, communication, and older adults. In M. L. Hummert, J. M. Wiemann, & J. F. Nussbaum (Eds), *Interpersonal communication in older adulthood.* Thousand Oaks, CA: Sage.

Villaume, W. A., Darling, R., Brown, M. H., Richardson, D., & Clark-Lewis, S. (1993). The multidimensionality of presbycusis: Hearing losses on the content and relational dimensions of speech. *Journal of the International Listening Association, 7,* 111–128.

Vincent, D. E. (2006). Exploring college students' family discussions about organ and tissue donation. *Communication Research Reports, 23,* 299–308.

von Gunten, C. F. (2002). Secondary and tertiary palliative care in US hospitals. *Journal of the American Medical Association, 286*(7), 875–881.

Walsh, D., & Gordon, S. (2001). The terminally ill: Dying for palliative medicine? *American Journal of Hospice and Palliative Care, 18,* 203–205.

Weitzner, M. A., McMillan, S. C., & Jacobson, P. B. (1999). Family caregiver quality of life: Differences between curative and palliative cancer treatment settings. *Journal of Pain and Symptom Management, 17,* 418–428.

Wiemann, J. M. (1977). Explication and test of a model of communicative competence. *Human Communication Research, 3,* 195–213.

Willard, J., Miller, K., Shoemaker, M., & Addison, P. (2008). Making sense of sibling responsibility for family caregiving. *Qualitative Health Research, 18,* 1673–1686.

Williams, A., & Nussbaum, J. F. (2001). *Intergenerational communication across the lifespan.* Mahwah, NJ: Lawrence Erlbaum.

Winker, M. A., & Flanagin, A. (1999). Caring for patients at the end of life. *JAMA, 282,* 1965.

Wolff, J. L., & Kasper, J. D. (2006). Caregivers of frail elders: Updating a national profile. *Gerontologist, 46,* 344–356.

Won, A., Lapane, K., Gambassi, G., Bernabei, R., Mor, V., & Lipsitz, L. A. (1999). Correlates and management of nonmalignant pain in the nursing home. *Journal of the American Geriatric Society, 47,* 936–942.

Zamborsky, L. J. (1996). Support groups for hospice staff. In D. C. Sheehan & W. B. Forman (Eds), *Hospice and palliative care: Concepts and practices* (pp. 131–137). Sudbury, MA: Jones and Bartlett.

Zechner, M. (2008). Care of older persons in transnational settings. *Journal of Aging Studies, 22,* 32–44.

Zerzan, J., Stearns, S., & Hanson, L. (2000). Access to palliative care and hospice in nursing homes. *Journal of the American Medical Association, 284,* 2489–2494.

Zhang, A. Y., & Siminoff, L. A. (2003). Silence and cancer: Why do families and patients fail to communication? *Health Communication, 15,* 415–429.

Part III

Social, Cultural, and Organizational Contexts

Chapter 4

Social Support and Health

Like most people, you probably feel better when you are experiencing problems at school, work, or in relationships, when you have friends or family members to talk with. Sometimes these individuals give us good advice or they help us to forget our problems for a while by involving us in activities, such as playing golf or going to the movies. At other times you may feel that your friends and family members will not understand the problem you are facing, or they give you bad advice, so you may turn to other sources of information to help you cope with the problem, such as looking up information on the Internet. According to Goldsmith and Albrecht (2011), supportive communication is "a necessary condition for the quality of life and for healthful living" (p. 335). In addition, communication plays a key role in the support process, whether it involves finding the best ways to discuss problems and obtain support, finding information about a problem on-line or through interpersonal relationships, or by empathically listening and finding the best way to support someone who is struggling with a health-related problem.

Our relationships with family, friends, and even acquaintances can have a positive effect on our physical and mental health throughout our lives through the various types of social support they offer us. We, in turn, can influence the health of our social network members through the support we provide them. This is true not only during times when we face a health crisis, but also when we are coping with everyday stressful events. Moreover, research suggests that our social network members can be beneficial in helping us to avoid stressful situations that could adversely affect our health, and the companionship of significant others can help us to be more resistant to certain types of illness. However, the relationship between social support and health outcomes is extremely complicated, and some types of support (or sources of support) can actually negatively affect health. Communication plays an important role in these

Health Communication in the 21st Century, Second Edition. Kevin Bradley Wright, Lisa Sparks, and H. Dan O'Hair.
© 2013 John Wiley & Sons, Inc. Published 2013 by John Wiley & Sons, Inc.

processes (Goldsmith, 2004), and while the relationship between social support and health appears to be simple, we will see that it is actually a quite complex process.

This chapter will examine the concept of social support, the various ways in which support networks can impact health, the central role of communication in social support, and benefits and problems with supportive messages. In addition, it discusses characteristics of support networks and support groups for people with health concerns.

History of Social Support and Health Research

In the early 1970s researchers from a number of disciplines began to focus their attention on how social support and relationships affect health (Goldsmith & Albrecht, 2011). Over the past several decades, across numerous studies (Cohen & Wills, 1985; House, Landis, & Umberson, 1988), researchers have been able to build empirical evidence for a link between social support and a variety of health outcomes (see Berkman & Syme, 1979; House, Landis, & Umberson, 1998; Uchino, Cacioppo, & Kielcolt-Glaser, 1996; Uchino, 2006), including improved immune system functioning, reduced stress, lower depression, shorter recovery times from illness and surgery, increased sense of well-being, and reduced mortality rates (i.e. longer life). Social support has even been linked to increased cardiovascular functioning and resistance to the common cold.

A variety of social scientists (such as psychologists) added to this body of research by examining personality traits, reactions to stress, coping strategies, and a host of individual variables that mediate the relationship between social support and health (see Sarason, Sarason, & Pierce, 1990; Turner, King, & Tremblay, 1992). Communication scholars have also made significant contributions to social support and health research over the years by conducting studies that examine relational issues and message characteristics that influence social support processes (see Albrecht & Adelman, 1987; Burleson, 1994). Today, social support researchers are attempting to understand how access to extended social networks through computer-mediated communication (i.e. social networking sites and on-line support groups) impact health outcomes (Tanis, 2008; Rains & Young, 2009; Walther & Boyd, 2002; Wright, 2000). In addition, there are many unanswered questions about the relationship between social support and health that will likely spur research in this area for many years to come.

Types and Functions of Social Support

Types of support

Social support is "an umbrella term for various theories and concepts that link involvement with social relationships to health and well-being" (Goldsmith & Albrecht, 2011, p. 335). However, within this larger definition are many other terms that reflect the complexity of social support. The reason for this is due to the fact that our social networks, such as friends, family members, and co-workers, and even acquaintances on social networking sites like Facebook, often provide us with many different types of social support (Goldsmith, 2004). In the following section, we examine several different types of social support and other related terms.

According to Goldsmith and Albrecht (2011), *instrumental support* refers to tangible types of assistance, such as when parents give children money so they can go to the movies with friends, or when a friend helps another friend with a household project. *Emotional support* refers to such diverse activities as listening to a person's troubles, validating his or her problems, offering encouraging words when someone is not feeling well, and simply "being there" during a time of need. *Esteem or appraisal support* deals with efforts to make a person who is facing a stressful situation feel validated, or that their problems are legitimate. *Informational support* can take many forms, such as when you receive good advice about a relationship problem from a close friend or if a person with pancreatic cancer receives information about medications in an Internet support group. *Enacted support* has to do with the conditions under which communication facilitates beneficial outcomes for people facing stress (Wills & Shinar, 2000). *Companionship* is a variation of social support in that it is typically entered into for the sake of enjoyment as opposed to social obligation (Rook, 1995). Companions tend to be friends who elevate our mood by just being with us, but they can also provide support in times of need.

Social support can also be *proactive* or *reactive* (Sarason, Sarason, & Pierce, 1990). *Proactive support* is any type of assistance that helps an individual to circumvent problems, such as if a doctor recommends a diet that helps a patient lower his or her risk of hypertension. *Reactive support* is usually assistance that is provided in response to some crisis a person is facing or a disruption of normal life events. For example, a diagnosis of cancer is a major crisis event, and members of the social network of a person with cancer typically provide emotional support or some other type of assistance to help him or her cope with the disease.

Social support takes place in some type of *social network*, or sets of overlapping relationships among people (Penner, Dovidio, & Albrecht, 2000). Social networks can be as small as family or close circle or friends, or they can be as large as an extended Facebook network of close friends, family members, coworkers, and acquaintances. Social networks serve as the context for the support we receive and provide to others, and patterns of communication within social networks tend to vary depending upon social norms. When network members engage in frequent overlapping communication, this is known as *density*. When people within social networks are similar to each other in terms of demographics, background, and attitudes, this is *homogeneity*, and when people are different from each other it is called *heterogeneity*. Finally, social networks can be *bounded* or *unbounded*, meaning that they can have strict or permeable boundaries. For example, a close-knit family might not interact with outsiders (bounded), whereas all of your Facebook friends may let you "friend" their friends (unbounded). Social support researchers who are interested in social networks frequently examine these and other characteristics of social networks in an attempt to assess how they influence social support processes.

Positive and negative functions of support

The various types of support mentioned above have been linked to positive psychological and physical health outcomes as well as improved quality of life (Cobb, 1976; Goldsmith, 2004; Hughes, 2005). However, people often differ as to the types of support they find useful due to factors such as the context of the stressful situation they are facing, their perceived coping skills, and their relationship with the support provider (La Gaipa, 1990). Depending upon the situation, a recipient of support may perceive some types of support negatively, and this may negate the positive effects of the supportive attempt or it may actually have a negative impact on health or quality of life.

For example, instrumental support is a common type of support that people provide individuals with health problems, and it is crucial for people who require long-term care due to an illness. In these situations, individuals who are sick often rely heavily on others to take care of physical needs, such as preparing meals, transportation, and basic daily tasks such as going to the bathroom, bathing, and providing medications. While individuals typically appreciate the support they receive in these situations, inappropriate instrumental support can be perceived negatively.

When people feel that they can successfully perform physical tasks, they may perceive tangible assistance negatively, especially if it is viewed as patronizing or if it undermines their sense of competence. People with disabilities often resent others who go out of their way to open doors or who engage in other types of instrumental support when they feel that they could accomplish these tasks themselves. In some cases, such as within nursing homes, older residents may initially resent some types of instrumental support, but they may eventually accept it if they feel they have little control over their situation. Older nursing home residents have been found to acquire a "learned helplessness" when it comes to many physical tasks as a result of workers engaging in over-accommodating behaviors when they provide tangible assistance (Grainger, 1995).

In cases when informational support is perceived as useful, people with health problems may feel they have more control over their situation (Roter & Hall, 1992). However, too much information about a disease or condition from a physician or other healthcare provider can be perceived negatively if the information overwhelms the patient or causes him or her to worry (Brashers, Neidig, & Goldsmith, 2004). For example, if a physician gives a patient a large amount of information about treatment options, side effects, and the progression of symptoms after an HIV-positive diagnosis, all of this information is likely to be perceived as overwhelming to the patient, particularly if he or she has not had a chance to think about all of the implications of the diagnosis. In this type of case, patients are often unable to cognitively process the information they receive from their doctor.

Informational support from family members and friends during times of stress can also be seen as inappropriate, especially when it takes the form of unwanted advice (Goldsmith & Fitch, 1997) or if it is perceived as patronizing or intrusive. For example, a caregiver who reminds a sick spouse that he needs to eat something prior to taking his medication might think that she is being helpful, while the spouse may see it as "butting in." As you can see, the provision of informational support can be quite complicated, depending upon how it is perceived. Albrecht and Goldsmith (2003) point out other complications when providing informational support:

> One may receive information and advice about how to cope with a health problem and yet find that the advice is uninformed and therefore of little use. Worse yet, the advice others give might lead an individual to feel that others are critical of his or her own coping efforts or that others are condescending by providing information that the individual already knows. (p. 270)

Emotional support is often perceived as more beneficial than informational support among people with health concerns, particularly in helping them to cope with the emotional distress of illness (Cwikel & Isreal, 1987; Magen & Glajchen, 1999). However, emotional support can also be perceived negatively, especially when the support provider denies or draws attention away from the feelings that the support recipient is experiencing or if the type of emotional support offered is perceived as inappropriate in other ways (Burleson, 1994). For example, a woman with breast cancer may want her partner to simply listen to and accept her fear about an upcoming mastectomy, but rather than acknowledging this fear the partner might say "Try not to worry so much—these operations are usually very successful." In this case the partner, while most likely having the best of intentions, is attempting to minimize the woman with cancer's fear by implying that she is perhaps worrying too much.

Esteem support is an important type of support in helping distressed individuals who feel socially stigmatized as a result of their health condition (e.g. people with HIV or people with visible disabilities) to feel valued at times when their self-esteem is low as a result of struggles dealing with their daily lives (Wills, 1985). As we will discuss in greater depth in Chapter 5, stigma refers to negative feelings attached to a health condition or a group of people who are living with it. Disabilities, HIV, cancer, and eating disorders are a few of the many health conditions that carry a social stigma, and the individuals who are living with them often experience communication problems with people who do not share their condition. Both the negative societal perceptions of these diseases and the communication problems associated with these perceptions may lead a person with one of these conditions to feel socially isolated or depressed. Esteem support or validation may help individuals increase their sense of self-worth when it is provided by an understanding loved one or others facing similar circumstances.

Not surprisingly, issues of social support are also important when it comes to family decision-making. Sparks (2008) posits that decisions within families can be classified into types such as: instrumental, affective, social, economic, and technical. Instrumental decisions are those that focus on issues of money, health, shelter, and food for the family members (Epstein, Bishop, & Baldwin, 1982). Affective decisions deal with choices related to feelings and emotions such as deciding about getting married, whereas social decisions are usually decisions related to the values, roles, and goals of the family (see e.g. Noller & Fitzpatrick, 1993). Such decisions may include whether the children will be raised going to one church or another or whether one parent will stay at home while the children are preschool age. Economic decisions focus on choices about using and gathering family resources such as whether an adolescent should get a job and contribute to the family income or buy his or her own car. Technical decisions consist of the smaller decisions that must be made to carry out a larger decision. For instance, if a family decides that one member must stop working in order to go back to school for an advanced degree, then a series of technical decisions must be made so the larger decision will materialize (Noller & Fitzpatrick 1993). Families use a variety of decision-making processes ranging from taking the same approach day in and day out with daily decision-making to more varied methods depending on the type of decision, their emotional state, and most often their stage of development across the life span from when the children are babies to when they are in school to mid-life and later-life issues (Sparks, 2008).

Family decisions are negotiated every day from family decisions in the childhood and adolescent years to middle and later life family decisions, many of which occur in healthcare environments (Sparks, 2008). Family decision processes in the healthcare environment are particularly difficult and complex because of the uncertainties, emotions, technical language, and subsequent health outcomes (e.g. Harzold & Sparks, 2007; Sparks, 2003). Conflicting information from various sources can be difficult to navigate and process to make the most informed healthcare decisions. Families make decisions about health issues using information from a variety of sources including insurance provider lists, Internet research, recommendations from primary care physicians and specialists, interpersonal communication with friends and family members, and mediated messages (see Pecchioni & Sparks, 2007).

However, support providers do not always view a person's situation as a legitimate problem, and they may not be able to adequately provide esteem support. For example, a father might see his daughter's struggle with anorexia as something that is within her control rather than as a psychological disorder. While wanting to be supportive, his perception of his daughter's condition may lead him to say things that reflect an inaccurate understanding of anorexia or that do not legitimize her condition or her feelings. When people have a better understanding of a health condition and see it as a legitimate concern, they are often better able to provide esteem support. This is one of the reasons why members of peer support groups are often able to provide a person with esteem support. Because members of peer support groups are facing a health condition themselves, it is often easier for them to validate the feelings of other members of the group. (See the discussion of support groups later in this chapter.)

Models of Social Support and Health

Stress and health

In order to understand the relationship between stress and psychological/physical health, it is important to have a basic understanding of the physiology of stress. While the general association between stress and physical health is easy to understand, researchers have actually found this relationship to be extremely complex. Similar to many species of animals, the physiological responses to stress have evolved in human beings to promote survival during times of crisis. Essentially, the body's response to a stressor prepares it for rapid physical action (fight or flight). In others words, the brain helps to ensure that there is sufficient oxygen and energy to the brain and muscles so that a person can survive a crisis situation by either fighting or running. Unlike the stressors that many animals face in the wild, such as encountering predators, few aspects of modern life are immediately life-threatening to human beings. However, exposure to everyday stressors, such as threats to our sense of financial security, a heavy workload at the office, relationship problems, and minor hassles such as traffic jams, taxes, and household chores, all trigger physiological responses from the body.

At the psychological level, people appraise stressful events in terms of their severity and duration (i.e. short-term problems and long-term problems) as well as their available resources and abilities to cope with or manage the stressor. The central nervous system plays an important role when people encounter stressful situations. The central nervous system consists of millions of specialized cells known as neurons. Sensory neurons sense changes to the body due to environmental stimuli such as stressors and relay information to the brain. The brain makes sense of this information, and if a situation is perceived as threatening, emotional responses to the stressor trigger physiological reactions from the body's limbic system. The limbic system can activate an area of the brain known as the hypothalamus. The hypothalamus regulates the body's stress response systems, which include the sympathetic adrenal medullary (SAM) response system and the hypothalamic–pituitary–adrenal (HPA) system (Clow, 2001). Neurons associated with both systems regulate cardiovascular activity, such as heart rate and blood pressure, and the immune system by releasing chemicals into the bloodstream known as neurotransmitters. These neurotransmitters stimulate the release of other chemicals into the bloodstream. For example, they activate the release of adrenaline from our adrenal glands (located above the kidney), known as the sympathetic adrenal medullary response system. Adrenaline provides the needed energy to the brain and muscles to make quick decisions in the face of threatening situations. It is likely that you have experienced an "adrenaline rush" after a stressful episode such as nearly hitting another vehicle while driving, being startled by someone, or after engaging in a conflict with a friend or family member.

Over time, when our body's stress response system is repeatedly activated, this can lead to wear and tear on the body's cardiovascular system (Clow, 2001). For instance, the increase in blood pressure and the release of cortisol associated with stress response (both of which are associated with the release of adrenaline) can damage certain blood vessels. When these blood vessels are damaged, it allows for the build-up of fatty nutrients within the damaged walls of the vessels, a condition known as atherosclerosis. When this process occurs within blood vessels located in the arteries supplying the heart, it can lead to heart disease (such as heart attacks). Moreover, the frequent release of cortisol into the bloodstream can disturb the balance of the body's immune system and make us more susceptible to disease. The release of cortisol (over an extended period of time) has also been linked to negative psychological states, such as depression (Clow, 2001). In short, our body's physiological response to stressful situations can lead to a variety of physical and mental health problems.

Stress and social support

Researchers have focused on the relationship between social support and health outcomes for several decades, and study findings indicate benefits to both mental and physical health (Aneshensel & Stone, 1982; Berkman & Syme, 1979; Cohen, 1988; Krause, 1990; Wills, 1985). In terms of specific health outcomes, a variety of studies have found a relationship between social support and stress (Aneshensel & Stone, 1982; Ballieux & Heijen, 1989; Berkman & Syme, 1979; Billings & Moos, 1981; Dean & Lin, 1977).

Two models explaining this relationship have emerged from the social support literature: (i) the buffering model and (ii) the main effects model. The *buffering model* suggests that social support shields individuals from the negative effects of stress, such as weakened immunity and depression, over time (Cohen & Wills, 1985; Dean & Lin, 1977; La Rocca, House, & French, 1980). The *main effects model* asserts that there is a direct rather than buffering relationship between social support and physical and psychological outcomes (Aneshensel & Stone, 1982; Thoits, 1982).

Researchers have linked both models to positive effects in terms of morbidity and mortality (Berkman & Syme, 1979; Cohen, 1988; Uchino, Cacioppo, & Kiecolt-Glaser, 1996). The reduction of stress associated with supportive behaviors appears to affect physical health in a variety of ways. As we have seen, prolonged exposure to stress has been found to impair immune system response (Ballieux & Heijen, 1989), and it can create damage to internal organ systems through the production and maintenance of chemicals such as cortisol. Elevated levels of other chemicals, such as adrenaline, have been found to be associated with colds and flu, tension and nervousness, and elevated systolic blood pressure (Kohn, 1996). In addition, physiological responses to stress may exacerbate other physical problems that a person is currently experiencing. Lockenhoff and Carstensen (2004) posited that "an intact social network serves as a buffer against physical and psychological stressors" (p. 1402). However, there are a number of variables that make the relationship between social support and health more complicated. These include differences in individual coping styles and adaptation to stressful situations (Kohn, 1996; Pierce, Sarason, & Sarason, 1996), and perceptions of support providers and recipients within the context in which support takes place (Barbee, 1990; Edwards & Noller, 1998).

Coping strategies and health outcomes

People cope with stressful situations in a variety of ways, and these individual differences in coping styles have been linked to health outcomes. For example, suppose a young man suspects there is a possibility that he has HIV given his sexual history. He may decide to avoid getting tested for HIV or obtaining information about the disease as a way of coping with this particular stressful situation. However, his partner might have similar suspicions regarding her HIV status, and she might obtain as much information about the disease as she can from her physician or she might get tested to resolve the uncertainty over her HIV status. This example shows two radically different ways of coping with a health-related stressful situation. The man chose to avoid the situation as a coping strategy whereas his partner chose a more active set of actions for coping with it.

Kohn (1996) identifies three general types of coping strategies that individuals use when confronted with a stressful situation. *Problem-focused coping* is a strategy that is "directed at remedying a threatening or harmful situation" (Kohn, 1996, p. 186). When people engage in active behaviors they think will reduce a threatening situation or at least help them to deal with it better, they are using problem-focused coping. For example, if a person gets tested for HIV, learns that she has the disease, and attempts to find as much information about it as possible, she might find ways to reduce the threat of the disease. In recent years, early diagnosis of HIV and advances in HIV medication have made it possible for HIV-positive individuals to live without HIV-related medical problems (or with minimal problems) for many years. By choosing a problem-focused coping strategy such as early diagnosis and treatment, a person with HIV might actually prolong his or her life. Problem-focused coping has been linked to positive adaptation to stressful situations in a variety of studies, and it is thought to reduce psychological and physical stress (Endler & Parker, 1990; Heady & Wearing, 1990).

Emotional-focused coping refers to behaviors such as venting frustrations about a stressful situation or expressing some type of emotional response to it rather than making an attempt to remedy or improve the situation (Kohn, 1996). For instance, a person who discovers that he has hypertension might complain about having the disease or his doctor's request to make changes to his diet (e.g. avoiding salt and foods with high fat content) rather than taking active steps to manage it. Not surprisingly, emotional-focused coping has been linked to negative adaptation to stressful situations (Edwards & Trimble, 1992; Turner, King, & Tremblay, 1992), although some of the research has produced mixed findings.

Finally, *avoidance-focused coping* refers to an "attempt to disengage mentally or even physically from threatening or damaging situations" (Kohn, 1996, p. 186). Many people choose to avoid threatening situations, particularly when dealing with health issues. Our mortality and susceptibility to illness are difficult concepts for most people to deal with, and many people use avoidance-focused coping when confronted with stressful health-related situations. Rather than actively obtaining information about diseases such as diabetes or breast cancer, some people would rather avoid talking about them or engage in some type of diversion as opposed to dealing with the threat of illness. Researchers have found mixed results for avoidance-focused coping strategies in terms of adaptation to stressful situations. For some people, avoiding stressful situations actually helps them to cope with them, while others find that avoidance leads to negative adaptation. In other situations, people may feel that they have no control over their health status, and this might lead to an avoidance-focused strategy.

For example, an individual who is facing a terminal illness might find that spending more time with family and friends serves as a diversion to thinking about the illness, and this actually helps to reduce stress. Sometimes dwelling upon problems that are out of our control leads to additional stress, and we find it less stressful when we divert our attention from the problem. However, some individuals who choose avoidance strategies when dealing with a stressful health situation might better adapt to it if they were to choose a more problem-focused coping strategy, such as seeking information about treatment options for a disease that might help their prognosis over time. *Problematic integration theory* helps to explain both how people engage in information-seeking behaviors and manage uncertainty when coping with an illness and why people may or may not choose information and other types of support. Babrow (2001) argued that the meaning of uncertainty is largely dependent on the values of the individual who is experiencing an illness, and those values guide the ways that information is used to manage uncertainty. For example, a person with cancer may decide to gather certain types of information about the most aggressive forms of chemotherapy if he or she primarily values stopping the progression of cancer, regardless of the side effects of the treatment, whereas another person might be more concerned with acquiring information that enhances the quality of his or her life.

Humor as a coping mechanism is receiving increased research attention in recent years (Wanzer, Sparks, & Frymier, 2009). Research on the benefits of humor for aging adults seems to support the premise that humor can assist in the aging process in a number of positive ways (Sparks-Bethea, 2001; Houston, McKee, Carroll, & Marsh, 1998; Nahemow, McCluskey-Fawcett, & McGhee, 1986; Richman, 1995; Ryff, 1989; Solomon, 1996; Wanzer, Sparks, & Frymier, 2009; Westburg, 2003). Humor can help facilitate successful aging when used as a means of coping with the challenges associated with aging (Pfeifer, 1993). Older adults who used humor to cope often report less distress or negative stress in their lives (Pfeifer, 1993). Similarly, older adults who can reframe and label stressful occurrences as beyond their control are able to manage stress more effectively by identifying comical distractions (Folkman, Lazarus, Pimley, & Novacek, 1987). Richman (1995) describes the "lifesaving" function of humor for the severely depressed and suicidal elderly. As a therapist who regularly treats severely depressed elderly patients, Richman feels that encouraging patients to laugh and use humor to cope may relieve depressive affective states. These studies have primarily exposed participants to humorous stimuli (e.g. movies or jokes) and then examined the outcome of that exposure to humor.

As Wanzer, Sparks, and Frymier (2009) explain, the relationship between humor production and coping effectiveness in everyday interaction has not received a great deal of research attention by communication scholars, particularly within the older adult segment of the population (see also McGhee, 1986; Sparks, 1994; Sparks-Bethea, 2001). Researchers have examined humor production as a coping strategy that affects life satisfaction and the role humor plays in coping with the aging process and ultimately improving residents' psychological well-being (Celso *et al.*, 2003; Houston *et al.*, 1998; Westburg, 2003). Houston and colleagues research found that when residents of a residential facility engaged in funny sing-alongs and similar humorous activities, they were less likely to report depression and anxiety than residents who did not participate in humorous activities (Houston *et al.*, 1998). Similarly, Westburg (2003) used the Funny Bone History to obtain residents' and care providers' perceptions of the importance of humor and sources of humor in an assisted living facility. Residents and staff members identified a variety of health-enhancing benefits from humor and laughter and revealed that interacting with family, friends, and younger people were valuable sources of humor. Thus, humor serves as a means of helping people relate effectively to one another as well as helping older adults to cope with stresses associated with aging and the assisted living environment.

Sparks-Bethea's (2001) study of older adults' use of humor further supports this finding. She found that nearly 95 percent of the older adult participants noted the importance of possessing a sense of humor throughout one's life. Sparks-Bethea (2001) noted that older adults seemed to strategically employ humorous communication as a means of coping with life stress, easing tensions, and increasing solidarity during social interaction. Similarly, Ryff (1989) interviewed groups of middle aged and older adults about their perceptions of factors related to psychological well-being. Both groups indicated that a heightened awareness of others and humor use were important components of good mental adjustment. The significance of humor production as it relates to our ability to cope and adapt throughout our lives, therefore, may be revealed through an examination of more mature personalities, who have developed a broader perspective of life and the self over time (see e.g. Nussbaum, 1989; Nussbaum, Pecchioni, Robinson, & Thompson, 2000; Sparks, 1994; Sparks-Bethea, 2001). Further, Wanzer, Sparks, & Frymier (2009) found a significant relationship between older adults' humor production, coping abilities and life satisfaction. Results of their study overall indicated these four variables function in communicatively complex ways for older adults. As predicted, humor-oriented individuals were more likely to use humor as a coping mechanism and reported greater coping efficacy. When examining individuals who varied in age (under 50, 51–74 and 74+ years), differences in humor orientation scores emerged among the three groups. As predicted by Folkman and Lazarus's (1987) transactional theory of coping and emotion, the relationship between self-reported humor orientation and life satisfaction was mediated by coping efficacy. In attempting to determine which variables best predicted life satisfaction, coping efficacy and health status explained unique variance in life satisfaction scores.

Because individuals vary greatly in their appreciation, propensity, and ability to communicate humorous messages (Booth-Butterfield & Booth-Butterfield, 1991), it is likely that these differences affect both coping effectiveness and life satisfaction. Booth-Butterfield and Booth-Butterfield (1991) developed the concept of humor orientation, which enables researchers to investigate individual differences in humor production as well as outcomes associated with the communication of humor.

Perceptions of Support Providers

In addition to individual differences in coping with stressful situations, our perceptions of our social support network members during times of stress influence whether or not we find helpful a person's attempts to be supportive. *Support appraisals*, or the perceptions of the appropriateness of social support behaviors (such as the degree to which an individual is satisfied with the support he or she receives), influence how people adjust to stressful situations (Albrecht, Burleson, & Goldsmith, 1994). In this section, we will examine perceptions of support providers and situations where supportive attempts can be perceived negatively and have negative effects on our stress levels.

Social comparison theory and social support

Our social networks provide many opportunities to give and receive social support, and while expanding our social networks is thought to increase opportunities for social support, our perceptions of others within these networks influence our evaluations of supportive behaviors. *Social comparison theory* (Festinger, 1954) is a useful framework for examining perceptions of people within our support networks and for understanding why support from these individuals may not always lead to positive outcomes. According to social comparison theory, individuals make assessments about their own health and coping mechanisms by comparing them to others in their social network (Helgeson & Gottlieb, 2000).

Helgeson and Gottlieb (2000) mention that *lateral comparisons*, comparisons to similar others, may normalize people's experiences and reduce uncertainty and stress for those dealing with health concerns. However, when individuals compare themselves to others, their self-assessment could be either positive or negative. For example, if a person with cancer feels that he is coping with problems less effectively than others in his network (such as a friend or relative who has or had cancer or a similar life-threatening illness), this may create *upward comparisons*, which could produce feelings of frustration or serve as a source of inspiration to the person to cope more effectively by emulating the successful behaviors of those other members. Conversely, *downward comparisons* to others in the social network, such as when an individual feels that he or she is coping better than other members, can lead to positive self-assessments and/or to negative feelings about people if interaction with the other members is perceived as being unhelpful.

Participants often glean information about the status of their health issues through social comparisons that take place within supportive interactions (Bennenbroek, Buunk, Van der Zee, & Grol, 2001; Davison, Pennebaker, & Dickerson, 2000). According to Sarasohn-Kahn (2008), the second most popular reason people seek health information through online social networks is to research other participants' experiences with a health condition. Such social comparison processes do not even require actual participation in the online group; rather, individuals may engage in these practices even if they do not actively contribute to the group discussion. However, the vast majority of studies using this framework have investigated face-to-face support groups (Davison, Pennebaker, & Dickerson, 2000), despite its potential utility for investigating social support processes within computer-mediated support groups.

Reciprocity and social support

Perceptions of *reciprocity* within supportive relationships are another important aspect of the social support process. According to equity theory (Deutsch, 1985), we tend to feel troubled in a relationship when we feel that we are *underbenefited*, that is, when we perceive that we are incurring too many costs in a relationship while simultaneously receiving too few rewards. For example, if you devoted many hours of time taking care of a friend when she was ill or providing emotional support when she was facing a health crisis, such as a miscarriage, but she never seems to have time to call you or listen to your problems when you are facing a similar stressful situation, you would probably feel underbenefited, or that the relationship was inequitable. A similar problem can occur when a person in a relationship feels *overbenefited*. In this case, you may have received help from a friend during a stressful time without having the opportunity to reciprocate. Most people feel uncomfortable in situations where they perceive themselves as overbenefited in a relationship, particularly when they feel unable to reciprocate support they have received.

Reciprocity issues are common in caregiving relationships (see Chapter 3), especially in cases when a healthy relational partner is caring for a loved one. For example, a woman who is caring for her husband with prostate cancer may spend a considerable amount of time offering tangible assistance and managing a large number of caregiver duties, such as monitoring symptoms, giving medication, and managing daily household chores. The husband in this scenario would likely feel overbenefited while the wife might feel underbenefited, although in marital relationships role obligations often lead people to accept these types of inequities. Receiving support without having the opportunity to reciprocate, which is common in caregiver–patient relationships, often leads individuals to feel overbenefited, and this can lead to feelings of inadequacy, helplessness, and demoralization (Bakas, Lewis, & Parsons, 2001). However, research suggests that caregivers often feel overwhelmed and frustrated by the inequitable nature of caregiver–patient relationships (Andrews, 2001; Sarna & McCorkle, 1996), yet they are often unable to express their frustrations about their situation to members of their social network because they do not want to burden friends and family with the added stress of thinking about these concerns or because they may fear being judged negatively by these individuals for expressing negative feelings about caring for a loved one (Bakas, Lewis, & Parsons, 2001; Laizner, Yost, Barg, & McCorkle, 1993).

Strong Tie Versus Weak Tie Support Networks

Most support takes place between close ties, such as family members and friends. Family members and friends are likely to be support providers during times of illness due to the role obligations that exist in these relationships. Family members are typically in the best position to provide us with tangible support during illness, such as taking care of our physical needs. Our relational histories with our family members and close friends also make them good candidates for being able to understand us and provide us with emotional support. While the role obligations and relational history associated with close tie networks are typically beneficial, they can also cause problems for people who are seeking support when facing a health problem. As we have seen, role obligations can lead to problems with reciprocity.

In addition, our intimate knowledge of close tie network members and our relational history with them can create problems in times when support is needed. While close ties know us intimately, they can also know us too well, and it is sometimes difficult to disclose certain topics to these individuals, particularly when we feel embarrassed by them or if they have a social stigma attached to them. Unfortunately, in the case of many health problems, there are a number of topics, such as symptoms and bodily functions, which can be difficult to talk about with people who are close to us. An alternative to close ties for support is weak tie support networks.

Weak tie relationships (Granovetter, 1973) occur between individuals who communicate on a relatively frequent basis but who do not consider one another to be members of their close personal network (e.g. close friends, family). Weak tie networks for most individuals typically consist of neighbors, service providers, people within Internet groups, and other individuals a person could turn to during times of stress when closer ties were unavailable. Individuals facing stressful situations, such as a life-threatening disease or other health problems, often find that weak tie networks offer them certain advantages over strong tie networks in terms of social support.

One reason why some individuals may decide to seek support through weak tie networks instead of within their strong tie network is that weak tie networks often provide access to diverse points of view and information that may not be available within more intimate relationships (Adelman, Parks, & Albrecht, 1987). Typically, many individuals form close relationships with others who are similar to them in terms of demographics, attitudes, and backgrounds. This homogeneous preference can limit the diversity of information and viewpoints obtained about topics, including health concerns. Access to more diverse viewpoints about health problems can provide individuals with more varied informational support about health issues, and interacting with varied types of people increases the number of social comparisons a person can make about his or her health condition vis-à-vis others (Adelman, Parks, & Albrecht, 1987).

For example, a person who has been recently diagnosed with cancer will probably not find many people within his or her traditional support network who also have cancer, and these network members may only have a limited perspective about how to cope with the disease. By moving outside of one's traditional support network and using weak tie networks, such as support groups for people who have cancer, a person with cancer can obtain more information about the disease from someone who also has it and who is likely to share similar feelings about it. By interacting with multiple individuals with cancer in a support group, assessments about how one is coping with the disease compared to others can be made, and this process can help reduce uncertainty. For instance, individuals who are in earlier stages of cancer can interact with others who are in the later stages and learn about possible trajectories of the disease, and/or glean first-hand information about the efficacy of treatment options. Other aspects of support groups for people facing health concerns are discussed later in this chapter.

Optimal matching model

The optimal matching model posits that an optimal match between the needs of support seekers and the resources/abilities of support providers is important in terms of coping with the many relational challenges associated with communicating social support (Cutrona & Russell, 1990). For example, if an individual is seeking emotional support and validation for an eating disorder and he or she perceives that members of his or her support network have competently listened, expressed empathy, and acknowledged the severity of the issue, then this would be considered an example of an optimal match between the support seeker and support providers. Conversely, if an individual desires emotional support, and members of his or her support network provide unwanted advice (a negative form of informational support), then this would be considered a bad (or less than optimal) match. Goldsmith (2004) contends that optimal matches in supportive episodes may lead to more positive perceptions of the relational partners and the type of support that is being offered, and this, in turn, may ultimately influence positive health outcomes.

While this model has been applied to a variety of face-to-face supportive contexts (see Goldsmith, 2004), relatively few researchers have used this framework to investigate computer-mediated support (some exceptions exist, i.e. Wright & Muhtaseb, 2005). Yet, this perspective may help to provide important insights into the supportive needs of individuals who seek computer-mediated support. For example, drawing upon an optimal matching theory framework, Eichhorn (2008) found that informational support through shared experiences was the most common type of support for members of an online support groups for eating disorders (followed by emotional support). Moreover, Sullivan (2003) found that men were more likely to seek informational support within online support groups, whereas women were more likely to seek emotional support and validation.

Communicating about illness in weak tie vs. close tie networks

Close tie support networks are sometimes perceived to be inadequate in providing satisfactory support for a variety of reasons, and this notion may influence a person's decision to use weak tie support networks as an alternative. Life-threatening illnesses are difficult topics for most people to discuss, especially when they affect a close relative or friend. In terms of talking about cancer, researchers have found that family members and friends often minimize the concerns of people with cancer, avoid interacting with them, and/or steer conversational topics away from emotional talk about the disease or refrain from any discussion of cancer (Dakof & Taylor, 1990; Helgeson, Cohen, Shultz, & Yasko, 2000; Wortman & Dunkel-Schetter, 1979).

By comparison, certain members of weak tie networks may be more willing to talk about illness since these individuals tend to be less emotionally attached to a person (Adelman, Parks, & Albrecht, 1987). Weak tie network members are often able to provide more objective feedback about a problem since they are less emotionally attached to a person with cancer than family and friends. According to La Gaipa (1990), "confidants are not likely to provide an accurate reflection of what a person is worth. Rather, one must turn to less intimate friends for more accurate feedback" (p. 126). People with whom we have close relationships, in an effort to spare our feelings when talking about a health problem, may be more likely to "sugar coat" the advice they give us or not be completely honest when discussing how they feel about our illness. According to Goldsmith and Albrecht (2011), stronger ties are often better at providing tangible aid over extended periods of time whereas weaker ties tend to be helpful when coping with a health issue requires new information or skills (that may be limited within a close-knit family or friendship social network).

In addition, studies have found that role obligations in close ties and reciprocity issues can lead to problems with the provision of social support. Support for a loved one who is ill in close ties can lead to increased conflict or negative feelings toward the person due to role obligations (Albrecht & Goldsmith, 2003; Chesler & Barbarin, 1984; La Gaipa, 1990; Pitula & Daugherty, 1995), despite the fact that people may care deeply for the person. According to La Gaipa (1990), "social obligations may override the positive effect of companionship and social support. Such constraints can have a negative effect on mental well-being that may not make up for the beneficial aspects of personal relationships" (p. 126).

According to socio-emotional selectivity theory (SST), factors such as age and whether or not a person is facing a terminal illness may also influence weak tie versus strong tie support network preference. According to Lockenhoff and Carstensen (2004), "perceived limitations on time lead to reorganizations of goal hierarchies such that goals related to deriving emotional meaning from life are prioritized over goals that maximize long-term payoffs in a nebulous future" (p. 1396). In other words, changes in a person's time perspective (due to factors such as growing older or facing a terminal illness) can result in associated changes in social preferences that influence the composition of his or her social network partners.

SST posits that younger individuals and people who perceive themselves to be in good health tend to be future-oriented when developing relationships, and they are interested in forming expanded and diverse social networks in an attempt to gain novel experiences, new information, and diverse social contacts (Carstensen & Fredrickson, 1998; Lockenhoff & Carstensen, 2004). By contrast, older people or younger individuals who are facing a terminal illness, tend to prefer smaller social network comprising familiar, emotionally close, and meaningful relational partners due to the perceptions they have relatively limited time in life (Lockenhoff & Carstensen, 2004).

The Internet appears to be an important context for individuals who wish to seek weak tie network support given the ease and convenience of locating and maintaining weak ties via the computer (Wright, Johnson, Bernard, & Averbeck, 2011), such as in computer-mediated support groups for people with health concerns and/or social networking sites like Facebook. We will explore the topic of computer-mediated support more thoroughly in Chapter 7.

The Role of Communication in the Social Support Process

Communication has been identified as a key component of social support (Albrecht & Goldsmith, 2003; Albrecht *et al.*, 1994), and it has been found to be important in helping individuals manage psychosocial stressors associated with a variety of illnesses and other health conditions (Walsh-Burke, 1992). Communication researchers have focused much of their attention on characteristics of supportive messages, perceptions of support providers and recipients, and appraisals of supportive behaviors (Adelman, Parks, & Albrecht, 1987; Albrecht & Goldsmith, 2003; Barnes & Duck, 1994).

Brant Burleson is a communication researcher who has extensively studied supportive communication, specifically characteristics of supportive messages that are exchanged between people during times of stress. Burleson (1990, 1994) argues that individuals vary in their ability to effectively communicate comforting messages to people experiencing stressful situations. In terms of providing support, Burleson (1990) contends that "since the helpee is already in a distressed state, failure of a relational partner to provide support (or the right kind of support) may exacerbate the stressful situation" (p. 67).

Comforting messages, or those messages that are intended to alleviate or lessen the emotional distress experienced by others (Burleson, 1990), require a certain degree of cognitive complexity and skill to accomplish. Burleson contends that individuals often differ in the *cognitive complexity* required to produce appropriate comforting messages. Cognitive complexity refers to a person's ability to differentiate between different aspects of a concept or situation and to use information in complicated and intricate ways (Crockett, 1965). For example, individuals with low cognitive complexity may see a person or a situation as either good or bad, whereas someone with higher cognitive complexity may be able to see both good and bad aspects.

Cognitive complexity is influenced by a number of factors, including intelligence and life experience. During the process of communication, cognitive complexity is linked to a person's ability to construct messages. In general, people with lower levels of cognitive complexity tend to construct relatively simplistic messages, while people with higher levels of cognitive complexity are able to construct more complex messages. For example, in terms of comforting messages, individuals with higher levels of cognitive complexity are often more sensitive to the self-esteem needs of others and are often able to produce supportive messages that are perceived as more helpful by the support recipient (Burleson, 1990).

Comforting messages generally tend to be viewed as more effective when they exhibit concern for the support recipient and legitimize his or her feelings, perspective, and situation. In addition, Burleson (1990) argues that sophisticated comforting messages, "compared to less sophisticated messages, project a greater degree of involvement with the distressed other, are more neutral evaluatively, are more feeling centered, are more accepting of the other, and contain more cognitively oriented explanations of feelings experienced by the other" (p. 70). In other words, producing satisfying comforting messages when attempting to support a person in his or her time of need is a relatively complex behavior, and many individuals may not possess the necessary skills to comfort others adequately. Studies have shown that more sophisticated comforting messages tend to be evaluated more positively and are perceived as more helpful by distressed individuals (see Goldsmith, 2004; Jones & Wirtz, 2006). Moreover, the physical and psychological experience of many health conditions is not easy for people who have not experienced them to understand or identify with. This may make it difficult for a support provider who has little or no experience of the health condition to identify effectively with the person facing the condition, and it could affect his or her ability to produce satisfying comforting messages. As you can see, although supporting others seems to be a relatively straightforward process and a common part of life, the ability to do so effectively can be a complex process and can be challenging for many people.

Interactive nature of support provision

Helping individuals to effectively cope with the many stresses of illness is also complicated by the perception the support provider has of the support recipient and his or her situation. The provision of support is transactional in nature, which means that both the support provider and recipient mutually influence each other's behaviors through communication. Barbee (1990) argues that support providers' perceptions of the person in need of support can influence the type of support they provide. For example, according to Barbee (1990), a support provider may attempt to (i) *solve the person's problem*, such as offering some type of assistance or resource; (ii) *support the person emotionally*, by listening empathetically or affirming his or her abilities to cope; (iii) *dismiss the person's problem*, such as telling the person not to worry so much; or (iv) *escape from dealing with the issue*, which would include behaviors such as changing the subject, ignoring the person, or leaving.

If a support provider perceives that she has the skills to help the individual with a problem, then she may attempt to solve it. In other cases, a provider may feel that she can only support the person emotionally. When the provider feels that the distressed person is worrying too much about a problem or if the problem is seen as controllable, then the provider may dismiss it. Finally, in situations where the problem or the distressed person's reaction to it are seen as too overwhelming or complex for the support provider, she may choose an escape strategy.

Communication within Social Networks, Social Support Processes, and Health

Communication within social networks in an effort to obtain social support can impact health in a number of ways (Goldsmith and Albrecht, 2011). First, participation in a network of relationships can help regulate health risk behaviors through feedback and social control. Feedback refers to messages and information that your social network members provide you during interaction. In some cases, feedback takes the form of companionship, such as when your friends make you feel happy, less lonely, or when you laugh after seeing a funny picture that your friends posted on your Facebook wall. Network members can also encourage healthy behaviors, such as eating right, exercise, and by encouraging stress reduction. Social control involves social constraints on certain behaviors. For example, your friends and family members may reinforce your decision to maintain a low-calorie diet by helping you avoid fattening foods or sweets. Family members who live with an alcoholic often hide bottles from the person who is drinking or limit the amount of money he or she has to spend on alcohol. Depending upon how health information is communicated, people's reactions to the support they receive can be positive or negative. Most research suggests that social control behaviors are perceived more negatively (especially when people really want to engage in unhealthy behaviors), and this may lead to withdrawing from one's social network or feeling resentful about attempts as social control (Tucker & Anders, 2001; Rook, 1990).

Second, social networks provide crucial information that help people make more informed decisions about health issues. For example, having a family friend who has recently been through a breast cancer screening may be able to provide you with information about the process that can help you manage your expectations and allay your fears before you make an appointment with the doctor. In computer-mediated support groups, people can gain access to information that is not readily available in their primary face-to-face social network (Wright *et al.*, 2011). For example, a person who is diagnosed with HIV may not know anyone in his family or friendship network that has the disease, and this can limit exposure to crucial information about treatment options, symptoms, and ways to emotionally cope with the social aspects of the disease (i.e. how to deal with negative societal perceptions when revealing your HIV status).

Third, social networks often provide instrumental, or tangible, support (Goldsmith, 2004). While informational and emotional support are extremely valuable, people facing health concerns are often faced with numerous physical needs, and social network members play an important role in terms of meeting them. Finally, people within our social networks help us to cope with stress more effectively when they provide us with appropriate social support (Lakey & Cohen, 2000). Again, the specific type of coping that is encouraged by social network members is important. As we saw earlier, most of the research suggests that problem-focused coping tends to lead to the most desirable outcomes whereas emotional-focused coping and avoidance-focused coping is somewhat mixed in terms of producing positive outcomes.

Support Groups for People with Health Concerns

Have you ever known a friend or family member who is a member of Alcoholics Anonymous or a similar type of 12-Step group? If not, it is likely that you have at least seen slogans from 12-Step groups, such as "One Day at a Time" or "Easy Does It." Support groups for people coping with a variety of illnesses have become a popular source of health information and comfort for over 25 million US Americans (Kessler, Mickelson, & Zhao, 1997), and they are the most common way that individuals in the United States attempt to change health behaviors (Davison, Pennebaker, & Dickerson, 2000). Support groups have a long history in the US, arising from a variety of grass-roots efforts in which people bypass professional healthcare institutions and structures to form communities based on their collective experience of facing similar illnesses and medical conditions (Katz, 1993; Katz & Bender, 1976; Yalom, 1995). These and other healthcare practices (e.g. residential care facilities) have added an important alternative voice to the traditional authorities (e.g. hospitals) that have defined health-care (see Adelman & Frey, 1997).

Currently, there are support groups for almost every conceivable physical or mental health condition. Most support groups follow the structure of early types of support groups, such as Alcoholics Anonymous, but they often differ in terms of their affiliation, structure, and focus. Some support groups are affiliated with hospitals and other healthcare facilities. Other support groups, such as those found on the Internet, operate independently of any healthcare organization. Support groups are also distinguished by whether they are facilitated by health professionals (typically, a counselor or an oncology nurse) or are self-led (often with informal or no leadership) (Cline, 1999). In addition, such groups differ in the type of support they offer members, with some groups focusing primarily on providing information about cancer (e.g. educating people about the nature of the disease, helping them to cope with lifestyle changes, and suggesting treatment options), some groups primarily providing peer-based emotional support, and some offering both informational and emotional support.

Reasons why people join support groups

Although many people who have been diagnosed with an illness or who are dealing with other health concerns never feel the need to join a support group, many other individuals experience difficulties with the social implications of having a health condition or illness and in communicating with others about it. In particular, some individuals with an illness appear to be drawn to support groups because of problems they experience with traditional support providers (e.g. physicians, family members, and close friends) in their existing social network who do not always behave in supportive ways when dealing with the issue of illness.

Inadequate support is not just a social problem for people facing illness; it has been linked to negative health outcomes, such as suppressed immune systems, prolonged recovery time, disease vulnerability, and increased stress (Cohen & Wills, 1985; DiMatteo & Hays, 1981). Conversely, satisfaction with one's support network has been found to be associated with positive health outcomes, including reduced stress and better adjustment to living with a disease (Lepore, Allen, & Evans, 1993; Wills, 1985). Such effects are important because successful adjustment to an illness has been associated with longer survival times (Jones & Reznikoff, 1989), improved psychological well-being and sense of control (Fritz, Williams, & Amylon, 1988; Sullivan & Reardon, 1985), and improved ability to cope with the experience of pain (Spiegel & Bloom, 1983).

Difficulties communicating about illness within traditional social networks As we have seen, many diseases and medical conditions have been found to carry a social stigma in the US, as they do in many other cultures (Goffman, 1963; Mathieson *et al.*, 1996; Sullivan & Reardon, 1985), and this may negatively affect the provision of social support (Bloom, 2008; MacDonald & Anderson, 1984). The stigma associated with various health conditions and the social implications of being diagnosed with them can lead people to struggle with their identity. This identity crisis is exacerbated because illness may limit people's ability to perform various taken-for-granted roles they engage in on a daily basis (e.g. work and family roles), and the strain of these changes in roles contributes to feelings of being socially and emotionally isolated (Bloom & Spiegel, 1984). For example, Spiegel (1992) found that discussion of cancer often arouses relational partners' fears, which may lead to avoidance of the person with cancer or a lack of discussion of cancer-related topics when interacting with him or her. Such responses can contribute to the person with cancer feeling alienated and isolated, feelings that can create even greater psychological stress, which in turn can exacerbate the person's physical health problems (Cohen & Wills, 1985; DiMatteo & Hays, 1981). Similarly, Rintamaki (2003) found that changes in support network size and structure were attributed to negative stigma surrounding HIV status.

People may feel socially isolated due to embarrassing aspects of disease symptoms and treatment. Weber, Roberts, and McDougall (2000) argued that "the diagnosis and treatment for prostate cancer may cause incontinence and sexual dysfunction, [and] men often feel embarrassment and shame" (p. 251). As another example, Bloom (1982) contended that mastectomy as a treatment for breast cancer often undermines a woman's sense of her attractiveness and that this can lead to both embarrassment and mutual withdrawal from relationships with significant others. A woman who has had a mastectomy may be hesitant to engage in intimate communication with her spouse; in turn, he "perceives her withdrawal as rejection and responds by further withdrawal" (Bloom, 1982, p. 1330). This mutual withdrawal can lead a woman with breast cancer to feel isolated and disconnected from a vitally important potential source of social support.

In addition, the difficulties of caring for a person with an illness can also damage relationships within an individual's primary support network due to factors such as stress and burnout (Chesler & Barbarin, 1984; Helgeson & Gottlieb, 2000), and this may foster a greater sense of isolation for the individual facing the illness. Researchers have suggested that simply expressing their needs can be problematic for people facing illness because this may lead to a secondary stigma of feeling inadequate, nonactive, and/or weak (Chesler & Barbarin, 1984; DiMatteo & Hays, 1981). Such isolation and alienation from traditional sources of support may help to make peer support groups attractive for people with health problems. According to Davison, Pennebaker, & Dickerson (2000), "Alienation from one's usual support network may be precisely the kind of social anxiety that in turn increases the value of the mutual support context" (p. 213). These researchers found that the amount of support that health-related support group participants sought was highly associated with their feelings of embarrassment due to the social stigma assigned to their disease or condition.

Illness can be a difficult topic to discuss because it may make people think about their mortality, lead to the expression of strong, often uncontrollable, emotional feelings (e.g. crying), and create general discomfort because people may not have the skills to communicate about sensitive topics such as illness (Bute, 2007). Because of these and other difficulties, members of the traditional support network of a person with an illness may not encourage him or her to express negative emotions about the illness, either because they feel that it is unhealthy or because it makes them feel uncomfortable. They may minimize the concerns of the person, avoid interacting with him or her, and/or steer conversational topics away from emotional talk about the disease or from discussion of it altogether (Dakof & Taylor, 1990; Helgeson *et al.*, 2000; Sullivan & Reardon, 1985; Wortman & Dunkel-Schetter, 1979).

Other factors influencing support group participation All of these issues may increase a person's decision to join a support group when facing a health problem. Of course, other variables, such as people's perceptions of these groups in general, whether or not they perceive them as helpful, and the availability of these groups, may influence whether or not they join them. Other factors, such as gender, race, and social status, are also important in determining whether or not people join support groups in our culture. Support group members tend to be white, middle class, well educated (compared to the national average), and female (Kessler, Mickelson, & Zhao, 1997). However, given that most support groups try to protect the anonymity of their members, it has been difficult for researchers to obtain data about the demographics of individuals who use them.

Communication Processes within Support Groups

Support researchers have identified a number of communicative features of support groups that appear to influence health outcomes. This section examines a variety of communication processes that occur in support groups and their possible health benefits to members.

Use of narrative

Support groups encourage participation among members through group norms of "telling one's story" to the group on a voluntary basis (Arntson & Droge, 1987; Cline, 1999; Yalom, 1995). This process usually begins with a member providing a brief history of his experience with the disease or illness and then discussing current issues and feelings with which he is dealing (Helgeson & Gottlieb, 2000). Rappaport (1993) contends that members of self-help groups use narratives like this as a means of forming a social identity. People with a variety of diseases and conditions often experience feelings of isolation, and support groups provide an environment where these individuals feel they share a common identity with the other members. Support group members learn to identify with other members' experiences and feelings about the illness through the sharing of narratives, and this appears both to validate their own experiences and feelings and to lessen their sense of isolation (Mok & Martinson, 2000; Wright & Bell, 2003). According to Davison, Pennebaker, & Dickerson (2000), "The stories told and heard in this context carry the weight of shared experience, the emotional potency of common suffering, and an avenue for social learning" (p. 206).

In addition to identifying with other members' experiences and feelings, newer members of support groups often find experienced members' stories particularly credible (Wright, 1997). Moreover, the experiences of other health-related support group members is often perceived as more credible than information obtained from other people, even healthcare professionals, especially information about the psychosocial aspects of their disease, due to the fact that other support group members are actually living with the disease on a daily basis.

Arntson and Droge (1987) point to some specific functions served by the sharing of narratives within support groups that may benefit both the narrator and those who listen to his or her story. For example, because narratives typically place events within a sequence, they "organize the relevant symbols in one's environment, making it possible to gain meaning from the past, give meaning to the present, and reduce uncertainty about the future" (p. 161). Hsieh (2004) found that members of a transplant support group used narratives to socialize, ask for help, bolster their self-image, indirectly share their beliefs with others, and as a means for managing uncertainty about their illness. Other researchers have found that the use of narratives provide several options for talking about health-related issues, depending upon how the stories are framed by participants (Golden & Lund, 2009).

Such ways of interpreting meaning may help people coping with illness to perceive health-related events as less unpredictable, which may strengthen their sense of control over their situation. Moreover, listening to stories told in support groups is a way to receive advice nondidactically, so that individuals are free to follow or disregard it (Arntson & Droge, 1987; Wright, 2000). For example, a narrator might disclose through a story that a certain type of medication was helpful in alleviating nausea during chemotherapy, without actually telling others that they should take the medication themselves. In this way, narratives may help serve the purpose of providing suggestions to others without overstepping relational boundaries (which may lead to perceptions of unwanted advice).

Being helped by helping

Helping others is usually part of a support group's ideology that is reinforced during group interaction (Antze, 1976; Frank & Frank, 1991; Wright, 1997). Support groups typically consist of individuals who vary in terms of the amount of time they have been members of the group, and members who have participated for longer periods of time are in a better position to proactively help others. They can be especially influential in providing new members with opportunities to learn vicariously about the illness, helping them to understand how to cope with physical, psychological, and social issues associated with the disease, offering them emotional support, and sharing information with them about treatment options (Wright, 2002).

Although newer members certainly receive a great deal of support from more experienced members, support groups are not a one-way street as regards helping behaviors: the act of helping others appears to have psychological benefits as well. Support groups thus encourage members who have been with the group for a longer period of time to share their experiences with newer members through the idea that helping others is important to one's own recovery. Helping others has been found to increase helpers' sense of self-worth and value and, simultaneously, to reduce their feelings of powerlessness (Spiegel, Bloom, & Yalom, 1981; Yalom, 1995). According to Spiegel, Bloom, & Yalom (1981), "Patients who feel helpless and demoralized learn that they can be enormously useful to others" (p. 528). Moreover, Rosenberg (1984) states: "members feel that by improving their own competence in handling the situation they are also improving the competence of other group members and perhaps the social conditions of the group as a whole" (p. 175).

Support group members often reap benefits by helping others within the support group. This phenomenon has been named "the helper principle" (Riessman, 1965). According to Cline (1999), the helper principle "encompasses a complex process of cognitive reframing during which rookie helpers become veterans" (p. 524). New support group members go through a socialization process in which they learn that helping others is an important part of the process of coping with the disease. Cline (1999) contends "as members make the transition from helpee to helper, retelling their stories validates their experiences and reminds them, as well as other members, of their progress" (p. 524). This transformation from helpee to helper also appears to help support group members gain a sense of personal control when discussing their illness (Arntson & Droge, 1987; Cline, 1999). In addition, the mentor role helps to reinforce positive attitudes, beliefs, and behaviors about the particular health issue for support group members.

Support Group Participation and Health Outcomes

Participation in health-related support groups has been linked to a variety of health outcomes, including reduced stress, lower depression, improved patient resistance to infection, faster recovery time, enhanced psychological well-being, less likelihood of relapsing into risky health behaviors, and reduced mortality rates (see Fogel *et al.*, 2002; Helgeson *et al.*, 2000; Helgeson & Gottlieb, 2000; Hogan, Linden, & Najarian, 2002; Kassel & Wagner, 1993; Rains & Young, 2009). However, as we have seen in this chapter, the relationship between social support and health outcomes is mediated by how social support is communicated within social settings. Unfortunately, studies have found that many people who initially join support groups quit the group after a short period of time (Gottlieb & Wachala, 2007; Helgeson *et al.*, 2000; Wright & Bell, 2003). In many of these cases, it appears that social/communicative issues may at least partially influence people's decisions to leave the group. Despite what we know about communication and social support, it is often difficult for researchers to gain access to social support groups (particularly in the face-to-face world) as participants often wish to protect their privacy. However, efforts to better understand and link social support processes within support groups to health outcomes are important, and will continue to be valuable in the future.

Social Support Interventions

Given all that we know about social support and its relationship to health outcomes, there is a strong need for communication research that utilizes social interventions to reinforce health behavior change (Goldsmith & Albrecht, 2011; Gottlieb, 2000). As we will see in Chapter 10, health intervention campaign design is an important aspect of health communication research, particularly because interventions help to translate communication and public health research into practice (Kreps, 2011). Communication researchers have known for a long time that social support can be a key component of health inventions in terms of helping to reinforce the maintenance of targeted health behaviors, such as using social networks to help people stick with a low-calorie diet or physical exercise program. As we saw earlier, social networks can reinforce health behaviors through social control, such as when people in our social network say something negative when we try to light up a cigarette. As we have seen, members of our social networks can have a strong influence on our health beliefs, attitudes, values, and behaviors through the different types and functions of social support they provide during interactions with us. Furthermore, social network members can help train individuals to seek support for their health concerns more efficiently, improve the overall quality of support resources (such assuring there is up-to-date information available within the community), and alter community norms (Goldsmith & Albrecht, 2011). Such social support features can be included as part of a larger intervention design.

A number of researchers have been successful using social support as a component of targeted health interventions (see review by Gottlieb & Wachala, 2007). For example, Levine *et al.* (2009) demonstrated that information from an on-line social support network for diabetes maintenance helped at-risk consumers to effectively manage their blood sugar levels. Goldsmith and Brashers (2008) describe a program that helps individuals who are newly diagnosed to with HIV to use social support and communication skills to manage the uncertainty (and associated stress) surrounding the disease. Other support interventions have been used to target health issues ranging from drug and smoking relapse prevention to diet and exercise programs that are designed to reduce the risk of heart disease (Shoham, Rohrbaugh, Trost, & Muramoto, 2006). In addition, social support interventions appear to have implications for caregivers of individuals living with health issues. For example, Joling *et al.* (2008) found that mobilizing social support for caregivers of Alzheimer's disease patients improved caregiver functioning and delayed placing patients in nursing homes.

Summary

The social support we receive from others is important to our physical and mental health. However, our perceptions of whether or not the support we receive is appropriate, our coping styles, and our personal and social resources mediate the relationship between social support and health outcomes. Many individuals are able to obtain sufficient support from the members of their primary social network. Other people find it difficult to receive adequate support from family members and friends, and they may opt to seek support from weak ties, including members of support groups. Support groups offer many advantages to people who are facing health concerns. The ability to find a concentrated setting where people share similar problems and feelings and the opportunity to help others are major advantages of support groups for people facing health issues.

References

Adelman, M. B., & Frey, L. R. (1997). *The fragile community: Living together with AIDS*. Mahwah, NJ: Lawrence Erlbaum.

Adelman, M. B., Parks, M. R., & Albrecht, T. L. (1987). Beyond close relationships: Support in weak ties. In T. L. Albrecht & M. B. Adelman (Eds), *Communicating social support* (pp. 126–147). Newbury Park, CA: Sage.

Albrecht, T. L., & Adelman, M. A. (1987). *Communicating social support*. Newbury Park, CA: Sage.

Albrecht, T. L., & Goldsmith, D. J. (2003). Social support, social networks, and health. In T. L. Thompson, A. M. Dorsey, K. I. Miller, & R. Parrott (Eds), *Handbook of health communication* (pp. 263–284). Mahwah, NJ: Lawrence Erlbaum.

Albrecht, T. L., Burleson, B. R., & Goldsmith, D. (1994). Supportive communication. In M. L. Knapp & G. R. Miller (Eds), *Handbook of interpersonal communication* (2nd ed., pp. 419–449). Newbury Park, CA: Sage.

Andrews, S. C. (2001). Caregiver burden and symptom distress in people with cancer receiving hospice care. *Oncology Nursing Forum, 28*, 1469–1474.

Aneshensel, C. S., & Stone, J. D. (1982). Stress and depression: A test of the buffering model of social support. *Archives of General Psychiatry, 39*, 1392–1396.

Antze, P. (1976). The role of ideologies in peer psychotherapy organizations: Some theoretical considerations and three case studies. *Journal of Applied Behavioral Science, 12*, 323–346.

Arntson, P., & Droge, D. (1987). Social support in self-help groups: The role of communication in enabling perceptions of control. In T. L. Albrecht, M. B. Adelman, & Associates (Eds), *Communicating social support* (pp. 148–171). Newbury Park, CA: Sage.

Babrow, A. S. (2001). Uncertainty, value, communication, and problematic integration. *Journal of Communication, 51*, 553–573.

Bakas, T., Lewis, R. R., & Parsons, J. (2001). Caregiving tasks among family caregivers of patients with lung cancer. *Oncology Nursing Forum, 28*, 847–854.

Ballieux, R. E., & Heijen, C. J. (1989). Stress and the immune response. In H. Weiner, I. Floring, R. Murison, & D. Hellhammer (Eds), *Frontiers of stress research* (pp. 51–55). Toronto: Huber.

Barbee, A. P. (1990). Interactive coping: The cheering-up process in close relationships. In S. Duck & R. Silver (Eds), *Personal relationships and social support* (pp. 46–65). Newbury Park, CA: Sage.

Barnes, M. K., & Duck, S. (1994). Everyday communicative contexts for social support. In B. R. Burleson, T. L. Albrecht, & I. G. Sarason (Eds), *Communication of social support: Messages, interactions, relationships, and community* (pp. 175–194). Thousand Oaks, CA: Sage.

Bennenbroek, F. T. C., Buunk, B. P., Van der Zee, K. I., & Grol, B. (2001). Social comparison and patient information: What do cancer patients want? *Patient Education and Counseling, 47*, 5–12.

Berkman, L. F., & Syme, L. S. (1979). Social networks, host resistance, and mortality: A nine-year follow-up study of Alameda County residents. *Journal of Epidemiology, 109*, 186–204.

Billings, A. G., & Moos, R. H. (1981). The role of coping responses and social resources in attenuating the impact of stressful life events. *Journal of Behavioral Medicine, 4*, 139–157.

Bloom, J. R. (1982). Social support, accommodation to stress and adjustment to breast cancer. *Social Science Medicine, 16*, 1329–1338.

Bloom, J. R. (2008). Improving the health and well-being of cancer survivors: Past as prologue. *Psycho-Oncology, 17*, 525–532.

Bloom, J. R., & Spiegel, D. (1984). The relationship of two dimensions of social support to the psychological well-being and social functioning of women with advanced breast cancer. *Social Science Medicine, 19*, 831–837.

Booth-Butterfield, M. & Booth-Butterfield, S. (1991). Individual differences in the communication of humorous messages. *Southern Communication Journal, 56*, 32–40.

Brashers, D. E., Neidig, J. L., & Goldsmith, D. J. (2004). Social support and the management of people living with HIV or AIDS. *Health Communication, 16*, 305–331.

Burleson, B. R. (1990). Comforting as social support: Relational consequences of supportive behaviors. In S. Duck & R. C. Silver (Eds), *Personal relationships and social support* (pp. 66–82). Newbury Park, CA: Sage.

Burleson, B. R. (1994). Comforting messages: Significance, approaches, and effects. In B. R. Burleson, T. L. Albrecht, & I. G. Sarason (Eds), *Communication of social support: Messages, interactions, relationships, and community*. Newbury Park, CA: Sage.

Bute, J. (2007). *Talking about infertility: A conceptual model.* (Unpublished doctoral dissertation). University of Illinois at Urbana-Champaign, Urbana, IL.

Carstensen, L. L., & Fredrickson, B. L. (1998). Influence of HIV status and age on cognitive representations of others. *Health Psychology, 17,* 494–503.

Ceslo, B. G., Ebener, D. J., & Burkhead, E. J. (2003). Humor coping, health status, and life satisfaction among older adults residing in assisted living facilities. *Aging & Mental Health, 7,* 438–445.

Chesler, M. A., & Barbarin, O. A. (1984). Difficulties of providing help in a crisis: Relationships between parents of children with cancer and their friends. *Journal of Social Issues, 40,* 113–134.

Cline, R. J. (1999). Communication within social support groups. In L. R. Frey (Ed.), D. S. Gouran, & M. S. Poole (Assoc. Eds), *The handbook of group communication theory and research* (pp. 516–538). Thousand Oaks, CA: Sage.

Clow, C. (2001). The physiology of stress. In F. Jones & J. Bright (Eds), *Stress: Myth, theory, and research* (pp. 47–61). Harlow: Prentice-Hall.

Cobb, S. (1976). Social support as a moderator of life stresses. *Psychosomatic Medicine, 38,* 300–314.

Cohen, S. (1988). Psychosocial models of the role of support in the etiology of physical disease. *Health Psychology, 7,* 269–297.

Cohen, S., & Wills, T. A. (1985). Stress, social support, and the buffering hypothesis. *Psychological Bulletin, 98,* 310–357.

Crockett, W. H. (1965). Cognitive complexity and impression formation. In B. A. Maher (Ed.), *Progress in experimental personality research* (Vol. 2, pp. 47–90). New York: Academic Press.

Cutrona, C. E., & Russell, D. W. (1990). Type of social support and specific stress. Toward a theory of optimal matching. In B. R. Sarason, I. G. Sarason, & G. R. Pierce (Eds), *Social support: An interactional view* (pp. 319–366). Oxford: Wiley.

Cwikel, J. M., & Isreal, B. A. (1987). Examining mechanisms of social support and social networks: A review of health-related intervention studies. *Public Health Review, 15,* 159–193.

Dainton, M., & Zelly, E. D. (2006). Social exchange theories: Interdependence and equity. In D. O. Braithwaite & L. A. Baxter (Eds), *Engaging theories in family communication: Multiple perspectives* (pp. 243–259). Thousand Oaks, CA: Sage.

Dakof, G. A., & Taylor, S. E. (1990). Victim's perceptions of social support: What is helpful from whom? *Journal of Personality and Social Psychology, 58,* 80–89.

Davison, K. P., Pennebaker, J. W., & Dickerson, S. S. (2000). Who talks? The social psychology of illness support groups. *American Psychologist, 55,* 205–217.

Dean, A., & Lin, N. (1977). The stress buffering role of social support: Problems and prospects for systematic investigation. *Journal of Health and Social Behavior, 32,* 321–341.

Deutsch, M. (1985). *Distributive justice: A social psychological perspective.* New Haven, CT: Yale University Press.

DiMatteo, M., & Hays, R. (1981). Social support and serious illness. In B. Gottlieb (Ed.), *Social networks and social support* (pp. 117–148). Beverly Hills, CA: Sage.

Eichhorn, K. C. (2008). Soliciting and providing support over the internet: An investigation of online eating disorder groups. *Journal of Computer-Mediated Communication, 14,* 67–78.

Edwards, H., & Noller, P. (1998). Factors influencing caregiver–care receiver communication and the impact on the well-being of older care receivers. *Health Communication, 10,* 317–342.

Edwards, J. M., & Trimble, K. (1992). Anxiety, coping, and academic performance. *Anxiety, Stress, and Coping, 5,* 337–350.

Endler, N. S., & Parker, J. D. A. (1990). Multidimensional assessment of coping: A critical evaluation. *Journal of Personality and Social Psychology, 58,* 844–854.

Epstein, N. B., Bishop, D. S., & Baldwin, L. M. (1982). McMaster model of family functioning (pp. 115-141). In F. Walsh (Ed.), *Normal family processes,* New York: Guilford Press.

Festinger, L. (1954). A theory of social comparison processes. *Human Relations, 2,* 117–140.

Fogel, J., Albert, S. M., Schnabel, E., Ditkoff, B. A., & Neugut, A. I. (2002). Internet use and social support in women with breast cancer. *Health Psychology, 21,* 398–404.

Folkman, S., Lazarus, R.S., Pimley, S., & Novacek, J. (1987). Age differences in stress and coping process. *Psychology & Aging, 2,* 171–184.

Folkman, S. & Lazarus, R.S. (1987). Transactional theory and research on emotions & coping. *European Journal of Personality, 1,* 141–169.

Frank, J. D., & Frank, J. B. (1991). *Persuasion and healing.* Baltimore, MD: Johns Hopkins University Press.

Fritz, G. K., Williams, J. R., & Amylon, M. (1988). After treatment ends: Psychosocial sequelae in pediatric cancer survivors. *American Journal of Orthopsychiatry, 54*, 552–561.

Golden, M. A., & Lund, D. A. (2009). Identifying themes regarding the benefits and limitations of caregiver support group conversations. *Journal of Gerontological Social Work, 52*, 154–170.

Goffman, E. (1963). *Stigma: Notes on the management of spoiled identity.* Englewood Cliffs, NJ: Prentice-Hall.

Goldsmith, D. J. (2004). *Communicating social support.* Cambridge: Cambridge University Press.

Goldsmith, D. J., & Fitch, K. (1997). The normative context of advice as social support. *Human Communication Research, 23*, 454–476.

Goldsmith, D. J., & Albrecht, T. L. (2011). Social support, social networks, and health: A guiding framework. In T. L. Thompson, R. Parrott, & J. F. Nussbaum (Eds), *The Routledge handbook of health communication, 2nd ed.* (pp. 335–348). New York: Routledge.

Goldsmith, D. J., & Brashers, D. E. (2008). Communication matters: Developing and testing social support interventions. *Communication Monographs, 75*, 320–330.

Gottlieb, B. H. (2000). Selecting and planning support interventions. In S. Cohen, L. G. Underwood, & B. H. Gottlieb (Eds), *Social support measurement and interventions: A guide for health and social scientists* (pp. 195–220). New York: Oxford University Press.

Gottlieb, B. H., & Wachala, E. D. (2007). Cancer support groups: A critical review of empirical studies. *Psycho-Oncology, 16*, 379–400.

Grainger, K. (1995). Communication and the institutionalized elderly. In J. F. Nussbaum & J. Coupland (Eds), *Handbook of communication and aging research* (pp. 417–436). Mahwah, NJ: Lawrence Erlbaum.

Granovetter, M. S. (1973). The strength of weak ties. *American Journal of Sociology, 78*, 1360–1380.

Harzold, E., & Sparks, L. (2007). Adult child perceptions of communication and humor when the parent is diagnosed with cancer: A suggestive perspective from communication theory. *Qualitative Research Reports in Communication, 7*, 67–78.

Heady, B. W., & Wearing, A. J. (1990). Subjective well-being and coping with adversity. *Social Indicators Research, 22*, 327–349.

Helgeson, V. S., & Gottlieb, B. H. (2000). Support groups. In S. Cohen, L. G. Underwood, & B. H. Gottlieb (Eds), *Social support measurement and intervention* (pp. 221–245). New York: Oxford University Press.

Helgeson, V. S., Cohen, S., Schultz, R., & Yasko, J. (2000). Group support interventions for women with breast cancer: Who benefits from what? *Health Psychology, 19*, 107–114.

Hsieh, E. (2004). Stories in action and the dialogic management of identities: Story telling in transplant support group meetings. *Research on Language and Social Interaction, 37*, 39–70.

Hogan, B. E., Linden, W., & Najarian, B. (2002). Social support interventions: Do they work? *Clinical Psychology Review, 22*, 381–440.

House, J. S., Landis, K. R., & Umberson, D. (1988). Social relationships and health. *Science, 241*, 540–544.

Houston, D. M., McKee, K. J., Carroll, L., & Marsh, H. (1998). Using humour to promote psychological well-being in residential homes for older people. *Aging & Mental Health, 2*, 328–332.

Hughes, H. (2005). Work stress differentials between psychiatric and general nurses. *British Journal of Nursing, 14*, 802–808.

Joling, S. M., van Hout, H. P. J., Scheltens, P., Vernooij-Dassen, M., van den Berg, B., Bosmans, J. *et al.* (2008). (Cost)-effectiveness of family meetings on indicated prevention of anxiety and depressive symptoms and disorders of primary family caregivers of patients with dementia: Design of a randomized controlled trail. *BMC Geriatrics, 8.* Doi:10.1186/1471-2318-2.

Jones, D. N., & Reznikoff, M. (1989). Psychosocial adjustment to a mastectomy. *Journal of Nervous and Mental Disease, 177*, 624–631.

Jones, S. M., & Wirtz, J. G. (2006). How does comforting communication work? An empirical test of an appraisal-based model of comforting. *Human Communication Research, 32*, 217–243.

Kassel, J. D., & Wagner, E. F. (1993). Processes of change in Alcoholics Anonymous: A review of possible mechanisms. *Psychotherapy, 30*, 222–234.

Katz, A. H. (1993). *Self-help in America: A social movement perspective.* New York: Twayne.

Katz, A. H., & Bender, E. I. (1976). Self-help groups in Western society: History and prospects. *Journal of Applied Behavioral Science, 12*, 265–282.

Kessler, R. C., Mickelson, K. D., & Zhao, S. (1997). Patterns and correlates of self-help group membership in the United States. *Social Policy, 27*, 27–46.

Kohn, P. M. (1996). On coping adaptively with daily hassles. In M. Zeidner & N. S. Endler (Eds), *Handbook of coping* (pp. 181–201). New York: John Wiley & Sons.

Krause, N. (1990). Stress, support, and well-being in later life: Focusing on salient social roles. In M. A. Stephens, J. H. Crowther, S. E. Hobfoll, & D. L. Tennenbaum (Eds), *Stress and coping in later-life families* (pp. 71–97). New York: Hemisphere.

Kreps, G. L. (2011). Translating health communication research into practice: The influence of health communication scholarship on health policy, practice, and outcomes. In T. L. Thompson, R. Parrott, & J. F. Nussbaum (Eds), *The Routledge handbook of health communication, 2nd ed.* (pp. 595–609). New York: Routledge.

La Gaipa, J. J. (1990). The negative effects of informal support systems. In S. Duck & R. C. Silver (Eds), *Personal relationships and social support* (pp. 122–139). Newbury Park, CA: Sage.

Laizner, A. M., Yost, L. M., Barg, F. K., & McCorkle, R. (1993). Needs of family caregivers of persons with cancer: A review. *Seminars in Oncology Nursing, 9*, 114–120.

Lakey, B., & Cohen, S. (2000). Social support theory and measurement. In S. Cohen, L. G. Underwood, & B. H. Gottlieb (Eds.), *Social support measurement and intervention: A guide for health and social scientists* (pp. 29–52). Oxford: Oxford University Press.

La Rocca, J., House, J., & French, J. R. (1980). Social support, occupational health, and stress. *Journal of Health and Social Behavior, 21*, 201–218.

Lepore, S. J., Allen, K. A. M., & Evans, G. W. (1993). Social support lowers cardiovascular reactivity to an acute stressor. *Psychosomatic Medicine, 55*, 518–524.

Levine, B. A., Turner, J. W., Robinson, J. D., Angelus, P., & Hu, M. (2009). Communication plays a critical role in web based monitoring. *Journal of Diabetes Science and Technology, 3*, 461–467.

Lockenhoff, C. E., & Carstensen, L. L. (2004). Socioemotional selectivity theory, aging, and health: The increasingly delicate balance between regulating emotions and making tough choices. *Journal of Personality, 72*, 1395–1423.

MacDonald, L. D., & Anderson, H. R. (1984). Stigma in patients with rectal cancer: A community study. *Journal of Epidemiology and Community Health, 38*, 284–290.

Magen, R. H., & Glajchen, M. (1999). Cancer support groups: Client outcome and the context of group process. *Research on Social Group Practice, 9*, 541–554.

Mathieson, C. M., Logan-Smith, L. L., Phillips, J., MacPhee, M., & Attia, M. L. (1996). Caring for head and neck oncology patients: Does social support lead to better quality of life? *Canadian Family Physician, 42*, 1712–1720.

McGhee, P. E. (1986). Humor across the life span: Sources of developmental change and individual differences. In L. Nahemow, K. A. McCluskey-Fawcett, & R. E. McGhee (Eds), *Humor and aging* (pp. 27–47). London: Academic Press.

Mok, E., & Martinson, I. (2000). Empowerment of Chinese patients with cancer through self-help groups in Hong Kong. *Cancer Nursing, 23*, 206–213.

Nahemow, L., McCluskey-Fawcett, K. A., & McGhee, R. E. (Eds), *Humor and aging.* London: Academic Press.

Noller, P., & Fitzpatrick, M. A. (1993). *Communication in Family Relationships.* Englewood Cliffs, NJ: Prentice-Hall.

Nussbaum, J. F. (1989). *Life-span communication: Normative processes.* Hillsdale, NJ: Erlbaum.

Nussbaum, J. F., Pecchioni, L., Robinson, J. D., & Thompson, T. (2000). *Communication and Aging* (2nd). Mahwah, NJ: Lawrence Erlbaum Associates, Inc.

Pecchioni, L., & Sparks, L. (2007). Health information sources of individuals with cancer and their family members. *Health Communication, 21*, 1–9.

Penner, L. A., Dovidio, J. F., & Albrecht, T. L. (2000). Helping victims of loss and trauma: A social psychological perspective. In J. H. Harvey & E. D. Miller (Eds), *Handbook of loss and trauma* (pp. 62–85). Philadelphia, PA: Brunner/Mazel.

Pfeifer, D. L. (1993). Humor and aging: A comparison between a younger and an older group. (Doctoral dissertation, University of Miami, 1993). *Dissertation Abstracts International, 53*, 4034–4035.

Pierce, G. R., Sarason, I. G., & Sarason, B. R. (1996). Coping and social support. In M. Zeidner & N. S. Endler (Eds), *Handbook of coping* (pp. 434–451). New York: John Wiley & Sons.

Pitula, C. R., & Daugherty, S. R. (1995). Sources of social support and conflict in hospitalized depressed women. *Nursing and Health, 18*, 325–332.

Rains, S. A., & Young, V. (2009). A meta-analysis of research on formal computer-mediated support groups: Examining group characteristics and health outcomes. *Human Communication Research, 35*, 309–336.

Rappaport, J. (1993). Narrative studies, personal stories, and identity transformation in the mutual help context. *Journal of Applied Behavioral Science, 29*, 239–256.

Rintamaki, L. S. (2003). *HIV identity trajectories and social interaction* (Unpublished doctoral dissertation). University of Illinois at Urbana-Champaign, Urbana, IL.

Richman, J. (1995). The lifesaving function of humor with the depressed and suicidal elderly. *The Gerontologist*, *35*, 271–273.

Riessman, F. (1965). The "helper" therapy principle. *Social Work*, *10*, 27–32.

Rook, K. S. (1990). Social relationships as a source of companionship: Implications for older adults' psychological well-being. In B. R. Sarason, I. G. Sarason, & G. R. Pierce (Eds), *Social support: An interactional view* (pp. 97–128). New York: Wiley.

Rook, K. S. (1995). Support, companionship, and control in older adults' social networks: Implications for well-being. In J. F. Nussbaum & J. Coupland (Eds), *Handbook of communication and aging research* (pp. 437–463). Mahwah, NJ: Lawrence Erlbaum Associates.

Rosenberg, P. P. (1984). Support groups: A special therapeutic entity. *Small Group Behavior*, *15*, 173–186.

Roter, D., & Hall, J. A. (1992). Improving talk through interventions. *Doctors talking with patients/patients talking with doctors: Improving communication in medical visits*. Westport, CT: Auburn House.

Ryff, C. D. (1989). In the eye of the beholder: Views of psychological well-being among middle-aged and older adults. *Psychology and Aging*, *4*, 195–210.

Sarasohn-Kahn, J. (2008). The wisdom of patients: Health care meets online social media. Retrieved July 23, 2012, from http://www.chcf.org/documents/chronicdisease/index.cfm?itemID=133631.

Sarason, B. R., Sarason, I. G., & Pierce, G. R. (1990). *Social support: An interactional view*. New York: Wiley.

Sarna, L., & McCorkle, R. (1996). Burden of care and lung cancer. *Cancer Practice*, *4*, 245–251.

Schimmel, S. R. (1999). *Cancer talk: Voices of hope and endurance from "The Group Room," the world's largest cancer support group*. New York: Broadway Books.

Shoham, V., Rohrbaugh, M. J., Trost, S. E., & Muramoto, M. (2006). A family consultation intervention for health-comprised smokers. *Journal of Substance Abuse Treatment*, *31*, 395–402.

Solomon, J.C. (1996). Humor and aging well. *The American Behavioral Scientist*, *39*, 249–271.

Sparks, L. (Ed.). (2003). Cancer communication and aging [Special Issue]. *Health Communication*, *15*(2), 123–258.

Sparks, L. (2003). An introduction to cancer communication and aging: Theoretical and research insights. *Health Communication*, *15*(2), 123–132.

Sparks, L. (2008). *Family decision-making*. In W. Donsbach (Ed.), *The international encyclopedia of communication*, 4, (pp. 1729–1733). Oxford, UK and Malden, MA: Wiley-Blackwell.

Sparks-Bethea, L. (2001). The function of humor within the lives of older adults. *Qualitative Research Reports in Communication*, *2*(3), 49–56.

Spiegel, D. (1992). Effects of psychosocial support on patients with metastatic breast cancer. *Journal of Psychosocial Oncology*, *10*, 113–121.

Spiegel, D., & Bloom, J. R. (1983). Pain in metastatic breast cancer. *Cancer*, *52*, 149–153.

Spiegel, D., Bloom, J. R., & Yalom, I. (1981). Group support for patients with metastatic cancer: A randomized prospective outcome study. *Archives of General Psychiatry*, *38*, 527–533.

Sullivan, C. F. (2003). Gendered cybersupport: A thematic analysis of two on-line cancer support groups. *Journal of Health Psychology*, *8*, 83–103.

Sullivan, C. F., & Reardon, K. K. (1985). Social support satisfaction and health locus of control: Discriminators of breast cancer patients' style of coping. In M. L. McLaughlin (Ed.), *Communication yearbook* (Vol. 9, pp. 707–722). Beverly Hills, CA: Sage.

Tanis, M. (2008). Health-related on-line forums: What's the big attraction? *Journal of Health Communication*, *13*, 698–714.

Thoits, P. (1982). Conceptual, methodological, and theoretical problems in studying social support as a buffer against life stress. *Journal of Health and Social Behavior*, *23*, 145–159.

Tucker, J. S., & Anders, S. L. (2001). Social control of health behaviors in marriage. *Journal of Applied Social Psychology*, *31*, 467–485.

Turner, R. A., King, P. R., & Tremblay, P. F. (1992). Coping styles and depression among psychiatric outpatients. *Personality and Individual Differences*, *13*, 1145–1147.

Uchino, B. N. (2006). Social support and health: A review of physiological processes potentially underlying links to disease outcomes. *Journal of Behavioral Medicine*, *29*, 377–387.

Uchino, B. N., Cacioppo, J. T., & Kiecolt-Glaser, J. K. (1996). The relationship between social support and physiological processes: A review with emphasis on underlying mechanisms and implications for health. *Psychological Bulletin*, *119*, 488–531.

Walther, J. B., & Boyd, S. (2002). Attraction to computer-mediated social support. In C. A. Lin & D. Atkin (Eds),

Communication technology and society: Audience adoption and uses (pp. 153-188). Creskill, NJ: Hampton Press.

Walsh-Burke, K. (1992). Family communication and coping with cancer. Impact of the We Can Weekend. *Journal of Psychosocial Oncology, 10,* 63–81.

Wanzer, M., Sparks, L., & Frymier, A. B. (2009). Humorous communication within the lives of older adults: The relationships among humor, coping efficacy, age, and life satisfaction. *Health Communication, 24,* 1–9.

Weber, B. A., Roberts, B. L., & McDougall, G. J. (2000). Exploring the efficacy of support groups of men with prostate cancer. *Geriatric Nursing, 41,* 250–253.

Westburg, N. G. (2003). Hope, laughter, and humor in residents and staff at an assisted living facility. *Journal of Mental Health Counseling, 25,* 16–32.

Wills, T. A. (1985). Supportive functions of interpersonal relationships. In S. Cohen & S. L. Syme (Eds), *Social support and health* (pp. 61–82). New York: Academic Press.

Wills, T. A., & Shinar, O. (2000). Measuring perceived and received social support. In S. Cohen, I. G. Underwood, & B. H. Gottlieb (Eds), *Social support measurement and intervention: A guide for health and social scientists* (pp. 86–135). New York: Oxford University Press.

Wortman, C., & Dunkel-Schetter, C. (1979). Interpersonal relationships and cancer. *Journal of Social Issues, 35,* 120–155.

Wright, K. B. (1997). Shared ideology in Alcoholics Anonymous: A grounded theory approach. *Journal of Health Communication, 2,* 83–99.

Wright, K. B. (2000). The communication of social support within an on-line community for older adults: A qualitative analysis of the SeniorNet community. *Qualitative Research Reports in Communication, 1,* 33–43.

Wright, K. B. (2002). Social support within an on-line cancer community: An assessment of emotional support, perceptions of advantages and disadvantages, and motives for using the community from a communication perspective. *Journal of Applied Communication Research, 30,* 195–209.

Wright, K. B., & Bell, S. B. (2003). Health-related support groups on the Internet: Linking empirical findings to social support and computer-mediated communication theory. *Journal of Health Psychology, 8,* 37–52.

Wright, K. B., Johnson, A. J., Bernard, D. R., & Averbeck, J. (2011). Computer-mediated social support: Promises and pitfalls for individuals coping with health concerns. In T. L. Thompson, R. Parrott, & J. F. Nussbaum (Eds), *The Routledge handbook of health communication,* 2nd ed. (pp. 349–362). New York: Routledge.

Wright, K. B., & Muhtaseb, A. (2005, May). *Perceptions of on-line support in health-related computer-mediated support groups.* Paper presented to the Health Communication Division at the annual International Communication Association Convention, New York.

Yalom, I. (1995). *The theory and practice of group psychotherapy.* New York: Basic Books.

Chapter 5

Culture and Diversity Issues in Healthcare

Imagine if you moved to a new country (where you did not speak the native language well) and you needed to go to the doctor's office. Not only would you likely struggle to communicate your needs with the physician and other staff members, you might find that there are important other cultural differences in beliefs about health or communication behaviors among healthcare providers compared to your country of origin. For example, in some cultures, people attribute illness to spirits or bad luck as opposed to viruses or environmental causes. Culture permeates all aspects of life and it influences our perceptions and experiences of life events, including health-related situations. Culture influences the most fundamental aspects of our existence, such as our assumptions about human nature, the nature of reality, and our relationships to one another and the environment (Gudykunst, 1998; Hofstede, 1984; Schein, 1985). Communication is central to this process because language is defined by, reflects, and transmits culture (Pecchioni et al., 2008).

Culture may best seen as a dynamic (rather than static) concept given that cultural meanings are typically always in a state of flux as individuals adapt to ever-changing environmental conditions, including acculturation, or adaptation from one's culture of origin to a new culture (Dutta & Basu, 2011). Conceptions of health and illness as well as ways to treat illness vary from culture to culture within the US and around the world. As more and more people from different cultures have immigrated to the US in recent years, there is greater diversity among patients than ever before. Providers can no longer approach healthcare from a single cultural perspective and be effective in treating patients from other cultures in a competent manner. As we will explore in this chapter, culture conceptions of illness and health can be radically different as people from different cultures come together in healthcare settings. Ignoring cultural differences in conceptions of illness and health can lead to a variety of problems

Health Communication in the 21st Century, Second Edition. Kevin Bradley Wright, Lisa Sparks, and H. Dan O'Hair.
© 2013 John Wiley & Sons, Inc. Published 2013 by John Wiley & Sons, Inc.

between providers and patients, including culturally inappropriate medical decision-making, increased anxiety, fear, and anger, and patient dissatisfaction with overall healthcare. Unfortunately, culture has historically been omitted from health communication studies (Dutta & Basu, 2011). However, this situation has changed in recent years as healthcare providers and health communication researcher have begun to recognize the pivotal role culture plays in health and healthcare. Further, there has been a surge in healthcare consumers' and providers' cultural competence, oral and written communication, and numeracy levels becoming increasingly important to achieve adequate health literacy for medical decision-making. The health literacy literature refers to cultural competence as one of the key indicators of being health literate (Kreps, Neuhauser, Sparks, & Villagran, 2008a; Kreps & Sparks, 2008). Kreps and Sparks (2008) define health literacy as involving one's literacy level, the structure and complexity of the material given, linguistic barriers, differing cultural contexts, and the efficacy of the method in which health messages are communicated. Their recent definition expands on Speros' conceptualization to include factors external to the consumers, such as information providers' communication competence. This inclusive definition thus conceives of health literacy as a mutual effort between health information providers and consumers. While there is a general lack of health literacy in many sectors of the population (Fagerlin *et al.*, 2007a), it is particularly disproportionate among certain demographic groups, showing that certain populations are marginalized (Sparks & Nussbaum, 2008).

In addition to the greater use of translators, many healthcare organizations are now implementing intercultural communication training programs. Cultural diversity has become more and more important in healthcare settings among providers and health campaign designers (Dutta, 2007). While healthcare settings have traditionally excluded women and minorities, healthcare provider diversity has increased in recent years. In addition, providers exhibit a great deal of professional diversity due to differences in training and expertise. In recent years, healthcare organizations have attempted to capitalize on the strength of diverse provider perspectives to help solve complex patient health issues through interdisciplinary healthcare teams.

This chapter will explore these issues and a variety of other communication concerns related to culture and diversity within health settings. Specifically, it will examine a variety of topics related to diversity and culture in healthcare, including patient diversity in the US healthcare system, cultural differences in concepts of health and medicine, the need to recognize cultural diversity in healthcare, alternative medicine, social implications of disease, spirituality and health, provider diversity, and interdisciplinary healthcare teams.

Patient Diversity and Issues with Healthcare

The US continues to become more culturally diverse as a nation. Over 55 million people speak a language other than English in the US (US Census Bureau, 2005). Traditionally, most patients in the US healthcare system have been white. However, in the last decade, the population of white Americans grew at about 3.5 percent while other racial and ethnic groups increased by over 43 percent (Ndiwane *et al.*, 2004). By 2030, the population of many minority groups in the US is expected to increase while the population of white Americans is expected to decrease by 10 percent. This presents a number of challenges to healthcare providers, who lack important knowledge about the groups and how to effectively communicate with them (Dutta & Basu, 2011). Currently, people of Latin American origin are the largest minority group in the US with a population of over 20 million, followed by people from various parts of Asia with numbers of over 10 million (US Census Bureau, 2005). In addition, various co-cultures within the US differ in terms of level of education, income, and housing status, all of which impact perceptions of health and access to healthcare services. There are many different problems related to patient diversity that affect quality healthcare and provider–patient communication. For example, many minority groups and recent immigrants often lack access to adequate healthcare, they often cannot afford these services, and/or they receive lower quality of healthcare from providers (Heisler, Rust, Patillo, & Dubois, 2005; Ku & Waidmann, 2003).

The National Cancer Institute (2006) defines health disparities as "differences in the incidence, prevalence, mortality, and burden of cancer and other adverse health conditions that exist among specific population groups in the United States." Healthcare disparities for immigrants include lack of knowledge about cancer care and research opportunities, and are driven in part by immigration status, cultural, and linguistic differences (Gany, Shah, & Changrani, 2006).

Vulnerable populations often have significant health literacy difficulties and are challenged by intercultural communication barriers to accessing and making sense of relevant health information (Kreps & Sparks, 2008; Sparks, in press). These consumers are often confused and misinformed about healthcare services, early detection guidelines, disease prevention practices, treatment strategies, and the correct use of prescription drugs, which can lead to serious errors and health problems (Kreps & Sparks, 2008).

Members of vulnerable immigrant populations who suffer significant health disparities are desperately in need of culturally relevant, accurate, and timely health information (Kreps, 2005; Kreps & Sparks, 2008). Many vulnerable immigrant consumers in the US are non-native English speakers and encounter serious language barriers and health literacy challenges that necessitate adaptive, culturally sensitive communication strategies to provide them with needed health information (Chew, Bradley, & Boyko, 2004; Hardin, 2005; Kreps, 2006b; Parker & Kreps, 2005).

Moreover, members of many ethnic groups mistrust the healthcare system for a variety of reasons, including historical injustices, such as the mistreatment of Native Americans and African Americans (Ferguson *et al.*, 1998) and the preponderance of Caucasian providers. A number of patients have trouble understanding the English language, and language barriers can lead to many problems such as misunderstandings between providers and patients, misdiagnoses, inappropriate treatments, and poor adherence to suggested treatments for medical problems (Hornberger, Itakura, & Wilson, 1997; Johnson, Roter, Powe, & Cooper, 2004; Rivadeneyra *et al.*, 2000). In addition to language barriers, many immigrants are unfamiliar with the US healthcare system. Given the complexities of managed care, referrals, medical terminology, and many other aspects of the healthcare system, even for people who grew up with it, you can easily understand how an immigrant might find healthcare in the US confusing and intimidating.

Cultural Differences in Concepts of Health and Medicine

Our understanding of the world and our experiences of illness and health are heavily influenced by our day-to-day communication with others. Some communication scholars have argued that people *create* reality through communication (Gergen, 1999; Pearce, 1995). This is not to say that physical reality is created through communication, but rather that our understanding of reality evolves from interaction with others and is based on and informed by previous interactions. In terms of health, when individuals discuss their conceptions of illness and health again and again, they learn about these concepts through repeated interaction. People who are socialized within a particular culture come to understand illness and health through repeated interactions with others. All cultures have beliefs about illness and health that are passed down from generation to generation (Galanti, 1991; Lupton, 1994).

Perspectives of health and illness in western society are largely dominated by the biomedical model of health, although this is slowly changing to reflect a balance with increases in patient centered care approaches (Sparks & Villagran, 2010). Biomedicine refers to medical practices and beliefs derived from the western scientific tradition, including germ theory, biology, biochemistry, and biophysics, and it is focused primarily on establishing physical causes for illness (Gillick, 1985; Sharf & Vanderford, 2003). However, the biomedical view of health is just one of many cultural conceptions of health around the world and within the US (Galanti, 1991; Spector, 1996). *Ethnomedical belief systems* are culturally unique beliefs and knowledge about health and disease (Witte, 1991). In addition, Airhihenbuwa and Obregon (2000) argue that communicating about health risks (such as the risk for HIV/AIDS) in ways that are based upon western cultural assumptions, such as privileging the individual over the group or culture as a whole and linear types of thinking (which have their base in the western scientific tradition), are often inadequate when communicating with people from certain regions and cultures, such as South America, Central America, the Caribbean, and Africa. Unfortunately, many providers lack adequate training in understanding the ethnomedical belief systems of their patients from other countries and co-cultures within the US. Ignorance or misunderstanding of these different belief systems can lead to a host of communication problems between providers and patients (O'Hair, O'Hair, Southward, & Krayer, 1987).

Another important issue to acknowledge is the ageism and racism that exist in the medical profession (Pecchioni *et al.*, 2008). For instance, when physicians do not provide older patients with information about clinical trials, even when they think they are acting in the patient's best interests, they are acting on assumptions that may be unfounded. In fact, the empirical evidence shows that older cancer patients fare well in clinical trials when compared with their younger counterparts. Older patients may well have physical differences from younger patients, but these differences should be established empirically rather than based on limited experience that may be filtered through negative attitudes toward aging (Pecchioni *et al.*, 2008).

Cultural differences in attributions of illness/health

Many cultures attribute illness to spiritual forces, and this is in direct conflict with the western biomedical model that attributes disease to microorganisms, such as viruses, or to lifestyle influences. For example, some cultures, such as the Hmong from Southeast Asia, often attribute disease to spiritual forces such as malevolent spirits or ghosts who bring ill health, or to the lack of protective spirits of ancestors (Johnson, 2002). Some cultural groups, such as Mexican immigrants, often exhibit strong cultural tendencies toward fatalism when it comes to health issues (Barron, Hunter, Mayo, & Willoughby, 2004), or the belief that health problems are meant to be or caused by God/supernatural forces. Individuals with fatalistic views of health often feel that they have no control over health problems, and they may perceive little personal ability or responsibility for the success or failure of health outcomes. Therefore, individuals from cultures that promote fatalistic views of health may have a more difficult time adhering to biomedical treatments suggested by healthcare providers or making significant lifestyle changes that influence health risks (Lupton, 1994).

The first important step is to acknowledge and be aware of the fact that all patients are not the same. As Pecchioni *et al.* (2008) recognized, this acknowledgement should extend not just to the physical realm. Most healthcare professionals continue to operate based on the biomedical model of health and illness, in which the body is treated as a machine in isolation from its environment. The biopsychosocial model, however, provides us with a broader lens for examining patient responses to illness because it acknowledges that individuals operate within a web of individual and social roles. Conrad (1987) proposed the use of *disease* to refer to the physical ailment and *illness* to refer to the social elements of the disease. Thus, an individual is not his or her diagnosis, but makes sense of that diagnosis within a web of cultural expectations. In this perspective, then, healthcare personnel must identify each patient's attitudes toward the causes of illness and treatment options, definitions of quality of life, availability of social support, and the like. The body is no longer a machine, but a living organism in communication with its physical and cultural environments (Pecchioni *et al.*, 2008).

Medical procedures that are commonplace in western culture, such as surgery, blood transfusions, and blood tests, are not part of some cultures around the world (such as the Hmong), and these often provoke fear and mistrust among immigrants (Helman, 2000; Smith, 1997). In terms of medical treatment options, some cultures value biomedical solutions to health problems, while others prefer more natural remedies for health problems or spiritual solutions to them. For example, researchers have found that a large number of immigrants from Mexico use herbal medications, massage, and relaxation techniques, which are often suggested by family members or *curanderos*, traditional Mexican folk healers (Hunt, Hamdi, & Arana, 2000; Keegan, 1996).

Acculturation

Immigrants often change their lifestyle in ways that can affect their health when they come to the US. For example, mainstream US culture often promotes sedentary life-styles, high fat/high food consumption, smoking, and a variety of other unhealthy behaviors. However, the cultures that many immigrants come from do not promote these lifestyles and diets, and taking on new diets and lifestyles can lead to a variety of health problems. For example, hypertension, diabetes, and substance abuse are becoming more common among immigrants from Southeast Asia and other countries who adopt US mainstream diets and lifestyles (Aldrich & Variyam, 2000; Cobas *et al.*, 1996; Popkin & Udry, 1998). Immigrants may find their ability to continue their tra-ditional diet somewhat difficult to maintain, since some of the traditional foods to which they are accustomed may not be available in the US, and children can become "Americanized," so that they take on unhealthy lifestyle habits. Moreover, because immigrants from these countries often attribute disease to spiritual forces, they may not understand the connection between lifestyle behaviors and poor health (Helman, 2000; Johnson, 2002).

Informed consent

In the US patients have the legal right to be fully informed about their health condi-tion, and many Americans perceive this law as ethical and would insist on having full knowledge of their health situation, especially if they were at risk of dying from cancer or high blood pressure. However, beliefs surrounding the issue of informed consent vary by culture, and informed consent should be delivered to people in cultur-ally sensitive ways (Carrese & Rhodes, 1995; Kakai, 2002). For example, the Hmong involve extended family in important decisions, including medical decisions if a family member becomes ill (Johnson, 2002). Moreover, Hmong culture is patriarchal, and decision-making is typically left to the oldest member of the family and male family members, such as a husband or father (Johnson, 2002).

Providers in the US often pressure family members to make decisions about treat-ment options relatively quickly, but this can lead to problems for a Hmong patient if an older family member (such as a grandfather) or a high-status male family member is not nearby, and other family members may be hesitant to make a decision about healthcare treatment for a family member without consulting this person (Johnson, 2002). In Japan, providers historically concealed terminal cancer diagnoses from patients (Kakai, 2002). Although Japanese physicians have adopted a policy of disclos-ing terminal cancer diagnoses to patients in recent years, and the majority of Japanese say that they prefer to be informed by their physician if they have cancer (Long, 2000), many individuals still prefer indirect or ambiguous communication from a physician if a family member is diagnosed with cancer (Kakai, 2002). This indirect communica-tion about a cancer diagnosis allows family members to be more hopeful about a loved one's recovery as opposed to viewing the diagnosis as a "death sentence." Complicat-ing the issue of informed consent further, medical interpreters are required to inter-pret information for providers and patients without omitting or changing anything

(Dysart-Gale, 2005). This can make it difficult to convey information to patients in a culturally sensitive way, especially if the physician or other provider who is attempting to convey information to the patient through an interpreter has little understanding of the health beliefs of the patient.

Cultural differences of people born in the US

Cultural differences in health beliefs and influences on health behaviors do not just affect immigrants in the US. There are many different co-cultures among people who were born in the US, and these co-cultures can influence health beliefs and health behaviors in a variety of ways. Co-cultural differences based on ethnicity, race, or nationality may be even more pervasive in healthcare than ageism because differences extend across the spectrum of care. Ethnic minorities have less access to healthcare, report lower levels of trust in healthcare professionals, delay going to doctors for tests, and are less likely to be offered high-quality care options with cutting-edge technology. This broad spectrum of differences in access make many healthcare experiences quite different depending on one's co-cultural group, at least in the US (Pecchioni *et al.* (2008). For example, in the southern US, many people eat foods that are high in calories and fat, such as barbeque, fried okra, and sweet tea (iced tea with large quantities of sugar), because this is often part of traditional Southern cuisine. However, these types of food can have a tremendous impact on health risks, such as obesity, diabetes, high blood pressure, and heart disease, especially if they are not consumed in moderation. Cultural issues implicate certain age groups as well.

The amount of information that the patient is provided also impacts the decision-making (Sparks, 2008). Older patients have been found to ask their physicians fewer questions (Beisecker & Beisecker, 1990) and to receive less information from the physician than younger patients (Street, 1991). patients have a tendency to prefer a communication style that contains less detail and is jargon free, whereas younger and middle aged adults expect more medical information in their messages (O'Hair, Behnke, & King, 1983), and have a number of unique age-related barriers (Sparks & Nussbaum, 2008).

As Sparks & Nussbaum state, the influx of people from varying countries and cultures has also increased demands for healthcare providers who are culturally sensitive to the specific needs of older men and women facing cancer diagnoses. Even in other cultures that practice western medicine, there are differing views as to how much to disclose to patients about their conditions. In the US, we proceed from the assumption and have enshrined as law, the idea that patients have a right to full disclosure of their medical condition. However, Hippocrates was among the first to realize that the mind had an effect on the body. As a result, some medical communities in other cultures consider it good medical practice to lie to patients about their true condition as well as enlist the complicity of the family to perpetuate the prevarication (Sparks & Nussbaum, 2008). All of our communication research points to stereotyping, memory issues, language issues, and intergenerational barriers that present a host of communication problems for older adults within the best of circumstances (Nussbaum, Baringer, & Kundrat, 2003; Sparks, 2003a; Sparks & Nussbaum, 2008), which can ultimately hinder satisfactory healthcare.

Recognizing Cultural Diversity in Health Beliefs

As we have seen, healthcare organizations have witnessed a number of demographic shifts among patients in recent years (Dysart-Gale, 2005). As a result, healthcare workers must learn to communicate effectively with people from other cultures in order to provide competent and quality healthcare (Ulrey & Amason, 2001). In order for healthcare providers to be culturally sensitive, they must have knowledge about the varying cultural beliefs of their patient population, understand and respect the cultural beliefs, attitudes, and values of patients, and be willing to use cultural knowledge when interacting with patients and making decisions about treatment options (Brislin, 1993; Ulrey & Amason, 2001). Providers need to be aware of cultural differences in beliefs about the nature of illness and health as well as the relationship between cultural practices and health.

Learning to communicate more effectively with patients from diverse cultural backgrounds has a number of implications for business-related outcomes within healthcare settings (Voelker, 1995). For instance, as competition between healthcare organizations increases, individual organizations must find ways to attract new patient populations and keep patients satisfied so that they will not go to a competitor to obtain health-related services. Conversely, culturally insensitive or inappropriate communication behaviors on the part of providers can lead to a host of problems, including patient dissatisfaction with healthcare and malpractice lawsuits (Kreps & Thornton, 1992).

A continuing problem in healthcare settings is the assumption that all stakeholders, but particularly patients, share the same perceptions as the host culture. Several studies have offered a view of how Americans perceive themselves and are perceived by others. One such study, conducted by Protocol International, suggested Americans see themselves as efficient, direct, competitive, action-oriented, outgoing, open, and self-reliant. Conversely, people from other cultures saw Americans as abrupt, confrontational, materialistic, pushy, insincere, transparent, and self-centered. Central to competent intercultural communication is having cultural partners who understand the perspective held by each person (Leong & Schneller, 1997). Understanding how healthcare stakeholders view one another is a critical challenge, one that can be overcome with some effort. For instance, American student nurses found that as they learned more about Russian culture, their stereotypes broke down and it was easier for them to understand key cultural aspects that could lead to better healthcare (Heuer, Bengiamin, & Downey, 2001).

Culture helps us to make coherent sense of our mortality, suffering, and death (Greenberg, Solomon, & Pyszczynski, 1997; Lynn, 2000). Such sensitive issues are influenced not just by culture and co-cultural groups, but also by religious beliefs and personal experiences (Lynn, 2000). Ethnic minorities in the US prefer a variety of preferences influenced by their cultural beliefs (Pecchioni *et al.*, 2008). African Americans are reluctant to share their treatment preferences with healthcare providers, but are more likely to prefer life-sustaining treatments than other groups and are less likely to use hospice care or agree to organ donation (Mouton, 2000). Hispanics are also less likely to agree to organ donation or autopsies (Talamantes, Gomez, & Braun, 2000). For both groups, the main reason for not selecting organ donation is the desire to present a whole body to God (Mouton, 2000; Talamantes, Gomez, & Braun, 2000). Further, both Hispanics and African Americans are more inclined to request life-prolonging treatments (Talamantes, Gomez, & Braun, 2000). As we will discuss in more detail later in this chapter, both groups express a desire to allow time for God to work miracles. Among Asian Americans and Pacific Islanders, considerable variability reflects the diversity of their countries of origin, their immigration histories, rural versus urban backgrounds, and education level (Yeo & Hikoyeda, 2000). However, as Asian groups often take a more collectivistic approach to life, issues surrounding illness and death are managed primarily within their co-cultural groups where there is a preference for the family to be involved in all decision-making (Yeo & Hikoyeda, 2000). In general, Asian Americans and Pacific Islanders are more likely to want life support because longevity is more important than quality of life (Pecchioni *et al.*, 2008). In order to provide a whole body to their ancestors, they prefer to avoid autopsy and organ donation (Yeo & Hikoyeda, 2000). Among Native Americans and Alaska Natives, who represent a diverse group with more than 300 federally registered tribes, death is seen as a natural part of the circular pattern of life, so they tend to have more positive attitudes toward dying than most other groups (Pecchioni *et al.*, 2008; Van Winkle, 2000).

Barriers to providing culturally sensitive healthcare

Unfortunately, many barriers to providing culturally sensitive healthcare exist within the current US healthcare system. Many providers do not have adequate knowledge of how changes in lifestyle from one culture to another can affect the health of immigrants. The majority of hospitals and healthcare facilities in the US today still do not have an adequate number of translators or personnel who understand the ethnomedical belief systems of patients (Schott & Henley, 1996).

As Collins, Villagran, and Sparks (2008) point out, structural and cultural barriers to care are especially problematic for immigrant populations who encounter variance in cultural norms and healthcare delivery systems in their new country. Structural barriers include material phenomena that prevent access to healthcare due to problems such as poverty, lack of transportation, illiteracy, and language difference. Health belief barriers are socially constructed ideas about health and wellness that can either inhibit or enable access to healthcare (Collins, Villagran, & Sparks, 2008).

In addition, as Collins, Villagran, and Sparks (2008) point out, efforts aimed at overcoming barriers to cancer care among Mexican immigrants must address structural and cultural issues that deter patients from seeking treatment. Health literacy efforts to increase prevention can benefit from the cultural notion of *bienestar* (good God theory) by building on Mexicans' beliefs about prevention and linking together positive behaviors such as screening, diet, and exercise habits. Emphasizing the balance of integrating healthier foods into the traditional Mexican diet could also help focus prevention measures on cultural ideals of well-being. Health education efforts must also explicitly distinguish between prevention efforts and actual causes of cancer. Such education efforts can enhance the residents' agency by reducing irrational fears about causing cancer through a toothache or a fight (Collins, Villagran, & Sparks, 2008).

Alternative Medicine

Alternative medicines, such as more holistic forms of medicine, have had a long history around the world and in the US, and many of the practices that are known as western mainstream or orthodox medicine are relatively recent innovations compared to the use of herbal remedies, acupuncture, osteopathy, chiropractics, yoga, massage, guided imagery, and therapeutic touch. Some studies estimate that about 42 percent of the US population, or around 83 million people, have used some form of alternative medicine or holistic therapy, spending an estimated $27 billion on such therapies (Barnes, Bloom, & Nahin, 2008; Eisenberg *et al.*, 1998). Studies also suggest that the majority of individuals who use alternative forms of medicine do not mention it to their physicians and other healthcare providers (Dunn & Perry, 1997). Despite the prevalence and use of alternative forms of medicine, many are hesitant to talk about their use of alternative medicine with providers because of the dominance of mainstream biomedical approaches to health in our culture (Goldner, 1998). US healthcare providers are aware of the growth in popularity of alternative medicines among patients, and there is greater interest among providers in talking with patients about the pros and cons of such approaches (Udani, 1998). For instance, there is concern among many physicians over the possible interaction effects that can occur when a patient is simultaneously using prescription medications and over-the-counter treatments (such as herbal remedies) for the same health problem.

As we saw in Chapter 1, there is a fundamental tension between the biomedical model of health and psychosocial approaches, a tension that includes different perceptions about the efficacy of mainstream medical approaches as opposed to alternative approaches to treating disease and enhancing health. This tension can be seen in the history of medicine within the US. For example, advances in the natural sciences and medical technology during the eighteenth and nineteenth centuries led physicians to begin to distinguish biomedical approaches to medicine from alternative forms of medicine (Schreiber, in press). For example, during this time, herbal remedies were popular treatments for a variety of illnesses, although their efficacy is difficult to document since people did not usually keep records of successes and failures. However, also during this time, there were a variety of traveling "medicine shows" that typically used performers to persuade audiences to purchase somewhat dubious remedies for their ailments (which often contained mostly alcohol).

To distance themselves from what they perceived as questionable approaches to medicine, and to set themselves apart from other types of medical practitioners, biomedical practitioners began to form societies such as the American Medical Association and write medical books that detailed biomedical approaches. However, the language they used to make these distinctions often privileged the biomedical approach or talked about more holistic approaches to medicine in derogatory and negative terms, for example describing them as unprofessional, lacking standards, or erratic (Schreiber, in press). As a result, many holistic approaches to health that have value in enhancing physical, psychological, and spiritual health came to be seen as unorthodox, suspicious, and ineffective. Today, many people dismiss homeopathic medicine and other approaches as quackery, and alternative medicine often carries a negative social stigma. Even terms like "alternative medicine," "complementary medicine," and "integrative medicine" are not without problems. The word "alternative" carries the connotation of being out of the ordinary, while "complementary" and "integrative" imply that these approaches should be used in conjunction with other, biomedical approaches rather than on their own. Some scholars have argued that these terms help to privilege the biomedical approach to medicine (Schreiber, in press; Wardwell, 1994).

However, holistic medicines may offer some advantages and disadvantages over biomedicine, although what is perceived as an advantage or disadvantage by the patient largely depends on his or her values regarding health, illness, and quality of life (Ho & Robles, 2011). For example, biomedical approaches to a disease such as cancer typically involve the use of chemotherapy, radiology, and surgery. While these procedures offer a number of advantages in terms of destroying cancerous cells and tissue, they also have a great number of side effects. For instance, people who are on chemotherapy often experience fatigue, nausea, hair loss, and a variety of other problems. While one of the authors was conducting research at a cancer center in Memphis, Tennessee, one patient described chemotherapy as like "using an atomic bomb to kill a terrorist hiding in New York City."

In other words, chemotherapy may help to kill the cancer, but it also destroys a lot of healthy tissue in the process. Holistic approaches may be an attractive alternative to treating disease for individuals facing chemotherapy and other biomedical approaches in that they offer a less invasive type of treatment or one that does not negatively impact their quality of life in a significant way. It should be pointed out that many traditional herbal remedies used for centuries have been adapted by pharmaceutical researchers. For instance, the herb *Periwinkle vinca rosea* contains insulin that can be used in the treatment of diabetes, and *Rauwolfia serpentine* is an herb that contains respirine, which is commonly used as a tranquilizer by biomedical practitioners (Airhihenbuwa, 1995).

However, while pharmaceutical companies often use natural ingredients when developing medications, they also frequently develop synthetic versions of chemicals found in nature as well as ways to make these chemicals more concentrated. In addition, because many holistic approaches do not treat disease in an aggressive manner, individuals who are given a good prognosis by their physician for overcoming a disease may consider traditional biomedical treatments along with complementary holistic therapies. Other individuals who are facing a terminal illness and who have been told they may have a relatively short survival time may choose to forgo aggressive biomedical treatments and use holistic approaches to allow for some treatment of symptoms without threatening their overall quality of life.

Spirituality, Culture, and Health

Religion and spirituality are important influences on health beliefs and behaviors, and many health-related practices observed in cultures around the world and within the US are rooted in religious and spiritual traditions. Religion can be conceptualized as "an organized system of beliefs, practices, rituals, and symbols," and spirituality as "one's transcendent relationship to some form of higher power" (Thoreson, 1998, p. 415). Egbert, Sparks, Kreps, and du Pré (2008) state that although there is no general agreement regarding how the terms *religiosity* and *spirituality* should be defined, scholars largely agree that the terms represent separate, although overlapping, concepts (Koenig, McCullough, & Larson, 2001; Paloutzian & Kirkpatrick, 1995; Parrott, 2004; Thoresen & Harris, 2002). Religion and spirituality have had a profound influence on views of health and illness in many cultures, and they have a number of implications for health communication, although relatively few health communication scholars have examined the impact of religious and spiritual influences on health (Parrott, 2004).

Historically, religiosity has received more scholarly attention than spirituality, especially in relation to health outcomes (Parrott, 2004), however, spirituality is often viewed as a more inclusive term and therefore preferred by many scholars (see e.g. Egbert *et al.*, 2008). In 1967, a classic work by Allport and Ross differentiated between *intrinsic* (living according to one's religious beliefs because one truly believes in them) and *extrinsic* religiosity (using one's religion to meet needs such as social support, tradition, or status). This differentiation has been maintained by researchers for the past 40 years and has shaped many scholars' understanding of how religion and religiosity are defined (Egbert *et al.*, 2008). For instance, Koenig, McCullough, and Larson (2001) define religion as "an organized system of beliefs, practices, rituals, and symbols designed (a) to facilitate closeness to the sacred or transcendent (God, higher power, or ultimate truth/reality) and (b) to foster an understanding of one's relationship and responsibility to others in living together in a community" (p. 18).

Spirituality, on the other hand, is a more expansive conceptualization of divinity. One may be a spiritual person, but not necessarily religious; likewise, being a member of a religion does not by definition make one spiritual. Whereas religion is associated with terms such as *formal*, *behavior-oriented*, and *doctrine-based*, spirituality is better characterized using words such as *individualistic*, *inward-directed*, and *not doctrine-oriented* (Koenig, McCullough, & Larson, 2001). Although both are concepts worthy of discussions related to cancer and aging, the central concept we highlight in this chapter is found in the term *spirituality*, meaning an individual's search for meaning in life (e.g. Dreyer, 1994; National Cancer Institute, 2005). Egbert *et al.* (2008) embrace Koenig, McCullough, and Larson's (2001) definition:

> Spirituality is the personal quest for understanding answers to ultimate questions about life, about meaning, and about relationships to the sacred or transcendent, which may (or may not) lead to or arise from the development of religious rituals and the formation of community. (p. 18)

Spirituality has been identified as a key variable that influences an individual's response to a cancer diagnosis and sense of identity as expressed in religious ritual practice (Haynes & Smedley, 1999; Lackey, Gates, & Brown, 2001). This is also the case for women diagnosed with a variety of diseases other than cancer. Several studies of illness and wellness in different segments of the larger African American community claim that many believe their degree of health or presence of illness to be God's will (Abrums, 2000). Hispanic cultural beliefs often align with this notion and often have a low desire for information about terminal illnesses, which is referred to in Spanish as "fatalismo" (see e.g. Collins, Villagran, & Sparks, 2008). Further, Collins, Villagran, and Sparks' (2008) Hispanic study participants reported avoidance of information about cancer as a means of control and as a demonstration in the power of God. Other members of this population may integrate the prayer process with their sense of *familismo*, known as the importance of family, or use it as a way to manage information needs. The strategies by which the participants negotiate the tensions between *bienestar* and "good God theory" illuminate perceptions about personal control in preventing, treating, and surviving cancer (Collins, Villagran, & Sparks, 2008).

Religious and spiritual beliefs can influence both generalized views about health and illness and specific behaviors. For example, fatalistic views about health among Mexican immigrants can be traced to the Roman Catholic religious worldview. According to Barron *et al.* (2004), "within this religious worldview, God controls all, and faith, not medical management, is essential to recovery from illness" (p. 333). Similarly, many Christian Scientists in the US avoid taking medications or seeing the doctor when they become ill. Instead, these individuals rely on their faith and prayer to help them through their health problems. In Japan, followers of Shintoism believe that the *kegare* is a source of spiritual contamination associated with events like death and terminal illness (Kakai, 2002). People in Japan who have these beliefs often avoid people who are terminally ill and their loved ones because they fear spiritual contamination. This belief leads many Japanese families to avoid publicly talking about their own or a family member's terminal illness. Moreover, Stephenson *et al.* (2008) found that individuals from Korea, Japan, and some groups within the US were reluctant to register as organ donors due to spiritual beliefs.

Religion and psychological/physical health outcomes

Religious beliefs and practices are often associated with social and psychological mechanisms that can enhance health and well-being, including improved outcomes for health conditions, better health behaviors, and reduced mortality rates (Dessio *et al.*, 2004; Levin, 1996; Robinson & Nussbaum, 2004). For example, one study found that African American women who used religion/spirituality for health reasons were more likely to have used complementary/alternative medicine and to have seen a medical doctor compared to those who did not (Dessio *et al.*, 2004). Many religions encourage healthy lifestyles, such as avoiding smoking, excessive alcohol consumption, and promiscuous sex. Regular church attendance has been linked to increased morale, less depression, reduced likelihood of being hospitalized, and reduced mortality rates (Koenig & Larson, 1998; Koenig *et al.*, 1999). Many providers are not prepared to discuss religious topics with patients, largely due to the emphasis on biomedical approaches to health during medical school, but medical schools are increasingly including courses on the influence of religion on health in the curriculum (Robinson & Nussbaum, 2004).

Church and spiritually based health interventions

A variety of populations have benefited from church and spiritually based health interventions (Holt, Lee, & Wright, 2008), particularly many groups that have been traditionally hard-to-reach by conventional mass media health interventions, such as African Americans and other racial and ethnic minorities. The church is often central to African American communities, and African American churches have served as a pivotal starting point for community-based health interventions, including those targeting hypertension, weight loss, breast cancer screening, smoking, and diet and weight loss (see Smith, 1999; Smith, Merritt, & Patel, 1997; Yanek *et al.*, 2001). Church and spiritually based health interventions have been successful with other minority groups as well, including Hispanic and Asian populations (Duan, Fox, Derose, & Carson, 2000; Kim & Sarna, 2004). Health communication researchers should continue to examine the influence of churches and spiritually based organizations on helping people change and maintain health behaviors within a variety of communities given the importance of these organizations in people's lives.

Religion and social support

Churches and other spiritually based organizations are also important sources of social support, which has been linked to a variety of positive psychological and physical health outcomes (see Chapter 4). Church membership provides opportunities to expand one's social network and to give and receive different types of social support. In our increasingly mobile society, religious organizations provide opportunities for people to develop and expand their social network when they are new to a community. According to Robinson and Nussbaum (2004), church membership can "provide a sense of belonging, fellowship, and cohesiveness, as well as provide instrumental and emotional resources, such as monitoring others for illness and providing encouragement, hope, and aid" (p. 65). Church membership can also help reduce a person's sense of social isolation, and this has important implications for psychological well-being (Levin, 2001). Religion also encourages behaviors that are related to social support, such as staying married and spending time with family (Levin, 1996). Hospitals and other health facilities in the US have had a long tradition of hiring clergy or using volunteers to provide patients with opportunities for spiritual guidance and support during times of illness. Finally, religious beliefs and spiritual talk are often extremely comforting to people who are dying from a terminal illness or who have experienced the death of a loved one (Keeley, 2004), and church social network members can provide instrumental help to people who are caregivers for a loved one facing an illness.

Recent studies suggest that culturally appropriate healthcare within the African American community is keyed to that community's strong base in spirituality, is combined with social support that accepts and extends that spirituality, and establishes opportunity for people to tell stories about their experience, recounting it in the ways they prefer (Lackey, Gates, & Brown, 2001; Newlin, Knafl, & Melkus, 2002; Taylor, 2001). Culturally appropriate care includes the ability to listen to communication patterns and nuances in order to identify cues that suggest the need for practitioner intervention. For example, McTavish, Pingree, Hawkings, and Gustafson (2003) reviewed differences in how African American and Caucasian women use online information and discussion groups, commenting that "for women of color, the overwhelming topic of conversation is treatment, while it is a distant second for Caucasian women" (McTavish *et al.*, 2003, p. 110). Wilmoth, Davis, and Sanders (2008) explored the narrative styles used in face-to-face focus groups by African American women with breast cancer, looking particularly at how their narratives signal linkages between spirituality and self-efficacy in their discussions of living with the disease, and then provide suggestions for what practitioners need to listen for when caring for these women. The authors found that African American women diagnosed with breast cancer draw strength from their belief in God and include references to God when describing their symptoms. It is not uncommon for these women to delay seeking diagnosis and treatment until they have "given it over" to God. As such, healthcare providers need to understand this and encourage them to continue to draw strength from their spirituality during treatment rather than chastise them for what may be perceived as needless delay in seeking treatment. Offering opportunities for prayer and including references to their faith during treatment are ways providers can offer culturally sensitive care. These narratives or stories, often occur in conjunction with references to spirituality (Wilmoth, Davis, & Sanders, 2008). Being award of these cultural, spiritual, and religious beliefs can be a very important component impacting healthcare delivery, and receptivity to treatment and adherence issues that may arise.

Many support groups are modeled after Alcoholics Anonymous, an organization influenced by religious and spiritual thought (Jenson, 2000). Alcoholics Anonymous was formed in 1935 by a New York stockbroker named Bill Wilson after what he referred to as a spiritual awakening resulting from his association with the Oxford Group, a Christian-based religious organization whose members believed in temperance and that belief in God was necessary to achieve sobriety.

People who join Alcoholics Anonymous learn about the Twelve Steps to recovery from alcoholism. Many of the Twelve Steps have their roots in the teachings of the Oxford Group (Kassel & Wagner, 1993; Wright, 1997). The Twelve Steps stress the importance of relying on a Higher Power to help recovering alcoholics get through situations that may tempt them to drink and to help them manage problems in their daily lives. According to the Alcoholics Anonymous worldview, recovering alcoholics are powerless over the temptation to drink, and a Higher Power is needed to help them through difficult situations. The Alcoholics Anonymous literature stresses the idea that members can choose their own conception of a Higher Power (this idea is also reinforced during Alcoholics Anonymous group meetings), and this spiritual pluralism allows people from different religious backgrounds to put aside individual differences in conceptions of a Higher Power in order to come together for the common purpose of recovery (Jenson, 2000; Wright, 1997).

Social Implications of Illness

Disease and illness not only affect us physically, they also have a variety of social implications. As we have seen, the ways in which we perceive health and illness are influenced by many different social forces, including the mass media, religion, institutions of higher learning, family and peers, and larger cultural perspectives of social life. These influences on our perceptions of health and illness, in turn, influence the way we communicate with others about health, and how we behave when we encounter health issues (O'Hair & Sparks, 2007; Palmer, Kagee, Coyne, & DeMichele, 2004). In addition, health-related behaviors, such as diet, exercise, smoking, and alcohol consumption, and sexual behaviors take place in social settings and are reinforced through social interactions. This section examines negative perceptions of illness, then looks at ways in which people who are afflicted with health problems socially construct more positive ways to view them.

Stigma and disease

Some health problems are viewed negatively by society. Many diseases carry a social *stigma*, or a mark of shame, disgrace, or taboo that is attached to people and their problem (Goffman, 1963; O'Hair *et al.*, 2003). In terms of health problems, we often view certain diseases and conditions negatively (and frequently the people who have them) because of the ways that society has influenced our perceptions. Cultural beliefs about the nature of diseases and stereotypes about the individuals who have them both influence the stigma of disease, and stigmatized individuals often face prejudice and discrimination as a result of their illness (Kreps & Thornton, 1992). Stigmatized individuals frequently feel devalued by others and often withdraw from people or attempt to conceal their health condition in an effort to cope with the negative social implications of being stigmatized (Smith & Hipper, 2010). However, research has shown that increased education about stigmatized diseases and positively framed exposure to people living with these conditions tends to reduce stigma and can lead to more positive perceptions of stigmatized (Estroff, Penn, & Toporek, 2004). Furthermore, consumers with serious and chronic medical conditions, as well as individuals who confront physical and mental disabilities, are often particularly vulnerable to health risks and have unique communication needs that have to be adequately addressed to provide them with the relevant health information they need for their particular healthcare needs (Kreps & Sparks, 2008).

While all health conditions have social implications, in the following sections we examine the stigma and related social issues surrounding four health concerns: HIV/AIDS, cancer, alcoholism, and mental illness.

HIV/AIDS According to Schwalbe and Staples (1992), US culture influences our perceptions of HIV/AIDS and our behaviors surrounding the disease in a variety of ways, including an obsession with sexuality (promoted by advertising and the media in general), a culture of homophobia, reluctance to openly discuss sexual matters, limited technical knowledge of HIV/AIDS among laypersons, and a tension between secular, scientific views and religious (often punishment-based) perceptions of HIV. In an effort to sell products, advertisers, filmmakers, and television producers regularly use sexual content to attract our attention. Unfortunately, this has had the secondary effect of helping us to become a culture that is preoccupied with sex. In an effort to gain the social rewards of being sexually active, many people engage in sexual behaviors without considering many of the dangerous consequences.

Because of the cultural norm to not openly discuss sexual matters, many couples are reluctant to talk about condom usage, previous sexual partners, or other highly relevant information about sexual history that may influence risk for HIV/AIDS. Moreover, there is often confusion among laypersons about the ways in which the HIV virus can be transmitted, the course of the disease, and ways that it can be treated. Some religious groups still see HIV/AIDS as a curse from God as opposed to the scientific view that HIV is caused by a retrovirus. In addition, because HIV/AIDS was first seen among gay men and intravenous drug users, and these groups have traditionally been perceived by many in mainstream America as unnatural or undesirable, HIV/AIDS carries a social stigma with it (Adelman & Frey, 1997; Greene, 2000).

Hiding the fact that one has HIV/AIDS due to the social stigma attached to it has been found to create a considerable amount for people living with the disease (Brown, Macintyre, & Trujillo, 2003; Greene, 2000; Thomas, 2006). In some cases, this stress may exacerbate the symptoms of the disease or lead to situations where people do not take their medications in social settings, such as around family members or at work (many HIV/AIDS anti-viral medications require strict adherence to taking them at certain time intervals). Although HIV/AIDS has been part of US culture for nearly three decades, the negative social stigma attached to it still leads to many problems for those individuals living with the disease.

Cancer Though not to the same degree as HIV/AIDS, cancer has also been found to carry a social stigma. Cancer is one of the most significant health challenges facing our society, being the second leading cause of death in the US (American Cancer Society, 2001). Over 9 million US citizens are currently living with some form of cancer, with about 1 million new cases diagnosed each year. Spiegel, Bloom, and Yalom (1981) contend that individuals within the social network of a person with cancer "often in subtle but unmistakable ways distance themselves from the dying" (p. 528) as a result of societally induced fears about disease and death. Ironically, members of social networks sometimes withdraw from us during times when we need them the most. For example, Samarel and Fawcett (1992) reported that a diagnosis of cancer often leads to difficulty maintaining the previous quality of interpersonal relationships and creates dissatisfaction with traditional sources of support (O'Hair & Sparks, 2008). There are many reasons for the stigma associated with cancer. One reason is that cancer is often associated with death and dying, both of which are difficult subjects for people to talk about in our culture. Few individuals like to bring up the subject, even when the person with cancer would like to talk about it (O'Hair *et al.*, 2003; Wortman & Dunkel-Schetter, 1979). The stigma attached to someone dying of a disease like cancer can lead to social isolation, which has been linked to both depression and mortality among cancer patients (Reynolds & Kaplan, 1990).

The nature and management of cancer for specialized populations, such as older adults, depends upon not only biological processes, but also psychological and social processes (Cohen, 1994). Communication not only plays a crucial role in assessing a patient's mental and physical health, but, additionally, after they are diagnosed with an illness such as cancer, their communicative relationships seem to influence how they will get well (Nussbaum, Pecchioni, Robinson, & Thompson, 2000; Pecchioni, Ota, & Sparks, 2004; O'Hair, Kreps, & Sparks, 2007; Sparks, 2007). Due to the complexities of the healthcare provider–older adult patient relationship, barriers that older adults and their partners and caregivers face in conversation and some implications of such barriers must be better understood as well as the connection to the ways in which older adults adapt to deficits acquired across the life span (Sparks, 2007).

Our research has suggested that there is a need for a paradigm shift among patients and practitioners in the cancer communication context. Patients who find themselves at the mercy of a complex and overwhelming delivery and recovery system often adopt an acquiescence profile in managing their cancer care (O'Hair, Kreps, & Sparks, 2007). Instead, we must find ways to promote a more proactive or "agency" approach to cancer care (O'Hair & Sparks, 2008; O'Hair *et al.*, 2003; O'Hair, Scannell, & Thompson, 2005). Agency is a strategy that promotes emotional and informational management processes that facilitate uncertainty management. Once patients manage their uncertainty, they position themselves to realize self-empowerment and to make decisions that correspond to their goals. Some patients come to terms with their terminal illness and make decisions that make them feel more comfortable and empowered (palliative care). Others exert agency by insisting on enrollment on the latest clinical trial that offers hope for a cure. The key to agency is being in control of information and emotions in order to make an informed and empowered decision. Health communication stands as the most obvious option for putting forth *patient agency*.

Alcoholism The disease model of alcoholism (Jellinek, 1952), which has been adopted by the medical profession, is a relatively new idea. Prior to the conceptualization of alcohol problems as a disease, they were seen primarily as a moral issue and were most often associated with individuals who were stigmatized as having a "low character" (Lender & Martin, 1987). When "normal" drinkers encounter individuals who cannot control their drinking behavior or who behave irresponsibly while drinking, they often view this type of behavior as abnormal, despite the fact that many people who experience alcohol problems have a physical dependence on alcohol coupled with a psychological craving that makes consumption difficult to control (Jellinek, 1952). Problem drinkers may be seen by "normal" drinkers as people who should be able to control their drinking, despite the fact that once an alcohol-dependent individual takes a drink, he or she may have little control over behaviors. When the body is deprived of alcohol, the alcohol-dependent person typically experiences intense cravings for drink, even when they may know that they won't be able to stop once this first drink is consumed (Jellinek, 1952).

Mental illness Over 44 million Americans suffer from a diagnosable mental disorder. The most common types of mental illness include major depression, bipolar disorder, schizophrenia, and obsessive–compulsive disorder (Regier *et al.*, 1993). In addition, eating disorders such as anorexia nervosa, bulimia nervosa, and binge-eating disorder are often classified as types of mental illness. Mental illness carries a social stigma for a variety of reasons (Corrigan, 2000). The mass media often portray mental illness in negative ways, such as showing people who are mentally ill as dangerous or out of control, despite the fact that these types of incidents are very rare among mentally ill individuals. In addition, there are a number of misconceptions about mental illness in our society, especially because for many Americans their primary exposure to mental illness is through the entertainment media (Link & Phelan, 1999). Negative words such as "loony," "psycho," and "crazy" are commonly used to describe mentally ill individuals in the mass media and are a common part of our society's vernacular. Not surprisingly, these negative perceptions of mental illness can cause a variety of social problems for mentally ill people, who are often feared or shunned when others discover they are dealing with a mental illness.

Although mental health is a biological process, the social stigma of mental illness often creates multiple challenges to patients' social identities (see e.g. Sparks & Villagran, 2010). Mental health has unique characteristics that other areas of healthcare do not have. Unlike other biological health concerns such as cancer, diabetes, or arthritis, mental health is often an invisible illness. For instance, mental health can start as a very subtle invisible illness that can be misdiagnosed for months, years, or in many cases, decades before it is detected as the biological issue affecting a patient's interactions, relationships, and overall behaviors.

The links among social identity, communication, and mental illness are numerous. First, although mental illness is a biological process the expression of it occurs through communication. Patients do not often self-diagnose mental illness as they would if they felt a lump in their breast. It is most often through interactions with others that mental illness becomes apparent to the patient and/or their family and friends. Second, unlike AIDS or cancer, mental illnesses cannot be diagnosed with a brain scan or a blood test. Instead, doctors mostly draw on their perceptions of verbal and nonverbal cues to determine to what extent a patient is healthy or sick. Third, therapeutic approaches to the treatment of mental illness are rooted in continued communication between the patient and a healthcare professional. Adherence to medication is also heavily reliant on discussions about the effectiveness of the treatment protocol.

Communication is central to the diagnosis and treatment of mental illness. Mental health is often experienced by close family, friends, and one's social support network long before the patient gets to a doctor's office. The history of interactions that emerge before diagnosis can greatly impact how we view ourselves as well as the way we orient to those around us via communication, which creates our social identities across the life span. The mental health continuum from the most severe cases to the more simplistic has communicative and behavioral characteristics that make it distinctively tied to our social identities. Such stigma creates barriers to open communication about mental illness with family members and other traditional sources of social support make patient provider interactions especially salient (Sparks & Villagran, 2010).

Changing Social Perceptions of Stigmatized Health Issues through Communication

Communication often plays a vital role in determining how people perceive health issues (Cline, 2003; Lupton, 1994). Individuals with alcoholism, cancer, HIV/AIDS, and a variety of other diseases and conditions often attempt to alter social perceptions of these health concerns in their interactions with others. Communication is important for helping people construct new health-related identities, especially in interactions between individuals sharing the same disease or health concern. For example, the term "cancer survivor" has largely replaced earlier designations like "cancer victim," largely due to people with cancer redefining the disease in light of their own experiences. Many people with cancer object to terms like "cancer victim" because it places them in a powerless position, preferring instead the more positive connotations of "cancer survivor" (O'Hair *et al.*, 2003). Language can be very powerful in altering cultural perceptions about health concerns. Through terms like "cancer survivor," many people facing the disease have attempted to use language to change cultural beliefs and attitudes toward the disease.

Social identity theory

Another common way that individuals facing similar health conditions can transform their own and others' perceptions is through the lens of Tajfel and Turner's social identity theory (1987) as a guiding framework in terms of how we talk to each other based on group memberships (see Harwood & Sparks, 2003; Sparks & Harwood, 2008; Sparks & Villagran, 2010). Patients diagnosed with a chronic or terminal disease gain membership in a group of people who share a common set of symptoms, side effects, and challenges in dealing with providers. The intersection of intergroup communication and health communication was initially revealed with the pioneering work of Jake Harwood and Lisa Sparks (2003) in their applications of social identity to health and cancer communication contexts (see also Dryden & Giles, 1987). The social identity theory further explains that a person is not really their "own self" but rather multiple selves that are a part of a larger group membership. Different social contexts may trigger an individual to think and act on the basis of their family or national "level of self" (Tajfel & Turner, 1987).

It is through communicating with others that patients diagnosed with an illness often see themselves differently and start to recognize that others may view them differently as well (see Harwood & Sparks, 2003; Sparks, 2003b; Sparks & Harwood, 2008). Barriers faced by groups of patients who deal with similar physical and psychological issues can have a major impact on the self-concept (Williams, 2008). For example, after a negative diagnosis some patients immediately begin to question their own identity with thoughts of biological degradation ("how could my body do this to me?"), to destiny ("Will I possibly be able to get through this?"), to transformations in self ("Losing my breast to cancer makes me feel that I'm no longer a woman"). Although illness is never a positive development in a person's life, the way illness is experienced is based on the patient's pre-diagnosis identity (see Villagran & Sparks, 2010).

As discussed throughout the book, health communication impacts a variety of disease conditions affecting our population such as heart disease and cancer, but also permeates our society in more difficult to detect illnesses that may be neurologically driven tremors, or early stages of cancer or mental illness. The asymmetrical nature of communication in healthcare contexts requires a coordinated negotiation of social identity (Sparks & Villagran, 2010), which can impact medical decision-making in the doctor–patient relationship (see Hajek, Villagran, & Wittenberg-Lyles, 2007; Sparks & Villagran, 2010; Villagran, Fox, & O'Hair, 2007; Villagran & Sparks, 2010). Providers use instrumental talk to give and receive information and maintain their in-group identity status, whereas patients often bring an existing social identity that may be transformed by a diagnosis of illness (Villagran & Sparks, 2010). Through communicating with others, patients diagnosed with an illness often see themselves differently and start to recognize that others may view them differently as well. Awareness of potential identity shifts as individuals experience a change in their health status is a coordinated effort involving all interactants within and outside of the healthcare environment (Sparks & Villagran, 2010; Villagran & Sparks, 2010). For example, the Hispanic culture tends to live in a collectivist fashion and identify themselves as not their own self but as part of the larger cohort they consider to be their family (Wills, Yaeger, & Sandy, 2003). More importantly research has found that based on social identity theory, the Hispanic population will continue to assimilate toward their own identity. Researchers Chattaraman, Lennon, and Rudd (2010) found that when Hispanic consumers were introduced to cultural mainstream brands there were no significant preference shifts. The only significant preference shifts were in response to similar cultural primes that embodied the Hispanic culture. Therefore, it seems that the Hispanic population will act on the values and opinions of their family or group membership before themselves. With this in mind, it is important to examine how much the media influences culturally based health habits, such as smoking, sunscreen protection, exercise, or food choices.

Social discrepancy theory

One common way that individuals facing similar health conditions can transform their own and others' perceptions is through the use of Higgins' (1987) social discrepancy theory as a secondary framework one can explain how individuals adjust their emotional states and attitudes based on conflicting beliefs about themselves. The theory states that there are two types of self-images: the actual self, and the ideal self. The actual self represents who the person actually is, the ideal self represents who the person believes that people think they should be. When there is a discrepancy between the two self-images, feelings of sadness, disappointment, and anxiety may occur in the person. When a person is consistently reminded of the discrepancy, they will engage in particular behaviors to try to overcome the discrepancy and relieve the emotional distress. These behaviors can include various health behaviors including overeating or eating disorders such as anorexia and bulimia (Higgins, 1992). Social cues in the environment could influence the pattern of self-discrepancy. In the media, for instance, images depicting the thin female body image have created a social environment that facilitates a self-guide for women encouraging the thin female body as being the only beautiful body (Harrison, 2000). Researchers Anshutz, Engels, Becker, and Strien (2009) found that college women exposed to thin models expressed a greater increase in body dissatisfaction than after exposure to normal weight models. Researchers have found that when women internalize this thin ideal body image, they will change their diet and exercise habits to try and diminish the discrepancy between their actual self and their ideal self to look more like the images they see in the media (Hargreaves & Tiggemann, 2003). Such perceptions of acceptable body image can and often do vary greatly by culture. For example, researchers Fitzgibbon, Blackman, and Avellone (2000) found that Hispanic women had a body image discrepancy only after they were overweight. Hispanic women are at a higher risk for obesity and for those entering midlife must face the effects of aging.

In other cases, widespread societal perceptions associated with diseases like cancer may lead some individuals to view themselves as victims of the disease, which may result in passive coping strategies (Kreps, 1993) or a type of self-fulfilling prophecy, in which they do not actively seek treatment for the disease or adhere to lifestyle changes that may improve their chances of survival. In cancer support groups, members learn to identify with others' experiences and feelings about cancer through sharing narratives, and this appears to both validate their own experiences and feelings and lessen their sense of isolation (Mok & Martinson, 2000; Wright & Bell, 2003).

People with similar health concerns can also use narratives to create and sustain a culture that offers a unique perspective on the issues they face. Cancer survivors, recovering alcoholics, and people with disabilities have been influential in changing public perceptions of these health issues by telling their stories to each other and through the mass media. For example, alcoholics were once seen as being morally weak, but through the stories of members of organizations such as Alcoholics Anonymous, recovering alcoholics have been instrumental in promoting the idea that alcoholism is a physical disease rather than a moral failing.

Culturally Centered Health Campaigns

In recent years, health communication researchers have become more aware of cultural issues when designing public health campaigns. Traditionally, campaigns have been designed using theories and practices that largely have Eurocentric biases (Dutta, 2008). However, given the limited impact of many health campaigns on minority groups in the US due to cultural biases (Snyder, 2003; Zoller & Dutta, 2008), and the fact that these same groups typically face the greatest health disparities (Kreps, 2006a; Kreps & Sparks, 2008), health campaign designers need to spend more time researching and understanding the worldview of minority groups so that more culturally sensitive campaigns can be developed and have a greater chance of influencing health outcomes (Dutta, 2007). Having a thorough understanding of the audience one wishes to influence is a crucial component of all health campaigns (see Chapter 10). Culturally sensitive approaches to health campaigns involve being aware of Eurocentric and social class biases and critically examining taken-for-granted assumptions about why people from different groups engage in health-related behaviors (Dutta & Basu, 2008). Moreover, developing culturally sensitive campaigns can often be more time consuming since it requires preliminary research, such as extensive interviews with members of the targeted minority population, so that campaign designer can assess cultural differences in beliefs, attitudes, and values about health, illness, and behavior. In addition, it is important to give members of the targeted group opportunities to become stakeholders in the campaign process, which can often lead to greater trust, understanding, and access to members of the community.

Provider Diversity

Communication by healthcare providers has been linked to patient satisfaction with care (Buller & Buller, 1987) and patient compliance (Cropley, 2003). Patients and providers from varying cultures enter in their healthcare interactions with different health beliefs and expectancies about care. These divergent perspectives can influence verbal and nonverbal communication patterns, which in turn can impact behavior and health outcomes.

As we have seen, patients exhibit a great amount of diversity in the current US healthcare system. Unfortunately, the racial and ethnic diversity of providers has not kept pace with the diversity of patients in recent years, and as we have discussed, this may lead to a number of communication problems. However, there is also considerable diversity among healthcare providers in terms of occupation, education levels, areas of expertise, and socioeconomic status (see Table 5.1 for a list of some of the many healthcare provider occupations). This section briefly explores healthcare provider diversity.

Table 5.1   Select healthcare provider occupations

Child life specialist
Dentist
Dental assistant
Dental hygienist
Hospital administrator
Medical sonographer
Occupational therapist
Pharmacy technician
Phlebotomist
Psychologist
Physician
Physician assistant
Registered nurse
Surgical technologist

The amount of training for jobs in the healthcare system varies widely. For example, phlebotomists can often receive a certificate after about 6 months of training, while radiologists and other types of medical personnel have much more extensive training. Nurses and physicians obviously require more advanced levels of education and training. In addition, the training specific to each type of provider and interactions among providers having the same occupation contributes to a variety of unique co-cultures within many healthcare settings. Even among medical doctors there is a great deal of diversity and status difference in medical specialty. Some medical doctors, such as pathologists, have little interaction with patients, and physicians often attribute a higher professional status to surgeons and other specialties due to the amount and sophistication of the training they receive.

Much like patients, providers are socialized into unique cultures based upon factors such as education and training. Further, lack of a common language between client and provider can result in diagnostic errors and inappropriate treatment (Woloshin *et al.*, 1995). Even within a relatively small healthcare organization, there are a wide variety of cultural conceptions of health and healthcare among providers. These differences can lead to conflict between providers from different backgrounds (see Chapter 6) and can affect communication with patients. For example, many physicians gravitate toward recommending certain procedures and medications as a result of their training, and may have relatively low tolerance for alternative treatments recommended by other providers or by the patient. While cultural differences among providers can often lead to negative outcomes, health organizations can capitalize on provider diversity in an effort to provide more comprehensive care. For example, Wright and Frey (2008) studied a state-of-the-art cancer center in Memphis, Tennessee, where oncologists provide patients with traditional biomedical cancer treatments along with complementary herbal treatments, relaxation therapy, and group/individual counseling. In addition, many of the larger modern healthcare organizations rely on an interdisciplinary team approach to patient care. With this approach, administrators within a healthcare organization assemble a team of providers with different types of training and experience in an effort to gain a more holistic understanding of a patient's health issues. For example, interdisciplinary teams are often composed of a wide range of providers, such as physicians, nurses, pharmacists, physical therapists, psychologists, and social workers. In short, patients need to actively seek information from providers, and ask for clarity when they do not understand. In this manner patients can positively increase their own health literacy through the acquisition of knowledge about their healthcare situations while simultaneously making their healthcare provider their partner in their health.

Providers can contribute to the improvement of patient health literacy though effective means of communication with patients. This simply means that providers should "engage in good communication practices with their patients by employing active listening techniques, and checking for understanding" (Sparks, & Villagran 2010, p. 17). Additionally, healthcare providers should provide health information to patients via as many different mediums as possible; utilizing verbal, written, and illustrations in order for patients to employ their preferred way of learning (Sparks *et al.*, 2010, p. 24). Finally, healthcare providers can increase health literacy through the use of plain language. Providers can employ plain language by avoiding medical jargon, technical and medical terms when speaking with patients (Quick Guide, US Department of Health and Human Services, p. 2.3). Overall, providers should attempt to remove themselves from the "culture of medicine" when communicating with patients, and recognize that their patients have very different cultural perspectives than their own (Quick Guide, US Department of Health and Human Services, p. 2.3). Moreover, interdisciplinary team members collaborate with each other to find holistic ways to treat patients, taking into account medical and social factors. We examine interdisciplinary healthcare teams in much greater depth in Chapter 11.

Summary

This chapter has taken on a topic—namely, cultural diversity—that is often emphasized in mission and vision statements and frequently recognized as an essential component of comprehensive healthcare delivery. Many healthcare organizations have succeeded in addressing cultural diversity issues with grace and enthusiasm. However, organizations still face the many challenges that diversity presents in relation to disease management, provider–patient relationships, and quality healthcare delivery. In this chapter we have promoted an agency approach to diversity whereby patients or consumers of healthcare services impose their rights to information and uncertainty management processes to achieve empowerment, which in turn provides increased options for making decisions about their healthcare.

We recognize that diversity in healthcare is a dynamic and constantly challenging factor that healthcare professionals are expected to consider. Diversity issues will impose their will on the delivery system regardless of preference or preparedness. Organizations will find that embracing an open and integrative approach to diversity will maximize their effectiveness for patient care and at the same recognize the value-added nature of diversity sensitivity.

Health communication scholars must do a better job of translating relevant communication theories and literature into the lives of patients, caregivers, and healthcare provider teams with foci on cultural and diversity issues that permeate modern healthcare environments. As Sparks (2007) suggests, communication theories from interpersonal relationship development and processes to persuasion and mass-mediated provide sound building blocks for those interested in using reliable research based empirical evidence to aid in explaining the critical features of a patient who has received the news of a scary and uncertain health diagnosis such as cancer. Thus, further understanding of how such diverse cultural communicative interactions play out in the construction and processing of such messages across the communication continuum (e.g. interpersonal, small group, organizational, public, mass) is an essential step that is greatly needed to increased health outcomes for patients and providers speaking different languages, with different cultural backgrounds and experiences. Recognizing the complexities of effective healthcare communication with diverse patients must no longer be ignored. Health communication messages must be designed and delivered to match the communication skills, needs, and pre-dispositions of such specific audiences.

References

Adelman, M. B., & Frey, L. R. (1997). *The fragile community: Living together with AIDS*. Mahwah, NJ: Lawrence Erlbaum.

Airhihenbuwa, C. O. (1995). *Health and culture: Beyond the Western paradigm*. Thousand Oaks, CA: Sage.

Airhihenbuwa, C. O., & Obregon, R. (2000). A critical assessment of theories/models used in health communication for HIV/AIDS. *Journal of Health Communication*, *5*, 5–16.

Aldrich, L., & Variyam, J. N. (2000). Acculturation erodes the diet quality of US Hispanics. *Diet Quality*, *23*, 51–55.

Allport, G. W., & Ross, J. M. (1967). Personal religious orientation and prejudice. *Journal of Personality and Social Psychology*, *5*, 432–443.

American Cancer Society. (2001). Cancer statistics. Retrieved July 12, 2012, from www.cancer.ogr/cancerinfo/.

Anschutz, D. J., Engels, R. C. M. E., Becker, E. S., & Van Strien, T. (2009). The effects of TV commercials using less thin models on young women's mood, body image, and actual food intake. *Body Image*, *6*, 270–276.

Barnes, P. M., Bloom, B., & Nashin, R. L. (2008). *Complementary and alternative medicine use among adults and children: United States, 2007*: CDC National Health Statistics Report #12.

Barron, F., Hunter, A., Mayo, R., & Willoughby, D. (2004). Acculturation and adherence: Issues for health care providers working with clients of Mexican origin. *Journal of Transcultural Nursing*, *15*, 331–337.

Beisecker, A. & Beisecker, T. (1990). Patient information-seeking behaviors when communicating with doctors. *Medical Care*, *28*(1), 19–28.

Brislin, R. W. (1993). *Understanding culture's influence on behavior*. Fort Worth, TX: Harcourt Brace.

Brown, L., Macintyre, K., & Trujillo, L. (2003). Interventions to reduce HIV/AIDS stigma: What have we learned? *AIDS Education and Prevention*, *15*, 49–69.

Buller, M. K., & Buller, D. B. (1987). Physicians' communication style and patient satisfaction. *Journal of Health and Human Behavior*, *28*(4), 375–388.

Carrese, J. A., & Rhodes, L. A. (1995). Western bioethics on the Navajo reservation. Benefit or harm? *JAMA*, *274*, 826–829.

Chattaraman, V., Lennon, S., & Rudd, N. (2010). Social identity salience: Effects onidentity-based brand choices of Hispanic consumers. *Psychology and Marketing*, *27*(3), 263–284.

Chew, L. D., Bradley, K. A., & Boyko, E. T. (2004). Brief questions to identify patients with inadequate health literacy. *Family Medicine*, *36*, 588–594.

Cline, R. J. W. (2003). Everyday interpersonal communication and health. In T. L. Thompson, A. M. Dorsey, K. I. Miller, & R. Parrott (Eds), *Handbook of health communication* (pp. 285–313). Mahwah, NJ: Lawrence Erlbaum.

Cobas, J. A., Balcazar, H., Benini, M. B., Keith, V. M., & Chong, Y. (1996). Acculturation and low-birthweight infants among Latino women: A reanalysis of HHANES data with structural equation models. *American Journal of Public Health*, *86*, 394–396.

Cohen, G. (1994). Age-related problems in the use of proper names in communication. In M. L. Hummert, J. M. Wiemann, & J. F. Nussbaum (Eds), *Interpersonal communication in older adulthood:Interdisciplinary theory and research* (pp. 40–57). Thousand Oaks, CA: Sage.

Collins, D., Villagran, M. M., & Sparks, L. (2008). Crossing borders, crossing cultures: Barriers to cancer prevention and treatment along the U.S./Mexico border. *Patient Education and Counseling*, *71*(3), 333–339.

Conrad, P. (1987). The experience of illness: Recent and new directions. In J. Roth & P. Conrad (Eds), *Research in the sociology of health care: A research manual* (Vol. 6, pp. 1–31). Greenwich, CT: JAI.

Corrigan, P. W. (2000). Mental health stigma as social attribution: Implications for research methods and attitude change. *Clinical Psychology: Science and Practice*, *7*, 49–67.

Cropley, C. J. (2003). The effect of health care provider persuasive strategy on patient compliance and satisfaction. *American Journal of Health Studies*, *18*, 117–125.

Dessio, W., Wade, C., Chao, M., Kronenberg, F., Cushman, L. E., & Kalmuss, D. (2004). Religion, spirituality, and healthcare choices of African-American women: Results of a national survey. *Ethnicity & Disease*, *14*, 189–197.

Dryden, C., & Giles, H. (1987). Language, social identity, and health. In H. Beloff & A. M. Coleman (Eds), *Psychology survey* (pp. 115–138). Leicester: British Psychological Society.

Dreyer, E. A. (1994). *Earth crammed with heaven: A spirituality of everyday life*. New York: Paulist Press.

Dunn, L., & Perry, B. L. (1997). Where your patients are. *Primary Care, 24*, 715–721.

Dutta, M. (2007). Communicating about culture and health: Theorizing culture-centered and culturally-centered approaches. *Communication Theory, 17*, 304–328.

Dutta, M. (2008). *Communicating about health: A culture-centered approach.* Cambridge: Polity.

Dutta, M. J., & Basu, A. (2011). Culture, communication, and health: A guiding framework. In T. L. Thompson, R. Parrott, & J. F. Nussbaum (Eds), *The Routledge handbook of health communication, 2nd ed.* (pp. 320–334). New York: Routledge.

Duan, N., Fox, S. A., Derose, K. P., & Carson, S. (2000). Maintaining mammography adherence through telephone counseling in a church-based trial. *American Journal of Public Health, 90*, 1468–1471.

Dysart-Gale, D. (2005). Communication models, professionalization, and the work of medical interpreters. *Health Communication, 17*, 91–103.

Egbert, N., Sparks, L., Kreps, G. L., & du Pré, A. (2008). Finding meaning in the journey: Methods of spiritual coping for aging cancer patients. In L. Sparks, H. D. O'Hair, & G. L. Kreps, (Eds), *Cancer communication and aging* (pp. 277–292). Cresskill, NJ: Hampton Press.

Eisenberg, D., Davis, R., Ettner, S., Appel, S., Wilkey, S., Van Rompay, M., & Kessler, R. (1998). Trends in alternative medicine use in the United States, 1990–1997: Results of a national follow-up study. *Journal of the American Medical Association, 280*, 1569–1575.

Estroff, S. E., Penn, D. L., & Toporek, J. R. (2004). Stigma to discrimination: An analysis of community efforts to reduce the negative consequences of having a psychiatric disorder and label. *Schizophrenia Bulletin, 30*, 493–509.

Fagerlin, A., Ubel, P. A., Smith, D. M., & Zikmund-Fisher, B. J. (2007a). Making numbers matter: Present and future research in risk communication. *American Journal of Health Behavior, 31*(Suppl 1), S47–S56.

Fagerlin, A., Zikmund-Fisher, B. J., Ubel, P. A., Jankovic, A., Derry, H. A., & Smith, D. J. (2007b). Measuring numeracy without a math test: Development of the subjective numeracy scale. *Medical Decision Making, 27*(5), 672–680.

Ferguson, J. A., Weinberger, M., Westmoreland, G. R., Mamlin, L. A., Segar, D. S., Green, J. Y., Martin, D. K., & Tierney, W. M. (1998). Racial disparity in cardiac decision making: Results from patient focus groups. *Archives of Internal Medicine, 158*, 1450–1453.

Fisher, W. R. (1987). *Human communication as narration: Toward a philosophy of reason, value, and action.* Columbia, NC: University of North Carolina Press.

Fitzgibbon, M., Blackman, L., & Avellone, M. (2000). The relationship between body image discrepancy and body mass index across ethnic groups. *Obesity, 8*(8), 582–589.

Galanti, G. (1991). *Caring for patients from different cultures: Case studies from American hospitals.* Philadelphia, PA: University of Pennsylvania Press.

Gany, F. M., Shah, S. M., & Changrani, J. (2006). New York City's immigrant minorities. Reducing cancer health disparities. *Cancer, 107*, 2071–2081.

Gergen, K. J. (1999). *An invitation to social construction.* London: Sage.

Gillick, M. (1985). Common-sense models of health and disease. *New England Journal of Medicine, 313*, 700–703.

Goffman, E. (1963). *Stigma: Notes on the management of spoiled identity.* Englewood Cliffs, NJ: Prentice-Hall.

Goldner, M. A. (1998). *Explaining the success of the alternative health care movement: How integrative medicine is expanding Western medicine.* Unpublished doctoral dissertation, Ohio State University, Columbus, OH.

Greenberg, J., Solomon, S., & Pyszczynski, T. (1997). Terror management theory of self-esteem and cultural worldviews: Empirical assessments and conceptual refinements. In M. Zanna (Ed.), *Advances in experimental social psychology* (Vol. 29, pp. 61–139). Orlando, FL: Academic Press.

Greene, K. (2000). Disclosure of chronic illness varies by topic and target: The role of stigma and boundaries in willingness to disclose. In S. Petronio (Ed.), *Balancing the secrets of private disclosures.* Mahwah, NJ: Lawrence Erlbaum.

Gudykunst, W. B. (1998). *Bridging differences: Effective intergroup communication* (3rd ed.). Thousand Oaks, CA: Sage.

Hardin, L. R. (2005). Counseling patients with low health literacy. *American Journal of Health-System Pharmacy, 62*, 364–365.

Hargreaves, D., & Tiggemann, M. (2003). Longer-term implications of responsiveness to "thin-idea" television: Support for a cumulative hypothesis of body image disturbance. *European Eating Disorder Review, 11*, 465–477.

Haynes, M. A., & Smedley, B. D. (1999). *The unequal burden of cancer.* Washington, DC: National Academy Press.

Heisler, M. B., Rust, G., Pattillo, R., & Dubois, A. M. (2005). Improving health, eliminating disparities: Finding solutions for better health care for all populations. *Ethnicity & Disease, 15*, S1–S4.

Helman, C. G. (2000). *Culture, health, and illness*. Oxford: Butterworth Heinemann.

Heuer, L., Bengiamin, M., & Downey, V. (2001). The impact of an international cultural experience on previously held stereotypes by American student nurses. *Multicultural Education*. Accessed September 26, 2006, from www.findarticles.com/p/articles/.

Harrison, K. (2000). The body electric: Thing-ideal media, self-discrepancies, and eating disorder symptomatology in adolescents. *Journal of Social Clinical Psychology, 20*, 289–323.

Harwood, J., & Sparks, L. (2003). Social identity and health: An intergroup communication approach to cancer. *Health Communication, 15*, 145–170.

Hajek, C., Villagran, M. &, Wittenberg-Lyles, E. (2007). The relationships among perceived physician accommodation, perceived outgroup typicality, and patient inclinations toward compliance. *Communication Research Reports, 24*(4), 293–302.

Higgins, E. T. (1987). Self-discrepancy: A theory relating self and affect. *Psychological Review, 94*(3), 319–340.

Ho, E., & Robles, J. S. (2011). Cultural resources for health participation: Examining biomedicine, acupuncture, and massage therapy for HIV-related peripheral neuropathy. *Health Communication, 26*, 135–146.

Hofstede, G. (1984). *Culture's consequences*. Beverly Hills, CA: Sage.

Holt, C. L., Lee, C., & Wright, K. (2008). A spiritually based approach to breast cancer awareness: Cognitive response analysis of communication effectiveness. *Health Communication, 23*, 13–22.

Hornberger, J., Itakura, H., & Wilson, S. (1997). Bridging language and cultural barriers between physicians and patients. *Public Health Reports, 112*, 410–417.

Hunt, L. M., Hamdi, A., & Arana, L. L. (2000). Herbs, prayer, and insulin: Use of medical and alternative treatments by a group of Mexican American diabetes patients. *Journal of Family Practice, 49*, 216–223.

Japp, P. M., Harter, L. M., & Beck, C. S. (2005). Vital problematics of narrative theorizing about health and healing. In P. Japp, L. Harter, & C. Beck (Eds), *Narratives, health, and healing: Communication theory, research, and practice* (pp. 7–30). Mahwah, NJ: Lawrence Erlbaum.

Jellinek, E. M. (1952). *The disease concept of alcoholism*. Highland Park, NJ: Yale Center of Alcohol Studies Press.

Jenson, G. H. (2000). *Storytelling in Alcoholics Anonymous: A rhetorical analysis*. Carbondale, IL: Southern Illinois University Press.

Johnson, R., Roter, D., Powe, N. R., & Cooper, L. A. (2004). Patient race/ethnicity and quality of patient–physician communication during medical visits. *American Journal of Public Health, 94*, 2084–2091.

Johnson, S. K. (2002). Hmong health beliefs and experiences in the Western health care system. *Journal of Transcultural Nursing, 13*, 126–132.

Kakai, H. (2002). A double standard in bioethical reasoning for disclosure of advanced cancer diagnosis in Japan. *Health Communication, 14*, 361–376.

Kassel, J. D., & Wagner, E. F. (1993). Processes of change in Alcoholics Anonymous: A review of possible mechanisms. *Psychotherapy, 30*, 222–234.

Keegan, L. (1996). Use of alternative therapies among Mexican Americans in the Texas Rio Grande Valley. *Journal of Holistic Nursing, 14*, 277–294.

Keeley, M. P. (2004). Final conversations: Survivors' memorable messages concerning religious faith and spirituality. *Health Communication, 16*, 87–104.

Kim, Y. H., & Sarna, L. (2004). An intervention to increase mammography use by Korean American women. *Oncology Nursing Forum, 31*, 105–110.

Koenig, H. G., & Larson, D. B. (1998). Use of hospital services, religious attendance, and religious affiliation. *Southern Medical Journal, 91*, 925–932.

Koenig, H. G., Hays, J. C., Larson, D. B., George, L. K., Cohen, H. J., McCullough, M. E. et al. (1999). Does religious attendance prolong survival? A six-year follow-up study of 3,968 older adults. *Journal of Gerontology, 54A*, M370–M376.

Koenig, H. G., Mc Cullough, M. E., & Larson, D. B. (2001). *Handbook of religion and health*. New York: Oxford University Press.

Kreps, G. L. (1986). Health communication and the elderly. *World Communication, 15*, 55–70.

Kreps, G. L. (1993). Refusing to be a victim: Rhetorical strategies for confronting cancer. In G. L. Kreps & B. C. Thornton (Eds), *Perspectives on health communication* (pp. 42–47). Prospect Heights, IL: Waveland Press.

Kreps, G. L.(2005). Communication and racial inequities in health care. *American Behavioral Scientist, 49*, 1–15.

Kreps, G. L. (2006a). Communication and racial inequalities in health care. *American Behavioral Scientist, 49,* 744–760.

Kreps G. L. (2006b). One size does not fit all: Adapting communication to the needs and literacy levels of individuals. *Annals of Family Med* (online), http://www.annfammed.org/cgi/eletters/4/3/205.

Kreps, G. L., & Sparks, L. (2008). Meeting the health literacy needs of vulnerable populations. *Patient Education and Counseling, 71*(3), 328–332.

Kreps, G. L., & Thornton, B. C. (1992). *Health communication: Theory and practice* (2nd ed.). Prospect Heights, IL: Waveland Press.

Kreps, G. L., Neuhauser, L., Sparks, L., & Villagran, M. (Eds) (2008a). Translational community-based health communication interventions to promote cancer prevention and control for vulnerable audiences [Special Issue] *Patient Education and Counseling, 71*(3), 315–350.

Kreps, G. L., Neuhauser, L., Sparks, L., Villagran, M. (2008b). The power of community-based health communication interventions to promote cancer prevention and control for at-risk populations. *Patient Education and Counseling, 71*(3), 315–318.

Ku, L., & Waidmann, T. (2003). *How race/ethnicity, immigration status, and language affect health insurance coverage, access to care, and quality of care among the low-income population.* Washington, DC: The Henry J. Kaiser Family Foundation.

Lackey, N. R., Gates, M. F., & Brown, G. (2001). African American women's experiences with the initial discovery, diagnosis, and treatment of breast cancer. *Oncology Nursing Forum, 28*(3), 519–527.

Lender, M. E., & Martin, J. K. (1987). *Drinking in America.* New York: Free Press.

Leong, F. T. L., & Schneller, G. (1997). White Americans' attitudes toward Asian Americans in social situations: An empirical examination of potential stereotypes, bias, and prejudice. *Journal of Multicultural Counseling and Development, 25,* 68–78.

Levin, J. S. (1996). How religion influences morbidity and health: Reflections on natural history, salutogenesis and host resistance. *Social Science and Medicine, 43,* 849–864.

Levin, J. S. (2001). *God, faith, and health: Exploring the spirituality–healing connection.* New York: Wiley.

Link, B. G., & Phelan, J. C. (1999). Labeling and stigma. In C. S. Aneshensel & J. C. Phelan (Eds), *Handbook of the sociology of mental health* (pp. 481–494). New York: Kluwer Academic.

Long, S. O. (2000). Public passages, personal passages, and reluctant passages: Notes on investigating disclosure practices in Japan. *Journal of Medical Humanities, 21,* 3–13.

Lupton, D. (1994). *Medicine as culture: Illness, disease, and the body in Western societies.* Thousand Oaks, CA: Sage.

Lynn, J. (2000). Preface. In K. L. Braun, J. H. Pietsch, & P. L. Blanchette (Eds), *Cultural issues in end-of-life decision making* (pp. ix–xi). Thousand Oaks, CA: Sage.

McTavish, F., Pingree, S., Hawkings, R., & Gustafson, D. (2003). Cultural differences in use of discussion group. *Journal of Health Psychology, 8,* 103–116.

Mok, E., & Martinson, I. (2000). Empowerment of Chinese patients with cancer through self-help groups in Hong Kong. *Cancer Nursing, 23,* 206–213.

Mouton, C. P. (2000). Cultural and religious issues for African Americans. In K. L. Braun, J. H. Pietsch, & P. L. Blanchette (Eds), *Cultural issues in end-of-life decision making* (pp. 71-82). Thousand Oaks, CA: Sage.

Murray, S. A., Kendall, M., Boyd, K., Worth, A., & Benton, T. F. (2004). Exploring the spiritual needs of people dying of lung cancer or heart failure: A prospective qualitative interview study of patients and their carers. *Palliative Medicine, 18,* 39–45.

National Cancer Institute. (2005, June 7). *Spirituality in cancer care.* Retrieved July 12, 2012 from http://www.cancer.gov/cancertopics/pdq/supportivecare/spirituality/healthprofessional/allpages#Section_4.

National Cancer Institute (2006). Overview of health disparities research [homepage on the internet]. Bethesda, MD: National Cancer Institute [cited 2006 September 10]. Available from: http://dccps.nci.nih.gov/od/hd-overview.html.

Ndiwane, A., Miller, K. H., Bonner, A., Imperio, K., McNeal, G., Amertil, N., & Feldman, Z. (2004). Enhancing cultural competencies of advanced practice nurses: Health care challenges in the twenty-first century. *Journal of Cultural Diversity, 11,* 118–121.

Newlin, K., Knafl, K., & Melkus, G.D. (2002). African-American spirituality: A concept analysis. *Advances in Nursing Science, 25*(2), 57–70.

Nussbaum, J. F., Baringer, D., & Kundrat, A. (2003). Health, communication, and aging: Cancer and the older adult [Special Issue]. *Health Communication, 15*(2), 185–194.

Nussbaum, J. F., Pecchioni, L., Robinson, J. D., & Thompson, T. (2000). *Communication and aging* (2nd ed.). Mahwah, NJ: Lawrence Erlbaum.

O'Hair, H. D., & Sparks, L. (2008). Relational agency during life-threatening illnesses. In K. B. Wright & S. D. Moore (Eds), *Applied health communication* (pp. 271–289). Cresskill, NJ: Hampton Press.

O'Hair, H. D., Behnke, R., & King, P. (1983). Age-related patient preferences for physician communication behavior. *Educational Gerontology*, 9, 147–158.

O'Hair, H. D., Kreps, G. L., & Sparks, L., (2007). Conceptualizing cancer care and communication. In H. D. O'Hair, G. L. Kreps & L. Sparks (Eds), *Handbook of communication and cancer care* (pp. 1–12). Cresskill, NJ: Hampton Press.

O'Hair, H. D., O'Hair, M., Southward, M., & Krayer, K. (1987). Patient compliance and physician communication. *Journal of Compliance in Health Care*, 2, 125–128.

O'Hair, H. D., Scannell, D., & Thompson, S. (2005). Agency through narrative: Patients managing cancer care in a challenging environment. In L. Harter, P. Japp, & C. Beck (Eds), *Narratives, health, and healing: Communication theory, research, and practice* (pp. 413–432). Mahwah, NJ: Lawrence Erlbaum.

O'Hair, H. D., Sparks, L., & Thompson, S. (2005). Negotiating cancer care through agency. In E. B. Ray (Ed.), *Health communication in practice: A case study approach* (pp. 81–94). Mahwah, NJ: Lawrence Erlbaum.

O'Hair, H. D., Villagran, M., Wittenberg, E., Brown, K., Hall, T., Ferguson, M., & Doty, T. (2003). Cancer survivorship and agency model (CSAM): Implications for patient choice, decision making, and influence. *Health Communication*, 15, 193–202.

Palmer, S. C., Kagee, A., Coyne, J. C., & DeMichele, A. (2004). Experience of trauma, distress, and posttraumatic stress disorder among breast cancer patients. *Psychosomatic Medicine*, 66, 258–264.

Paloutzian, R. F., & Kirkpatrick, L. A. (1995). Introduction: The scope of religious influences on personal and societal well-being. *Journal of Social Issues*, 51(2), 1–11.

Parker, R., Kreps, G. L. (2005). Library outreach: Overcoming health literacy challenges. *Journal of the Medical Library Association*, 93(4), 78–82.

Parrott, R. (2004). "Collective amnesia": The absence of religious faith and spirituality in health communication research and practice. *Health Communication*, 16, 1–5.

Pearce, W. B. (1995). A sailing guide for social constructionists. In W. Leeds-Hurwitz (Ed.), *Social approaches to communication* (pp. 88–113). New York: Guilford.

Pecchioni, L., Krieger, J. C., Sparks, L., Pitts, M., & Ota, H. (2008). Investigating cancer and ageing from a cultural perspective. In L. Sparks, H. D. O'Hair, & G. L. Kreps, (Eds), *Cancer communication and aging* (pp. 239–257). Cresskill, NJ: Hampton Press.

Pecchioni, L., Ota, H., & Sparks, L. (2004). Cultural issues in communication and aging (2nd ed.). In J. F. Nussbaum, & J. Coupland (Eds), *Handbook of communication and aging research* (pp. 167–207). Mahwah, NJ: Lawrence Erlbaum.

Popkin, B. M., & Udry, J. R. (1998). Adolescent obesity increases significantly in second and third generation US immigrants: The National Longitudinal Study of Adolescent Health. *Journal of Nutrition*, 128, 701–706.

Quick Guide to Health Literacy, U.S. Department of Health and Human Services. Retrieved on July 12, 2012, from www.health.gov/communication/literacy/quickguide/quickguide.pdf.

Regier, D. A., Narrow, W. E., Rae, D. S., Manderscheid, R. W., Locke, B. Z., & Goodwin, F. K. (1993). The de facto mental and addictive disorders service system. Epidemiologic Catchment Area prospective 1-year prevalence rates of disorders and services. *Archives of General Psychiatry*, 50, 85–94.

Reynolds, P., & Kaplan, G. A. (1990). Social connections and risk for cancer: Prospective evidence from the Alameda County study. *Behavioral Medicine*, 16, 101–110.

Rivadeneyra, R., Elderkin-Thompson, V., Silver, R. C., & Waitzkin, H. (2000). Patient centeredness in medical encounters requiring an interpreter. *American Journal of Medicine*, 108, 470–474.

Robinson, J. D., & Nussbaum, J. F. (2004). Grounding research and medical education about religion in actual physician–patient interaction: Church attendance, social support, and older adults. *Health Communication*, 16, 63–85.

Samarel, N., & Fawcett, J. (1992). Enhancing adaptation to breast cancer: The addition of coaching to support groups. *Oncology Nursing Forum*, 19, 591–596.

Schott, J., & Henley, A. (1996). *Culture, religion, and childbearing in a multiracial society: A handbook for health professionals*. Oxford: Butterworth Heinemann.

Schein, E. H. (1985). *Organizational culture and leadership*. San Francisco, CA: Jossey-Bass.

Schreiber, L. M. (in press). The importance of precision in language: Communication research and (so-called) "alternative" medicine. *Health Communication*.

Schwalbe, M. L., & Staples, C. L. (1992). Forced blood testing: Role taking, identity, and discrimination. In J. Huber & B. E. Schneider (Eds), *The social context of AIDS*. Newbury Park, CA: Sage.

Sharf, B. F., & Vanderford, M. L. (2003). Illness narratives and the social construction of health. In T. L. Thompson, A. M. Dorsey, K. I. Miller, & R. Parrott (Eds), *Handbook of health communication* (pp. 9–35). Mahwah, NJ: Lawrence Erlbaum.

Smith, E. D. (1992). Hypertension management with church-based education: A pilot study. *Journal of the National Black Nurses Association, 6,* 19–28.

Smith, E. D., Merritt, S. L., & Patel, M. K. (1997). Church-based education: An outreach program for African Americans with hypertension. *Ethnicity & Health, 2,* 243–253.

Smith, L. S. (1997). Critical thinking, health policy, and the Hmong culture group, Part I. *Journal of Cultural Diversity, 4,* 5–12.

Smith, R. A., & Hipper, T. J. (2010). Label management: Investigating how confidants encourage the use of communication strategies to avoid stigmatization. *Health Communication, 25,* 410–422.

Snyder, R. (2003). Development communication campaigns. In B. Mody (Ed.), *International and development communication: A 21st-century perspective.* Thousand Oaks, CA: Sage.

Sparks, L. (Ed.). (2003a). Cancer communication and aging [Special Issue]. *Health Communication, 15*(2), 123–258.

Sparks, L. (2003b). An introduction to cancer communication and aging: Theoretical and research insights. *Health Communication, 15*(2), 123–132.

Sparks, L. (2007). Cancer care and the aging patient: Complexities of age-related communication barriers. In H. D. O'Hair, G. L. Kreps & L. Sparks (Eds), *Handbook of communication and cancer care* (pp. 233–249). Cresskill, NJ: Hampton Press.

Sparks, L. (2008). Family decision-making. In W. Donsbach (Ed.) *The international encyclopedia of communication, 4* (pp. 1729–1733). Oxford, UK and Malden, MA: Wiley-Blackwell.

Sparks, L. (in press). Health communication and caregiving research, policy, and practice: A health literacy approach to reducing health disparities. *Reducing health disparities: Communication interventions.* New York and Berlin: Peter Lang.

Sparks, L., & Harwood, J. (2008). Cancer, aging, and social identity: Development of an integrated model of social identity theory and health communication. In L. Sparks, H. D. O'Hair, & G. L. Kreps, (Eds), *Cancer communication and aging* (pp. 77–95). Cresskill, NJ: Hampton Press.

Sparks, L., & Nussbaum, J. F. (2008). Health literacy and cancer communication with older adults. *Patient Education and Counseling, 71*(3), 345–350.

Sparks, L., & Villagran, M. (2010). *Patient and provider interaction: A global health communication perspective.* Cambridge: Polity Press.

Sparks, L., Villagran, M. M., Parker-Raley, J., & Cunningham, C. B. (2007). A patient centered approach to breaking bad news: Communication guidelines for healthcare professionals. *Journal of Applied Communication Research, 35,* 177–196.

Spector, R. (1996). *Culture and diversity in health and illness.* Stamford, CT: Appleton Lange.

Spiegel, D., Bloom, J. R., & Yalom, I. (1981). Group support for patients with metastatic cancer: A randomized prospective outcome study. *Archives of General Psychiatry, 38,* 527–533.

Stephenson, M. T., Morgan, S. E., Roberts-Perez, S. D., Harrison, T., Afifit, W., & Long, S. D. (2008). The role of religiosity, religious norms, subjective norms, and bodily integrity in signing an organ donation donor card. *Health Communication, 23,* 436–447.

Street, R. L., Jr. (1991). Information-giving in medical consultations: The influence of patients' communicative styles and personal characteristics. *Social Science and Medicine, 32,* 541–548.

Tajfel, H., & Turner, J. C. (1987). The social identity theory of inter-group behavior. In S. Worchel & L. W. Austin (Eds), *Psychology of intergroup relations.* Chicago: Nelson-Hall.

Talamantes, M. A., Gomez, C., & Braun, K. L. (2000). Advance directives and end-of-life care: The Hispanic perspective. In K. L. Braun, J. H. Pietsch, & P. L. Blanchette (Eds), *Cultural issues in end-of-life decision making* (pp. 83–100). Thousand Oaks, CA: Sage.

Taylor, E. J. (2001). Spirituality, culture, and cancer care. *Seminars in Oncology Nursing, 17*(3), 197–205.

Thomas, F. (2006). Stigma, fatigue and social breakdown: Exploring the impacts of HIV/AIDS on patient and carer well-being in the Caprivi Region, Namibia. *Social Science & Medicine, 63,* 3174–3187.

Thoreson, C. E. (1998). Spirituality, health, and science: The coming revival? *The emerging role of counseling psychology in health care* (pp. 409–431). New York: Norton.

Thoresen, C. E., & Harris, A. H. (2002). Spirituality and health: What's the evidence and what's needed? *Annals of Behavioral Medicine, 24,* 3–13.

Udani, J. (1998). Integrating alternative medicine into practice. *Journal of the American Medical Association, 280,* 1620.

Ulrey, K. L., & Amason, P. (2001). Intercultural communication between patients and health care providers: An exploration of intercultural communication effectiveness, cultural sensitivity, stress, and anxiety. *Health Communication, 13,* 449–463.

US Census Bureau (2005). 2005 American community survey data: Race and ethnicity. Retrieved July 12, 2012, from www.factfinder.census.gov.

Van Winkle, N. W. (2000). End-of-life decision making in American Indian and Alaska Native cultures. In K. L. Braun, J. H. Pietsch, & P. L. Blanchette (Eds), *Cultural issues in end-of-life decision making* (pp. 127–144). Thousand Oaks, CA: Sage.

Villagran, M. M., Fox, L., & O'Hair, H. D. (2007). Patient communication processes: An agency-identity model for cancer care. In D. O'Hair, G. L. Kreps, & L. Sparks. (Eds), *Handbook of communication and cancer care* (pp. 127–143). Cresskill, NJ: Hampton Press.

Villagran, M. M., & Sparks, L. (2010). Social identity and health contexts. In H. Giles, S. Reid, & J. Harwood (Eds), *The dynamics of intergroup communication* (pp. 235–248). New York & Berlin: Peter Lang.

Voelker, R. (1995). Speaking the language of medicine and culture. *JAMA, 273,* 1639–1642.

Wardwell, W. I. (1994). Alternative medicine in the United States. *Social Science and Medicine, 38,* 1061–1068.

Williams, C. C. (2008). Insight, stigma, and post-diagnosis identities in schizophrenia. *Psychiatry, 71,* 246–255.

Wills, T., Yaeger, A., & Sandy, J. (2003) Buffering effect of religiosity for adolescent substance use. *Psychology of Addictive Behaviors, 17*(1). 24–31.

Wilmoth, M. C., Davis, B., & Sanders, L. D. (2008). When black women talk about breast cancer: How health care workers need to learn to listen. In L. Sparks, H. D. O'Hair, & G. L. Kreps (Eds), *Cancer communication and aging* (pp. 147–168). Cresskill, NJ: Hampton Press.

Witte, K. (1991). The role of culture in health and diseases. In L. Samovar and R. Porter (Eds), *Intercultural communication: A reader* (6th ed., pp. 199–207). Belmont, CA: Wadsworth.

Woloshin, S., Bickell, N., Shwartz, L., Gany, F., & Welch, G. (1995). Language barriers in medicine in the United States. *JAMA, 273:* 724–728.

Wortman, C., & Dunkel-Schetter, C. (1979). Interpersonal relationships and cancer. *Journal of Social Issues, 35,* 120–155.

Wright, K. B. (1997). Shared ideology in Alcoholics Anonymous: A grounded theory approach. *Journal of Health Communication, 2,* 83–99.

Wright, K. B., & Bell, S. B. (2003). Health-related support groups on the Internet: Linking empirical findings to social support and computer-mediated communication theory. *Journal of Health Psychology, 8,* 37–52.

Wright, K. B., & Frey, L. R. (2008). Communication and care in an acute cancer center: The effects of patients' willingness to communicate about health, healthcare environment perceptions, and health status on information seeking, participation in care practices, and satisfaction. *Health Communication, 23,* 369–379.

Yanek, L. R., Becker, D. M., Moy, T. F., Gittelsohn, J., & Koffman, D. M. (2001). Project job: Faith based cardiovascular health promotion for African American women. *Public Health Reports, 116,* 68–81.

Yeo, G., & Hikoyeda, N. (2000). Cultural issues in end-of-life decision making among Asians and Pacific Islanders in the United States. In K. L. Braun, J. H. Pietsch, & P. L. Blanchette (Eds), *Cultural issues in end-of-life decision making* (pp. 101–125). Thousand Oaks, CA: Sage.

Zoller, H., & Dutta, M. (2008). *Emerging perspectives in health communication: Meaning, culture, and power.* New York: Routledge.

Chapter 6

Communication and Healthcare Organizations

Several years ago, a friend of one of the authors of this book received new lungs for a much-needed and long-awaited transplant. It was not until the 23rd month of the two-year waiting period that she finally received them. Interestingly, this woman would never have received her new lungs if a nurse who had befriended her had not argued on her behalf. The nurse played a pivotal role in influencing the hospital administration, who would not have given her the lungs were it not for the strategic communication the nurse provided to the decision-makers. The nurse was asked how the patient was doing in the hospital, to which the nurse answered, "Oh, she's doing quite well," which was a bit of a stretch. However, if the nurse had answered more bluntly, for example "She's having trouble breathing," then it is near certain that our friend would not be living today. She still has to take more than 30 pills a day, but she is alive and well now nearly 12 years after the transplant—and that is a miracle! Communication played a significant role in the health outcome (i.e. the life) of this incredible woman. An update on this story a few years later: She has been in and out of the hospital numerous times and has nearly died at least twice. They are considering another lung transplant as her lungs continue to slowly fill with fluid, but know it is extremely unlikely that they will get another one so they are mentally preparing for what that will bring (that which we Americans have difficulty talking about . . . the death and dying process). She knows that each day she has is a precious gift and has an amazing attitude. Her husband continues to be extremely supportive, yet he also is stressed out (as one could imagine). He works out almost every day, and is a bit of a workaholic, which is also easy to imagine in terms of coping. They both use humor a lot to cope with the difficulties of daily living and what is likely in the future. They are truly an amazing couple navigating the uncertain and complex healthcare environment almost daily in one way or another and yet they still seem to enjoy life.

As this story illustrates, most of the health communication situations we experience take place within some type of healthcare organization, and our ability to understand

Health Communication in the 21st Century, Second Edition. Kevin Bradley Wright, Lisa Sparks, and H. Dan O'Hair.
© 2013 John Wiley & Sons, Inc. Published 2013 by John Wiley & Sons, Inc.

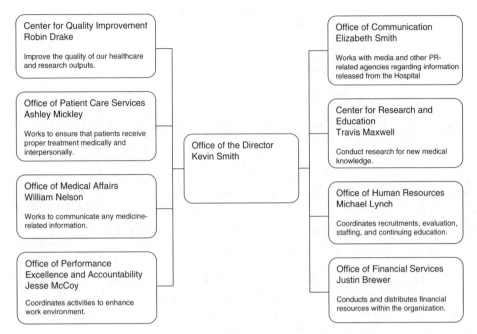

Figure 6.1 Health organizational hierarchy 1: Organizational chart from Oklahoma General Health Care Center.
Source: From the Office of Human Resources at the University of Oklahoma Health Sciences Center: http://hr.ou.edu/. Reprinted with kind permission.

these organizations can have important implications for our health. Our interactions with physicians, dentists, nurses, laboratory technicians, and many other types of providers are often influenced by characteristics of the larger healthcare organization and that organization's relationship with stakeholders in networks of other organizations. While we have seen that provider–patient communication can be quite complex even when it occurs between just you and your doctor, it is important to remember that these interactions are embedded within the norms and practices of a larger complex and confusing healthcare system.

Few organizations are more complex than modern-day healthcare organizations, such as hospitals, nursing homes, and health insurance companies, and communication is an essential part of an organization's ability to function effectively.

This chapter examines a variety of communication issues related to healthcare organizations, including communicative characteristics of organizations, types of healthcare organizations, and some of the major influences on communication within healthcare organizations in today's healthcare system.

Healthcare Organizations as Systems

One helpful way to examine healthcare organizations is to view them as systems. O'Hair, Friedrich, and Dixon (2010) define a system as an interdependent collection of

Figure 6.2 Health organizational hierarchy 2: Organizational chart from Oklahoma General Health Care Center.
Source: From the Office of Human Resources at the University of Oklahoma Health Sciences Center: http://hr.ou.edu/. Reprinted with kind permission.

components that are related to one another and combine their relative strengths to respond to internal changes and external challenges. For example, a hospital can be viewed as a complex system that contains many smaller systems or interrelated units, such as the hospital's administration, radiology department, and nursing department. In addition, hospitals are typically embedded within larger systems that oversee or influence the daily operations of the hospital (e.g. government agencies) or provide it with necessary resources, such as medical supplies (e.g. pharmaceutical companies).

The ways in which healthcare systems function have important implications for patient care. For example, a few years ago another dear friend of one of the authors was fighting fourth-stage esophageal cancer with a nearly three-inch malignant tumor that had metastasized to the liver. The surgeon at one hospital had told him to have the difficult and aggressive chemotherapy and radiation treatment to shrink the tumor down enough to do surgery. The surgeon said, "We can do it. It will be difficult, but if you do your part I can definitely get the tumor out of the esophageal area, move the stomach up and you will survive. The average survival rate is around five years, but you are younger and stronger than those statistics." The surgeon continued to explain the ways in which the tumors have to shrink, particularly the ones in the liver, which may be more difficult depending on where they are located and how much they shrink from the chemotherapy and radiation, but he further expressed that "this operation is absolutely doable." However, the "system" in which a surgeon operates may not be as optimistic about a patient's prognosis due to the cost of such proce-dures. For example, the "system" at another hospital where the author's friend obtained a "second opinion" told him to get his affairs in order, and that no chemo-therapy or radiation would help. In fact, after a courageous fight he died about a year after his initial diagnosis. Both systemic opinions were correct, but coming from dif-ferent perspectives and presenting the information in different ways. Many hospital administrators and other key decision-makers within healthcare systems often find they must focus on the bottom line, while patient care that is tailored to the individual rather than to the system can often take a back seat.

Characteristics of systems

According to *systems theory*, systems have certain characteristics that can influence the communication behaviors of individuals within them. Complex systems such as healthcare organizations are more than the sum of their individual parts. Different units of a system are *interdependent*, and they interact in ways that create outcomes that would not be possible otherwise.

A hospital could not function if it relied only on the services of providers. A physi-cian would have trouble diagnosing and treating a patient's health problems if he or she did not have medical supplies or support from other units in the organization (e.g. nurses, technicians, laboratory personnel), a patient could not treat his or her health problem without the services of pharmacies and health insurance organizations, and the hospital itself could not exist without proper licensing from government health agencies and an administration that managed the business and legal aspects of the hospital (e.g. managing costs, ordering supplies, handling malpractice lawsuits). Each of these units (as well as many others) must work together and coordinate its actions for the hospital to function, and communication within and between different ele-ments of the organization is vital to the organization's ability to function effectively.

Systems have other qualities, such as *homeostasis*, or the ability of a system to self-regulate or achieve a sense of balance when faced with changing conditions. Similar to the thermostat in your home that adjusts to changing temperatures by turning on and off the heater or air conditioner, systems such as healthcare organizations must adapt to changing situations. For example, a normally busy medical clinic that finds itself with fewer patients than average for several months must advertise its services or make other arrangements to attract a suitable number of patients for the business to function. During the cold and flu season, a department of public health may need to take steps to insure a steady supply of flu shots to keep up with the increased demand. In both cases, the organizations are reacting to shifts in the system.

Systemic problems can be costly to health organizations. In fact, during the past decade there has been unprecedented national attention directed toward the safety of patients in hospitals. A "zero tolerance" approach has been put forward for certain healthcare-associated infections (HAIs) deemed preventable. Indeed, a sweeping alliance of professional organizations has fueled a national call to action to eliminate HAIs including the Institute of Medicine, Centers for Disease Control and Prevention, Infectious Diseases Society of America, Association of Professionals in Infection Control and Epidemiology, and the Society for Healthcare Epidemiology of America (Spellberg *et al.*, 2008). This growing movement to protect patients from preventable infections is consistent with the proverbial adage of medicine, *"primum non nocere."*

Generally, there is broad consensus that the burden of HAIs is unacceptably high. An estimated 1.4 million people worldwide have an HAI at any given time (Weinstein, 2008). In the US, there are approximately 2 million annual HAIs among newborns, children and adults that are responsible for nearly 100 000 deaths each year (Klevens, Edwards, & Richards, 2007). This ranks HAIs as the fifth leading cause of death in acute care hospitals (Klevens, Edwards, & Richards, 2007). Data suggest that 5 to 10 percent of hospitalized patients develop an HAI over the course of hospital admission (Weinstein, 2008). If these data are valid estimates today, the number of annual HAIs and attributable deaths may be even higher, given that there are 39.5 million hospitalizations in the US each year (Stewardson *et al.*, 2011).

The financial burden of such systemic problems is staggering. Recent estimates suggest the annual hospital cost of HAIs ranges from $28 billion to $45 billion in the US alone (Kyne, Hamel, Polavaram, & Kelly, 2002). Upwards of 60 percent of HAIs are further due to multi-drug resistant organisms that cannot be treated with most antibiotics and are associated with increased costs, hospital length of stay, and mortality (Spellberg *et al.*, 2008). For example, the excess cost due to HAIs involving methicillin-resistant *Staphylococcus aureus* is known to be $4,000 per infection, whereas the attributable cost of hospital-acquired *Clostridium difficile*-associated diarrhea is $4,500 per patient (Kyne *et al.*, 2002).

In addition, systems exhibit a characteristic known as *equifinality*, which can be defined as the "many different ways by which a system may reach the same end state" (Infante, Rancer, & Womack, 1997, p. 92). In other words, systems such as healthcare organizations often use many different strategies to achieve a desired goal or outcome. For example, if a hospital is faced with a high nursing turnover rate, it can hire new nurses to replace those who have left the organization or find ways to retain existing nurses in an attempt to improve the situation. Increased medical costs within a healthcare organization can be addressed by laying off staff, finding more efficient ways to provide care, and/or focusing on preventive measures to reduce the number of patients who require costly services to treat certain illnesses.

Communication among members of a system is important to achieving homeostasis and the process of equifinality. In order to achieve a sense of balance or improve the situation when faced with challenging conditions, healthcare organizations rely on input from their members. Individuals and units of an organization are needed to provide solutions to issues that threaten the normal functioning of the organization when they arise. While we have seen that there are often many ways an organization can solve problems or meet goals, healthcare organizations need to find the best strategy for reducing costs and providing quality healthcare. This can be an extremely difficult task for healthcare organizations in today's dynamic and competitive healthcare environment. We will examine how members of healthcare organizations communicate with one another to adapt to changing conditions later in this chapter.

Types of Healthcare Organizations

There are currently more types of healthcare organizations than at any other time in history, ranging from small clinics and practices to large government agencies. The growth of these organizations in the modern-day healthcare system is due to many factors, including increased specialization, competition in the healthcare marketplace, managed care, changing professional and legal standards, and the diverse health needs of the US population.

Lammers, Barbour, and Duggan (2003) identify some of the many types of healthcare organizations that we see today (see Table 6.1). Some of these organizations are primarily concerned with financing and regulating health services and products, while others are important in terms of accrediting hospitals and other healthcare delivery organizations or influencing healthcare standards and practices, and many are

Table 6.1   Types of healthcare organizations

Organizations concerned with financing and regulating health services and products
    Centers for Medicare and Medicaid
    Insurance and managed care
Organizations concerned with healthcare delivery
    Departments of public health
    Hospice centers
    Hospitals
    Medical groups
    Nursing homes
    Parish nurse programs
    Physicians' offices
    Pharmaceutical and biotechnological organizations
Professional organizations that influence other healthcare organizations
    Accreditation organizations
    Trade and professional associations

Source: Adapted from Lammers, Barbour, and Duggan (2003).

important in terms of healthcare delivery. In addition to these organizations, other organizations are focused on health-related research. It is important to remember that many of these organizations are interdependent or are influenced by one another in other significant ways.

Health insurance organizations are important for helping consumers to access healthcare services, managing the costs of healthcare, and paying providers for their services. The federal government also provides health insurance through Medicaid and Medicare to serve older adults and individuals with lower incomes. We will examine health insurance, Medicare, and Medicaid in more depth later in this chapter.

Healthcare delivery service organizations exist in both the public and private sector, and they can range from small physicians' offices to large hospitals. While some physicians still work out of private offices, many cannot afford the tremendous costs of running an office, paying staff, and using outside services (such as diagnostic laboratories). These costs have led many doctors to join medical groups where they can share the costs with a small number of other physicians by pooling together resources. Investor-owned and nonprofit hospitals and hospital systems are important healthcare delivery organizations that bring together even more resources than medical groups. Other healthcare organizations include nursing homes, teaching hospitals, hospice services for chronically ill patients, and parish nurse programs in which nurses are hired by churches and other religious organizations to service the needs of their members.

The federal government provides healthcare services for veterans through the Veterans' Administration Healthcare System and it supports other types of hospitals through federal income tax revenue. Federal government organizations overseen by the Department of Health and Human Services, such as the Center for Disease Control and Prevention and the National Cancer Institute, engage in various types of research that influence healthcare practices within healthcare delivery organizations. State and many local governments have departments of public health or other agencies that provide vital services, such as immunizations, HIV and other sexually transmitted disease screening, prenatal care, and psychological counseling. Pharmaceutical and biotechnology organizations as well as hospital supply companies support all of these healthcare delivery organizations.

Finally, organizations such as JCAHO make sure that hospitals and other healthcare facilities meet certain standards of quality healthcare on a two- to three-year basis. JCAHO assesses and accredits almost 15 000 healthcare organizations in the US in a variety of care delivery functions (JCAHO, 2006). According to Lammers, Barbour, and Duggan (2003), "JCAHO accreditation is important to health organizations because it is required by many third-party payers, state licensing agencies, managed care organizations, and financial institutions" (p. 324). In addition to accreditation, professional associations such as the American Medical Association, the American Hospital Association, and the American Nurses Association influence healthcare organizations by advocating certain standards of practice and lobbying for their interests in Congress.

Communication within Healthcare Organizations

Organizational information theory and healthcare organizations

Healthcare organizations must confront many challenges on a daily basis at both the macro and micro levels, such as finding ways to cut costs by efficiently managing resources, taking decisions about how to improve healthcare for consumers, making efforts to retain staff, and promoting the organization in an effort to attract consumers and improve business conditions. Communication is central to successfully meeting these and a host of other challenges typically faced by healthcare organizations. Healthcare organizations must use communication to acquire, manage, disseminate, evaluate, and act upon various types of information to function effectively, and communication is a vital component of the interrelationships within an organization (e.g. administrator–provider relationships, provider–provider relationships, and provider–patient relationships) and the interrelationships among healthcare organizations and other organizations within the healthcare system, such as relationships among hospitals, diagnostic laboratories, pharmaceutical companies, and health insurance organizations.

Organizational information theory is a useful framework to assess the various ways in which healthcare organizations use information to function on a daily basis and to meet organizational goals. Karl Weick (1979) developed organizational information theory to describe the process by which organizations collect, manage, and use information they receive. Two important tenets of this theory are that change is a constant within organizations, and that confronting change successfully is necessary for the survival of organizations. For example, in the last 50 years, we have seen hospitals and other healthcare organizations respond to many changes in the health landscape, including provider specialization, the rise of managed care, healthcare legislation (such as the Health Insurance Portability and Accountability Act), an increase in the number of female physicians, nursing shortages, an aging population, diseases like HIV and Severe Acute Respiratory Syndrome (SARS), and the threat of biological terrorism. Healthcare organizations cannot ignore significant changes and trends such as these in health and healthcare and expect to remain competitive in today's healthcare market. Organizations must adjust to these types of changes as they occur, and communication plays an important role in the process of adapting to them.

Organizations rely on members within the organization who are skilled in certain areas to interpret information, or the organization can find people outside of the organization (i.e. using affiliations with other organizations or resources) to help interpret the information. Based upon the interpretation of the information, organizations first decide whether the information is relevant or useful to the goals of the organization, then they must decide how to use the information or adapt to it so that organizational goals are met. For example, suppose hospital administrators learn that poor physician handwriting has led to a high percentage of mistakes in filling prescriptions at the hospital pharmacy. While it may be relatively easy to interpret that this information is relevant to the organization and poses a problem to organizational goals (such as providing quality patient care and avoiding lawsuits), finding ways to solve the problem can be somewhat ambiguous. By consulting with a team of experts within the organization, a computer specialist might suggest that physicians use a personal data assistant (PDA) device, where they could select from a list of medications when prescribing for patients, and then the information could be sent by wireless technology from the PDA directly to a computer in the pharmacy. The administrators might conclude that this is the best way to manage the issue, or after consulting with other experts within the organization (such as an accountant) they may feel that this option would be too expensive, and they may continue to seek other information about ways to solve the problem.

According to Weick (1979), organizations engage in communication patterns known as *cycles*, which include an action, a response, and an adjustment. An action might be a question someone within the organization raises when confronted with an ambiguous problem he or she encounters, such as if a nurse asks why so many children are coming into the clinic with otitus media (an ear infection). A response to this action might be: "I saw this problem last winter during flu season" from a fellow nurse. The first nurse might adjust to this information by alerting physicians that they might expect to see a number of cases in the near future. Of course, when the physicians hear about this problem, it may lead to additional cycles (e.g. more questions, responses, and adjustments). These multiple cycles are known as *double interact loops* according to Weick (1979).

Most healthcare organizations have formal rules and policies for interpreting and acting upon ambiguous information as it surfaces. In organizations with formal organizational structures, ambiguous information is typically delegated to individuals who specialize in certain areas of knowledge, and many healthcare organizations rely upon hierarchical structures to process information. Hierarchies often have the advantage of processing information quickly and efficiently, but they can be problematic if organizations rely too much on individuals at the top of the hierarchy, such as managers, directors, and administrators, to interpret, process, and disseminate equivocal information. Ambiguous information is often encountered at various levels of organizations. For example, sometimes issues that can affect an entire hospital are first encountered by administrators, while at other times they are first recognized by people on the "front lines" of healthcare, such as nurses and receptionists. Other times pertinent information about an issue that will have a major impact on the organization can come from a particular department within the organization, such as the hospital security department.

O'Hair, O'Rourke, and O'Hair (2001) identify three common forms of message flow within healthcare organizations. When upper managers or administrators identify issues and messages are then communicated to the lower levels of the hierarchy, this is known as *downward communication*. Conversely, when people at the lower levels of the hierarchy, such as maintenance personnel, encounter information that may be useful to the organization and communicate messages to people at higher levels, this is known as *upward communication*. When messages are communicated among individuals who share a similar status within the organization, such as information exchanged among nurses, this is known as *horizontal communication*. Healthcare organizations with traditional hierarchical structures tend to privilege downward communication, and this can be detrimental to the organization since people at lower levels of healthcare organizations often possess important information about day-to-day operations and events that the higher levels of the organization may not be aware of, even though this information can be vital to the organization's success. For example, charge nurses are some of the most vital members of hospital organizations since they assist other nurses, order medicine, and organize schedules and other duties that appear out of the blue. All too often these important organizational resources are not consulted on the very issues they deal with on a daily basis. Instead, they receive emails and memos dictating policy for the very floors of the hospital they serve.

Messages can also be communicated through *formal and informal organizational communication networks* (Kreps & Thornton, 1992). Formal communication networks are tied to the structure of the organization, and messages may include emails, memos, handbooks, and other forms of written or oral communication, while informal channels tend to be more interpersonal and are linked to workers' need for additional information about organizational events and issues. Informal communication networks often consist of relationships that develop within the organization through day-to-day interactions. For example, supervisors make friends with subordinates, employees from different areas of the organization eat lunch and go to happy hour together, and people begin to rely on one another for various types of organizational information, including everyday gossip about personalities and opinions about policy changes and regulations. While a hospital memo might announce that the administration is considering hiring a new director of nursing from within the organization, employees may use friends in different departments or among the administration to find out which individuals might be the best candidates.

Informal leaders can emerge from these networks, and these individuals can sometimes become more powerful than formal leaders, especially when people trust them more than formal leaders. As we will see in the next section, informal networks are an important part of organizational culture, and administrators need to be aware of the influence of informal networks on employee perceptions of the organization and behaviors.

Healthcare Organization Culture

Healthcare organizations use communication for more than processing information and managing uncertainty: communication is central to the development and maintenance of relationships and the creation of organizational culture. A culture can be defined as the beliefs, assumptions, attitudes, and values a group of individuals share about the world based upon common experiences. In other words, when people share similar experiences on a regular basis, they often develop similar ways of seeing the world. All of us are members of many different cultures that are based upon common interests or shared realities due to common experiences (e.g. communication majors, sororities and fraternities, religious organizations, clubs), and like the cultures of these groups, members of healthcare organizations develop unique ways of seeing the organization and their experiences within it through day-to-day interactions.

Communication scholars who take a cultural approach to organizations argue that individuals within organizations create meanings for everyday events that occur in organizations, and they ultimately develop a unique sense of organizational reality (Eisenberg & Riley, 2001; O'Reilly, Chatman, & Caldwell, 1991; Pacanowsky & O'Donnell-Trujillo, 1982). These scholars contend that organizational members constantly create meanings for the behaviors they observe within the organization in an attempt to make sense of their world. The meanings that individual members create are shared with others through different forms of communication within the organization, such as symbols, stories, and rituals. These messages as well as the physical layout of hospitals, clinics, and other healthcare organizations can reflect the beliefs, attitudes, and values of an organization.

For example, in a hospital that values a holistic approach to healthcare, such as addressing patients' emotional needs in addition to providing care for physical health problems, stories about organizational heroes, such as a story about a nurse who called a patient at home on several occasions following a mastectomy to see how she was coping emotionally after the procedure, might be frequently told by members. Such a story would legitimize the organization's culture value of going beyond physical health when providing patient care, and by portraying the nurse's actions as heroic or favorable the story suggests that her behavior should be emulated by other employees. Other stories, such as those about organizational "villains" or individuals who behaved in ways that were contrary to the beliefs, attitudes, and values of the organization, might also be told to indirectly disseminate information about culturally undesirable behaviors.

Several years ago, one of the authors conducted a study (Wright & Frey, 2008) that examined a comprehensive cancer center in Memphis, Tennessee. This cancer center wanted to create a "home-like" environment for its clients as opposed to a more institutionalized medical setting (such as the sterile environment that is often seen in large hospitals). This desire to create a warm and friendly environment at the center was reflected in the physical surroundings, which resembled a comfortable living room, including a kitchen and meeting rooms for clients, rather than the look of a traditional medical clinic. The clients indicated that they perceived the center to be more like a home than an institution, and this perception influenced their communication with staff members and satisfaction with the center.

Insights into the beliefs, attitudes, and values of other healthcare organizations can often be gained by examining organizational promotional materials, such as pamphlets and television commercials. In several cities, hospitals and medical centers have purchased state-of-the-art medical technology and often advertise these services as a way of conveying to potential patients that they have the ability to provide "cutting-edge" medical care. However, because technology is often perceived as cold and inhuman in our culture, many of these organizations also wish to convey to consumers that they still value caring relationships with patients despite the technology. For example, one hospital in Oklahoma City uses advertising slogans such as: "We provide the touch beyond the technology."

In addition to the overall cultural values of healthcare organizations, numerous co-cultures, or smaller groups of individuals with their own unique system of beliefs, attitudes, and values, exist within them. As we will discuss in greater detail in Chapter 11, healthcare organizations consist of individuals from a wide variety of backgrounds in terms of education and training. The unique socialization of administrators, physicians, nurses, technicians, and other healthcare workers creates distinct co-cultures within health organizations, and differences in worldviews between each of these co-cultures can lead to misunderstandings, different expectations of healthcare, and sometimes conflict between groups (O'Hair, Thompson, & Gilchrist, 2004).

Influences on Healthcare Organization Communication

Pharmaceutical and biotechnology companies

Pharmaceutical companies are an important influence on healthcare organizations because they are the main suppliers of the prescription drugs that are commonly used to treat a multitude of health conditions. Major pharmaceutical companies, such as Pfizer, Merck, and Bristol Myers Squibb, are under tremendous pressure to generate quarterly profits for their investors, and the promotion of prescription drugs represents a growing source of pharmaceutical marketing. These companies market new prescription drugs to providers through the use of pharmaceutical sales representatives and to consumers through direct-to-consumer advertising (see Chapter 8).

Pharmaceutical companies spend a substantial portion of their marketing budgets promoting prescription medications to health organizations. Physicians and other providers frequently attend seminars, lunches, and other promotional events sponsored by drug companies, and pharmaceutical sales representatives make frequent visits to hospitals, clinics, and other major health facilities in an effort to persuade providers to prescribe their company's medications. Many pharmaceutical companies do not necessarily rely on convincing medical arguments to persuade physicians to adopt their products. Pharmaceutical companies often try to hire attractive individuals as sales representatives who provide physicians and other providers with free sample packets of medications. Many of the events sponsored by drug companies are designed to "wine and dine," or persuade providers by offering free lunches and other perks for attending a sales event. For example, one of the authors worked as a researcher at a family medicine center in Oklahoma City and was invited to a free pharmaceutical company luncheon that included a huge barbeque buffet, including ribs, fried chicken, and free cocktails. The purpose of the event, ironically, was to promote a new appetite suppressant medication.

Direct-to-consumer marketing is an effective marketing tool for pharmaceutical companies (Holmer, 1999). Direct-to-consumer advertising urges consumers to "ask your doctor about" a particular medication. Undoubtedly you have seen some of the many direct-to-consumer advertisements for various medications on television in recent years, including Viagra, cholesterol-reducing medications, allergy pills (such as Claritan), hormone replacement therapy (HRT) drugs for women facing menopause, and a host of anti-anxiety and depression medications. Both pharmaceutical sales representatives and direct-to-consumer advertising appear to influence provider prescribing behaviors. For example, Ubel, Jepson, and Asch (2003) found that physician prescription practices were associated with the provision of free samples of medications by pharmaceutical representatives. We will examine drug advertisements in more depth in Chapter 10.

While patients certainly need these medications for treating their health problems and providers need them to help patients, the rising cost of many of these medications (particularly newer ones) has raised many questions about whether more expensive drugs are more effective than cheaper drugs, and about ethical issues surrounding the process of prescription drug marketing.

For example, many health problems, such as certain types of heart disease, can be treated with relatively inexpensive medications such as beta-blockers, but cardiologists and other physicians often continue to favor more expensive medications like angiotensin-converting enzyme (ACE) inhibitors and calcium channel blockers as their first choice for treating patients largely due to the influence of pharmaceutical sales representatives who promote these higher-priced drugs (Ubel, Jepson, & Asch, 2003). Prescribing more expensive drugs increases profits for pharmaceutical companies, but it can have a negative impact on patients in a variety of ways. The practice of prescribing higher-priced medications can unfairly favor higher-income patients who can pay for them. Lower-income patients and older patients on fixed incomes often find it difficult to afford prescription medications. Medicaid and Medicare are two organizations that were created to help lower-income and older patients, but they often only pay for a small percentage of drug costs, resulting in more money the patient has to spend to purchase the medication. This may lead to lower compliance on the part of the patient when it becomes too expensive to continue taking the drug.

One questionable practice that occurs in many hospitals and medical centers is clinical *preceptorships*. During a preceptorship, a pharmaceutical company representative spends the day with the physician seeing patients "as an educational experience," but the physician receives an honorarium (often hundreds of dollars) from the drug company in return. While sales representatives may indeed learn much about medicine during a preceptorship, the primary reason for this activity is ultimately to build relationships between sales representatives and providers for the purpose of selling the company's medications.

In addition, patients who learn about medications through direct-to-consumer marketing may influence their providers to prescribe medications they don't really need. The over-prescribing of antibiotics in the US is related to patient requests during office visits for these drugs, and many times providers will prescribe them even when they know the medication will have little effect. While direct-to-consumer marketing of medications may be educational for patients and facilitate communication between providers and patients when they are discussed, these medications can have unwanted side effects or may be inappropriate for patients in other ways, and this can lead to other health problems if the doctor feels pressured by the patient to prescribe them.

Providers often do not question the practices of pharmaceutical marketing or do not critically examine conflicts of interest that may develop as a result of their relationships with drug sales representatives. For example, one study found that medicine residents and faculty had relatively low levels of knowledge about physician–

pharmaceutical industry relationships (Watkins & Kimberly, 2004). Research suggests that pharmaceutical companies will most likely continue these marketing strategies in the future (Holmer, 1999), and more education about the many ethical issues surrounding the relationships between pharmaceutical companies and health organizations is needed.

Health Insurance and Accountability Act

In 1996 the US Congress passed the Health Insurance Portability and Accountability Act (HIPAA), which was designed to lower healthcare costs, safeguard identifiable patient data, and promote e-commerce in health. The law required that healthcare organizations identified by HIPAA be compliant by April of 2003. The implementation of HIPAA has affected healthcare organizations in a variety of ways.

Patient privacy Efforts to become compliant with the patient privacy section of HIPAA have been very costly for healthcare organizations. The patient privacy section of HIPAA requires healthcare organizations to protect verbal, written, and electronic patient data. Health organizations have had to spend billions of dollars making changes to the way that patient information is handled in order to comply with these standards. For example, HIPAA requires health organizations to hire a privacy officer (who coordinates efforts to meet privacy regulations), to set up new privacy policies and procedures, to train employees to safeguard identifiable patient data, and to periodically review daily operations to insure that the privacy standards are being met. Verification of organizational compliance can occur through random unannounced visits by the Department of Health and Human Services, the Office of Civil Rights, or through health information privacy complaints filed against an individual or the organization (Bradley, 2004).

According to Gunter (2002), "the privacy rule is estimated to have a $3 billion financial impact on the US economy over the next 10 years" (p. 50). These costs will ultimately be passed on to consumers in the form of higher health insurance premiums. Failure to comply with HIPAA privacy protocols can be expensive, including fines for wrongful disclosure of health information ranging from $50 000 to $250 000 and imprisonment from one to ten years (Gunter, 2002). The law also allows for civil lawsuit awards up to $25 000 per violation.

While HIPAA privacy standards are costly for healthcare organizations, the privacy section offers benefits to patients. In recent years, many consumers have become concerned about third parties gaining access to their health records. Sensitive information within health records, including HIV status or history of other diseases and conditions, unhealthy lifestyle information (such as whether or not a patient smokes or drinks), and personal information, are typically not the types of information most people want revealed to insurance companies, researchers, hospital staff, or other third parties such as pharmaceutical companies and marketing firms. Physicians and other healthcare workers frequently write notes about patients in medical charts, particularly information about patient behaviors, such as when they are confrontational, moody, or perceived to be problem patients. In the past, receptionists, nurses, and other individuals working within the organization could easily access this information. Under HIPAA, sensitive patient information is more secure than in the past, although the law has not completely eliminated all third parties from seeing this type of information.

HIPAA's effect on medical research Hospitals and medical facilities are not only places where people come to be treated for health problems, they are also sites for medical research. Researchers need access to patient populations to test new medications, medical procedures, and new approaches to healthcare delivery (including health communication studies). Under HIPAA, researchers must obtain detailed written permission from patients to use individually identifiable patient data, and this new rule is making it more costly for healthcare organizations to conduct research. Prior to HIPAA, researchers could access patient records and other information more easily, requiring in many cases only a brief review by the organization's Institutional Review Board. According to Kulynych and Korn (2002), "Erecting new regulatory barriers to the use or disclosure of medical information imposes costs, not only in terms of real dollars, but also in terms of research delayed or perhaps forgone" (p. 204). However, the more stringent policies toward protecting patient data in the research process may encourage greater patient participation because potential participants will have assurances that sensitive information will remain private.

HIPAA's effect on providers and patients Under HIPAA, doctors are required to obtain a patient's permission before sending their information to pharmacies, laboratories, and insurance companies. Patients can also request a report of all parties who have seen their health information, and patients must be permitted to review and amend their medical records. Providers are required to explain privacy issues to every patient they treat and answer any questions a patient may have about the HIPAA privacy policies. Many providers feel that this new requirement may take time away from other activities during appointments with patients. As we have seen earlier, providers face a number of time constraints during provider–patient interactions, and many providers feel that the HIPAA requirements add to an already heavy workload. However, Ross and Lin (2003), in a review of studies that examined the effects of patient access to medical records due to HIPAA, found that the increased opportunities for providers and patients to talk about the patient's medical records could enhance provider–patient communication.

Medicare and Medicaid

The US government provides health insurance to about 74 million Americans through the Centers for Medicare and Medicaid. The Centers for Medicare and Medicaid were created in 1965 and provide a safety net for US citizens who may find it difficult to obtain health insurance from other sources due to factors such as living on a fixed income, difficulty obtaining employment because of a disability, and living beneath the poverty level. Individuals 65 years of age and older are eligible for Medicare benefits as well as people (old or young) with a permanent disability, while Medicaid provides health insurance to lower-income individuals and their children. The Centers for Medicare and Medicaid impose many rules and regulations on providers in terms of how they will be reimbursed for healthcare services. Each US state is allowed to determine eligibility requirements for Medicare and Medicaid, and the health services that are reimbursed by these programs vary from state to state (Lammers, Barbour, & Duggan, 2003).

There is great concern over the ability of the federal government to continue covering medical expenses through Medicare and Medicaid due to rising healthcare costs and the aging of the US population. Medicare currently covers two-thirds of the healthcare costs for older adults in the US, and with the number of individuals 65 and older projected to grow substantially over the next decade, the Medicare program will need to find new ways to assure quality healthcare services for US citizens. Medicare currently has a number of restrictions on types of services that individuals can obtain from providers, and many individuals on Medicare find it difficult to afford prescription drugs because in many cases Medicare will only reimburse individuals for a small portion of the cost of these medications. This problem is exacerbated by the rising cost of prescription drugs and the tendency for pharmaceutical companies to promote more expensive products. Many hospitals and other health facilities provide only limited services to individuals being reimbursed by Medicaid, and during financial downturns certain Medicaid services can be eliminated as a cost-cutting measure (Vock, 2005).

In 1985 the US Congress passed legislation to extend Medicare benefits to people living in nursing homes, and under this newer legislation Medicare now covers the costs of approved hospice programs for terminally ill individuals. However, these services are often underused because of delayed referrals and lack of information about them (Miller & Mor, 2001). Medicare and Medicaid restrictions on the reimbursement of providers, medical procedures, and medications will likely continue to influence the practices of health organizations in the future.

Insurance and managed care

The introduction of managed care in the US has transformed healthcare delivery from an activity controlled by providers to one controlled by healthcare bureaucracies (Hafferty & Light, 1995; Moore, O'Hair, & Ledlow, 2002). According to Anthony (2002), "the purpose of managed care is to effectively coordinate and oversee the delivery of care such that excessive and possibly unnecessary care is eliminated, thereby improving quality while reducing costs" (p. 2033). Managed care organizations help bring providers and patients together in a way that is financially beneficial to both parties (and to the managed care organization). These organizations help providers gain access to consumers by offering consumers attractively priced health plans, advertising the plans, and working with employers who offer health plans to recruit potential consumers. In addition, managed care organizations create binding contracts with physicians, other providers, hospitals, and other health facilities, making them legally obligated to participate in managed care health plans, but the contracts also insure that they will be reimbursed for their services. Consumers prepay for services through monthly premiums, but they have the benefit of being able to access providers and health facilities when needed, while providers and health facilities have the advantage of being able to rely on a steady inflow of patients who need their services.

There are many types of managed care organizations today. According to Street (2003), "as we enter the 21st century, managed care has grown into a complex and multifaceted phenomenon with no singular identity." However, Street goes on to say that "practically all medical care is 'managed' in some way" (p. 72). Consumers can choose many types of managed care plans, ranging from traditional prepaid indemnity insurance policies that cover catastrophic events to access (albeit limited by the stipulations of the health plan) to networks of providers, facilities, and services for a fixed amount of money per year. This section discusses three major types of managed care: traditional health insurance, health maintenance organizations, and preferred provider organizations. Of course, there are many hybrid managed care plans, and these often combine features of each of these types of managed care.

Traditional health insurance, similar to car or home insurance, can be expensive for most consumers, although there are many different plans that are currently offered in today's market. Most of these plans pay for services in times of severe need, such as if an individual needs an operation or if he or she has been in an accident. These plans typically carry a deductible, and consumers have to pay a premium for the insurance. Like other types of insurance, the amount of premium will typically rise as a consumer makes more insurance claims. These types of plans are helpful for disastrous events, but they may not be ideal when less costly health services are needed for preventive health services, such as check-ups and diagnostic tests (e.g. blood tests).

Health maintenance organizations (HMOs) are an example of an early type of managed care organization, and they are still a popular option for consumers today. HMOs typically allow consumers access to a hospital system or a relatively small network of providers, facilities, and services. Consumers prepay a set amount for access to the HMO, and they can obtain healthcare when necessary. One disadvantage of HMOs is that patients are typically assigned a primary care physician, who serves as a gatekeeper allowing patients to access services and other providers (such as specialists). Typically, a patient must obtain a referral from his or her primary physician in order to gain access to services and other providers within the HMO. In some cases patients must call in to a triage center where a health professional determines their level of care and makes a recommendation (Ledlow, O'Hair, & Moore, 2003). In addition, patients are only allowed to access providers, facilities, and services that are within the domain of the HMO, and they are not covered if they use services outside of the HMO. The HMO Act of 1973 required larger employers to make an HMO plan available for workers, and this led to the rapid rise of these organizations (Lammers, Barbour, and Duggan, 2003). However, newer managed care options have provided consumers with other choices besides HMOs.

Preferred provider organizations (PPOs) "are a less unified form of managed care that offers patients wider (though still limited) choices of physicians and hospitals at varying levels of costs reflecting discounts providers are willing to give to attract patients" (Lammers, Barbour, & Duggan, 2003). Under PPO plans, consumers are allowed to choose from a list of providers and services, including specialists. One advantage of PPOs is that consumers do not need to see a primary care physician when they require health services. If a patient is experiencing foot problems, she is free to choose a podiatrist from a list of podiatrists offered by the PPO rather than having to see a primary care physician first. The list of providers offered by most PPO plans typically includes most types of specialists and several providers working within each specialty. The wider amount of health service choices within PPOs has led to an increase in their popularity. However, like HMOs, providers are often limited by the plan to certain treatment options, and consumers are penalized financially or not covered in some cases if they choose a provider or service that is outside of the PPO services network.

Effects of managed care on provider–patient relationships While managed care has made health insurance more affordable for consumers, many patients feel their provider's behaviors (e.g. treatment decisions) are dictated by managed care organizations, and this has negatively affected patient perceptions of trust towards providers (Davies & Rundall, 2000). Costs are often contained under managed care by managing the number of referrals made to specialists (Halm, Causino, & Blumenthal, 1997). Because specialty care is associated with higher medical costs (Greenfield *et al.*, 1992), providers often play the role of gatekeeper by limiting patient access to specialists and more expensive procedures through the referral process. Under managed care, primary care providers are limited to a list of approved providers to whom they can refer patients. Patients and providers often resent the restrictions on health services that are placed upon them by managed care plans. Patients want to have more choices in terms of which providers they can see and the services they can obtain, and providers often desire greater flexibility in referring patients to the best specialists and services possible. Cost-cutting associated with managed care in recent decades has led to an increase in clinical workload, downsizing of staff, and redefinitions of caregiver roles (Apker, 2001; Ray & Apker, 2011). In addition, physicians employed in managed care settings report greater job dissatisfaction, reduced autonomy, higher patient loads, and communication problems. All of these can produce strain on provider–patient interactions. Increased provider workloads may also lead to longer waiting times for patients, and this has been linked to lower patient satisfaction with providers and the larger healthcare organization (Cassidy-Smith, Baumann, & Boudreaux, 2007; Moore, Wright, & Bernard, 2009). As we will see in the next section, these and other aspects of managed care have had a major impact on provider stress and relationships with patients.

Provider Stress, Conflict, and Support within Healthcare Organizations

Healthcare organizations are inherently stressful environments for providers, and this can lead to employee burnout and problems with patient care (Ray & Apker, 2011). For example, stressors that have traditionally existed within healthcare organizations include staff shortages, work overload, time pressures, having to answer to multiple supervisors, administrative and co-worker conflict, dealing with organizational bureaucracy, lack of support from superiors and peers, and uncertainty concerning ability to treat patients (Simoni & Patterson, 1997; Tyler & Cushway, 1995).

Communicating with patients can be stressful for providers in a variety of ways. Patients may be worried or anxious about their health condition, embarrassed by questions asked by providers, angry or abusive, and they may have difficulty expressing their thoughts and feelings to providers (Maslach & Jackson, 1982). Providers may find it difficult to discuss emotional topics, deliver bad news to the patient, or deal with the patient's family members (O'Hair *et al.*, 2003).

A major contributor to healthcare provider job stress is role conflict and role ambiguity. According to Apker and Ray (2003), *role conflict* "refers to a person having to engage in two or more incompatible roles simultaneously," while *role ambiguity* "refers to a lack of clarity regarding the definition and expectations for a particular role" (p. 351). For example, nurses may experience role conflict when taking on the role of patient advocate (e.g. protecting the rights of patients and being sensitive to their needs) while simultaneously playing the role of a "good employee" who needs to answer to physicians and administrators. In terms of role ambiguity, under-managed care practices nurses are being asked to perform more administrative duties, such as documenting insurance information for patients, and they may question whether the main focus of their job is to care for patients' physical and emotional needs or to take care of their insurance needs. Many other duties that nurses are sometimes expected to perform, such as answering telephones and admitting new patients, are not clearly defined by hospital administrators as part of their job description, and nurses often find it frustrating when asked to perform duties that are incompatible with their expectations of what their job actually entails.

Additionally, stress among healthcare workers can result from *emotional labor*, or the job-related need to display socially appropriate emotions when interacting with others within healthcare contexts (Apker & Ray, 2003). For example, providers such as nurses often must display empathy and concern for patients in an effort to comfort them, and have to suppress emotions such as anger when interacting with uncooperative patients or sadness when interacting with a terminally ill patient (so they do not upset the patient further), and they must suppress other emotions in an effort to act "professional" when communicating with co-workers. Management of these emotions can be a difficult task to accomplish for providers, and it can lead to stress and emotional exhaustion. Many providers also must contend with *work–life* conflict (Ray & Apker, 2011), which involves with managing their emotions and the frequent competing demands of work and obligations outside of the workplace (such as family and social demands). For example, after a stressful day, providers often do not want to display emotions such as anger, sadness, or frustration to their family members or loved ones, and they suppress these emotions (which may lead to increased stress).

In recent years a variety of changes have redefined the healthcare profession, and in many cases these changes have led to increased stress for healthcare workers. The increased surveillance of medical expenses by managed care organizations has led to a situation where providers must think more about the costs of procedures and medications, a patient's insurance coverage, and administrative duties (documenting adherence to managed care regulations), and these changes can negatively affect the quality of provider–patient communication (Lammers & Geist, 1997). Under-managed care, providers may feel they have less time to address patients' emotional concerns, their communication with patients may become more formal, and patients often feel more dehumanized (Lammers & Geist, 1997). In addition, according to Buiser (2000), current trends such as case management, downsizing, restructuring of the workforce, and changes in patient profile have negatively affected job satisfaction among healthcare workers. For example, recent trends point to increased overtime for healthcare workers to cover staff shortages related to downsizing, and increases in overtime have been linked to a greater likelihood of medical errors, stress, fatigue, and burnout (Garrett, 2008; Letvak, 2001).

Stress and conflict

Stress and conflict within healthcare organizations are often interrelated. Managing the multiple demands placed upon healthcare workers inside and outside of the workplace (e.g. incompatible personalities in the workplace, financial problems, family problems) increases stress and can lead to conflict among healthcare workers and between healthcare workers and their loved ones outside of the workplace (Decker, 1997; Miller & Gilles, 1996). Conflict, in turn, tends to produce more stress for healthcare workers, and this may lead to additional conflict. Healthcare workers tend to work closely together in a fast-paced environment where they often have to deal with multiple patients, carry out unpleasant duties (e.g. removing bedpans from hospitalized patients), perform administrative duties, cope with the bureaucracy of the healthcare organization (e.g. forms and procedures set forth by administrators), and work in an environment where people vary widely in terms of status and education (Apker & Ray, 2003).

Individuals differ in the way they handle conflict and tend to exhibit patterns of conflict that are trait-like, or relatively stable and consistent over time (Hample, 1999). Some people tend to be argumentative, which involves focusing on issues (presenting and defending one's own position and refuting another's), while other individuals tend to be verbally aggressive (using personal attacks as opposed to focusing on the issues) or conflict avoidant (refusing to engage in an argument or withdrawing from the setting). (For reviews of this research see Deutsch & Coleman, 2000; Infante & Wigley, 1986; Rahim, 2001.) When individuals with different conflict traits engage in conflict, this can lead to unsatisfying outcomes. For example, a radiology technician who is argumentative will find it frustrating when arguing with a physician who tends to be verbally aggressive, and she may resent the physician for making personal attacks rather than focusing on the issues. Wright (2011) found that healthcare workers who had higher levels of communication competence were more likely to use productive conflict styles when managing conflict with their coworkers, such as collaborative styles, and they had lower levels of stress and burnout, and higher levels of job satisfaction. Conversely, healthcare workers with lower levels of communication competence were more likely to use unproductive conflict styles, such as aggression and conflict avoidance, and they had higher levels of stress and burnout (and lower levels of job satisfaction).

In addition, healthcare workers frequently encounter unpleasant patients or patients who are unhappy because of their fear of seeing a provider or uncertainty over their health status, and this can lead to conflict between providers and patients. Like any other workplace, unpleasant personalities, inflated egos, and other interpersonal issues can lead to conflict among workers, but these problems are often magnified in stressful healthcare settings.

Effects of job stress

Stress appears to be inevitable in healthcare organizations, and stress can lead to many negative outcomes for healthcare workers, including, fear, uncertainty, insecurity, frustration, resentment, anger, sadness, depression, guilt, betrayal, and distrust (Young & Brown, 1998). One effect of job stress is _burnout_, or a "syndrome of emotional exhaustion, depersonalization, and reduced personal accomplishment" (Maslach & Jackson, 1982, p. 228). When healthcare workers experience burnout, they may see little value in their job or no longer care about performing their duties well. Stress and burnout can lead to higher job dissatisfaction, and dissatisfaction may exhibit itself in the form of lower productivity, higher absenteeism, increased work errors, poor judgement, defensive behavior, hostility, reduction in creativity, and higher job turnover (Ray & Apker, 2011; Buiser, 2000). For example, in recent years there has been a shortage of nurses in the US, and a major contributing factor to the nursing shortage is dissatisfaction with stressful conditions in the workplace (Apker, 2001; _Nursing World_, 2001). Bacharach, Bamberger, and Conley (1991) found that high levels of role conflict experienced by nurses at work were predictive of higher levels of job burnout and lower levels of satisfaction. This situation has become especially acute among younger nurses (Shrader _et al._, 2001).

In addition, low job satisfaction may adversely affect the quality of patient care (Douglas, Meleis, Eribes, & Kim, 1996) and reduced productivity (Ray & Apker, 2011). Preventable medical errors are the eighth most common cause of death in the US (Sexton, Thomas, & Helmreich, 2000), and when healthcare workers are dissatisfied, they may become less sensitive to patient needs, and less concerned or neglectful in terms of performing duties. Moreover, dissatisfaction in the workplace and job stress can lead to other problems that can affect patient care. Substance abuse, for example, is common among healthcare workers and is often related to job stress and job dissatisfaction (Shattner & Coman, 1998).

Support and stress in the workplace

Support networks in the workplace have been found to protect healthcare workers from adverse mental and physical health consequences of job stressors (Dignam & West, 1988; Voltmer & Spahn, 2009). Perceived availability of support in hospitals has been linked to a reduction in emotional exhaustion and burnout among healthcare workers (Cronin-Stubbs & Rooks, 1985; Firth, McIntee, McKeown, & Britton, 1986; Hare, Pratt, & Andrews, 1988; Ogus, 1990). For example, studies have) found that nurses who had more supervisory support experienced reduced burnout, depersonalization, and emotional exhaustion (Halbesleben, 2008; McGilton *et al.*, 2007). Studies have found that both social support and positive coping activities (such as problem-focused coping, see Chapter 4) are associated with the ability to solve problems more effectively and fewer sick days in healthcare organizations (Koleck *et al.*, 2000). Wright, Banas, Bessarabova, & Bernard (2010) found that healthcare workers who had greater communication competence in their interactions with coworkers were more likely to be satisfied with the support they received in the workplace and were less likely to experience stress and job burnout.

Summary

Healthcare organizations are an integral part of healthcare delivery and an important context for examining health communication. Healthcare organizations facilitate healthcare by pooling together many resources, and these resources are used by organizations to adapt to changing conditions. In addition, healthcare organizations can be viewed as cultures with their own unique beliefs, attitudes, and values. Interactions at the smallest levels of healthcare organizations, such as talk between providers and patients, are often influenced by forces at higher levels of the organization and the larger healthcare system. Pharmaceutical companies, government agencies, and managed care organizations have considerable influence on the day-to-day operations of healthcare organizations. Finally, healthcare organizations are stressful and demanding environments for healthcare workers, and this can lead to many negative outcomes, such as health problems, burnout, and conflict. However, social support networks within these organizations can help individuals cope with stress, reduce burnout, and improve the quality of care.

References

Anthony, D. (2002). Changing the nature of physician referral relationships in the US: The impact of managed care. *Social Science and Medicine, 56*, 2033–2044.

Apker, J. (2001). Role development in the managed care era: A case in hospital-based nursing. *Journal of Applied Communication Research, 29*, 117–136.

Apker, J., & Ray, E. B. (2003). Stress and social supporting health care organizations. In T. L. Thompson, A. M. Dorsey, K. I. Miller, & R. Parrott (Eds), *Handbook of health communication* (pp. 347–368). Mahwah, NJ: Lawrence Erlbaum.

Bacharach, S., Bamberger, P., & Conley, C. (1991). Work–home conflict among nurses and engineers: Mediating the impact of role stress on burnout and satisfaction at work. *Journal of Organizational Behavior, 12*, 39–53.

Bradley, D. (2004). HIPAA compliance efforts. *Pediatric Emergency Care, 20*(1), 68–70.

Buiser, M. (2000). Surviving managed care: The effect on job satisfaction in hospital-based nursing. *MEDSURG Nursing, 9*, 129–134.

Cassidy-Smith, T. N., Baumann, B. M., & Boudreaux, E. D. (2007). The disconfirmation paradigm: Throughput times and emergency department patient satisfaction. *Journal of Emergency Medicine, 32*, 7–13.

Cronin-Stubbs, D., & Rooks, C. A. (1985). The stress, social support, and burnout of critical care nurses: The results of research. *Heart and Lung, 14*(1), 31–39.

Daft, R. L., & Lengel, R. H. (1986). Organizational information requirements, media richness, and structural design. *Management Science, 22*, 554–571.

Davies, H., & Rundall, T. (2000). Managing patient trust in managed care. *Milbank Quarterly, 778,* 609–624.

Decker, F. H. (1997). Occupational and nonoccupational factors in job satisfaction and psychological distress among nurses. *Research in Nursing and Health, 20,* 453–464.

Deutsch, M., & Coleman, P. T. (Eds). (2000). *The handbook of conflict resolution: Theory and practice.* San Francisco, CA: Jossey-Bass.

Dignam, J. T., & West, S. G. (1988). Social support in the workplace: Tests of six theoretical models. *American Journal of Community Psychology, 16,* 701–724.

Douglas, M. K., Meleis, A. I., Eribes, C., & Kim, S. (1996). The work of auxiliary nurses in Mexico: Stressors, satisfiers, and coping strategies. *International Journal of Nursing Studies, 33,* 495–505.

Eisenberg, E., & Riley, P. (2001). Organizational culture. In F. Jablin & L. Putnam (Eds), *The new handbook of organizational communication* (pp. 291–322). Beverly Hills, CA: Sage.

Firth, H., McIntee, J., McKeown, P., & Britton, P. (1986). Burnout and professional depression: Related concepts? *Journal of Advances in Nursing, 11*(6), 633–641.

Garrett, C. (2008). The effect of nurse staffing patterns on medical errors and nurse burnout. *Association of perioperative Registered Nurses, 87,* 1191–1204.

Greenfield, S., Nelson, E., Zubkoff, M., Manning, W., Rogers, W., Kraviz, R., Keller, A., Tarlov, A., & Ware, J. E. (1992). Variations in resource utilization among medical specialties and systems of care. *Journal of the American Medical Association, 267,* 1624–1630.

Gunter, K. P. (2002). The HIPAA privacy rule: Practical advice for academic and research institutions. *Healthcare Financial Management, 56,* 50–54.

Hafferty, F., & Light, D. (1995). Professional dynamics and the changing nature of medical work. *Journal of Health and Social Behavior, 35,* 132–153.

Halm, E. A., Causino, N., & Blumenthal, D. (1997). Is gatekeeping better than traditional care? A survey of physicians' attitudes. *Journal of the American Medical Association, 278,* 1677–1681.

Hample, D. (1999). The life space of personalized conflicts. In M. E. Roloff & G. D. Paulson (Eds), *Communication yearbook 22* (pp. 172–201). Thousand Oaks, CA: Sage.

Hare, J., Pratt, C. C., & Andrews, D. (1988). Predictors of burnout in professional and paraprofessional nurses working in hospitals and nursing homes. *International Journal of Nursing Studies, 25*(2), 105–115.

Halbesleben, J. R. B. (Ed.). (2008). *Handbook of stress and burnout in health care* (3rd ed.). Hauppauge, NY: Nova.

Holmer, A. F. (1999). Direct-to-consumer prescription drug advertising builds bridges between patients and physicians. *Journal of the American Medical Association, 281,* 380–382.

Infante, D., & Wigley, C. (1986). Verbal aggressiveness: An interpersonal model and measure. *Communication Monographs, 53,* 61–69.

Infante, D. A., Rancer, A. S., & Womack, D. F. (1997). *Building communication theory* (3rd ed.). Prospect Heights, IL: Waveland Press.

Joint Commission on Healthcare Organizations (JCAHO). (2006). Facts about the Joint Commission. Retrieved September 2, 2006, from www.jointcommission.org/AboutUs/.

Klevens, R. ., Edwards, J., & Richards, C. L. (2007). Estimating healthcare-associated infections and deaths in U.S. hospitals, 2002. *Public Health Reports, 122,* 160–166.

Kyne, L., Hamel, M. B., Polavaram, R., & Kelly, C. P. (2002) Health care costs and mortality associated with nosocomial diarrhea due to *Clostridium difficile. Clinical Infectious Diseases, 34,* 346–353.

Koleck, M., Bruchon-Schweitzer, M., Thiebaut, E., Dumartin, N., & Sifakis, Y. (2000). Stress, coping, and burnout among French general practitioners. *European Review of Applied Psychology, 50,* 309–314.

Kreps, G. L. (1990). *Organizational communication: Theory and practice* (2nd ed.). White Plains, NY: Longman.

Kreps, G. L., & Thornton, B. C. (1992). *Health communication: Theory and practice* (2nd ed.). Prospect Heights, IL: Waveland Press.

Kulynych, J., & Korn, D. (2002). The effect of the new federal medical-privacy rule on research. *New England Journal of Medicine, 346,* 201–204.

Lammers, J. C., & Geist, P. (1997). The transformation of caring in the light and shadow of "managed care." *Health Communication, 9,* 46–60.

Lammers, J. C., Barbour, J. B., & Duggan, A. P. (2003). Organizational forms of the provision of health care: An institutional perspective. In T. L. Thompson, A. M. Dorsey, K. I. Miller, & R. Parrott (Eds), *Handbook of health communication* (pp. 319–345). Mahwah, NJ: Lawrence Erlbaum.

Ledlow, G., O'Hair, H. D., & Moore, S. (2003). Predictors of communication quality: The patient, provider, and nurse call center triad. *Health Communication, 15,* 431–455.

Letvak, S. (2001). Nurses as working women. *Association of perioperative Registered Nurses, 73,* 675–682.

Maslach, C., & Jackson, S. E. (1982). Burnout in health professions: A social psychological analysis. In G. S. Sanders & J. Suls (Eds), *Social psychology of health and illness.* Hillsdale, NJ: Lawrence Erlbaum.

McGilton, K. S., McGillis Hall, L, Wodchis, W. P., & Petroz, U. (2007). Supervisory support, job stress, and job satisfaction among long-term care nursing staff. *Journal of Nursing Administration, 37,* 1–6.

Miller, D., & Gilles, P. (1996). Is there life after work? Experiences of HIV and oncology health staff. *AIDs Care: Psychological and Socio-Medical Aspects of AIDS/ HIV, 8,* 167–182.

Miller, S. C., & Mor, V. (2001). The emergence of Medicare hospice care in US nursing homes. *Palliative Medicine, 15,* 471–480.

Moore, S. D., O'Hair, H. D., & Ledlow, G. (2002). The effects of health delivery systems and self-efficacy on patient compliance and satisfaction. *Communication Research Reports, 19*(4), 362–371.

Moore, S. D., Wright, K. B., & Bernard, D. R. (2009). Influences on health delivery system satisfaction: A partial test of the ecological model. *Health Communication, 24,* 285–294.

Nursing World. (2001, November 5). American Nurses Association applauds introduction of Nurse Retention and Quality of Care Act 2001. Retrieved January 20, 2004, from www.nursingworld.org/.

Ogus, E. D. (1990). Burnout and social support systems among ward nurses. *Issues in Mental Health Nursing, 11*(3), 267–281.

O'Hair, H. D., Friedrich, G., & Dixon, L. (2010). *Strategic communication in business and the professions* (6th ed.). Boston, MA: Houghton Mifflin.

O'Hair, H. D., O'Rourke, J., & O'Hair, M. (2001). *Business communication.* Cincinnati, OH: South-Western.

O'Hair, H. D., Thompson, S., & Gilchrist, E. (2004). *Physician referral: Exploring the culture.* Paper presented at the annual meeting of the International Communication Association, New Orleans.

O'Hair, H. D., Villagran, M., Wittenberg, E., Brown, K., Hall, T., Ferguson, M., & Doty, T. (2003). Cancer survivorship and agency model (CSAM): Implications for patient choice, decision making, and influence. *Health Communication, 15,* 193–202.

O'Reilly, C., Chatman, J., & Caldwell, D. (1991). People and organizational culture: A Q-sort approach to assessing person–organization fit. *Academy of Management Journal, 34,* 487–516.

Pacanowsky, M. E., & O'Donnell-Trujillo, N. (1982). Organizational communication and organizational cultures. *Western Journal of Speech Communication, 46,* 115–130.

Rahim, M. A. (2001). *Managing conflict in organizations* (3rd ed.). Westport, CT: Quorum Books.

Ray, E. B., & Apker, J. (2011). Stress, burnout, and supportive communication. In T. L. Thompson, R. Parrott, & J. F. Nussbaum (Eds), *The Routledge handbook of health communication,* 2nd ed. (pp. 428–440). New York: Routledge.

Ross, S. E., & Lin, C. T. (2003). The effects of promoting patient access to medical records: A review. *Journal of the American Medical Informatics Association, 10,* 129–138.

Sexton, J. B., Thomas, E. J., & Helmreich, R. L. (2000). Error, stress, and teamwork in medicine and aviation: Cross-sectional surveys. *British Medical Journal, 320,* 745–749.

Shattner, P., & Coman, G. (1998). The stress of metropolitan general practice. *Medical Journal of Australia, 169,* 133–137.

Shrader, K., Marion, E., Broome, C. D., West, M. E., & Nash, M. (2001). Factors influencing satisfaction and anticipated turnover for nurses in an academic medical center. *Journal of Nursing Administration, 3*(4), 210–216.

Simoni, P. S., & Patterson, J. J. (1997). Hardiness, coping and burnout in the nursing workplace. *Journal of Professional Nursing, 13,* 178–185.

Stewardson, A., Allegranzi, B., Sax, H., Kilpatrick, C., & Pittet, D. (2011). Back to the future: Rising to the Semmelweis challenge in hand hygiene. *Future Microbiology, 6,* 855–876.

Spellberg, B., Guidos, R., Gilbert, D., Bradley, J., Boucher, H. W., Scheld, W.M., Bartlett, J. G., & Edwards, J.; Infectious Diseases Society of America. (2008). The epidemic of antibiotic-resistant infections: A call to action for the medical community from the Infectious Diseases Society of America. *Clinical Infectious Diseases, 46,* 155–164.

Street, R. L., Jr. (2003). Communication in medical encounters: An ecological perspective. In T. L. Thompson, A. M. Dorsey, K. I. Miller, & R. Parrott (Eds), *Handbook of health communication* (pp. 63–80). Mahwah, NJ: Lawrence Erlbaum.

Tyler, P. A., & Cushway, D. (1995). Stress in nurses: The effects of coping and support. *Stress Medicine, 11,* 243–251.

Ubel, P. A., Jepson, C., & Asch, D. A. (2003). Misperceptions about beta-blockers and diuretics: A national survey of primary care physicians. *Journal of General Internal Medicine, 18*, 997–983.

Vock, D. C. (2005). Medicaid cuts could target drug costs. Stateline.org. Retrieved July 12, 2012, from www.stateline.org/live/ViewPage.action?siteNodeId=136&languageId=1&contentId=53376.

Voltmer, E., & Spahn, C. (2009). Social support and physicians' health. *Zeitschrift für Psychosomatische Medizin und Psychotherapie, 55*, 51–69.

Watkins, R. S., & Kimberly, J., Jr. (2004). What residents don't know about physician–pharmaceutical industry interactions. *Academic Medicine, 79*, 432–437.

Weick, K. (1979). *The social psychology of organizing* (2nd ed.). Reading, MA: Addison-Wesley.

Weinstein, R. A. (2008). Nosocomial infection update. *Emerging Infectious Diseases, 4*, 416–420.

Wright, K. B. (2011). A communication competence approach to healthcare worker conflict, job stress, job burnout, and job satisfaction. *Journal of Healthcare Quality, 33*, 7–14.

Wright, K. B., Banas, J., Bessarabova, E., & Bernard, D. R. (2010). A communication competence approach to examining healthcare support, stress, and job burnout. *Health Communication, 25*, 375–382.

Wright, K. B., & Frey, L. R. (2008). Communication and care in an acute cancer center: The effects of patients' willingness to communicate about health, healthcare environment perceptions, and health status on information seeking, participation in care practices, and satisfaction. *Health Communication, 23*, 369–379.

Young, S., & Brown, H. N. (1998). Effects of hospital downsizing on surviving staff. *Nursing Economics, 16*, 258–262.

Part IV

Influences of Technologies and Media

Chapter 7

New Technologies and Health Communication

Have you ever looked up information about an illness on-line or used your health insurance company website to find a physician who is in your provider network? If so, you are one of millions of people who search for health information on the Internet each day. New communication technologies have permeated virtually every area of the healthcare delivery system in recent years, including provider–patient email exchanges, electronic records, access to laboratory results via the Internet, text messaging reminders, and the use of iPhone applications that allow you to have quick access to pertinent health information as well as to take a picture of your prescription and text it to your pharmacy for a refill.

The US healthcare system has a long and distinguished history of innovation, and when new technological advances are found to benefit healthcare delivery and the prevention of disease, it is often on the cutting edge of adopting them. For example, even the advent of the telephone was once considered a major technological advancement in terms of increasing a provider's ability to conveniently reach patients. Later, beginning in the 1980s, providers began using email to communicate with other providers, followed by the use of email to communicate with patients in the 1990s (Avtgis, Polack, Staggers, & Wieczorek, 2011). In recent years we have witnessed the growth of other new communication technologies that have led to major changes in health communication. The convergence of the Internet, wireless computer technology, global satellite positioning, and computer tailoring of messages are just a few examples of the high-tech revolution that has led to communication changes within the health delivery system. The extent to which these newer technologies will transform health communication remains to be seen, but it appears that technology will continue to be used by the healthcare system in the future.

Healthcare organizations hope that the application of these technologies will reduce the costs associated with traditional channels of communication (e.g. telephone,

Health Communication in the 21st Century, Second Edition. Kevin Bradley Wright, Lisa Sparks, and H. Dan O'Hair.
© 2013 John Wiley & Sons, Inc. Published 2013 by John Wiley & Sons, Inc.

paper-based patient charts, memoranda from healthcare organization administrators) and increase convenience and efficiency. New technologies can also be used in health prevention and education efforts to disseminate and access health information as well as facilitate relationships (provider–provider, provider–patient, and patient–patient). The costs of the current US healthcare system were estimated to be over $1 trillion in 2001 (US Census Bureau, 2010) and are projected to rise over the next decade.

New communication technologies have the ability to impact health communication both positively and negatively (Neuhauser & Kreps, 2003). In some cases the cost of adopting them may not be beneficial to health practitioners, so it is important for health communication scholars to understand the advantages and disadvantages these technologies offer in terms of disseminating health information and facilitating interaction among different stakeholders in the health arena. This chapter examines some of the prominent ways in which new communication technologies are currently being used in the US healthcare system and their potential impact on health outcomes.

Health Information on the Internet

More and more people are using the Internet to search for health information than ever before. Tu and Cohen (2008) found that in 2007 56 percent of US adults sought information about personal health concerns through health-related websites. Furthermore, the enmeshment of healthcare systems, globalization of media systems, convergence of media technologies, smartphone applications, text messaging, and the Internet as an information-gathering tool have transformed the decision-making practices of those seeking healthcare. While the growth and popularity of using the Internet for health information may provide consumers with up-to-date information about various aspects of disease prevention, illness, treatment, and control, there are many questions concerning the quality of health-related information that is currently on-line. In addition, there are many concerns about access to the Internet, particularly among traditionally underserved segments of the population (Kreps & Sparks, 2008; Sparks & Nussbaum, 2008).

Health information access

At no other point in history has access to health information been so convenient for both providers and consumers (Sundar, Rice, Kim, & Sciamanna, 2011). A recent Pew survey found that 61 percent of US adults had used the Internet for health information (Fox & Jones, 2009). Today, people can gain access to much of the same information as healthcare providers on government and research institution websites or electronic databases on the Internet that are free or charge a fee (e.g. MedLine), yet relatively few people have the education level or technical expertise to understand much of this information in the same way as providers (Shieh, Mays, McDaniel, & Yu, 2009). However, understanding health information, including information gathered from the Internet, influences health in a wide variety of ways. For example, according to

Galarce, Ramanadkan, and Viswanath (2011), "accessing and correctly using health information has an enormous influence on health-related lifestyle factors, early detection and diagnosis, coping with disease, managing symptoms, engaging in in active medical decision-making, understanding different treatment options, and ultimately, facing end of life challenges" (p. 167).

Consumers can find a variety of websites sponsored by government organizations, such as the National Institutes of Health (NIH) and the Center for Disease Control (CDC), and on-line medical journals, and they can even pose questions and receive information from healthcare specialists on some websites (e.g. WebMD). On-line health information is continuously available, accessible, and can be acquired anonymously (Viswanath, Ramanadhan, & Kontos, 2007), which is particularly helpful when people are dealing with sensitive health issues (i.e. diet, sexually transmitted diseases, etc.). Access to health information via the web has led to patients bringing information they have found there to discussions with their physicians during office visits (Aspden & Katz, 2001), more talk about information acquired from the Internet during medical interviews (Aspden & Katz, 2001; Ferguson, 1998), and greater patient ability to discuss more specific details of diseases and conditions (Napoli, 2001). According to Sundar *et al.* (2011), more recent trends in the use of on-line health information include increases in the amount of information people are seeking about diet and exercise, information from other people's experiences (blogs and on-line support groups), and on-line ratings of physicians and other providers (similar to prominent non-health-related rating websites like *Angie's List*).

Many search engines (e.g. Yahoo and Google) often lack an efficient way to access specific health-related websites. A keyword search for a specific disease, such as HIV/AIDS, will result in links to hundreds of sites that may vary in terms of their intended audience, information quality, and specificity of information about the disease (Bass, 2003). People accessing information about HIV/AIDS are often interested in very different aspects of the disease. For example, some people are interested in HIV prevention, while others might be concerned about specific treatment options or finding an on-line support group for people living with the disease. Other individuals interested in HIV/AIDS, such as physicians and researchers, frequently obtain information from HIV/AIDS websites dealing with highly technical aspects of the disease. The major search engines can make it difficult to locate information about health that is tailored specifically to the education level and interests of individuals. This makes it extremely cumbersome to sift through hundreds of links to websites that may not provide the desired information, or information may be presented in language that is too technical or too basic depending upon the background of the searcher (Eng, 2001).

In addition, just because people have access to information does not necessarily mean they will use it, understand it, or change their attitudes and behaviors because of it. For years people have had access to health information from university libraries and many other sources, but they have not necessarily used the information, had the capacity to understand it, or they have lacked the motivation to enact the suggested behaviors for improving health outcomes.

The evolution of the new technologies has also led to the advent of the mobile Internet, where individuals not only access health information via smartphones, but they also can download applications that monitor health behaviors (Hurling *et al.*, 2007; Kim & Kim, 2008), such as accelerometers to monitor physical activity, or disease management, such as mobile web-based applications that monitor blood glucose level and that provide recommendations). One of the authors of this book, who is a vegan, uses an iPhone application to scan bar codes on processed food products that indicates whether it contains animal products enablingdietary decisions at the grocery store. Health campaign designers are increasingly turning to smartphone applications for health campaigns (which often draw on web video platforms like *YouTube*), such as smoking cessation interventions, abstinence campaigns, and organ donation campaigns (Sundar *et al.*, 2011; Tian, 2010).

Credibility

It is often difficult to assess the credibility of health information found on the Internet. A number of researchers have expressed concerns about credibility in evaluating information on health-related websites (Barnes *et al.*, 2003; Cummins *et al.*, 2003; Wang, Walther, Pingree, & Hawkins, 2008). While government, university, and research organization-sponsored websites typically provide the most credible information, some websites created by interest groups and individuals can also contain credible information. For example, sometimes a cancer survivor or a person who is a caregiver for someone with Alzheimer's disease may have credible information to offer others because of his or her first-hand experience with the disease. Complicating the issue further, consumers often differ in terms of what they perceive to be credible information. Some people find scientific studies about a disease to be credible whereas others think that accounts of personal experience have more credibility.

Unfortunately, early studies found that much of the health information on the Internet is either inaccurate or incomplete (Bierman, Golladay, & Baker, 1999; Hersch, Gorman, & Sacherek, 1998), and many websites do not conform to standards set by professional medical associations, such as the American Medical Association (Rice, 2001). Typically, standards for credible websites include the provision of informed consent for consumers, editorial control over messages (e.g. controlling spam and other unwanted messages through the use of moderators or website content editors), and disclosure of all website sponsors, such as pharmaceutical companies or other health-related businesses (Rice, 2001). However, Metzger (2007) found that most web users do not undertake recommended information-verification steps, but focus more on design and navigation aspects when assessing website credibility. Researchers are still concerned about health website inaccuracies, particularly since a variety of studies have found a great deal of misinformation (Sundar *et al.*, 2011). Assessing the credibility of websites is often a difficult task for laypersons, and even for researchers and health professionals there are few consistent guidelines. Some researchers have attempted to create guidelines for health information on the Internet (see Cummins *et al.*, 2003; Weiler & Pealer, 2000), but whether or not these will ultimately be adopted on a large scale remains questionable. Yet, more and more people report that their health-related behaviors have been significantly influenced by information they receive on the Internet (Fox & Jones, 2009), leading them to ask doctors more questions, alter their diet, exercise level, or ways of dealing with stress, and affecting how they cope with chronic illness (Sundar *et al.*, 2011).

In recent years, we have witnessed the growth of Web 2.0 technologies that have made the Internet and websites more interactive. Health-related blogs, on-line support groups, and health wikis have proliferated in the past several years, and studies have found that these sources are often perceived as highly credible by people seeking health information (Kovic, Lulic, & Brumini, 2008). When the first author of this textbook inquired about this phenomenon from a blog user recently, he was told "an oncologist can tell you technical things about cancer, but people who live with cancer can tell you all kinds of things that an oncologist does not know." These included such things as emotions (such as fear and hope) that go along with living with cancer, personal experience with cancer medications, and detail about the many day-to-day challenges of living with the disease. According to Sundar *et al.* (2011), blogs, wikis, and other interactive web-based applications allow consumers of health information to receive both personal and mass communication. Moreover, it also gives people an opportunity to share their experiences and receive feedback from others. The "first hand" experience they receive from others and the increased ability to clarify information appears to bolster perceptions of credibility (particularly compared to traditional medical expert-based, one-way communication). However, Buis and Carpenter (2009) found that most commentary pertaining to medical issues in health-related blogs cited external media sources to back up statements (such as books, newspapers, and websites), but they contained very little actual medical information.

Literacy issues/underserved populations

Despite the large amount of health information that is currently available on the Internet, there are many underserved populations, including older adults, individuals from lower socioeconomic households, people with low literacy levels or little experience with technology, individuals with disabilities, and people living in rural areas who cannot access the Internet or who have limited access. Although the digital divide has become smaller in recent years due to a decline in the cost of computers and access to the Internet, many members of underserved populations still have difficulty gaining access to health information on-line (Rice, 2001). Unfortunately, these individuals are often also members of high-risk groups for many diseases and conditions, and they would benefit most from the health information that exists on the Internet. Consumers' unique cultural backgrounds and orientations have powerful influences on their interaction patterns that must be carefully accounted for in health communication efforts (Kreuter & McClure, 2004). It is very important to identify and examine the most important and influential cultural issues that are likely to influence the ways members of vulnerable populations, respond to communication about health and healthcare (Kreps & Kunimoto, 1994; Kreps & Sparks, 2008, Pecchioni *et al.*, 2008; Sparks & Nussbaum, 2008). Several of the key cultural variables that influence health communication outcomes include the unique health beliefs, values, norms, and expectations that different consumers bring to health situations (Kreps & Kunimoto, 1994). It is also important to assess consumers' culturally based language skills, barriers, their health literacy levels, their motivations to seek health information, and their unique media use patterns (Youmans & Schillinger, 2003; Andrus & Roth, 2003). Examination of these key cultural factors provides crucial information for determining how to best design and deliver key messages for effectively communicating complex health information to diverse populations (Kreps & Sparks, 2008). For instance, Pecchioni, Ota and Sparks (2004) found that in the US older adults are perceived highly negatively and often receive negative remarks or experiences from people in younger age groups. However, the authors found that in Hispanic cultures, the elderly have authority in their families and are treated with respect. Elderly Hispanic men and women emigrating to the US may go through culture shock as they are faced with negative stereotypes that the American culture places on them as older adults relative to the higher status they had in their native countries.

Sometimes, healthcare providers may have trouble communicating in cross-cultural conversations due to language barriers. These instances can lead to what seem like confounding messages regarding causes of illness and appropriate treatment when cancer patients are from different cultures (see e.g. Pecchioni *et al.*, 2008). Additionally, stereotypes can also inhibit openness among patients and providers when they view their patients' differing cultural beliefs or values about illness and treatments as inferior to their own (Pecchioni, Ota, & Sparks, 2004). Due to this factor, researchers have found that people frequently seek out healthcare providers who share similar cultural backgrounds as their own, with the belief that they share the same values, or they may commonly rely on family members (who may or may not have medical knowledge) to provide care (Pecchioni *et al.*, 2008). This is a type of conversion strategy in which people seek out others who are similar to themselves. Culturally sensitive health communication is a crucial component to providing vulnerable consumers with useful information about health promotion and healthcare.

Efforts have been made to reach members of underserved populations, including organizations such as SeniorNet that attempt to provide access to computers and computer training for older individuals within senior centers, software applications that allow people with disabilities (e.g. people who are visually impaired) to use web browsers, and corporate programs that provide donations of older computers and Internet access to poor communities (Kreps & Sparks, 2008; Mo, Malik, & Coulson, 2009; Sparks & Nussbaum, 2008; Stalberg *et al.*, 2008). However, a great deal of work still needs to be done in order to reduce the digital divide in the US (e.g. Kreps, Neuhauser, Sparks, & Villagran, 2008). Seniors, for example, are half as likely as younger adults to access the Internet for health information, and many ethnic/racial minority groups as well as less educated populations are less likely to rely on the Internet for health decision-making (Tu & Cohen, 2008). Addressing these types of problems will take efforts on many fronts, including making improvements to the Internet infrastructure to allow access in a variety of locations, computer literacy programs, and community efforts to provide locations where individuals can access the Internet for free, such as libraries and community centers. In addition, public health campaigns need to be directed toward helping individuals find information that is tailored to their health needs and helping them make sense of the health information that exists on-line.

New Technologies and Patient–Patient Communication

Health-related web communities and computer-mediated support groups

The development of the Internet has created possibilities for increased patient–patient communication, mostly through web communities, social networking sites like Facebook, and specialized computer-mediated support groups. Computer-mediated support groups have become more prevalent in recent years as a source of information and support for numerous health concerns as a result of the Internet's increasing popularity and its ability to connect people who have similar health issues. An estimated 90 million Americans have participated in some type of computer-mediated support group (Sarasohn-Kahn, 2008). A number of scholars, including health communication researchers, have focused their attention on these groups in an attempt to study their benefit to participants and to understand how the nature of supportive communication is affected by both the constraints and advantages of the computer medium (Rains & Young, 2009; Shaw *et al.*, 2006; Tanis, 2008; Wright, Johnson, Bernard, & Averbeck, 2011).

Computer-mediated support groups and health outcomes There is a growing body of evidence that these groups provide a wide variety of health benefits for users (such as individuals with cancer, diabetes, and substance abuse problems), including reduced stress, increased positive coping, increased quality of life, increased self-efficacy in terms of managing one's health problems, reduced depression, and increased physical health benefits (Beaudoin & Tao, 2007; Gustafson *et al.*, 2005; Houston, Cooper, & Ford, 2002; Jones *et al.*, 2008; Rains & Young, 2009; Shaw *et al.*, 2006; Wright, 2000a).

Advantages and disadvantages of computer-mediated support groups Query and Wright (2003) developed a model of on-line support group participation for people facing health concerns to help explain why some people use these groups while others do not. Not everyone who is concerned about a health issue seeks social support: some people choose individually based strategies for coping with stressful events, while others are more socially oriented in coping with stressful situations, such as seeking various types of social support (Kohn, 1996; Pierce, Sarason, & Sarason, 1996). Many people feel that they have sufficient support from family and friends, and they may never feel the need to join an on-line support group. However, as we saw in Chapter 4, there are times when people facing an illness find it difficult to communicate with close ties, such as family members and friends. For example, researchers have found that life-threatening illnesses are difficult topics for most people to discuss, especially when they affect a close relative or loved one, and family members and friends often minimize the concerns of people with a serious illness, avoid interacting with them, steer conversational topics away from emotional talk about the disease, or refrain from any discussion of illness (Dakof & Taylor, 1990; Helgeson, Cohen, Shultz, & Yasko, 2000).

Problems communicating about health with traditional face-to-face support network members may lead some individuals to seek support on-line. Papacharissi and Rubin (2000) concluded that individuals use computer-mediated communication as a "functional alternative" when face-to-face communication is perceived as difficult or not preferred. For individuals facing illness whose support needs are not met by their traditional support network, the Internet allows them to find other people with similar health concerns and provides an opportunity to obtain support from a much larger network than would be possible in the face-to-face world. The Internet is considered an *unbounded network* because, unlike the face-to-face world, on-line relationships are not hampered by temporal and geographical restrictions. Thus, it is possible for on-line support group participants to meet and obtain support from a large network of other people who come together to discuss very specific health concerns (e.g. prostate cancer groups, HIV/AIDS) as opposed to more general health issues. The Internet can also be seen as a weak tie support network (see Chapter 4), and people may be able to obtain more diverse points of view about health-related problems and talk about difficult issues with less interpersonal risk.

Other features of the Internet may be advantageous to those who use on-line support groups. Wellman (1997) contends that reduced nonverbal and appearance cues in email and other popular text-based forms of computer-mediated communication facilitate relationships that may be inhibited in the face-to-face world. Many of us are reluctant to form relationships with people in the face-to-face world due to cues such as age, gender, race, and appearance. However, in text-based computer-mediated communication, people do not see these cues and relationships tend to form around topics in which people have a mutual interest.

Additionally, *social information processing theory* (Ramirez, Walther, Burgoon, & Sunnafrank, 2002; Walther, 1996) asserts that in computer-mediated communication, message senders portray themselves in a socially favorable manner to draw the attention of message receivers and foster anticipation of future interaction. Message receivers, in turn, tend to idealize the image of the sender due to overvaluing minimal, text-based cues. In addition, the asynchronous format of most computer-mediated interaction (and to some extent in synchronous formats, such as chat rooms) gives the sender and the receiver more time to edit their communication, making computer-mediated interactions more controllable and less stressful compared to the immediate feedback loop inherent in face-to-face interactions. Idealized perceptions and optimal self-presentation in the computer-mediated communication process tend to intensify in the feedback loop, and this emphasis often leads to what Walther (1996) labels "hyperpersonal interaction," or a more intimate and socially desirable exchange than face-to-face interactions.

Hyperpersonal interaction is enhanced when no face-to-face relationship exists, so that users construct impressions and present themselves "without the interference of environmental reality" (Walther, 1996, p. 33). Hyperpersonal interaction has been found to skew perceptions of relational partners in positive ways, and in some cases computer-mediated relationships may exceed face-to-face interactions in intensity, including within on-line support groups (King & Moreggi, 1998; Ramirez *et al.*, 2002; Walther, 1996; Wright & Bell, 2003). Interestingly, Houston, Cooper, and Ford (2002) found that 40 percent of the individuals in their study preferred on-line support groups instead of face-to-face counseling, and this was attributed to skewed perceptions due to the computer-mediated environment.

The text-based nature of computer-mediated communication has other advantages. Weinberg, Schmale, Uken, and Wessel (1995) argue that the therapeutic value of writing down problems in text-based computer-mediated support groups may allow for more reflection and distance from others without worrying about other people's immediate responses. In addition, writing down problems creates distance between people and their dilemmas (Diamond, 2000), and this may help people view their health concerns more objectively. More recent research suggests that the very act of composing affectionate messages in supportive on-line exchanges is related to reduced total cholesterol levels and cortisol levels (Floyd, Mikkelson, Hesse, & Pauley, 2007). Both cholesterol and cortisol are physiological products of stress and have been linked to heart disease and strokes among individuals facing long-term stressful situations.

All of these features of computer-mediated support groups, along with the anonymity and 24-h availability of these groups, may lead people to a support network that fulfills their needs. In addition, some people may augment their support network using on-line support groups rather than replacing their traditional face-to-face network members with virtual ones. Research on health-related computer-mediated support groups indicates that the people who use these groups tend to be satisfied with the support they receive, and they are often able to obtain more (and better-quality) support than would be possible within their face-to-face network (Wright et al., 2011).

Of course, on-line support groups have their disadvantages, and researchers have found that there are other sources of dissatisfaction among people using them (Galinski, Schopler, & Abell, 1997; King & Moreggi, 1998; Preece & Ghozati, 2001; Walther & Boyd, 2002; Wright, 2000b). Participants often find the lack of immediacy when communicating with others frustrating. Other reasons for dissatisfaction include difficulty when expressing and interpreting emotions due to reduced non-verbal cues; dissatisfaction with the inability to touch others; frustration with unwanted messages from unsolicited parties participating in the group (including spam messages); and increased opportunities for some individuals to misrepresent themselves to the group.

New Technologies and Provider–Provider Communication

The Internet and other new communication technologies are transforming provider interaction and access to information in a variety of health settings, such as hospitals, clinics, pharmacies, and research facilities. In the past, long-distance telephone calls, overnight letters, and creation and storage of patient records contributed to the tremendous costs of running a health organization (costs that are eventually passed along to consumers). New communication technologies may present cheaper, more convenient, and more efficient alternatives to traditional ways of communicating within health organizations. This section examines several ways that new communication technologies are facilitating communication among providers.

Email, wireless/satellite communication, and electronic records

Email and wireless communication   Email is a relatively simple computer application, but it has transformed communication among providers in many important ways. Physicians and other providers can now obtain information and opinions from other key health personnel within and between organizations. The attachment feature of email has allowed providers to send one another detailed information about patient histories, relevant research articles about specific conditions, insurance records, and other important information that can be used to facilitate the healthcare process. In addition, the asynchronous nature of email allows providers to transcend temporal and geographical barriers. Providers at rural health clinics can quickly and cheaply access information from larger urban hospitals and research facilities, consult with specialists, and keep up with current information regarding health conditions from websites sponsored by medical research institutions and government websites (e.g. the NIH and the CDC). Communication researchers have found that most providers have positive attitudes toward email and see its value in improving communication among providers, although there appears to be some resistance among many older physicians to adopt this technology (Aspden, Katz, & Bemis, 2001). However, in the future, more and more physicians and other providers are expected to use email as more Internet training programs are introduced and older physicians retire (Aspden, Katz, & Bemis, 2001).

Satellite technology   The convergence of satellite technology and the Internet has led to health information organizations such as HealthNet (www.healthnet.org/), which provides a global communication network that links healthcare workers around the world via email. HealthNet and similar organizations use email and satellite technology to connect healthcare providers and to provide them with access to information such as on-line medical journals and other health-related databases. This technology has been particularly useful to health professionals in the developing world. For example, HealthNet has helped healthcare professionals in Africa and in developing countries fight the HIV/AIDS pandemic. In remote parts of developing countries, such access to medical journals and other up-to-date information sources can be vital for preventing and treating disease. Satellite/Internet technology is thus an important means of disseminating information to providers who work in these environments.

Wireless communication devices   Wireless devices, such as iPads, allow providers to enter information about patients during or shortly after medical interviews and to send information via wireless email to other providers, pharmacologists, technicians, and other health professionals (Eder & Wise, 2001). Patient prescriptions can be easily be photographed by a cell phone and emailed to a pharmacy to be refilled, and the process of making additional appointments and referrals is facilitated through wireless technology when messages can be sent quickly and conveniently to receptionists and other medical staff. In the past, physicians often made notes in charts after a meeting with patients, and then used transcription services to provide detailed information about patients. Wireless devices aid providers in supplying more detail about medical conditions for patient records, and also help to circumvent problems with poor handwriting or other difficulties associated with taking notes about patients.

Electronic medical records Over a decade ago, Eder and Wise (2001) estimated that "nearly 75% of all business activities in healthcare are related to the capture and manipulation of information, most of which is paper based" (p. 310). Today, electronic medical records (EMRs) are revolutionizing the healthcare industry (Jones, 2008) by helping to reduce costs by making records easier to store and more easily accessible, by providing greater continuity of care to patients, and by eliminating oversights that might lead to problems such as adverse drug interaction (i.e. if a patient does not remember all of the medications he or she is currently taking). Among healthcare organizations that have not adopted electronic records, a patient's vital medical information is often scattered across medical records kept by many different caregivers in many different locations, and valuable information such as drug allergies and preexisting health conditions is often unavailable at the time of care. Electronic records and web-based technologies have tremendous potential in terms of capturing and storing information in healthcare settings. According to Hillestad *et al.* (2005), a 90 percent adoption rate of EMRs within the US healthcare system could potentially lead to an average savings of over $77 billion per year. As you can imagine, US government agencies such as the NIH are urging healthcare organizations to move toward EMRs. It is hoped that electronic records will ultimately improve healthcare quality by preventing medical errors, improving administrative efficiencies, reducing paperwork, and by increasing access to affordable healthcare.

Electronic patient records can now be easily created through standardized electronic forms and stored in web-based programs on computer servers within health organizations. Many hospitals have computer programs that allow providers to enter information about the patient on computer within examination rooms, and prompts within the computer programs remind providers to ask patients about detailed aspects of their medical history, lifestyles, and health condition. X-rays and the results of other diagnostic tests can be quickly sent to providers or attached to electronic patient records. Server storage of patient records takes up less space than rooms designated for paper charts, and computer programs allow physicians, receptionists, nurses, technicians, and other medical personnel to quickly and conveniently retrieve patient medical records. In addition, when referring patients to other healthcare providers, sending electronic patient records helps to save time and money because it allows for more detailed information to be transmitted due to the increased bandwidth of electronic formats. EMRs also provide the ability for physicians to track the frequency of patient screenings for chronic disease, and this may help disease prevention efforts (Avtgis *et al.*, 2011). In addition, EMRs may help providers identify oversights regarding the treatment of disease in other health organizations where a patient has been seen in past, and this can help minimize costly mistakes that can lead to medical malpractice lawsuits by ensuring that the patient receives the appropriate treatment. Furthermore, information on patient charts that has been entered electronically is simply much easier to read than handwritten notes, and this appears to reduce misinterpretation of records and costly medical errors (Eder & Wise, 2001). Yet, several barriers to the widespread adoption of EMRs currently exist. The cost of EMR systems, particularly during times of economic weakness, patient privacy concerns, and the complexity of transferring information from a paper-based system to an electronic system will likely plague the growth and development of EMRs in the future (Jones, 2008).

Disadvantages of new communication technologies

While there are numerous advantages of web-based communication and electronic medical records in terms of cost savings and greater efficiency for providers and health organizations, there are disadvantages as well. According to Eder and Wise (2001), "there is no single, universally accepted standard for formatting electronic health records" (p. 316). This may cause problems in accessing and interpreting information about patients when information is shared between organizations using different types of electronic records or systems for organizing and accessing patient data. Less is known about how the use of computers in the examination room affects the interaction between providers and patients. However, it is likely that using a computer to enter patient information detracts from direct interaction with patients both verbally and nonverbally. The health communication literature has documented a variety of interaction problems that can occur between providers and patients in examination rooms without computers, such as problems assessing patient cues, time constraints, and provider domination of the interaction (see Geist & Hardesty, 1990; Roter, Hall, & Katz, 1988; von Friedrichs-Fitzwater, Callahan, Flynn, & Williams, 1991; Zyzanski, Stange, Langa, & Flocke, 1998), and it is reasonable to assume that the introduction of computers will make provider–patient interaction even more complex and potentially problematic.

For example, electronic prompts to enter certain types of information about the patient (e.g. symptoms) in current medical interview software may distract a physician from asking more relevant information that comes up during a medical interview, such as risky lifestyle behaviors or psychosocial concerns. Moreover, eye contact, listening, and attention to the patient might be compromised by the use of computer programs to collect patient information. Future research would benefit from assessing the impact of the presence of computers or other electronic communication devices on provider–patient interaction.

In recent years there have been growing concerns over privacy and confidentiality issues surrounding the use of electronic patient records. According to Katz and Aspden (2001), there are a number of questions relating to patient privacy associated with the use of electronic records that need to be addressed. First, during medical interviews patients often disclose a great deal of sensitive information about their lifestyle behaviors, including substance abuse problems, psychological problems, and sexual history. This information can be potentially damaging financially to the patient if it is accessed by third parties such as insurance companies, who may decide to raise insurance premiums for the patient based upon what they might perceive to be increased risk factors from the information they access from his or her records. Also, other third-party access to patient information can be damaging to patients socially, particularly if a history of mental illness or the HIV status of a patient is inappropriately discussed by hospital staff and this information gets back to members of his or her social network. Moreover, there have been cases where attorneys have examined medical records to look for a history of malpractice claims among patients, which could be used to cancel insurance or deny access to healthcare. The Department of Health and Human Services (DHHS) has been collaborating in recent years with the private sector and other federal agencies to identify and endorse voluntary standards that are necessary for health information to be shared safely and securely among healthcare providers. The implementation of HIPAA (see Chapter 6) has also set guidelines for the use of electronic records and patient information.

Finally, there is concern that certain information about patients, such as disease status, risk factors, and lifestyles, could be sold to marketing firms for pharmaceutical companies or other health-related industries, resulting in unwanted solicitations for products aimed at patients. Researchers and other individuals often request access to electronic patient information, and they should be concerned with the ethical issues involved when dealing with this type of sensitive information. These and other issues present challenges for the future of electronic record use, and ethical concerns about how patient information could be used inappropriately as this technology advances need careful consideration. Some health organizations have been experimenting with new forms of electronic security, such as digital signatures, encrypted data, or the use of improved Intranets, which are closed computer networks that limit access to information to certain health facilities.

According to Rains and Bosch (2009), as consumers are asked to enter more and more sensitive information about themselves and their health conditions on-line, and with the increased information sharing among health providers, pharmacies, and insurance companies, this has led to a situation where there are more and more privacy violations. Most health-related websites provide some type of privacy policy statement, which tells the consumer who data is collected and used. However, Rains and Bosch (2009), in a study of 97 health websites, found that fewer than 3 percent of the websites met all five of the Federal Trade Commission's Fair Information Practices guidelines. Despite HIPAA reform and other efforts to ensure patient privacy, the Internet allows individuals to circumvent regulations through the ease of sharing information. On-line health information privacy will likely remain a problematic issue in the future until better safeguards and guidelines for protecting patient information are developed.

Continuing education

Most providers, including physicians, physician assistants, nurses, technicians, and other key health organization personnel, are required in most states to complete continuing education requirements in order to renew their license as a health provider. This is also true for many other types of health providers, including physical therapists, dentists and dental hygienists, and pharmacists. Most states require a certain number of continuing education hours each year, and providers must submit proof of continuing education hours when reapplying for state licensure. Continuing education credit is given for attending a variety of health-related courses offered by scholars and other experts in health-related topics at universities and other sites in communities across the country. In the past, providers have had to take continuing education courses on weekends or days off, or the health organization schedules time for providers to attend them.

Over the last several years a variety of web-based continuing education courses have appeared, and many allow providers to complete the course at their own pace, some even allowing providers to download a certificate of completion at the end of the course. According to Whitten, Eastin, and Cook (2001), "the Internet provides a very low-cost way of presenting CME [continuing medical education], avoiding expensive meeting spaces, the rental of audiovisual equipment needed, as well as travel expenses and accommodation costs for faculty and staff" (p. 265). Web-based continuing education courses support the use of multimedia, and they are relatively inexpensive to design, implement, and maintain. However, the variety and quality of Internet-based continuing education courses vary (Kim, 1998), and this needs to be assessed in future research along with the other cost-cutting benefits these courses offer to the healthcare system.

New Technologies and Provider–Patient Communication

On-line communication technology and provider–patient interaction

Patients now have potentially greater access to physicians and other providers via the Internet than in the past, particularly through email and on-line health-related websites such as WebMD. However, despite the advantages these technologies offer in terms of facilitating communication between providers and patients, such as reduced expense, greater convenience, and the ability to attach documents containing health information, providers have largely been reluctant to adopt email as a means of communicating with patients (Delbanco & Sands, 2004; Roter *et al.*, 2008). While the majority of patients in the US report that they desire email and other types of web access to their physicians (Roter *et al.*, 2008), one study found that fewer than 10 percent of individuals with Internet access have actually contacted their physician on-line (Baker, Wagner, Singer, & Bandorf, 2003). However, Fox and Rainie (2000) found that 50 percent of participants reported that information from the Web led them to ask their doctor questions during regular medical visits. As we will see in this section, on-line access to physicians alters the traditional provider–patient interaction in a variety of other ways, so it is important for health communication scholars to study this trend. Yet, even today, access to email, high-speed Internet, education, and computer literacy continues to limit patient access to the Internet and the ability to interact with physicians on-line (Avtgis *et al.*, 2011; Pelletier, Sutton, & Walker, 2007).

Physician resistance Physicians often view the idea of interacting with patients via email or through other web-based means in a negative light (Podichetty & Penn, 2004). Despite the early widespread use of email in our culture, there is little evidence to suggest that provider–patient interaction has increased substantially as a result of this technology. According to Rice and Katz (2001), "The fact that these technologies were not adopted, we would argue, is not because the technology limits or permits access to physicians. Rather, it is the social structure that balances full access against managed boundaries" (p. 425). In other words, while email has the ability to increase doctor–patient communication, many physicians are reluctant to transcend traditional provider–patient relational boundaries because of such issues as patient privacy, the reduced ability to provide psychosocial dimensions of healthcare, and increased vulnerability to medical malpractice litigation (Bovi, 2003; Houston, Sands, Nash, & Ford, 2003; Roter *et al.*, 2008). In addition, given the many demands on physicians' time in most healthcare organizations, responding to multiple web-based interactions with patients increases their workload and may be another reason why we have not seen substantial physician–patient interaction via the Internet (Houston *et al.*, 2003).

Advantages of on-line provider–patient communication The use of the Internet for provider–patient communication could potentially have a number of benefits for patients. Scholars have found that email exchanges between providers and patients are associated with patient satisfaction, feelings of safety, and quality of care (Brooks & Menachemi, 2006; Roter *et al.*, 2008). Pelletier, Sutton, and Walker (2007) found that 78 percent of the patients in their study had a preference for on-line communication with their doctor over face-to-face communication. The reasons for this appear to range from issues such as the asynchronous nature of email might help apprehensive patients by giving them more time to compose their thoughts when asking questions or expressing concerns about their health (Strasser *et al.*, 2002). Unfortunately, providers and general have not taken advantage of the many features new communication technologies could potentially provide patients in terms of health information and healthcare. Given the technological advantages associated with devices like smartphones, providers could easily use links and attachments to send patients information about diseases and conditions, and patients could be easily linked to on-line social support groups or face-to-face support groups in their community through global positioning system (GPS) applications. Some research suggests that provider–patient email exchanges tend to be used for more mundane information exchange purposes, such as appointment scheduling and prescription refills (Delbanco & Sands, 2004). More research is needed to assess additional potential benefits of provider–patient communication via new technologies. However, traditional barriers between provider and patients, such as unequal power/status, as well as time constraints will likely continue to undermine the potential of using new technologies to their fullest potential in the near future.

Changes in face-to-face provider–patient interaction due to the Internet

Rice and Katz (2006) found that a growing number of patients are talking to their physicians specifically about health information they have acquired from the Internet. The abundance of health information on the Internet has altered face-to-face provider–patient interaction in a variety of ways. First, doctors now spend more time answering questions from patients about health information obtained on-line (Sundar *et al.*, 2011). Patients reportedly want their physicians to recommend websites with additional information about their health condition (Diaz *et al.*, 2005), and they appear to be more satisfied with the medical encounter when physicians answer their questions or address their concerns about information gathered via the Internet. Physicians want to help clarify health information that patients bring to them from the web, but physicians also feel that this makes visit time less efficient and it detracts from the quality of healthcare (Sundar *et al.*, 2011). Certainly, the trend is toward more talk between patients and providers during face-to-face visits about health information obtained from the Internet. Given the relationship between quality provider–patient communication and important outcomes such as patient satisfaction and compliance (see Chapter 2), health communication scholars need to continue researching the varied ways in which information from the Internet may alter face-to-face provider–patient interaction in both positive and negative ways.

Websites and patient access to providers

Some health websites, such as WebMD, occasionally schedule chats with physicians and other providers or allow consumers to pose questions through the use of bulletin boards. These types of websites allow patients to obtain health information free of charge from providers who are willing to participate. Providers who interact with patients through these websites are often paid by the website administrators, who ultimately make their money from sponsors who pay for advertising on the website. Sponsors are typically organizations that provide health services (such as hospitals and specialized health clinics) or companies who sell health-related products, such as prescription drugs (e.g. Eli Lilly, Pfizer), diet products, or medical supplies. The commercial sponsorship of such websites raises a number of ethical concerns. For example, is the desire to raise revenue through these websites more important than the promotion of public health? While these websites may have both these goals, their heavy commercial sponsorship raises questions about whether products and services are in the best interest of the consumer, and low-cost health alternatives may not be promoted simply because the organizations offering these services have chosen not to advertise on these websites.

In addition, while providers who appear on WebMD and other health-related websites give consumers advice, they typically qualify the advice they provide with the recommendation that consumers see their primary physician. The advice consumers receive may help them to allay fears or manage uncertainties about their health status, and it may lead them to seek additional information or explore treatment options. However, since providers on these websites cannot diagnose illnesses or prescribe medications, it is essential that consumers follow up on the advice they receive with their physician. Problems may arise if consumers feel that they need not be concerned about their health as a result of interacting with providers on these websites or if the advice raises unwarranted fears. Because many diseases and conditions are difficult to diagnose without the use of laboratory tests, web-based providers can only make educated guesses about a consumer's health condition based upon the information given by the consumer. More research needs to be conducted on how consumers process and act upon (or do not act upon) advice received from providers on these websites.

Telemedicine and patients

Telemedicine has become more prominent as a research topic for health communication researchers in recent years (Whitten, Cook, & Cornacchione, 2011). Although early forms of telemedicine have been around since the late 1950s (i.e. provider–patient interaction via closed-circuit television), the advent of the personal computer, the Internet, and mobile/wireless technology has significantly transformed telemedicine in recent years. Telemedicine (also known as *telehealth*) is an umbrella term that refers to the use of technologies to provide healthcare services over distances to individuals (American Telemedicine Association, 2009), and it includes physician–patient interaction via computer or teleconferencing as well as *teleradiology*, or sending radiological images via Internet, and *telepathology*, or transmitting microscopic images on-line. In addition, heart information (via an electronic stethoscope or a wireless electro-cardiogram [ECG]), blood pressure, and other physiological information can be monitored by providers through the Internet despite large geographic distance between providers and patients (Avtgis *et al.*, 2011; Hong *et al.*, 2009). Computers and the Internet also offer the ability to have a low-cost telephone conversation (via Skype technology) with a physician for a fee (Miller, 2009). The current picture of telemedicine is somewhat mixed, although most scholars agree that it will continue to be an important context of health communication in the future. The following sections present a brief overview of some of the major advantages and disadvantages of telemedicine.

Advantages of telemedicine Telemedicine services are extremely important in terms of providing low-cost access to healthcare for underserved individuals living in rural areas of the country or for people who have limited mobility (Whitten, Cook, & Cornacchione, 2011). Studies suggest that patients are largely satisfied with the experience of telemedicine, and they appreciate the ability to communicate with specialists (Gutske, Balch, West, & Rogers, 2000; Turner, 2003). However, Whitten, Cook, and Cornacchione (2011) caution that more studies of patient satisfaction with telemedicine need to be conducted due to methodological problems with existing studies. Moreover, telemedicine has been found to lead to a decrease in office visits, higher perceived quality of care and patient satisfaction (Chen *et al.*, 2009). The medical cost savings to patients and healthcare organizations due to telemedicine can be extraordinary. According to Bynum, Irwin, Cranford, and Denny (2003), in a study of the impact of telemedicine in rural Arkansas, found that the use of telemedicine saved $32 in fuel costs for 92 percent of the patients, $100 in wages for 84 percent of the patients due to not having to take time off from work for the medical visit, and an additional $75 to $150 for additional expenses for 74 percent of the patients. Moreover, telemedicine helps to reduce the cost of building and staffing rural healthcare centers since it uses technology to reach patients.

Disadvantages of telemedicine Despite the benefits of telemedicine, there are some potential drawbacks as well. Provider reimbursement and licensure are two key issues that are still being resolved since the advent of telemedicine. Both Medicare and private health insurance has been limited in terms of reimbursing expenditures related to telemedicine practices in most of the US. According to Whitten, Cook, and Cornacchione (2011), only five states (California, Kentucky, Texas, Louisiana, and Oklahoma) require private insurance coverage of healthcare services provided by telemedicine. In short, this has led to a large gap between the cost of services and what insurance agencies are willing to pay, and what is not covered is typically billed as out-of-pocket expenses to the patient. Moreover, according to Stanberry (2006), physicians are licensed by a particular state, and this can lead to legal problems when the telemedicine services cross state borders (i.e. when a doctor in California provides telemedicine services to a patient in Nevada). As you can imagine, this can present problems for patients and attorneys who wish to launch malpractice litigation against a physician since it brings up issues of legal jurisdiction and state licensing accountability. Telemedicine may lead to communication problems as well. Some studies report that the majority of the interaction within telemedicine consultations tends to occur between the primary physician and the specialist, largely excluding the patient (Turner, 2003). Miller (2003) contends that telemedicine may depersonalize provider–patient interaction due to reduced nonverbal cues, although other research has found that patients are satisfied with the interaction (Whitten & Buis, 2008). Although research on provider–patient communication is abundant in face-to-face settings (see Chapter 2), there is far less research on provider–patient interaction in telemedicine contexts. However, given the growth and impact of telemedicine, it is likely that this and other types of communication research will expand in the future.

Managed care organization efforts to reach patients via the Internet

Managed care organizations are increasingly using the Internet to provide information to patients. A central tenet of managed care is the reduction of cost to health organizations and the consumer by controlling access to health resources and through prevention efforts. The Internet offers managed care organizations a cheap and convenient way to provide patients with information about lifestyle changes, diagnostic testing for diseases, and other means of preventing susceptibility to health problems that can be costly to the organization. In addition, websites developed by these organizations often contain interactive features such as tutorials about diseases and conditions, risk factors, and diet and exercise, and they provide links to related websites. Consumers can access specific health information tailored to their needs by providing information about their lifestyles and health history, and interactive forms (similar to those used by search engines) direct them to information based upon their input.

However, interactive features on these websites tend to emphasize health information (on web pages) as opposed to interaction with actual providers. In an analysis of prominent health maintenance organization (HMO) websites in the US, Witherspoon (2001) found that none of the websites in the study offered email links to specific doctors or other practitioners, and none offered a bulletin board or chat room where they could interact with providers. Instead, consumers are typically directed to web pages that provide information such as facts about diseases and conditions, information about exercise classes, and recipes for healthy diets. Most sites provided links to support groups for various health conditions or to government-sponsored websites (e.g. the CDC or the National Cancer Institute). While HMO and other managed care websites offer great possibilities for influencing health behaviors, few websites currently take advantage of the full potential of the multimedia and interactive features that current web technologies provide.

New Technologies and Health Campaigns

Tailoring health messages

Advances in computer programming and software have enabled individuals interested in health campaigns to use computers to tailor messages to specific characteristics of target audiences. According to Kreuter, Farrell, Olevitch, and Brennan (2000), *tailored health promotion materials* refer to "any combination of information and behavior change strategies intended to reach one specific person, based on characteristics that are unique to that person, related to the outcome of interest, and derived from an individual assessment" (p. 5). Tailored systems provide messages that are appropriate for specific individuals based upon their responses to questions provided by a computer program (Hawkins *et al.*, 2008).

Computer tailoring of health messages can be used to produce materials for health campaigns using any communication channel, including print materials, television and radio advertisements, and Internet-based campaigns. Computers facilitate the tailoring of messages through the use of algorithms in computer programming that are used to create messages according to certain criteria designated by the researcher. Thus, a computer program can be written to create different messages depending upon whether participants in the target population are members of certain groups based on demographics, psychological characteristics, and communication behaviors (Rimal & Adkins, 2003), such as whether a person is male or female, belongs to a certain age group, or has scored high or low on a health self-efficacy measure.

Computer programs allow the creation of tailored messages by quickly linking together specific messages to targeted individuals through the use of algorithms created for the programming process. For computer programmers, creating a program based on algorithms does not typically require extensive programming skills. However, many health communication personnel working on campaigns do not have the computer science background to create message tailoring programs, and they often have to hire individuals to help with this part of the campaign.

Advantages of message tailoring According to Kreuter *et al.* (2000) and Strecher and Kreuter (1999), tailored messages offer many advantages over more generic types of messages in health campaigns. First, tailored messages are more likely to be personally relevant to members of the target audience since they are created using demographic, psychological, and communication characteristics for specific individuals within the audience. For example, if 20 individuals out of 100 within a target audience scored high on a sensation-seeking measure prior to a campaign attempting to change risky sexual behaviors, only these 20 individuals would receive a message that specifically addressed high sensation-seeking tendencies. Second, Kreuter *et al.* (2000) maintain that people pay more attention to personally relevant information in health campaigns, and this is an important first step in changing attitudes and ultimately behaviors. Third, superfluous information found in more generic messages is eliminated, and only the information that matches the characteristics of a particular individual is used in the message for that person. When messages attend to the specific needs of individuals, Kreuter *et al.* (2000) argue that the information will be more thoughtfully processed, which is an important prerequisite for lasting attitudinal and behavioral change according to the elaboration likelihood model (Petty & Cacioppo, 1981). In two studies of message tailoring, Kreuter *et al.* (2006) and Kreuter, Alcaraz, Pfeiffer, and Christopher (2008) found that using computer kiosks that employed message tailoring for breast cancer education in the community setting led to improved attitude and knowledge change. According to Sundar *et al.* (2011), the positive outcomes associated with message tailoring campaigns seem to be due largely to the heightened self-awareness associated with entering one's own personal date into the computer (or kiosk) coupled with enhancement of the messages due to the feedback process.

Process of message tailoring According to Kreuter *et al.* (2000), there is ideally a nine-step process for creating tailored messages, including extensive background research on target audience characteristics, creating assessment measures for demographic, psycho logical, and communication variables, designing appropriate messages for each possible segment of the target audience, creating algorithms and the computer program for the campaign, and implementing and evaluating the campaign.

In addition to creating specific messages for members of a target audience, another important issue to consider in health campaigns is how to best reach individuals. Rimal and Adkins (2003) argue that successful tailored health message campaigns offer an optimal balance between audience reach and specificity. According to these authors, more attention should be devoted to finding ways to use appropriate channels of communication based upon audience characteristics. For example, some people, such as college students, might pay more attention to health messages disseminated via the Internet, whereas older adults might pay more attention to print material given to them by their physician.

Summary

New communication technologies will most likely continue to influence how consumers seek health information and communicate with other consumers and providers about health issues. These technologies appear to offer health organizations and providers many advantages in terms of gathering, storing, and disseminating health information, such as electronic patient charts and information from diagnostic tests.

In addition, telemedicine presents new opportunities for providers to collaborate during the process of caring for patients, and the Internet and other new computer technologies will continue to be used for public health campaigns. However, despite the optimism over these technologies for improving healthcare, many cultural, educational, financial, and legal barriers exist that will certainly shape the future of new technologies and health communication.

References

Andrus, M. R., & Roth, M. T. (2002). Health literacy: A review. *Pharmacotherapy, 22*, 282–302.

Aspden, P., & Katz, J. E. (2001). Assessments of quality of health care information and referrals to physicians: A nationwide survey. In R. E. Rice & J. E. Katz (Eds), *The Internet and health communication: Experiences and expectations* (pp. 99–106). Thousand Oaks, CA: Sage.

Aspden, P., Katz, J. E., & Bemis, A. (2001). Use of the Internet for professional purposes: A survey of New Jersey physicians. In R. E. Rice & J. E. Katz (Eds), *The Internet and health communication: Experiences and expectations* (pp. 107–119). Thousand Oaks, CA: Sage.

American Telemedicine Association. (2009). *Telemedicine defined*. Retrieved July 23, 2012, from http://www.americantelmedorg/.

Avtgis, T. A., Polack, E. P., Staggers, S. M., & Wieczorek, S. M. (2011). Healthcare provider-recipient interactions: Is "on-line" interaction the next best thing to "being there?" In K. B. Wright & L. M. Webb (Eds), *Computer-mediated communication in personal relationships* (pp. 266–281). New York: Peter Lang.

Baker, I., Wagner, T. H., Singer, S., & Bundorf, M. K. (2005). Use of the Internet and e-mail for health care information: Results from a national survey. *JAMA, 289*, 2400–2406.

Barnes, M., Penrod, C., Neiger, B., Merrill, R., Eggett, D., & Thomas, E. (2003). Measuring the relevance of evaluation criteria among health information seekers on the Internet. *Journal of Health Psychology, 8*, 71–82.

Bass, S. B. (2003). How will Internet use affect the patient? A review of computer network and closed Internet-based system studies and the implications in understanding how the use of the Internet affects patient populations. *Journal of Health Psychology, 8*, 25–38.

Beaudoin, C. E., & Tao, C. C. (2007). Benefiting from social capital in online support groups: An empirical study of cancer patients. *CyberPsychology & Behavior, 10*, 587–590.

Biermann, J. S., Golladay, G., & Baker, J. (1999). Evaluation of cancer information on the Internet. *Cancer, 86*, 381–390.

Bovi, A. M., & Council on the Ethical and Judicial Affairs of the American Medical Association. (2003). Ethical guidelines for the use of electronic mail between patients and physicians. *American Journal of Bioethics, 3*, W43–W47.

Brooks, R., & Menachemi, N. (2006, January). Physicians' use of email with patients: Factors influencing electronic communication and adherence to best practices. *Journal of Medical Internet Research, 8*(1), e2.

Buis, L. R., & Carpenter, S. (2009). Health and medical blog content and its relationships with blogger credentials and blog host. *Health Communication, 24*, 703–710.

Bynum, A. B., Irwin, C. A., Cranford, C. O., & Denny, G. S. (2003). The impact of telemedicine on patients' cost savings: Some preliminary findings. *Telemedicine and e-health, 9*, 361–367.

Chen, C., Garrido, T., Chock, D., Okawa, G., & Liang, L. (2009). The Kaiser Permanente electronic health record: Transforming and streamlining modalities of care. *Health Affairs, 28*, 323–333.

Cummins, C., Prochaska, J. O., Driskell, M., Evers, K., Wright, J., Prochaska, J. M., & Velicer, W. (2003). Development of review criteria to evaluate health behavior change websites. *Journal of Health Psychology, 8*, 55–62.

Dakof, G. A., & Taylor, S. E. (1990). Victim's perceptions of social support: What is helpful from whom? *Journal of Personality and Social Psychology, 58*, 80–89.

Delbanco, T., & Sands, D. Z. (2004). Electrons in flight—e-mail between doctors and patients. *New England Journal of Medicine, 350*, 1705–1707.

Diamond, J. (2000). *Narrative means to sober ends: Treating addiction and its aftermath*. New York: Guilford Press.

Diaz, J. A., Sciamanna, C. N., Evangelou, E., Stamp, M. J., & Ferguson, T. (2005). Brief report: What types of

Internet guidance do patients want from their physicians? *Journal of General Internal Medicine, 20,* 787–788.

Eder, L. B., & Wise, D. E. (2001). Web-enabled hospitals in the United States: Influences on adoption processes. In R. E. Rice & J. E. Katz (Eds), *The Internet and health communication: Experiences and expectations* (pp. 309–327). Thousand Oaks, CA: Sage.

Eng, T. R. (2001). *The eHealth landscape: A terrain map of emerging information and communication technologies in health and health care.* Princeton, NJ: The Robert Wood Johnson Foundation.

Ferguson, T. (1998). Digital doctoring: Opportunities and challenges in electronic patient–physician communication (Editorial). *Journal of the American Medical Association, 280,* 1261–1262.

Floyd, K., Mikkelson, A. C., Hesse, C., & Pauley, P. M. (2007). Affectionate writing reduces total cholesterol: Two randomized, controlled trials. *Human Communication Research, 33,* 119–142.

Fox, S., & Rainie, L. (2000). The online health care revolution: How the Web helps Americans take better care of themselves. A Pew Internet and American Life Project Online Report. Retrieved January 2, 2004, from www.pewinternet.org.

Fox, S., & Jones, S. (2009, June 11). *The social life of health information* (online health information use). Retrieved July 17, 2012 from http://www.pewInternet.org/Reports/2009/8-The-Social-Life-of-Health-Information.aspx.

Galarce, E. M., Ramanadhan, S., & Viswanath, K. (2011). Health information seeking. In T. L. Thompson, R. Parrott, & J. F. Nussbaum (Eds), *The Routledge handbook of health communication,* 2nd ed. (pp. 167–180). New York: Routledge.

Galinski, M. J., Schopler, J. H., & Abell, M. D. (1997). Connecting group members through telephone and computer groups. *Health and Social Work, 22,* 181–189.

Geist, P., & Hardesty, M. (1990). Reliable, silent, hysterical, or assured: Physicans assess patient cues in their medical decision making. *Health Communication, 2,* 69–90.

Gustafson, D. H., McTavish, F. M., Stengle, W., Ballard, D., Hawkins, R., Shaw, B. R., Jones, E., Julesberg, K., McDowell, H., Wei, C. C., Volrathongchai, K., & Landucci, G. (2005). Use and impact of ehealth system by low-income women with breast cancer. *Journal of Health Communication, 10,* 195–218.

Gutske, S., Balch, D., West, V., & Rogers, L. (2000). Patient satisfaction with telemedicine. *Telemedicine Journal, 6,* 5–13.

Hawkins, R. P., Kreuter, M., Resnicow, K., Fishbein, M., & Dijkstra, A. (2008). Understanding tailoring in communicating about health. *Health Education Research, 23,* 454–466.

Helgeson, V. S., Cohen, S., Schultz, R., & Yasko, J. (2000). Group support interventions for women with breast cancer: Who benefits from what? *Health Psychology, 19,* 107–114.

Hersch, W., Gorman, P., & Sacherek, L. (1998). Applicability and quality of information for answering clinical questions on the Web. *Journal of the American Medical Association, 280,* 1307–1308.

Hillestad, R., Bigelow, J., Bower, A., Girosi, F., Meili, R., & Scoville, R. (2005). Can electronic medical record systems transform health care? Potential health benefits, savings, and costs. *Health Affairs, 24,* 1103–1117.

Hong, S., Yang, Y., Kim, S., Shin, S., Lee, I., Jang, Y. *et al.* (2009). Performance study of the wearable one-lead wireless electrocardiographic monitoring system. *Telemedicine and e-Health, 15,* 166–175.

Houston, T. K., Cooper, L. A., & Ford, D. E. (2002). Internet support groups for depression: A 1-year prospective cohort study. *American Journal of Psychiatry, 159,* 2062–2068.

Houston, T., Sands, D. Z., Nash, B. R., & Ford, D. E. (2003). Experiences of physicians who frequently use e-mail with patients. *Health Communication, 15,* 515–525.

Hurling, R., Catt, C., Boni, M. D., Fairley, B. W., Hurst, T., Murray, P. *et al.* (2007). Using Internet and mobile phone technology to deliver an automated physical activity program: Randomized controlled trial. *Journal of Medical Internet Research, 9,* e7. Retrieved July 17, 2012 from http://www.jmir.org/2007/2/e7/.

Jones, D. S. (2008, December). Quality, defensibility, and the electronic medical record. *Journal of Healthcare Compliance, 41,* 71–72.

Jones, M., Luce, K. H., Osborne, M. L., Taylor, K., Cunning, D., Doyle, A. C. *et al.* (2008). Randomized, controlled trial of an internet-facilitated intervention for reducing overeating and overweight in adolescents. *Pediatrics, 121,* 453–462.

Katz, J. E., & Aspden, P. (2001). Networked communication practices and the security and privacy of electronic health care records. In R. E. Rice & J. E. Katz (Eds), *The Internet and health communication: Experiences and expectations* (pp. 393–415). Thousand Oaks, CA: Sage.

Kim, H. (1998, August). CME: A whole new World (Wide Web). *American Medical News*, pp. 1–3.

Kim, S. I., & Kim, H. S. (2008). Effectiveness of mobile and Internet intervention in patients with obese type 2 diabetes. *International Journal of Medical Informatics, 77*, 399–404.

King, S. A., & Moreggi, D. (1998). Internet therapy and self-help groups: The pros and cons. In J. Gackenbach (Ed.), *Psychology and the Internet: Intrapersonal, interpersonal, and transpersonal implications* (pp. 77–109). San Diego, CA: Academic Press.

Kohn, P. M. (1996). On coping adaptively with daily hassles. In M. Zeidner & N. S. Endler (Eds), *Handbook of coping* (pp. 181–201). New York: John Wiley & Sons.

Kovic, I., Lulic, I., Brumini, G. (2008). Examining the medical blogosphere: An online survey of medical bloggers. *Journal of Medical Internet Research, 10*, e10. Retrieved July 17, 2012, from http://www.jmir.org/2008/3/e28/.

Kreps, G.L., Neuhauser, L., Sparks, L., & Villagran, M. (Eds) (2008). Translational community-based health communication interventions to promote cancer prevention and control for vulnerable audiences [Special Issue] *Patient Education and Counseling, 71*(3), 315–350.

Kreps, G. L., & Sparks, L. (2008). Meeting the health literacy needs of vulnerable populations. *Patient Education and Counseling, 71*(3), 328–332.

Kreps, G. L., & Kunimoto, E. (1994). *Effective communication in multicultural health care settings.* Newbury Park, CA: Sage.

Kreuter, M. W, & McClure, S. M. (2004) The role of culture in health communication. *Annual Review of Public Health, 25*, 439–455.

Kreuter, M. W., Alcaraz, K. I., Pfeiffer, D., & Christopher, K. (2008). Using dissemination research to identify optimal community settings for tailored breast cancer information kiosks. *Journal of Public Health Management, 14*, 160–169.

Kreuter, M. W., Black, W. J., Friend, L., Booker, A. C., Klump, M. P., Bobra, S. et al. (2006). Use of computer kiosks for breast cancer education in five community settings. *Health Education & Behavior, 33*, 625–642.

Kreuter, M., Farrell, D., Olevitch, L., & Brennan, L. (2000). *Tailoring health messages: Customizing communication with computer technology.* Mahwah, NJ: Lawrence Erlbaum.

Metzger, M. J. (2007). Making sense of credibility on the Web: Models for evaluating online information and recommendations for future research. *Journal of the American Society for Information Science and Technology, 58*, 2078–2091.

Miller, C. C. (2009, January 6). Doctors will make web calls in Hawaii. *The New York Times.* Retrieved July 17, 2012, from http://www.nytimes.com/2009/01/06/technology/internet/06health.html.

Miller, E. A. (2003). The technical and interpersonal aspects of telemedicine: Effects on doctor-patient communication. *Journal of Telemedicine and Telecare, 9*, 1–7.

Mo, P. K. H., Malik, S. H., & Coulson, N. S. (2009). Gender differences in computer-mediated communication: A systematic literature review of online health-related support groups. *Patient Education and Counseling, 75*, 16–24.

Napoli, P. M. (2001). Consumer use of medical information from electronic and paper media: A literature review. In R. E. Rice & J. E. Katz (Eds), *The Internet and health communication: Experiences and expectations* (pp. 79–98). Thousand Oaks, CA: Sage.

Neuhauser, L., & Kreps, G. L. (2003). Rethinking communication in the e-health era. *Journal of Health Psychology, 8*, 7–23.

Papacharissi, Z., & Rubin, A. M. (2000). Predictors of Internet use. *Journal of Broadcasting and Electronic Media, 44*, 175–196.

Pecchioni, L., Ota, H., & Sparks, L. (2004). Cultural issues in communication and aging. In Nussbaum, J. F., & Coupland, J. (Eds), *Handbook of communication and aging research,* (pp. 167–207). Mahwah, NJ: Erlbaum.

Pecchioni, L., Krieger, J. C., Sparks, L., Pitts, M., & Ota, H. (2008). Investigating cancer and ageing from a cultural perspective. In L. Sparks, H. D. O'Hair, & G. L. Kreps (Eds), *Cancer communication and aging* (pp. 239–257). Cresskill, NJ: Hampton Press.

Pelletier, A. L., Sutton, G. R., & Walker, R. R. (2007). Are your patients ready for electronic communication? *Family Practice Medicine, 14*, 25.

Petty, R. E., & Cacioppo, J. T. (1981). *Attitudes and persuasion: Classic and contemporary approaches.* Dubuque, IA: William C. Brown Company.

Pierce, G. R., Sarason, I. G., & Sarason, B. R. (1996). Coping and social support. In M. Zeidner & N. S. Endler (Eds), *Handbook of coping* (pp. 434–451). New York: John Wiley & Sons.

Podichetty, V., & Penn, D. (2004). The progressive roles of electronic medicine: Benefits, concerns, and costs. *American Journal of Medical Science, 328,* 94–99.

Preece, J. J., & Ghozati, K. (2001). Experiencing empathy on-line. In R. E. Rice & J. E. Katz (Eds), *The Internet and health communication: Experiences and expectations* (pp. 237–260). Thousand Oaks, CA: Sage.

Query, J. L., Jr., & Wright, K. B. (2003). Assessing communication competence in an on-line study: Towards informing subsequent interventions among older adults with cancer, their lay caregivers, and peers. *Health Communication, 15,* 203–218.

Rains, S. R., & Bosch, L. A. (2009). Privacy and health in the information age: A content analysis of health web site privacy policy statements. *Health Communication, 24,* 435–446.

Rains, S. A., & Young, V. (2009). A meta-analysis of research on formal computer-mediated support groups: Examining group characteristics and health outcomes. *Human Communication Research, 35,* 309–336.

Ramirez, A., Walther, J. B., Burgoon, J. K., & Sunnafrank, M. (2002). Information-seeking strategies, uncertainty, and computer-mediated communication. Toward a conceptual model. *Human Communication Research, 28,* 213–228.

Rice, R. E. (2001). The Internet and health communication. In R. E. Rice & J. E. Katz (Eds), *The Internet and health communication: Experiences and expectations* (pp. 5–46). Thousand Oaks, CA: Sage.

Rice, R. E., & Katz, J. E. (2001). Concluding thoughts. In R. E. Rice & J. E. Katz (Eds), *The Internet and health communication: Experiences and expectations* (pp. 417–429). Thousand Oaks, CA: Sage.

Rice, R. E., & Katz, J. E. (2006). Internet use in physician practice and patient interaction. In M. Murero & R. E. Rice (Eds), *The Internet and health care: Theory, research and practice* (pp. 149–176). Mahwah, NJ: Erlbaum.

Rimal, R. N., & Adkins, D. A. (2003). Using computers to narrowcast health messages: The role of audience segmentation, targeting, and tailoring in health promotion. In T. L. Thompson, A. M. Dorsey, K. I. Miller, & R. Parrott (Eds), *Handbook of health communication* (pp. 497–513). Mahwah, NJ: Lawrence Erlbaum.

Roter, D. L., Hall, J. A., & Katz, N. R. (1988). Patient–physician communication: A descriptive summary of the literature. *Patient Education and Counseling, 12,* 99–119.

Roter, D. L., Sands, D. Z., Ford, D. E., & Houston, T. (2008). Can e-mail messages between patients and physicians be patient centered? *Health Communication, 23,* 80–86.

Sarasohn-Kahn, J. (2008). *The wisdom of patients: Health care meets online social media.* Retrieved August 21, 2008, from http://www.chcf.org/documents/chronicdisease/HealthCareSocialMedia.pdf.

Shaw, B. R., Hawkins, R., McTavish, F., Pingree, S., & Gustafson, D. H. (2006). Effects of insightful disclosure within computer-mediated support groups on women with breast cancer. *Health Communication, 19,* 133–142.

Shieh, C. Mays, R., McDaniel, A., & Yu, J. (2009). Health literacy and its association with the use of information sources and with barriers to information seeking in clinic-based pregnant women. *Health Care for Women International, 30,* 971–988.

Sparks, L., & Nussbaum, J. F. (2008). Health literacy and cancer communication with older adults. *Patient Education and Counseling, 71*(3), 345–350.

Stalberg, P., Yeh, M., Ketteridge, G., Delbridge, H., & Delbridge, L. (2008). E-mail access and improved communication between patient and surgeon. *Archives of Surgery, 143,* 164–168.

Stanberry, B. (2006). Legal and ethical aspects of telemedicine. *Journal of Telemedicine and Telecare, 12,* 166–175.

Strasser, F., Fisch, M., Bodurka, D. C., Sivesind, D., & Bruera, E. (2002). E-emotions: Email for written emotional expression. *Journal of Clinical Oncology, 20,* 3352–3355.

Strecher, V. J., & Kreuter, M. W. (1999). Health risk appraisal from a behavioral perspective: Present and future. In G. C. Hyner, K. W. Peterson, J. W. Travis, J. E. Dewey, J. J. Foerster, & E. M. Framer (Eds), *Society of Prospective Medicine handbook of health assessment tools* (pp. 75–82). Pittsburgh, PA: Society of Prospective Medicine.

Sundar, S. S., Rice, R. E., Kim, H., & Sciamanna, C. H. (2011). On-line health information: Conceptual challenges and theoretical opportunities. In T. L. Thompson, R. Parrott, & J. F. Nussbaum (Eds), *The Routledge handbook of health communication,* 2nd ed. (181–202). New York: Routledge.

Tanis, M. (2008). Health-related on-line forums: What's the big attraction? *Journal of Health Communication, 13,* 698–714.

Tian, Y. (2010). Organ donation on Web 2.0: Content and audience analysis of organ donation videos on YouTube. *Health Communication, 25,* 238–246.

Tu, H. T., & Cohen, G. R. (2008). Striking job in consumer seeking health information. *Tracking Report* (Center for Studying Health System Change), 20.

Turner, J. W. (2003). Telemedicine: Expanding health care into virtual environments. In T. L. Thompson, A. M. Dorsey, K. I. Miller, & R. Parrott (Eds), *Handbook of health communication* (pp. 515–535). Mahwah, NJ: Lawrence Erlbaum.

US Census Bureau. (2010). Press release. Retrieved July 23, 2012, from www.census.gov/Press-Release/www/2010/

Viswanath, K., Ramanadhan, S., & Kontos, E. Z. (2007). Mass media and population health: A macrosocial view. In S. Galea (Ed.), *Macrosocial determinants of population health* (pp. 275–294). New York: Springer.

von Friedrichs-Fitzwater, M. M., Callahan, E. J., Flynn, N., & Williams, J. (1991). Relational control in physician–patient encounters. *Health Communication*, 1, 17–36.

Walther, J. B. (1996). Computer-mediated communication: Impersonal, interpersonal, and hyperpersonal interaction. *Communication Research*, 23, 3–43.

Walther, J. B., & Boyd, S. (2002). Attraction to computer-mediated social support. In C. A. Lin & D. Atkins (Eds), *Communication technology and society: Audience adoption and uses* (pp. 153–188). Cresskill, NJ: Hampton Press.

Wang, Z., Walther, J. B., Pingree, S., & Hawkins, R. P. (2008). Health information, credibility, homophily, and influence via the Internet: Web sites versus discussion groups. *Health Communication*, 23, 358–368.

Weiler, R. M., & Pealer, L. N. (2000). The sitelegend: Twelve components of a new strategy for providing website documentation. *Journal of School Health*, 70, 148–152.

Weinberg, N., Schmale, J. D., Uken, J., & Wessel, K. (1995). Computer-mediated support groups. *Social Work with Groups*, 17, 43–55.

Wellman, B. (1997). An electronic group is virtually a social network. In S. Kiesler (Ed.), *Culture of the Internet* (pp. 179–205). Mahwah, NJ: Lawrence Erlbaum.

Whitten, P., & Buis, L. (2008). Use of telemedicine for haemodialysis: Perceptions of patients and health-care providers, and clinical effects. *Journal of Telemedicine and Telecare*, 14, 75–78.

Whitten, P., Cook, D., & Cornacchione, J. (2011). Telemedicine: Reviewing the past, looking toward the future. In T. L. Thompson, R. Parrott, & J. F. Nussbaum (Eds), *The Routledge handbook of health communication*, 2nd ed. (84-99). New York: Routledge.

Whitten, P. S., Eastin, M. S., & Cook, D. (2001). The role of the organization in the success of web-based continuing medical education programs. In R. E. Rice & J. E. Katz (Eds), *The Internet and health communication: Experiences and expectations* (pp. 261–285). Thousand Oaks, CA: Sage.

Witherspoon, E. (2001). A pound of cure: A content analysis of health information on web sites of top-ranked HMOs. In R. E. Rice & J. E. Katz (Eds), *The Internet and health communication: Experiences and expectations* (pp. 189–212). Thousand Oaks, CA: Sage.

Wright, K. B. (1999). Computer-mediated support groups: An examination of relationships among social support, perceived stress, and coping strategies. *Communication Quarterly*, 47, 402–414.

Wright, K. B. (2000a). Social support satisfaction, on-line communication apprehension, and perceived life stress within computer-mediated support groups. *Communication Research Reports*, 17, 139–147.

Wright, K. B. (2000b). Computer-mediated social support, older adults, and coping. *Journal of Communication*, 50, 100–118.

Wright, K. B., & Bell, S. B. (2003). Health-related support groups on the Internet: Linking empirical findings to social support and computer-mediated communication theory. *Journal of Health Psychology*, 8, 37–52.

Wright, K. B., Johnson, A. J., Bernard, D. R., & Averbeck, J. (2011). Computer-mediated social support: Promises and pitfalls for individuals coping with health concerns. In T. L. Thompson, R. Parrott, & J. F. Nussbaum (Eds), *The Routledge handbook of health communication*, 2nd ed. (349-362). New York: Routledge.

Youmans SL, Schillinger D. (2003). Functional health literacy and medication use: The pharmacist's role. *Annals of Pharmocotherapy*, 37, 1726–1729.

Zyzanski, S. J., Stange, K. C., Langa, D., & Flocke, S. A. (1998). Trade-offs in high volume primary care practices. *Journal of Family Practice*, 46, 397–402.

Chapter 8

Mass Communication and Health

Television and other mass media play an important role in influencing our perceptions of health and our health behaviors in a variety of ways. In addition to entertainment, television, films, newspapers, the Internet, and other media regularly convey information that can influence our health, such as advertisements for fast food, popular film characters engaging in unhealthy behaviors, celebrities who may influence unrealistic body images, and news stories about medical breakthroughs. Americans are avid consumers of the mass media, and our exposure to media content begins when we are young children. Many of our perceptions about health, illness, medicine, and healthcare professionals are shaped by what we see, hear, and read in the mass media. While our family members, peers, and educators also are strong social influences on our health perceptions and behaviors, what we learn from these sources interacts with the mass media to socialize us about health in very complex ways. Increasingly, new media technologies are playing a much larger role in the development and consumption of messages for general target audiences through community-based participation and segmented by social media usage (i.e. Facebook and Twitter) and blogging. Recent events in Egypt, Libya, and Japan have all demonstrated the relevance and power of social media during times of crisis and further propel messages to a larger audience for very little cost (excluding the initial cost for the computer and internet service provider). Thus, media use in the 21st century is evolving and rapidly changing with each new techno toy introduced into the marketplace. As such, it is changing the gatekeepers of how media are able to disseminate health information.

This chapter explores the role of mass media in influencing our perceptions of health and our health behaviors. It primarily focuses on traditional mass media, such as television, film, radio, and print, although we will briefly introduce aspects of new media as well. We begin by discussing two popular theories of media influence and research linking mass media images of health and portrayals of health situations to

Health Communication in the 21st Century, Second Edition. Kevin Bradley Wright, Lisa Sparks, and H. Dan O'Hair.

health behaviors. Next, we explore issues concerning how health-related stories are presented in the news media and the implications of reporting practices on public conceptions of health and health behaviors.

Two Perspectives of Media Influence

Most communication scholars feel that the mass media influence our perceptions and behaviors in a number of ways, including those related to health. However, it is has been difficult for researchers to demonstrate a direct link between specific media content and health behaviors. As you will see in this chapter, the relationship between mass media content and behaviors is complex, and many variables mediate the degree to which the mass media influence our behaviors. This chapter presents two broad perspectives of the relationship between media usage and behaviors. These theoretical frameworks are important to understand before talking about specific health behaviors that appear to be influenced by the mass media, such as eating habits, substance abuse, and violence, which we will explore later in this chapter.

Cultivation theory

A popular theory that has been used to explain the effects of mass media (particularly television) is *cultivation theory* (Gerbner, 1998; Gerbner & Gross, 1972; Gerbner, Gross, Morgan, & Signorielli, 1982). Cultivation theorists argue that the reality portrayed in the mass media influences our perceptions of reality in the real world over an extended period of time. In other words, cultivation theory posits that long-term repeated exposure to mass media messages shapes our understanding of the world in ways that are consistent with how reality is portrayed in the media. Cultivation theory holds that television can have a "normalizing" effect in terms of influencing perceptions, and televised behaviors may become perceived as acceptable or desirable over time (Shrum, 1999). Most cultivation theorists have examined the influence of television on behaviors because Americans use television more than any other medium, and because television is relatively inexpensive compared to other media (e.g. the Internet) and does not require consumers to be literate (Gerbner *et al.*, 1978).

Heavy viewers of television often tend to have attitudes and beliefs about the world that are congruent with the reality promoted by television, a concept known as *mainstreaming* (Gerbner, 1998). Television can also influence perceptions of reality in subtle ways. For example, *first-order effects* refer to information about a topic that people learn by watching television, and *second-order effects* are more generalized perceptions about topics and the world that people learn from television (Gerbner, Gross, Morgan, & Signorielli, 1986). For example, a heavy viewer of "Grey's Anatomy" might learn some basic terminology used in emergency room settings (a first-order effect), but she might also come to believe that biomedical and technological solutions to health problems (used most often in the show) are the most effective ways to deal with them (a second-order effect).

Similar to other perceptions of reality, our perceptions of health are most likely influenced in a variety of ways by our exposure to media content. Given the high prevalence of health-related dramatic entertainment in the mass media and health-related news stories, the mass media present a version of reality surrounding health issues that is often much different than what occurs in the real world (Turow & Coe, 1993). Yet, just because certain images of health are presented in the mass media, critics of cultivation theory argue that this does not necessarily mean that people will pay attention to all of these messages, interpret them, or react to them in the same way. In other words, for some individuals, the effects of encountering media content may be limited due to the reasons they use media. In the next section, we present an alternative framework for examining the influence of the mass media on perceptions and behaviors.

Uses and gratifications theory

While early theories about the influence of television and other mass media on individual behavior proposed that the mass media are very powerful in changing behaviors, later theories began to examine the idea of how the effects of the mass media are mediated by audience members as active users of media and choice makers when it comes to interpreting media content. For example, *uses and gratifications theory* proposes that the effects of media are tempered by the ways in which people use them. Specifically, the theory posits that people actively choose certain types of media and media content to gratify various psychological and social needs or to accomplish certain goals (Katz, Blumler, & Gurevitz, 1974). The reasons why individuals choose one type of media over another or choose specific media content are as diverse as people themselves, but what we choose to view, read, and listen to mediates the influence of the mass media. In the next section, we will explore various needs that the mass media fulfill concerning health.

Needs Fulfilled by the Mass Media Concerning Health

Information seeking

Media fulfill the need for information about the world or specific interests. Given the rapid changes we have experienced in society in recent years, with the advent of diseases such as HIV and SARS and health threats due to terrorism, most people desire up-to-date news and accurate information about health-related events. The mass media help to fulfill our desire to reduce uncertainty about health issues by gathering information that will help us to make better choices about how we should respond to daily events. Some people may gratify their information-seeking needs about health by paying attention to health stories on CNN or their local television news station. For other individuals, radio, newspapers, and magazines such as *Time* or *Men's Health* or Internet sources such as WebMD may be more important sources of news and information than television. Many consumers are getting the majority of their health information from new media sources such as Twitter and Facebook to augment more traditional media sources. For example, check out the chapmanhcomms Twitter account for weekly updates and feeds germane to health communication issues. Many students just like you are starting their own Twitter feeds and blogs on a variety of topics. It is indeed a new era of health information seeking, consumption, and creation.

Entertainment, diversion, and tension release

Others may learn about health issues by watching shows such as "Grey's Anatomy" or "House" or even reality shows such as "The Doctors," "Dr. Phil," or "Celebrity Rehab," "In Treatment," or "The Biggest Loser" for entertainment or as a diversion from the stress of everyday life. While people may initially watch a show to fulfill entertainment needs, they can often learn about a variety of health-related issues that are part of the story of the program episode. For example, "Grey's Anatomy" deals with many timely health issues (albeit sometimes indirectly) as part of the show's stories, including medical malpractice litigation, advanced care directives, issues of cultural competence and patient use or denial of treatment, and a variety of up-to-date medical procedures. For many people, television shows like "Grey's Anatomy" are one of the few places where they acquire information about the world of medicine and current health issues, particularly if they tend to avoid more traditional news stories about health on television or other media.

Individuals may also develop expectations about provider–patient interaction based on this type of entertainment, and characters on television often serve as role models for the ways individuals are expected to behave in health encounters. This may be problematic if people identify with providers who tend to be paternalistic toward patients, and this influences their behaviors when they actually visit their physicians and other providers in real life. However, shows like "Grey's Anatomy" sometimes show patients behaving in assertive ways, and the stories often give an insight into the stressful lives of healthcare professionals. In these cases, watching such programs can provide people with positive role models or help them see the perspective of providers. These programs also provide a venue for social comparison to others. According to social comparison theory (Festinger, 1954; see also Chapter 4), individuals compare themselves to other individuals in society and make a variety of judgements about their own lives, such as their abilities, opinions, and behaviors. For example, people may perceive themselves to be more or less healthy than the people they see on television. This can sometimes motivate people to engage in diet and exercise programs or be proactive about their health in other ways if they feel that they are relatively unhealthy compared to the people they see on television. However, as we have seen, negative aspects of television and other media, such as advertisements for fast food or role models engaging in unhealthy behaviors, can negatively affect health behaviors.

The media also provide content that can help us divert our attention from the stress of everyday life and fulfill various affective needs, including the need to appreciate aesthetic, emotional, and pleasurable experiences. Watching a situation comedy or emotional drama can help people temporarily forget about their problems and elevate their moods. There is some evidence that humor is linked to positive health outcomes (du Pré, 1998; Lambert & Lambert, 1995; Wanzer, Sparks, & Frymier, 2009). Humor tends to lift a person's mood and reduce stress levels, both of which are linked to positive psychological and physical health outcomes. However, while experiencing pleasure through using media can have a positive effect on health, diverting attention from problems does not make them go away, and avoidance of problems can sometime create more stress for individuals in the long run. In addition, spending too much time using passive media like television may lead to a sedentary lifestyle in which people limit their physical and mental activity. Sedentary lifestyles have been linked to obesity and other health problems, and there is some evidence that choosing to watch television over more mentally challenging activities (e.g. reading) on a long-term basis may lead to cognitive problems over time (Friedland *et al.*, 2001).

Media use to fulfill social needs

Television and other mass media provide people with the substance for conversations with members of their social network. Katz, Gurevitch, and Haas (1973) referred to this as the *personal integrative function*. The personal integrative function of media occurs when the knowledge we gain from the media about the world, current events, or happenings in the lives of media characters helps to enhance our credibility and status in conversations with others. For example, media provide us with content about health issues for conversations with members of our social network, such as sharing information from a news story about a new medical procedure.

Interactive media such as the Internet can fulfill interpersonal needs. In the last few decades, on-line health communities have become important places where people can meet others with similar health concerns and obtain health information from health-care professionals and other consumers, as well as emotional support and encouragement when coping with health problems (see Chapter 7). Even noninteractive media help to foster a sense of connection with others, particularly when people view the same content on a television program. For example, after the terrorist attacks on 9/11, watching television stories on CNN about how people were coping with the threat of terrorism helped many people feel that they were not alone, and this may have helped them to feel less anxious. Social media communities such as Facebook and Twitter can provide quick and easy access to health information from people's trusted interpersonal networks as well as health-related organizations and blogs.

Finally, people often choose a certain medium to fulfill their needs because it is convenient to do so. For example, some individuals may find navigating the Internet to be cumbersome, so they prefer to obtain health information from health-related news stories on television, in newspapers, and in magazines. Other people find the Internet to be a cheap and convenient way to discuss health issues with other people, particularly when they are geographically separated from their conversational partner(s). In addition, some people are more active than others when seeking health information, and this may motivate them to use resources like the Internet to find a variety of sources of health information, for example www.cdc.gov, instead of consulting one or two articles in a magazine.

Health information-seeking behavior is almost addictive use of new technologies. Information is "stimuli from a person's environment that contribute to his or her knowledge or beliefs" (Brashers, Goldsmith, & Hseih, 2002, p. 259) and can be obtained by way of a number of communication channels (Dutta-Bergman, 2004a). Health information can be obtained in a variety of interesting ways via multiple sources. For example, Burkell, Wolfe, Potter, & Jutai (2006) note that health information is typically sought via interpersonal and media sources. Initially, individuals seeking health information are likely to consult personal sources such as family or friends (Buller, Callister, & Reichert, 1995), though media sources such as television, newspapers, and the Internet, are also subsequent, important sources for health information (Brashers, Goldsmith, & Hseih, 2002). The media is certainly an integral health information source, as it defines illness and health, features services and products that that can help consumers manage their health, and provides a representation of others who have specific health conditions to a large number of individuals (Cotten & Gupta, 2004). In fact, Fox (2006) suggests 80 percent of adults surveyed have searched for health information online and 53 percent of them indicated they used the information found in health decisions.

Dutta-Bergman (2004b) examined interpersonal and media health information sources that included TV, radio, newspapers or magazines, hotlines, the Internet, and family or friends. We utilize these information sources here to understand how the public seeks and evaluates information about health care information such as health-care reform (Bevan *et al.*, 2012). Dutta-Bergman found that individuals who utilized active sources encourage the gathering of information and require participants to communicate with others including family or friends, newspapers and magazines, and the Internet. Further, his research revealed that individuals obtaining that information were more likely to have strong health beliefs and to be health conscious than those employing passive sources such as TV and radio. Pecchioni and Sparks' (2007) research found that family members of patients reported being significantly more satisfied with the Internet in terms of health information sources, whereas patients themselves reported more satisfaction with doctors and nurses as health information sources. Madden and Fox (2006) found that 58 percent of the caretakers surveyed reported that the Internet was an important tool for making health decisions. Additional research from the NCI 2005 Health Information National Trends Survey revealed that when participants were asked "Where would you go for cancer information" 50 percent stated they would go to their provider followed by Internet (34%), library (5%), family (4%), and print media (4%). Time constraints, competing demands for attention, and a lack of training in effective communication most certainly influences patient health information-seeking behaviors (Sparks & Villagran, 2010), and can greatly impact medical adherence and decision-making for patients (Tinley *et al.*, 2004). Buller, Callister, & Reichert (1995) found that the more individuals sought skin cancer information from print media (i.e. newspapers, magazines, newsletters, or pamphlets), the more they protected their skin. Further, use of healthcare providers and magazines or newspapers as an information source, as opposed to the Internet and toll-free phone numbers, was positively related to requesting a specific prescription medication (Lee, 2009). Lee also found that using the Internet as an information source facilitated consumers to discuss specific prescription medication with their health providers, an effect that grew substantially between 1999 and 2002. As such, using different media and interpersonal sources for obtaining health information has a number of potentially important implications.

Media Usage, Health Portrayals, and Health Behaviors

The mass media play a significant role in their ability to influence health behaviors. Americans are keen consumers of the mass media, and they are exposed to many different messages and images of health through media content. By the time an average American reaches 19 years of age, he or she will have spent more time watching television than most people spend at a full-time job in a year (Dworetzky, 1993). According to Bahk (2001), "because health occupies an essential part of human living, dramatic media presentations frequently depict health-related events for developing their story lines" (p. 188). In addition, the popular media are an important source of health-related information for most Americans (Atkin & Arkin, 1990; Signorielli, 1993), even when health information comes in the form of entertainment. As we have mentioned, information about health issues encountered through entertainment programs such as "Grey's Anatomy" can potentially raise awareness about health issues and risks, and this information can sometimes motivate positive behavioral changes (Montgomery, 1990; Scharf, Freimuth, Greenspon, & Plotnick, 1996).

However, portrayals of health situations in the mass media are often unrealistic, and they tend to emphasize certain messages about health while excluding others. The following sections explore unrealistic portrayals of health situations and unhealthy role models associated with the entertainment media.

Unrealistic portrayals of health situations

While some television and film dramas have somewhat accurate portrayals of healthcare settings, the mass media can also distort our perceptions of health situations in a variety of ways. Medical procedures and other solutions to health problems are presented as being far more successful in the media than in real life (Diem, Lantos, & Tulsky, 1996; Wallack & Dorfman, 1992). Key healthcare organization members such as administrators, physician assistants, laboratory technicians, and other medical personnel are rarely seen in media portrayals of healthcare situations, while physicians are the healthcare professional that viewers see most frequently. Constraints on providers imposed by managed care and other bureaucratic influences are seen much less than they occur in real healthcare situations. Healthcare teams, telemedicine, and other newer approaches to healthcare are also rarely seen in media portrayals of health situations. Patients on television are more likely to be depicted as having acute medical conditions rather than long-term chronic health conditions (which are more common), and most discussion between providers and patients centers on biomedical rather than psychosocial issues (Turow & Coe, 1993). Individuals with mental illness are often portrayed in stereotypical ways (du Pré, 2005; Sparks & Villagran, 2010), promoting the idea that people with mental illness are dangerous and unstable. Characters with disabilities in the media, when they do appear at all, are rarely depicted as living ordinary lives (Signorielli, 1993). Instead, the media often focus too much attention on a character's disability or portray people with disabilities in stereotypical ways. Older individuals dealing with health problems are often disproportionately underrepresented in health-related film and television content (Turow & Coe, 1993). When they do appear, health problems are often attributed to age rather than disease, and issues common among older patients, such as polypharmacy or the impact of companions on provider–older patient interaction, do not appear in media portrayals of healthcare situations as often as they occur in real life. Despite these problems, film and television audience members frequently identify with characters who portray physicians and other healthcare professionals. The popularity of television shows like "Grey's Anatomy," "House," "Scrubs," "Nip/Tuck," and other health-related programs reflects the enormous interest many Americans have in healthcare situations.

Unhealthy role models and the promotion of unhealthy behaviors in advertising

Most sources of entertainment and advertising in the mass media have been criticized for promoting unhealthy perceptions of health and health behaviors among media consumers (Bahk, 2001; Terre, Drabman, & Speer, 1991; Signorielli, 1993). The media characters that are most attractive to media consumers often serve as role models for a variety of health behaviors, but unfortunately many of the health-related behaviors they engage in are negative (Kline, 2003, 2011). For example, central characters in popular television shows and movies often engage in a variety of unhealthy behaviors, including smoking, drinking alcohol, practicing unsafe sex, and eating unhealthy foods. In many cases it makes little difference whether media role models are real or fictitious in terms of influencing health behaviors (Kline, 2003, 2011). People often look up to television and film actors due to their attractiveness and celebrity status. The media often send competing messages when it comes to health.

For example, while we may often want to look like movie stars, we also associate these actors with behaviors we see them performing in the media. When the characters these actors portray eat unhealthy foods, smoke, drink alcohol, or engage in other unhealthy behaviors, it sends audience members an indirect message that these behaviors are desirable since they are associated with characters to whom we are attracted. To be fair, it should be pointed out that popular films such as "Patch Adams" and television shows like "Grey's Anatomy" do show positive aspects of healthcare, such as humor and health, alternative medicines, and provider commitment to quality healthcare. Yet, positive portrayals of health situations are often offset by unhealthy role models in health-related entertainment as well as unhealthy lifestyles promoted by advertisements in the media. The following sections explore research on the effects of encountering unhealthy role models on a regular basis in the mass media.

The influence of media on eating habits

Obesity Most Americans love eating cheeseburgers, pizza, french fries, and just about anything fried, or full of carbs, especially if we can wash them down with a high-fructose corn syrup drink like a Coke or Mountain Dew. In addition, people in the US love desserts like cheesecake, cookies, and chocolate in just about any form. Unfortunately, however, obesity has become a major public health concern in the US. According to the Centers for Disease Control and Prevention, in 2006, 67 percent of adults and 17 percent of children were overweight and 34 percent of adults were obese. Obesity is linked to a number of health problems, including diabetes, heart disease, hypertension, and cancer (Allison *et al.*, 1999; Centers for Disease Control and Prevention, 2004; Must *et al.*, 1999). The economic costs of heart disease, diabetes, and cancer treatment alone to the US economy are staggering given their high prevalence and the cost of maintaining these chronic conditions. The risk for obesity often begins at an early age. In the US, nearly 15 percent of children between the ages of 6 and 11 years can be classified as obese, a percentage that has nearly tripled since the 1960s (Ogden, Flegan, Carroll, & Johnson, 2002).

Many aspects of the mass media are related to obesity. The path toward obesity begins at an early age. US children see nearly 5500 messages per year that promote unhealthy food products (Federal Trade Commission, 2007), and health authorities believe that unhealthy food product advertising on television is the leading cause of unhealthy eating habits among children (Brownell & Horgen, 2004). Harrison and Marske (2005) found that during TV programs most frequently watched by children, 83 percent of the advertised foods were fast foods and sweets that far exceeded the daily recommended values of fat, saturated fat, and sodium. Moreover, television personalities often serve as poor role models for healthy eating. According to Byrd-Bredbenner, Finckenor, and Grasso (2003), television actors "constantly talk about, handle, or consume foods and alcoholic beverages, but almost none are overweight or suffer the consequences of overconsumptions" (p. 336). Research suggests that watching TV increases children's preferences for unhealthy foods (Signorielli & Staples, 1997), and these early patterns of unhealthy food preference tend to become stable and last into adulthood (Harris & Bargh, 2009).

In addition, television advertisements routinely promote unhealthy food products, and the popularity of television and related media in the US has contributed to sedentary lifestyles for many Americans. The food industry spends over $10 billion annually to promote largely unhealthy food products to the American public (Brownell & Horgen, 2004). Both children and adults spend more time watching TV than any other leisure activity (Roberts, Foehr, & Rideout, 2005). For children, there has been a significant shift over the last several decades from physical activities to sedentary behavior that has been linked to media usage, particularly the increased use of computers, DVDs, and electronic games (Hofferth & Sandberg, 2001). Although some video games encourage physical activity, the vast majority of them involve moving little more than one's fingers. And while there are many other factors related to obesity, including genetics, socioeconomic variables, and a family history of obesity, sedentary activities coupled with an increase in consuming unhealthy fast foods promoted by the mass media appear to be a major contributor to the problem (Greenberg *et al.*, 2009).

Despite this bleak picture, some research has found that parent–child communication interventions may show some promise in terms of helping children understand the potential health risks of frequently consuming the high-fat, high-calorie products that they see advertised on television (Austin & Chen, 2003). When parents engage in *mediation*, or the critical analysis of media content with their children, this may increase a child's ability to understand the health dangers of consuming the advertise products, which may help to make them more resistant to food advertisements in the future (Austin, 2001; Boush, 2001). For adults, things can be a bit more difficult, especially when unhealthy eating has become a habit. However, all is not lost when it comes to media exposure as things are slowly changing and some opinion leaders, researchers, and film-makers are paying attention to this evolving problem. Relatively new documentaries such as Morgan Spurlock's (2004) film "Supersize Me," Lee Fulkerson and Brian Wendel's "Forks Over Knives" (2011), or Michael Pollan's "Food, Inc." (2008) are raising awareness about what we are putting in our bodies. However, given the negative impact of obesity in the US on morbidity and mortality rates as well as the economic costs associated with obesity-related diseases, health communication researchers should continue to find interventions to educate people about the influence of the mass media on diet and change the eating habits of people from all age groups.

Eating disorders The standard of beauty for men and women has changed throughout history. However, in the past century, the media have perpetuated the thin ideal for women. While fewer than 5 percent of people in the US suffer from anorexia and bulimia, there has been an increase in these types of eating disorders over the last several decades, particularly among women (Becker, Grinspoon, Klibanski, & Herzog, 1999). Although some men suffer from eating disorders, only an estimated 5 to 15 percent of people with anorexia or bulimia and an estimated 35 percent of those with a binge-eating disorder are male. People with anorexia feel distress about eating and are compelled to avoid eating or take other actions to keep from gaining weight (such as exercise or diet medications), despite the fact that they are in danger of being underweight. Individuals with bulimia have the compulsion to purge after eating in an effort to lose weight. Both types of eating disorders can lead to a variety of serious health problems, including cardiac arrest, kidney failure, severe malnutrition, and death.

While there are many factors that may contribute to a person developing anorexia or bulimia, there is some evidence that the mass media influence unhealthy eating habits by distorting perceptions of ideal body weight, especially given the thin body images of characters on television, films, and in fashion magazines (Harrison, 2000; Sung-Yeon, 2005). Although television tends to promote thin as the ideal for both men and women, this is discrepant from body weight averages that are considered healthy in the real world (Greenberg *et al.*, 2003). Brown and Walsh-Childers (2002) contend that research over the past 20 years has shown that the women who appear in the media are substantially thinner (typically 25% thinner) than the average American woman. Brown and Walsh-Childers (2002) also found in a study that nearly all the *Playboy* centerfolds and three-fourths of fashion industry models had body mass indexes (BMIs) of 17.5 or below—the American Psychological Association's criteria for anorexia nervosa.

Consistent with uses and gratifications theory, there is some evidence that the type of media people use is related to healthy and unhealthy eating habits. For example, Dutta-Bergman (2004b) found that healthy eating habits were associated with newspapers, magazines, and the Internet, particularly when individuals used these media for information-seeking purposes. However, the same author found that watching sports and comedy on television and using the Internet for entertainment purposes was associated with unhealthy eating habits. It is also important to note that this study did not provide evidence that these types of media necessarily *cause* unhealthy eating habits, and the results can also be partially explained by other variables associated with using media for information purposes, such as age, gender, and education level, which are also linked to unhealthy eating habits (Dutta & Youn, 1999; Swenson & Wells, 1995).

Media content and cosmetic surgery

Have you ever wanted to have the face or the body of your favorite movie star? We are born with certain features, but more and more people are altering the cards that genetics has dealt them through cosmetic surgery. The popularity of television shows such as "Nip/Tuck," "Extreme Makeover," and "The Swan" reflect our culture's obsession with cosmetic surgery. It is not abnormal to want to be physically attractive in our society. Perceptions of physical attractiveness are associated with a variety of other favorable perceptions, such as intelligence, honesty, and persuasiveness (Hatfield & Sprecher, 1986), despite the fact that physically attractive people may be unintelligent, dishonest, and relatively unskilled at influencing others. While there is evidence that some aspects of what human beings find attractive is innate (Langlois, Roggman, & Rieser-Danner, 1990), our perceptions of what we find attractive are largely based upon culture and appear to be heavily influenced by the mass media (Hatfield & Sprecher, 1986).

In recent years researchers have become interested in the relationship between perceptions of attractiveness in the media and cosmetic surgery (Sarwer, 1997), especially given the rise of the "reality television" programs that promote plastic surgery as a transformative practice in the lives of women. Many of these shows, such as "The Swan," promote the idea that women need to have cosmetic surgery in order to achieve a high sense of self-esteem and happiness. The problem, of course, is that stereotypical notions of beauty are promoted, such as being ultra-thin or having a small nose and large lips for women, and these shows tend to downplay the risks associated with cosmetic surgery. As with any operation there are risks, ranging from bad reactions to anesthesia to technical problems that may arise during surgery. Many people who have cosmetic surgery are dissatisfied with the results (especially when they find they do not necessarily look like the supermodel or movie star they admire). As a result, some individuals opt for additional cosmetic surgery to "correct" these problems. In extreme cases individuals may develop body dysmorphic disorder, in which an individual has cosmetic surgery multiple times in an effort to achieve an unrealistic ideal of beauty.

Media content and acts of violence

We are often shocked by the brutality of mass murderers, such as the horrible crimes that occurred at Virginia Tech or Columbine High School, yet violence is the norm in television and movies. People are enthralled by organized crime and violence in movies like "The Town" and television series like "The Sopranos." Researchers have estimated that most children will witness 8000 murders and 100 000 other types of violent acts before finishing elementary school (Donnerstein, Slaby, & Enron, 1994). Some of the first images we see on television as children are violent acts, such as the abusive behaviors between characters in popular cartoons, and we continue to witness violence as our cognitive development takes place and our preferences shift to programs such as dramas and news programs. Communication researchers have been interested in the effects of television violence on children for decades. Yet, despite exposure to violent content, a number of variables, including cognitive and emotional maturity, intelligence, gender, and viewing habits, mediate the effects of violent content on aggressive or violent behavior (Atkin, Greenberg, Korzenny, & McDermott, 1979; Robinson & Bachman, 1972; Van Erva, 1998). Less is known about the relationship between other media, such as video games, and aggressive or violent behavior. Funk (1993) found that 50 percent of video games contained some form of violence against human or fantasy characters. In addition, the *interactive* nature of video games, or the ability of children to be an active participant in the game, is thought to have negative effects on children when playing violent types of games (Dill & Dill, 1998) since children are more involved with the mediated characters compared to more passive media (e.g. television).

The relationship between media and substance abuse

Alcohol A number of researchers have found that alcohol advertising plays an important role in shaping perceptions of alcohol use, including the idea that drinking alcohol is a normal, exciting, and favorable activity (Fleming, Thorson, & Atkin, 2004; Sargent *et al.*, 2006). In addition, alcohol advertising regularly associates alcohol usage with images of wealth, prestige, power, and social approval (Cassell, 1995; Fleming, Thorson, & Atkin, 2004). Alcohol advertisers typically direct a far greater number of advertisements toward younger consumers in an attempt to influence drinking behaviors early (Fleming, Thorson, & Atkin, 2004; Grube & Wallack, 1994). The use of alcohol is also highly prevalent in the mass media, particularly among characters in television programs and films (Christenson, Henriksen, & Roberts, 2000)

Other researchers have found similar patterns for the prevalence of alcohol use in prime-time television, feature films, and music videos (Durant *et al.*, 1997; Everett, Schnuth, & Tribble, 1998; Kean & Albada, 2003; Mathios, Avery, Bisogni, & Shanahan, 1998). Drinking in the media is portrayed as sophisticated and intelligent, and it usually occurs among characters who are well liked, attractive, and wealthy (Mathios *et al.*,

1998). Atkin and Block (1983) found that celebrity endorsers of alcohol have a much stronger impact on influencing drinking behaviors than ordinary people. In addition, female characters who drink alcohol are often portrayed more positively than male characters (Mathios *et al.*, 1998). For example, on the popular HBO series "Sex and the City" and recent Hollywood movies based on the show, the lead character Carrie Bradshaw and her friends regularly drink large quantities of alcohol in glamorous surroundings. We see similar glamorization of substance use patterns in shows like "Mad Men," and "Breaking Bad." However, despite the plethora of television shows, films, and other media that glamorize alcohol consumption, there are relatively few cases where popular media present content that emphasizes the harmful effects of long-term alcohol usage or problems related to alcohol abuse (Signorielli, 1993).

When the alcoholic beverage industry does caution consumers about alcohol abuse in advertisements, it often promotes the idea of self-control and responsibility in consuming alcoholic beverages. However, this perspective ignores many individuals, such as alcoholics, who often feel they have little control over the amount of alcohol they consume once they begin drinking, and who report engaging in behaviors that they would not consider while sober (Wright, 2001).

Tobacco products Researchers have identified a relationship between tobacco advertising and consumption of tobacco products (Biener & Siegel, 2000; Green, Murphy, & McKenna, 2002). Essentially, as tobacco product advertising increases, so does consumption of these products. Illnesses related to tobacco use, such as cancer, respiratory diseases, and cardiovascular diseases, account for more than 440 000 deaths annually and cost consumers billions of dollars each year (US Surgeon General, 2004). Although radio and television cigarette advertisements were banned in 1971, cigarette and other tobacco product advertising is alive and well within magazines. Several researchers have found that tobacco product advertising in men's magazines glamorize smoking and largely frame smoking and other tobacco use as "macho," or masculine (See Dutta & Boyd, 2007; Kline, 2003). Smoking characters on television programs and in feature films are typically portrayed as more romantically and sexually active than nonsmokers (Signorielli, 1998; McIntosh, Bazzini, Smith, & Wayne, 1998). In addition, smoking is often glamorized in other ways. For example, while cigar smoking was once associated with blue-collar workers, in recent years it has been promoted by the media as a glamorous and sophisticated type of smoking behavior, and this has led to an increase of over 250 million cigar sales a year (DeSantis & Morgan, 2003; Satcher, 1999). Magazines like *Cigar Aficionado* (which sells over 400 000 copies a year) regularly link cigar smoking with being wealthy and living the "good life," and they have become an important outlet for cigar advertisers to reach consumers (DeSantis & Morgan, 2003). In a study of *Cigar Aficionado* magazine, DeSantis and Morgan (2003) found that cigar advertisements often attempt to pitch the idea that cigars are qualitatively superior to cigarettes (with the implication that cigarette smoking is more of a lower-class activity). In addition, advertisers presented the argument that cigar smoking is inherently less dangerous than other types of behaviors (such as eating junk food), reduces stress, and is fine in moderation, and also made claims refuting scientific evidence that has linked smoking with cancer. However, these claims were based on questionable evidence, and more reputable studies have found that cigar smoking is actually linked to the same cancers and other health problems as cigarette smoking (Baker *et al.*, 2000). In terms of traditional cigarettes, Dutta and Boyd (2007) found that smoking advertisements in prominent men's magazines presented men who were smoking as sensual, independent, and mysterious, and few articles within these magazines discussed the dangers of smoking.

Media and sexual behavior

One in four Americans will become infected with a sexually transmitted disease (STD) during his or her lifetime, and the US has the highest rate of non-HIV STDs in the industrialized world (Institute of Medicine, 1997). The cost of treating STDs within the US healthcare system amounts to more than $10 billion each year (Institute of Medicine, 1997). The mass media may be particularly significant in influencing perceptions about sex and sexual behavior, especially given the high prevalence of sexual activity in television shows and films. Television and movies have been found to influence early onset of sexual activity (Brown *et al.*, 2006). Popular media portrayals of sexual behavior often emphasize its positive aspects while ignoring the potential consequences, such as pregnancy and STDs (Lowry & Towles, 1989; Olson, 1995). For example, sexual activity with multiple partners is often associated with popular characters and rewards (popularity, being macho, etc.) in television shows and films. However, it is rare to see discussions about the use of condoms or other safe-sex practices. While some films and television programs have characters who are HIV-positive, the behaviors that led to their HIV-positive status are rarely discussed. In addition, other types of STDs that are common in the US, such as syphilis, herpes, the human papilloma virus (which causes genital warts), and chlamydia, are rarely discussed in the entertainment media.

Direct-to-consumer advertising of prescription medications

Medications such as Prozac, Viagra, and Claritin have become household names, largely because they have been aggressively promoted by pharmaceutical companies through direct-to-consumer advertisements in the mass media (Holmer, 1999). Direct-to-consumer marketing attempts to create consumer demand for medications by constructing advertising messages in the popular media that promote the attractiveness of the product to the public along with messages encouraging people to ask their doctor about the drug (Bradley & Zito, 1997; Hollon, 1999). Direct-to-consumer marketing first emerged as a marketing strategy in the pharmaceutical industry in 1981, and it has since become a multi-billion dollar industry, with the pharmaceutical industry spending over $4 billion annually (Cline & Young, 2004; Macias, Pashupati, & Lewis, 2007). Like all advertisements, direct-to-consumer advertisements serve to sell a particular product, which may or may not be useful to the audience.

The question of whether the advent of direct-to-consumer advertising has had a positive or negative effect on consumers is a subject of debate among health professionals and health scholars (Wilkes, Bell, & Kravitz, 2000). Proponents of direct-to-consumer marketing cite greater consumer awareness of health conditions, increased knowledge of medications, and the ability of such advertisements to stimulate discussions between providers and patients and to promote more active patient roles as positive outcomes of this type of marketing (Cline & Young, 2004; Pines, 2000). Those who are concerned about the negative effects of direct-to-consumer advertisements have focused on the cost of advertised medications vis-à-vis less expensive drugs that are just as effective in treating consumer health problems, misleading or inaccurate information about the benefits and risks of the medications, unrealistic expectations about treatment outcomes, conflicts with patients who demand medications, and unnecessary visits to providers (Cline & Young, 2004; Pinto, 2000; Sellers, 2000).

In terms of message characteristics of direct-to-consumer advertisements, Cline and Young (2004) found that direct-to-consumer advertisements tend to be directed toward white consumers, and most advertisements do not use characters that reflect members of minority groups or older adults. Some racial differences appear to exist when it comes to drug advertising. For example, Mastin, Andsager, Choi, & Lee (2007) found that direct-to-consumer advertisements for sexually transmitted diseases were more likely to appear in Black magazines whereas drug advertisements for heart disease were more frequent in White magazines (despite the fact that heart disease is the number one cause of death for both groups). In addition, these advertisements tend to be aimed at individuals with higher incomes. While legally drug advertisements that make positive claims about products also have to present negative information (du Pré, 2005), advertisers often use tactics such as promoting the positive aspects of the product for the majority of the television commercial, then quickly mentioning the list of potential side effects at the end of the commercial (Hunter & Thompson, 2004; Macias, Pashupati, & Lewis, 2007). Some advertisers present ambiguous information about the product and avoid directly making positive claims so that they do not have to mention negative aspects (Wogalter, Smith-Jackson, Mills, & Paine, 2002).

The promotion of medications through direct-to-consumer advertising has strongly influenced patient preferences and prescribing patterns (Holmer, 1999). For example, during 1998, following aggressive advertising of Viagra, doctor visits for impotence rose by 113 percent (Maguire, 1999). Sales of Viagra, Prozac, and other heavily marketed drugs have skyrocketed in recent years, resulting in billions of dollars in sales for pharmaceutical companies.

Health News Stories in the Media

Health-related stories are highly prevalent in the news media. In fact, stories dealing with health issues are among the most frequent types of stories in television news, newspapers, and magazines (Kline, 2003). For example, Wang and Gantz (2010) found that 8.1 percent of local news stories focused on health topics in four major television markets between 2004 and 2005. In addition, the news media have a long-standing relationship with health promoters at the national, state, and local levels, and the news media have been actively involved in promoting a variety of health campaigns and initiatives during the past several decades (Boutwell, 1995; Cooper, Burgoon, & Roter, 2001; Dubren, 1977). However, Cooper, Burgoon, & Roter (2001) found that audience members do not remember much of the health information they encounter through the news media, and attention to health-related news media stories is influenced by variables such as the personal relevance of a news story, whether or not the story is novel, and its shock value. In addition, the types of health-related stories and the way these stories are presented are influenced by the needs and agendas of news media organizations. The following section takes an in-depth look at problems associated with the reporting of health-related stories in the news media.

Problems in the reporting of health news stories

Agenda-setting theory Agenda setting refers to how the daily selection and display of news stories by the media influences audience perceptions about the importance of news topics and issues (Protess & McCombs, 1991). The decision to select or not to select a news story is dependent on a number of factors, including the perceived importance of the story by the public and members of media organizations, time constraints, and whether a story is ongoing or "breaking news." *Media gatekeepers* are members of news media organizations who make decisions about which stories will be disseminated to the public and how the information will be presented. According to agenda-setting theory, these individuals play an important role in shaping public perceptions about which issues, including health issues, are important. Gatekeeper decisions to tell or not to tell a story are often linked to political views and news coverage policies that are part of the culture of media organizations. By making conscious decisions to cover some health issues and not others, news organizations can influence public perceptions of the relative importance of these issues. Agenda-setting theory is a useful framework for understanding how the *underreporting* or *overreporting* of a health problem or issue (or inaccuracies when reporting it) by a news organization can ultimately affect the public's understanding of the issue and their behaviors toward it. Roberts, Wanta, and Dzwo (2002) found that local television newscasts may affect the public health agenda not only by the news stories that they decide to air, but also by the ways in which they motivate viewers to seek postviewing information (such as following up on a news story on websites and/or online discussions).

A good example of how underreporting of a health problem by the media can impact public perceptions and behaviors is the HIV/AIDS epidemic in the US. James Kinsella's (1989) study of AIDS and the American media demonstrates the agenda-setting practices of media organizations in the early years of the HIV/AIDS epidemic in the US. According to Kinsella, news organizations avoided covering AIDS stories because the infected population at that time was primarily gay men. Gatekeepers within news organizations did not want to offend mainstream audiences with stories about individuals who may have contracted the disease through what the gatekeepers perceived to be deviant sexual behaviors. Unfortunately, because HIV/AIDS first spread among people whose behaviors mainstream America found to be somewhat offensive (e.g. gay men having sex, intravenous drug use), when stories did appear in the mainstream media they tended to be ambiguous about the risk behaviors for the disease (even though they were known at the time). As the HIV/AIDS epidemic began to spread, the media eventually gave it more coverage. However, Kinsella (1989) argues that most AIDS stories that did receive news coverage dealt with individuals who acquired the disease through heterosexual contact or through blood transfusions (so-called "innocent victims" of HIV/AIDS).

By limiting the coverage of HIV/AIDS stories in the early days of the epidemic, many heterosexual people did not perceive HIV/AIDS to be an issue they needed to worry about, and many heterosexuals continued to engage in unsafe sexual behaviors despite the fact that they were at risk for the disease. In addition, by downplaying the crisis in the media, money for HIV/AIDS research from the government was stalled (Dearing & Rogers, 1992). Even as new antiviral medications for HIV begin to be developed, media organizations are accused of not disseminating information about how these drugs may prolong the life of people with HIV, provided that they get tested for the disease while it is in its early stages (Kahn, 1993).

Of course, the media have underreported many other health problems as well. Wang and Gantz (2007) found that 70 percent of health stories on local television news were less than one minute, which is hardly enough time to cover the many implications of most health issues. Deaths from asthma, diabetes, heart disease, stroke, tobacco-related problems, and environmental and occupational influences on health tend to be underreported in the US relative to their incident rates in the population (Frost, Frank, & Maiback, 1997; Seale, 2002; Signorielli, 1993). Davidson and Wallack (2004), in a content analysis of popular print news media, found substantial under-reporting of STDs, particularly STDs other than HIV/AIDS. In addition, they found that most articles dealing with STDs did not cover routes of transmission, causes, or signs and symptoms of various STDs. Underreporting of health problems tends to occur even more often when the problems affect minority populations in the US (Kline, 2003; Vargas & dePyssler, 1999). For example, Armstrong, Carpenter, and Hojnacki (2006) found that print and broadcast media pay less attention to diseases that disproportionately affect African American individuals compared to white Americans.

Overreporting of health-related issues is also quite common in the mass media (Kline, 2003). For example, while catastrophic events such as tornadoes, homicides, and motor vehicle accidents claim many lives each year in the US, the number of people who die in these events is relatively small compared to deaths from diseases such as heart disease and cancer (Frost, Frank, & Maiback, 1997). However, news stories are much more likely to report deaths resulting from catastrophic events than deaths resulting from diseases and other common health problems (Frost, Frank, & Maiback, 1997; Singer, 1990). One of the reasons for the overreporting of tornadoes, homicides, and other traumatic events is that they tend to be more sensational, attention-grabbing, emotional spike type stories than stories about people dying from diseases and health problems (who tend to die less dramatically in healthcare facilities). Compared to natural disasters and homicides, the way that most people die from health problems may appear somewhat mundane. The producers of mass media news stories, who are interested in attracting the attention of audience members to gain advertising revenue, typically choose health-related stories that are more visually stimulating, graphic, or sensational. For example, you may have heard the news media saying: "If it bleeds it leads." Unfortunately, overreporting of traumatic events may lead people to overestimate their risk of dying from a catastrophic event (Singer, 1990).

When the news media decide to focus their attention on more common health problems, health risks are sometimes overreported. For example, although more people die of lung and colon cancer than skin cancer or breast cancer each year, many US media sources run a much higher percentage of skin cancer and breast cancer stories than stories about lung and colon cancer (Gerlach, Marino, & Hoffman-Goetz, 1997; Lantz & Booth, 1998; Kline, 2003). Researchers have found that breast cancer tends to be overreported in comparison to lung cancer and cardiovascular disease in newspapers, magazines, and television, despite higher incident rates of both diseases (Slater, Long, Bettinghaus, & Reinke, 2008). Women's magazines often devote excessive attention to diet, fitness, and reproductive health at the expense of major health risks for women, such as heart disease (Seale, 2002). One of the reasons why these types of stories tend to be overreported may be due to our culture's obsession with appearance and youth. For example, surgery for skin cancer and breast cancer can often lead to changes in physical appearance, such as visible scars left behind after the removal of melanomas or the removal of a breast due to a mastectomy, and because these changes are tied to cultural conceptions of beauty and sexuality, many women fear these types of cancer. Because of these fears, mass media organizations know that women will pay attention to stories about these types of cancer. However, this can be problematic when other types of cancers and health problems that pose greater risks to women are not given as much attention.

Media bias and inaccuracies in reporting health issues

Related to agenda-setting theory is the *framing* of news stories, or the "selection and emphasis of certain aspects of issues" (Andsager & Powers, 2001, p. 163). In other words, even when the news media decide to cover a particular story, they tend to discuss certain aspects of the issue while excluding other aspects. Although the news media often strive for "fair and balanced" reporting of issues, the reporting of news stories is influenced by a variety of social, cultural, and economic factors within news organizations and news organization personnel that can shape the way a particular story is presented (Andsager & Powers, 2001; Parrott & Condit, 1996). For example, news stories often emphasize the biomedical perspective of health and/or dominant cultural conceptions of health while downplaying psychosocial issues and alternative viewpoints (Parrott, 1996; Ruzek, Olesen, & Clarke, 1997). Since pharmaceutical companies and other corporations with vested interests in biomedical approaches to medicine are often sponsors of media news programming, these organizations have a vested interest in promoting the biomedical model of healthcare.

Exposure to health-related news stories may have second-order effects, or more subtle effects due to long-term exposure, on audience member perceptions. For example, health-related stories tend to emphasize the idea that avoiding health problems is largely in the control of the individual, and messages tend to focus on individual solutions to health problems while downplaying health issues that are largely outside of most people's control (Seale, 2002), such as health problems related to the environmental waste practices of corporations. In addition, few news stories emphasize collective responses to public health issues, such as ways to organize political efforts to deal with health issues facing larger communities.

The news media often rely heavily on sources for health-related stories, such as government officials, key members of the medical establishment, and members of the pharmaceutical industry, to bolster the credibility of their stories (Shaw & McCombs, 1989; Shoemaker & Reese, 1996). However, these sources often have a somewhat narrow and privileged view of health issues, and they may be interested in preserving the status quo and/or financial interests when discussing health concerns (Dearing & Rogers, 1992; Wright, 1999). In addition, health-related news stories often pay little attention to risks involved with certain "breakthrough" medical procedures, or they may emphasize harmful aspects of some procedures while downplaying benefits if it provides a more sensational story (Ruzek, Olesen, & Clarke, 1997; Vanderford & Smith, 1996). News stories about new pharmaceutical products rarely present a balanced view of the benefits and the potential risks of these medications, and information about new drugs that is provided in the media tends to emphasize their potential benefits while downplaying problems, such as side effects and cost vis-à-vis competing medications (Entwistle & Sheldon, 1999).

While news organizations strive to present accurate information to the public, inaccuracies in the reporting of health-related news stories are quite common in the media (Carlson, Li, & Holm, 1997; Kline, 2003). Due to the limited amount of time and space the news media can devote to any story, there is always the potential that some information will be left out of a health-related item. In addition, news reporters may find it difficult in some cases to accurately convey a health-related story because of a variety of factors, including the nature of the story, the amount of medical or scientific expertise required to understand the health-related event, a reporter's level of education, or the experience a reporter has with a health issue.

Summary

The mass media influence our perceptions of health and health-related issues in a variety of ways. Increased popularity of social media outlets is changing the media landscape and the way we access and talk about health information, healthcare, and conditions. Some communication theorists contend that the media influence us by altering our perceptions of the world through repeated long-term exposure to the reality portrayed through media content. Other researchers argue that the reasons behind why we use media and the ways in which we use them ultimately mediate the effects of media messages. However, researchers have found a relationship between exposure to health-related images and messages in the mass media and both positive and negative health outcomes. Unfortunately, despite the potential of the media to influence healthy behaviors, they tend to be more of a negative influence, leading to problems such as poor eating habits, substance abuse, and sometimes the tendency to accept violence or aggressive behavior. We rely heavily on the news media for up-to-date and accurate information about health issues, although this is changing somewhat with the influx of social media. However, it is important to note that news media organizations often have their own agendas when presenting the news that may influence the way health stories are covered. In addition, these organizations are also influenced by larger social norms surrounding health issues. Finally, the limited amount of time and space that media organizations can devote to health stories may lead to inaccuracies and other problems in the reporting of health-related news.

References

Allison, D. B, Fontaine, K. R., Manson, J. E., Stevens, J., & Van Itallie, T. B. (1999). Annual deaths attributable to obesity in the United States. *Journal of the American Medical Association, 282*, 1530–1538.

Andsager, J. L., & Powers, A. (2001). Framing women's health with a sense-making approach: Magazine coverage of breast cancer and implants. *Health Communication, 13*, 163–185.

Armstrong, E. M., Carpenter, D. P., & Hojnacki, M. (2006). Whose deaths matter? Mortality, advocacy, and attention to disease in the mass media. *Journal of Health Politics, 31*, 729–772.

Atkin, C., & Arkin, E. B. (1990). Issues and initiatives in communicating health information. In C. Atkin & L. Wallack (Eds), *Mass communication and public health: Complexities and conflicts* (pp. 13–40). Newbury Park, CA: Sage.

Atkin, C., & Block, M. (1983). Effectiveness of celebrity endorsers. *Journal of Advertising Research, 23*, 57–61.

Atkin, C., Greenberg, B., Korzenny, F., & McDermott, F. (1979). Selective exposure to televised violence. *Journal of Broadcasting, 23*, 5–14.

Austin, E. W. (2001). Effects of family communication on children's interpretation of television. In J. Bryant & J. A. Bryant (Eds), *Television and the American family* (pp. 377–395). Mahwah, NJ: Lawrence Erlbaum.

Austin, E. W., & Chen, Y. J. (2003). The relationship of parental reinforcement of media messages to college students' alcohol-related behaviors. *Journal of Health Communication, 8*, 157–169.

Bahk, C. M. (2001). Drench effects of media portrayal of fatal virus disease on health locus of control beliefs. *Health Communication, 13*, 187–204.

Baker, F., Ainsworth, S. R., Dye, J. T., Crammer, C., Thun, M. J., Hoffman, D. *et al.* (2000). Health risks associated with cigar smoking. *Journal of the American Medical Association, 284*, 735–747.

Becker, A. E., Grinspoon, S. K., Klibanski, A., & Herzog, D. B. (1999). Eating disorders. *New England Journal of Medicine, 340*, 1092–1098.

Bevan, J. L., Sparks, L., Ernst, J., Francies, J., & Santora, N. (2012). Health care reform information sources in relation to information quality, information seeking, and uncertainty. *Health Communication in Contexts: Research and Applications*.

Biener, L., & Siegel, M. (2000). Tobacco marketing and adolescent smoking: More support for a causal inference. *American Journal of Public Health, 90*, 407–411.

Boush, D. M. (2001). Mediating advertising effects. In J. Bryant & J. A. Bryant (Eds), *Television and the American family* (pp. 397–412). Mahwah, NJ: Lawrence Erlbaum.

Boutwell, W. B. (1995). The under cover skin cancer prevention project: A community-based program in four Texas cities. *Cancer, 75*, 657–660.

Bradley, L. R., & Zito, J. M. (1997). Direct-to-consumer prescription drug advertising. *Medical Care, 35*, 86–92.

Brashers, D. E., Goldsmith, D. J., & Hsieh, E. (2002). Information seeking and avoiding in health contexts. *Human Communication Research, 28*, 258–271.

Buller, D. B., Callister, M. A., & Reichert, T. (1995). Skin cancer prevention by parents of young children: Health information and sources, skin cancer knowledge, and sun-protection practices. *Oncology Nursing Forum, 22*, 1559–1566.

Burkell, J. A., Wolfe, D. L., Potter, P. J., & Jutai, J. W. (2006). Information needs and information sources of individuals living with spinal cord injury. *Health Information and Libraries Journal, 23*, 257–265.

Brown, J. D., & Walsh-Childers, K. (2002). Effects of media on personal and public health. In. J. Bryant & D. Zillman (Eds), *Media effects: Advances in theory and research*. Mahwah, NJ: Lawrence Erlbaum.

Brown, J. D., L'Engle, K. L., Pardun, C. J., Guang, G., Kenneavy, K., & Jackson, C. (2006). Sexy media matter:

Exposure to sexual content in music, movies, television, and magazines predicts black and white adolescents' sexual behavior. *Pediatrics, 117,* 1018–1027.

Brownell, K. D., & Horgen, K. B. (2004). *Food fight: The inside story of the food industry, America's obesity crisis, and what we can do about it.* New York: McGraw-Hill.

Byrd-Bredbenner, C., Finckenor, M., & Grasso, D. (2003). Health-related content in prime-time television programming. *Journal of Health Communication, 8,* 329–341.

Carlson, E. S., Li, S., & Holm, K. (1997). An analysis of menopause in the popular press. *Health Care Women International, 18,* 557–564.

Cassell, S. (1995). Public discourse on alcohol: Implications for public policy. In H. Holder & G. Edwards (Eds), *Alcohol and public: Evidence and issues* (pp. 190–211). Oxford: Oxford University Press.

Centers for Disease Control and Prevention (2004). *Deaths: Final data for 2004.* Retrieved July 17, 2012, from http://www.cdc.gov/nchs/products/pubs/pubd/hestats/finaldeaths04/finaldeaths04.htm.

Christenson, P. G., Henriksen, L., & Roberts, D. F. (2000). *Substance use in popular prime time television.* Retrieved July 23, 2012, from www.mediascope.org/

Cline, R. J. W., & Young, H. N. (2004). Marketing drugs, marketing health care relationships: A content analysis of visual cues in direct-to-consumer prescription drug advertising. *Health Communication, 16,* 131–157.

Cooper, C. P., Burgoon, M., & Roter, D. L. (2001). An expectancy-value analysis of viewer interest in television prevention news stories. *Health Communication, 13,* 227–240.

Cotten, S. R., & Gupta, S. S. (2004). Characteristics of online and offline health information seekers and factors that discriminate between them. *Social Science & Medicine, 59,* 1795–1806.

Davidson, A. E., & Wallack, L. (2004). A content analysis of sexually transmitted diseases in the print news media. *Journal of Health Communication, 9,* 111–117.

Dearing, J. W., & Rogers, E. M. (1992). AIDS and the media agenda. In T. Edgar, M. A. Fitzpatrick, & V. S. Freimuth (Eds), *AIDS: A communication perspective* (pp. 165–189). Hillsdale, NJ: Lawrence Erlbaum.

DeSantis, A. D., & Morgan, S. E. (2003). Sometimes a cigar [magazine] is more than just a cigar [magazine]: Pro-smoking arguments in *Cigar Aficionado,* 1992–2000. *Health Communication, 15,* 457–480.

Diem, S. J., Lantos, J. D., & Tulsky, J. A. (1996). Cardiopulmonary resuscitation on television: Miracles and

misinformation. *New England Journal of Medicine, 334,* 1578–1582.

Dill, K. E., & Dill, J. C. (1998). Video game violence: A review of the empirical literature. *Aggression and Violent Behavior, 3,* 407–482.

Donnerstein, E., Slaby, R. G., & Enron, L. D. (1994). The mass media and youth aggression. In L. D. Enron, J. H. Gentry, & P. Schlegel (Eds), *Reason to hope: A psychological perspective on violence and youth* (pp. 219–250). Washington, DC: American Psychological Association.

Dubren, R. (1977). Evaluation of a televised stop-smoking clinic. *Public Health Reports, 92,* 81–84.

du Pré, A. (1998). *Humor and the healing arts: A multimethod analysis of humor use in health care.* Mahwah, NJ: Lawrence Erlbaum.

du Pré, A. (2005). *Communicating about health: Current issues and perspectives* (2nd ed.). Boston: McGraw-Hill.

Durant, R. H., Rome, E. S., Rich, M., Allred, E., Emans, S. J., & Woods, E. R. (1997). Tobacco and alcohol use behaviors portrayed in music videos: A content analysis. *American Journal of Public Health, 87,* 1131–1135.

Dutta, M. J., & Boyd, J. (2007). Turning "smoking man" images around: Portrayals of smoking in men's magazines as a blueprint for smoking cessation campaigns. *Health Communication, 23,* 253–263.

Dutta, M. J., & Youn, S. (1999). Profiling healthy consumers: A psychographic approach to social marketing. *Social Marketing Quarterly, 5,* 5–21.

Dutta-Bergman, M. J. (2004a). Primary sources of health information: Comparisons in the domain of health attitudes, health cognitions, and health behaviors. *Health Communication, 16,* 273–288.

Dutta-Bergman, M. J. (2004b). Reaching unhealthy eaters: Applying a strategic approach to media vehicle choice. *Health Communication, 16,* 493–506.

Dworetzky, J. P. (1993). *Introduction to child development* (5th ed.). St. Paul, MN: West.

Entwistle, V., & Sheldon, T. (1999). The picture of health? Media coverage of the health service. In B. Franklin (Ed.), *Social policy, the media and misrepresentation.* London: Routledge.

Everett, S. A., Schnuth, R. L., & Tribble, J. L. (1998). Tobacco and alcohol in top-grossing American films. *Journal of Community Health, 23,* 317–324.

Federal Trade Commission (2007). Bureau of Economics staff report. *Children's exposure to TV advertising in 1977 and 2004.* Retrieved July 17, 2012, from http://www.ftc.gov.

Ferris, J. E. (2003). Parallel discourses and "appropriate" bodies: Media constructions of anorexia and obesity in the cases of Tracy Gold and Carnie Wilson. *Journal of Communication Inquiry*, 27, 256–263.

Festinger, L. (1954). A theory of social comparison processes. *Human Relations*, 2, 117–140.

Flegal, K. M., Carroll, M. D., Ogden, C. L., & Johnson, C. L. (2002). Prevalence and trends in obesity among US adults, 1999–2000. *Journal of the American Medical Association*, 288, 1723–1727.

Fleming, K., Thorson, E., & Atkin, C. K. (2004). Alcohol advertising exposure and perceptions: Links with alcohol expectancies and intentions to drink or drinking in underaged youth and young adults. *Journal of Health Communication*, 9, 3–29.

Freed, G. L., Katz, S. L., & Clark, S. J. (1996). Safety of vaccinations: Miss America, the media, and public health. *Journal of the American Medical Association*, 276, 1869–1872.

Friedland, R. P., Fritsch, T., Smyth, K. A., Koss, E., Lerner, A. J., Chen, C. H. *et al.* (2001). Patients with Alzheimer's disease have reduced activities in midlife compared with healthy control-group members. *Proceedings of the National Academy of Sciences*, 98, 3440.

Frost, K., Frank, E., & Maiback, E. (1997). Relative risk in the news media: A quantification of misrepresentation. *American Journal of Public Health*, 87, 842–845.

Funk, J. B. (1993). Reevaluating the impact of video games. *Clinical Pediatrics*, 32, 86–90.

Gerbner, G. (1998). Cultivation analysis: An overview. *Mass Communication and Society*, 1, 175–194.

Gerbner, G., & Gross, L. (1972). Living with television: The violence profile. *Journal of Communication*, 26, 173–199.

Gerbner, G., Gross, L., Jackson-Beeck, M., Jeffries-Fox, S., & Signorelli, N. (1978). Cultural indicators: Violence profile No. 9. *Journal of Communication*, 28, 176–206.

Gerbner, G., Gross, L., Morgan, M., & Signorelli, N. (1982). Charting the mainstream: Television's contribution to political orientations. *Journal of Communication*, 32, 100–127.

Gerbner, G., Gross, L., Morgan, M., & Signorelli, N. (1986). Living with television: The dynamics of the cultivation process. In J. Bryant & D. Zillman (Eds), *Perspectives on media effects* (pp. 17–40). Hillsdale, NJ: Lawrence Erlbaum.

Gerlach, K. K., Marino, C., & Hoffman-Goetz, L. (1997). Cancer coverage in women's magazines: What information are women receiving? *Journal of Cancer Education*, 12, 240–244.

Green, L. W., Murphy, R. L., & McKenna, J. W. (2002). New insights into how mass media works for and against tobacco. *Journal of Health Communication*, 7, 245–248.

Greenberg, B. S., Hofschire, L., Lachlan, L. K., Eastin, M., & Brownell, K. (2003). Portrayals of overweight and obese individuals on commercial television. *American Journal of Public Health*, 93, 1342–1348.

Greenberg, B. S., Rosaen, S. F., Worrell, T. R., Salmon, C. T., & Volkman, J. E. (2009). A portrait of food and drink in commercial TV series. *Health Communication*, 24, 295–303.

Grube, J., & Wallack, L. (1994). Television beer advertising and drinking knowledge, beliefs, and intentions among school children. *American Journal of Public Health*, 84, 254–259.

Harris, J. L., & Bargh, J. A. (2009). Television viewing and unhealthy diet: Implications for children and media interventions. *Health Communication*, 24, 660–673.

Harrison, K. (2000). The body electric: Thin-ideal media and eating disorders in adolescents. *Journal of Communication*, 50(3), 119–143.

Harrison, K., & Marske, A. L. (2005). Nutritional content of foods advertised during the television programs children watch most. *American Journal of Public Health*, 95, 1568–1574.

Hatfield, E., & Sprecher, S. (1986). *Mirror, mirror: The importance of looks in everyday life*. Albany, NY: State University of New York Albany Press.

Hofferth, S. L., & Sandberg, J. F. (2001). How American children spend their time. *Journal of Marriage and Family*, 63, 295–308.

Hollon, M. F. (1999). Direct-to-consumer marketing of prescription drugs: Creating consumer demand. *Journal of the American Medical Association*, 281, 382–384.

Holmer, A. F. (1999). Direct-to-consumer prescription drug advertising builds bridges between patients and physicians. *Journal of the American Medical Association*, 281, 380–382.

Hunter, K. M., & Thompson, S. R. (2004, November). *Mass media medicine: A weighted content analysis and effects assessment of direct-to-consumer pharmaceutical ads*. Paper presented at the annual National Communication Association Convention, Chicago.

Institute of Medicine. (1997). *The hidden epidemic: Confronting sexually transmitted diseases*. Washington, DC.

Kahn, A. D. (1993). *AIDS: The winter war*. Philadelphia, PA: Temple University Press.

Katz, E., Blumler, J. G., & Gurevitz, M. (1974). Utilization of mass communication by the individual. In J. G. Blumler & E. Katz (Eds), *The uses of mass communication: Current perspectives on gratifications research* (pp. 19–32). Beverly Hills, CA: Sage.

Katz, E., Gurevitch, M., & Haas, H. (1973). On the use of mass media for important things. *American Sociological Review, 38,* 164–181.

Kean, L. G., & Albada, K. F. (2003). The relationship between college students' schema regarding alcohol use, their television viewing patterns, and their previous experiences with alcohol. *Health Communication, 15,* 277–298.

Kinsella, J. (1989). *Covering the plague: AIDS and the American media.* New Brunswick, NJ: Rutgers University Press.

Kline, K. N. (2003). Popular media and health: Images, effects, and institutions. In T. L. Thompson, A. M. Dorsey, K. I. Miller, & R. Parrot (Eds), *Handbook of health communication* (pp. 557–581). Mahwah, NJ: Lawrence Erlbaum.

Kline, K. N. (2011). Popular media and health: Images and effects. In T. L. Thompson, R. Parrott, & J. F. Nussbaum (Eds), *The Routledge handbook of health communication, 2nd ed.* (pp. 252–267). New York: Routledge.

Lambert, R. B., & Lambert, N. K. (1995). The effects of humor on secretory immunoglobulin A levels in school-aged children. *Pediatric Nursing, 21,* 16–19.

Langlois, J. H., Roggman, L. A., & Rieser-Danner, L. A. (1990). Infant's differential social responses to attractive and unattractive faces. *Developmental Psychology, 26,* 153–159.

Lantz, P. M., & Booth, K. M. (1998). The social construction of the breast cancer epidemic. *Social Science Medicine, 46,* 907–918.

Lee, A. L. (2009). Changing effects of direct-to-consumer broadcast drug advertising information sources on prescription drug requests. *Health Communication, 24,* 361–376.

Lowry, D., & Towles, D. (1989). Prime time TV portrayals of sex, contraception and venereal diseases. *Journalism Quarterly, 66,* 347–352.

Macias, W., Pashupati, K., & Lewis, L S. (2007). A wonderful life or diarrhea and dry mouth? Policy issue of direct-to-consumer drug advertising on television. *Health Communication, 22,* 241–252.

Madden, M. & Fox, S. (2006). Finding answers online in sickness and in health. Retreived July 17, 2012, from http://pewinternet.com/~/media/Files/Reports/2006/PIP_Health_Decisions_2006.pdf.pdf.

Maguire, P. (1999). How direct-to-consumer advertising is putting the squeeze on physicians. *ACP-ASIM Observer* [on-line]. Retrieved August 21, 2004, from www.aconline.org/journals/.

Mastin, T., Andsager, J. L., Choi, J., & Lee, K. (2007). Health disparities and direct-to-consumer prescription drug advertising: A content analysis of targeted magazine genres, 1992–2002. *Health Communication, 22,* 49–58.

Mathios, A., Avery, R., Bisogni, C., & Shanahan, J. (1998). Alcohol portrayals on prime time television: Manifest and latent messages. *Journal of Studies on Alcohol, 59,* 305–310.

McIntosh, W. D., Bazzini, D. G., Smith, S. M., & Wayne, S. M. (1998). Who smokes in Hollywood? Charcteristics of smokers in popular films from 1940 to 1989. *Addictive Behaviors, 23,* 395–398.

Montgomery, K. C. (1990). Promoting health through entertainment television. In C. Atkin & L. Wallack (Eds), *Mass communication and public health: Complexities and conflicts.* Newbury Park, CA: Sage.

Must, A., Spadano, J., Coakley, E. H., Field, A. E., Colditz, G., & Dietz, W. H. (1999). The disease burden associated with overweight and obesity. *Journal of the American Medical Association, 282,* 1523–1529.

Ogden, C. L., Flegan, K. M., Carroll, M. D., & Johnson, C. L. (2002). Prevalence and trends in overweight among US children and adolescents, 1999–2000. *Journal of the American Medical Association, 28,* 1728–1732.

Olson, B. (1995). Sex and the soaps: A comparative content analysis of health issues. *Journalism Quarterly, 71,* 840–850.

Parrott, R. L. (1996). A women-centered "sense-making" approach to communicating about women's reproductive health. In R. L. Parrott & C. M. Condit (Eds), *Evaluating women's health messages* (pp. 414–425). Thousand Oaks, CA: Sage.

Parrott, R. L., & Condit, C. M. (1996). Priorities and agendas in communicating about women's reproductive health. In R. L. Parrott & C. M. Condit (Eds), *Evaluating women's health messages* (pp. 1–11). Thousand Oaks, CA: Sage.

Pecchioni, L. L. and Sparks, L. (2007). Health information sources of individuals with cancer and their family members. *Health Communication, 21(2),* 143–151.

Pines, W. L. (2000). Direct-to-consumer advertising. *Annals of Pharmacology, 34,* 1341–1344.

Pinto, M. B. (2000). On the nature and properties of appeals used in direct-to-consumer advertising of prescription drugs. *Psychological Reports, 86,* 597–606.

Protess, D. L., & McCombs, M. E. (1991). *Agenda-setting: Readings on media, public opinion, and policy-making.* Hillsdale, NJ: Lawrence Erlbaum.

Roberts, D. F., Foehr, U. G., & Rideout, V. J. (2005). *Generation me: Media in the lives of 8–18 year-olds.* Retrieved July 17, 2012, from http://www.kff.org.

Roberts, M., Wanta, W., & Dzwo, T. (2002). Agenda setting and issue salience online. *Communication Research, 29,* 452–465.

Robinson, J., & Bachman, J. (1972). Television viewing habits and aggression. In G. Comstock & E. Rubenstein (Eds), *Television and social behavior: Television and adolescent aggressiveness* (pp. 372–382). Washington, DC: US Government Printing Office.

Ruzek, S. B., Olesen, V. L., & Clarke, A. E. (1997). *Women's health: Complexities and differences.* Columbus, OH: Ohio State University Press.

Sarwer, D. B. (1997). The "obsessive" cosmetic surgery patient: A consideration of body image dissatisfaction and body dysmorphic disorder. *Plastic Surgical Nursing, 17,* 193–209.

Satcher, D. (1999). Cigars and public health. *New England Journal of Medicine, 340,* 1829–1831.

Scharf, B. F., Freimuth, V. S., Greenspon, P., & Plotnick, C. (1996). Confronting cancer on *Thirty Something*: Audience response to health content on entertainment television. *Journal of Health Communication, 1,* 133–138.

Seale, C. (2002). *Media and health.* Thousand Oaks, CA: Sage.

Sellers, J. A. (2000). The two faces of direct-to-consumer advertising. *American Journal of Health-Systems Pharmacy, 51,* 1401.

Shaw, D. L., & McCombs, M. E. (1989). Dealing with illicit drugs: The power, and limits, of mass media agenda-setting. In P. J. Shoemaker (Ed.), *Communication campaigns about drugs: Government, media, and the public* (pp. 113–120). Hillsdale, NJ: Lawrence Erlbaum.

Shoemaker, P. J., & Reese, S. D. (1996). *Mediating the message: Theories of influences on mass media content* (2nd ed.). White Plains, NY: Longman.

Signorielli, N. (1993). *Mass media images and impact on health.* Westport, CT: Greenwood Press.

Signorielli, N. (1998). Health images on television. In L. D. Jackson (Ed.), *Health communication research: A guide to developments and directions* (pp. 163–179). Westport, CT: Greenwood.

Signorielli, N., & Staples, J. (1997). Television and children's conceptions of nutrition. *Health Communication, 9,* 289–301.

Shrum, L. J. (1999). Television and persuasion: Effects of the programs between the ads. *Psychology and Marketing, 16,* 119–140.

Singer, E. (1990). A question of accuracy: How journalists and scientists report research on hazards. *Journal of Communication, 40,* 102–116.

Slater, M. D., Long, M., Bettinghaus, E. P., & Reineke, J. B. (2008). News coverage of cancer in the United States: A national sample of newspapers, television, and magazines. *Journal of Health Communication, 13,* 523–537.

Sparks, L., & Villagran, M. M. (2010). *Patient and provider interaction: A global health communication perspective.* Cambridge, UK: Polity Press.

Sparks, L., Villagran, M. M., Parker-Raley, J., & Cunningham, C. B. (2007). A patient centered approach to breaking bad news: Communication guidelines for healthcare professionals. *Journal of Applied Communication Research, 35,* 177–196.

Sung-Yeon, P. (2005). The influence of presumed media influence on women's desire to be thin. *Communication Research, 32,* 594–614.

Swenson, M. R., & Wells, W. D. (1995). Target marketing for health communication. *Social Marketing Quarterly, 2,* 5–9.

Terre, L., Drabman, R. S., & Speer, P. (1991). Health-relevant behaviors in the media. *Journal of Applied Social Psychology, 21,* 1303–1319.

Tinley, S. T., Houfek, J., Watson, P., Wenzel, L., Clark, M. B., Coughlin, S., & Lynch, H. T. (2004). Screening adherence in BRCA1/2 families is associated with primary physicians' behavior. *American Journal of Medical Genetics A, 125A*(1), 5–11.

Turow, J., & Coe, L. (1993). Curing television's ills: The portrayal of health care. In B. C. Thornton & G. Kreps (Eds), *Perspectives on health communication* (pp. 130–145). Prospect Heights, IL: Waveland.

US Surgeon General (2004). *The health consequences of smoking: A report by the surgeon general.* Washington, DC: Government Printing Office.

Vanderford, M. L., & Smith, D. H. (1996). *The silicone breast implant story.* Mahwah, NJ: Lawrence Erlbaum.

Van Erva, J. P. (1998). *Television and child development* (2nd ed.). Mahwah, NJ: Lawrence Erlbaum.

Vargas, L. C., & dePyssler, B. J. (1999). US Latino newspapers as health communication resources: A content
analysis. *Howard Journal of Communications, 10,* 189–
205.

Wallack, L., & Dorfman, L. (1992). Health messages on
television commercials. *American Journal of Health Promotion, 6,* 190–196.

Wallack, L., Grube, J., Madden, P. R., & Breed, W. (1990).
Portrayals of alcohol on prime-time television. *Journal
of Studies on Alcohol, 51,* 428–433.

Wang, Z., & Gantz, W. (2007). Health content in local
television news. *Health Communication, 21,* 213–221.

Wang, Z., & Gantz, W. (2010). Health content in local
television news: A current appraisal. *Health Communication, 25,* 230–237.

Wanzer, M., Sparks, L., & Frymier, A. B. (2009). Humorous communication within the lives of older adults:
The relationships among humor, coping efficacy, age,
and life satisfaction. *Health Communication, 24,* 1–9.

Wilkes, M. S., Bell, R. A., & Kravitz, R. L. (2000). Direct-
to-consumer advertising: Trends, impact, and implications. *Health Affairs, 19,* 110–128.

Wogalter, M. S., Smith-Jackson, T. L., Mills, B. J., & Paine,
C. S. (2002). The effects of print format in direct-to-
consumer prescription drug advertising on risk knowledge and preference. *Drug Information Journal, 36,*
693–705.

Wright, K. B. (1999). AIDS, the status quo, and the elite
media: An analysis of the guest lists of "The MacNeil/
Lehrer News Hour" and "Nightline." In W. N. Elwood
(Ed.), *Power in the blood: A handbook on AIDS, politics,
and communication.* Mahwah, NJ: Lawrence Erlbaum.

Wright, K. B. (2001, April). *Perceptions of responsibility,
stigmatization, and control in college student drinking situations: An analysis of undergraduate student perceptions of
alcohol issues on campus.* Paper presented at the annual
Southern States Communication Association Convention, Lexington, KY.

Part V

Risk, Campaigns, Communities, and Teams

Chapter 9

Risk and Crisis Communication

"Terror threat orange," "A category four hurricane is heading toward Florida," "Eat foods that are high in fiber," and even "Put on sunscreen before you go outside today!" are common preventive risk messages we all frequently hear. Even at college you have likely heard your friends sending messages to you or other friends such as "Don't drink too much," "Be sure to have a designated driver," and "Take condoms just in case." As you get older, you are likely to hear more and more messages about changing diet and exercise habits, and messages about mammograms, colonoscopies, and prostate cancer exams as preventive measures for disease when you reach a high-risk age group. While many individuals in the US may not perceive that they are at risk for health problems, we are all vulnerable to some type of physical, psychological, or social health threat. From the examples given above, you may have noticed that health threats range from widespread threats (global and regional) to community and individual threats. As a result, health communication researchers have become increasingly interested in identifying groups of people who are at the greatest risk for specific types of threats and finding ways to design appropriate messages to help individuals avoid or reduce them.

The 21st century is a time in which people are much less likely to die from acute diseases such as pneumonia or an injury caused by a bad fall and far more likely to be harmed by chronic diseases like heart disease and cancer. The good news about these more modern times in terms of our disease susceptibility is that thanks to scientific advances people do live much longer, with the average life span for women around 76 and for men around 74 years. Another bit of good news is that effective, evidence-based communication efforts can dramatically reduce the harm that comes from chronic illness and actually result in better health outcomes and longer, more fruitful lives. However, we also are discovering that as science and technology advance, we increasingly understand that the causes of many chronic diseases such as cancer

Health Communication in the 21st Century, Second Edition. Kevin Bradley Wright, Lisa Sparks, and H. Dan O'Hair.
© 2013 John Wiley & Sons, Inc. Published 2013 by John Wiley & Sons, Inc.

are quite confusing with no real end in sight. As one can gather, risk communication is very important and interesting!

We have also seen the world at greater risk for global and large-scale health threats, such as HIV/AIDS, environmental threats (e.g. pollution and toxic waste), and politically motivated threats, such as bioterrorism. The terrorist attacks on September 11, 2001, the anthrax mailings in the months following September 11, and viruses such as SARS and avian "bird" 'flu have made many people in the US realize just how vulnerable they are to health threats in our ever-shrinking world. Communication between government agencies, media sources, scientists, and healthcare providers around the world is crucial during times of health-related crises and in order to cope with pandemics, such as HIV/AIDS. In addition, health communicators must now be conscious of disseminating messages about some health risks to a worldwide audience.

In addition to these health threats, there are many populations within the US and all over the world who are at risk for various health problems due to reasons such as poverty, age, race, hunger, inadequate education, insanitary environmental conditions, and lack of access to appropriate healthcare. Many of these populations are marginalized groups who are at risk for health problems due to larger social issues, including political and cultural conditions, racial injustice, and lack of financial and social resources. Increasingly, we are seeing a greater divide between those who have the resources to deal with these health issues and those who do not. Communicating health risk and coordinating disease prevention and control efforts within these populations can be complex and challenging situations for healthcare promoters.

This chapter explores health risk and crisis communication issues at the global/large-scale, community, and individual levels. Specifically, it begins by defining risk communication and crisis communication. This is followed by a discussion of global threats to health, including HIV and terrorism, as well as communication strategies for coping with these threats. Next it examines several factors that are related to being at risk for health problems in the US and strategies for communicating about risk at the community level. Finally, it examines strategies for communicating about risk at the provider–patient level.

Defining Risk Communication

What exactly is risk communication?

Risk communication involves creating shared understanding about uncertain loss or danger. Historically, risk communication has evolved to examine theory and research related to the communication of scientific information about environmental, agricultural, food, health, and nutritional risks. It concentrates on social theories related to risk perception and behavior. Scholars interested in risk communication issues examine case studies involving pesticide residues, waste management, water quality, environmental hazards, and personal health behaviors. The multi-disciplinary risk communication field emerged in the 1970s and 1980s. In those decades, members of the public, scientists, engineers, corporate leaders, and government officials were coping with Love Canal, a Niagara Falls, New York neighborhood where 21 000 tons of toxic waste were discovered buried beneath neighborhood homes; the Three Mile Island nuclear accident in Pennsylvania; and the Bhopal, India, disaster, where thousands died from accidental release of hazardous chemicals. As Leiss and Powell (2004) explain, modern day risk communication investigates mad cow disease, climate change and genetic technologies, as well as oil spills, nuclear leaks, *E. coli*, vaccinations, etc. For instance, the story of the bovine spongiform encephalopathy (BSE) outbreak started in the UK in the 1980s. BSE is still being discovered in UK herds, and cases of mad cow disease have been found in twenty countries across the European continent and as far away as Japan with devastating consequences for the food industry. BSE has now been discovered on the North American continent in two cows born in Canada. The original cause of these two new cases is almost certainly importation of infected cattle, cattle feed, or both from the UK. Canadian government regulators and those in the cattle industry have failed to correctly assess the risks of the disease in the Canadian herd, take the precautionary measures needed to prevent the spread of disease, and communicate risks and precautionary measures to the public (Liess & Powell, 2004). Global warming and climate change are hot risk communication topics. Not only is every aspect of this risk debate both contentious and difficult for the public to understand, but the potential consequences of the risks extend all the way to global catastrophe for human civilization. Genomic science is a risk communication context that taps into both the health benefits expected from genetic manipulation and some of the risk factors associated with it.

Risk can take on a number of meanings depending upon the lens one places onthe operationalization of the definition. For example, in the business and finance world, risk usually refers to the strategies surrounding the volatility of an investment or the likelihood that a certain use of money will cause unpredictable losses or gains.

In the sciences (social, behavioral, life, or technical), risk is often viewed as an index of the severity of some harm and the chances it will adversely affect people or the environment. For instance, when a new pesticide helps farmers keep their crops from being eaten by pests is a good thing, but when that same pesticide use becomes toxic or harmful and the bad outweighs the good, then we have a problem to solve via risk communication. People constantly debate the risks and benefits of phenomena such as whether or not to take the three doses of the human papilloma (HPV) vaccine before the age of 26, smoking cessation, sunscreen protection, food, alcohol or drug use or abuse, safe sex practices, texting or drinking while driving, as well as pesticides, genetically modified organisms, processed foods, vaccination, and nuclear power. Therefore, effective risk communication is key.

The risks that upset people are not always those that kill them, and the risks that kill them may not be the ones that upset them. For instance, accidents at nuclear power plants, terrorist attacks, and contamination of processed foods cause considerable concern and outrage. Nevertheless, the numbers of people killed or harmed by these phenomena are far fewer than those killed daily by activities such as smoking and automobile accidents. Half of the 47 million Americans who smoke, and continue to do so, will die from tobacco-related diseases, according to the US Centers for

Disease Control and Prevention. Those between the ages of 4 and 33 years are more likely to die in an automobile accident than in any other way, according to the US National Highway Traffic Safety Administration.

Roger Kasperson and associates studying risk perception issues developed the Social Amplification and Attenuation of Risk Framework to explain how social and communicative institutions and processes dramatize some disasters or harms and minimize others. A classic example is the 1989 Exxon-Valdez accident in the Prince William Sound of Alaska that involved 11 million gallons of crude oil fouling roughly 1 000 miles of once-pristine coastline. Media coverage of the accident was instantly accessible with vivid images of oil-soaked animals. The Chief Executive Officer of Exxon at the time, Lawrence G. Rawl, made a huge mistake by not immediately traveling to the site. Each of these elements amplified and dramatized public outrage, causing the Exxon Valdez to become one of the most widely known oil spills of all time. Literally dozens of other oil spills have impacted communities across the decades, but few have received the media attention and outrage of the Alaskan accident.

Oil spills are a telling example of the hundreds of hazards that interpersonal, organizational, mass communication, and social media processes dramatize or minimize. Many remember Hurricane Katrina as the worst disaster of 2005, a storm that killed over 1 300. However, according to the International Disaster Database in Brussels, Belgium, also in 2005, an earthquake in Pakistan killed over 73 000 people. It is important to remember that the location of a hazard and the ways it is communicated, from organizational leaders to the media to social networks, affect the degree to which that hazard is detected, recalled, discussed, and managed.

Risk communication vs. crisis communication

Risk communication and crisis communication are different from one another in one important sense. Generally, risk communication deals principally with communication about physical hazards such as tornadoes, toxic chemicals, and so forth (Rowan *et al.*, 2008). Risk communication deals mainly with communication about physical hazards such as tornadoes, toxic chemicals, and so forth. Crisis communication may, but does not have to concern, physical hazards. For example, an unexpectedly negative news article could constitute a crisis for an organization or an unexpected disaster such as the 2011 Japan earthquake and Pacific tsunami could raise worldwide awareness in disaster preparedness as the near 9.0 earthquake has greatly devastated the country, impacted the economy, etc. Hurricane Katrina could constitute a crisis for Louisiana and the entire country by raising awareness of a nation lacking in preparedness and effective communication exchange among officials and the affected communities.

Risk communication also deals with a range of issues involving health/risk information and preparation strategies to the public and key state and local government and non-government response partners before a tragic event occurs. Risk communication strategies for public health preparedness often concern agriculture, food, water issues; infectious disease and vaccines; mental health and general public health; as well as chemical, biological, nuclear, and radiological threats (see jhsph.edu/preparedness, http://www.bt.cdc.gov/cerc/pdf/CERC-SEPT02.pdf, for detailed information). The Centers for Disease Control (see cdc.gov) have prioritized risk communication and health information dissemination since 2004. Risk communication topics can range from frightening diseases such as cancer and AIDS, to mental health, to earthquakes and tsunamis (e.g. Japan), and violence in schools (e.g. Virginia Tech University). Scientific uncertainty about diseases sometimes leads people to wonder about the possible ways in which they may have contracted them. Consequently, groups as diverse as trade associations, medical associations, public relations offices, and many government groups currently devote considerable effort to learning how best to communicate with the public about risk and safety.

Crisis communication

After September 11, 2001, the term "crisis communication" took on greater meaning and urgency in the US. The phrase had been in use for decades, particularly by scholars studying military operations and international relations. In the post 9/11 crisis and terrorism environment, government officials, first responders, providers/practitioners, community leaders, community members, and researchers confront an alarming range of communication obstacles that can limit the effectiveness of responses to risk and terrorist events. Terrorism, not surprisingly, has become a significant topic in crisis management, academe, industry, and in our communities. The issues surrounding terrorism have now become an integral part of our daily conversations in America and throughout the world.

In the field of communication, crisis communication research involves the application of the use of strategically designed messages delivered through selected sources (mediated and interpersonal) to convey relevant information to targeted audiences in crisis situations that have the following features: (i) uncertainty; (ii) intense emotion; (iii) disparate target audience; (iv) time is of the essence; and (v) communication of appropriate and effective strategic message(s) is urgent. None of these aspects is unique to crisis communication (e.g. in health communication contexts, we know that a physician breaking bad news of a cancer diagnosis often faces a difficult emotional response), but when we consider these aspects jointly, we have a unique new communicative challenge worthy of systematic and thorough examination. Further, crisis communication involves creating ways for people to gather important information in a timely manner, while being able to adequately protect themselves when the information available is uncertain or equivocal.

Typically, a crisis is an event that occurs unexpectedly. When a crisis occurs, it may not be within a government or private organization's control, and may cause harm to the organization's good reputation or viability. An example of an organization facing a crisis is one where there has been an occurrence of a mass shooting of employees by a disgruntled employee. Or, as we saw with Hurricane Katrina, government agencies received criticism for not being sufficiently prepared to handle this particular crisis. In most instances, organizations face some legal or moral culpability for the crisis (unlike a disaster in which a tornado wipes out the production plant), and stakeholders and the public are judging the organization's response to the crisis. The underlying thread in crisis communication is that the communicating organization is experiencing an unexpected crisis and must respond. Crisis also implies lack of control by the involved organization in the timing of the crisis event.

An important goal of health communication scholars is to raise public awareness of the importance of communication following a crisis, why communication about hurricanes, terrorist attacks, health epidemics, and other unknown disasters can be so difficult, and what people can do to improve these communication processes.

Global and Large-Scale Health Threats

This section explores some of the major threats to health around the world, including environmental threats, hunger, pandemics, and terrorism. In addition, we will explore several responses to these threats posed by health communication scholars.

Environmental threats/world hunger

Environment-related diseases and injuries cause millions of preventable deaths each year. Hazardous waste disposal, overpopulation, smog, and pollution are just a few of the many adverse environmental factors that have been linked to health problems. As we discussed earlier in this chapter, people who are poor and/or marginalized tend to be at most risk for many of these health problems. Overpopulation is most common in developing countries, many of which already lack sufficient financial and structural resources. In countries with overpopulation problems, more people mean that there are greater demands on farm land, water supplies, and other natural resources, many of which are often affected by pollution due to the number of people. Around the world, millions of tons of hazardous waste are produced annually by industries, and these materials are often linked to many different health problems. Unfortunately, minority and/or low-income populations within many countries face *environmental injustice*, or disproportionate exposure to environmental dangers due to race, ethnicity, or socioeconomic status (Anderton, Anderson, Oakes, & Fraser, 1994). Hazardous waste disposal often occurs in locations that are in close proximity to where minority and/or low-income populations live, areas which are considered "undesirable" by higher-income individuals within the greater community. While most of these hazardous materials are contained within landfill, toxic emissions from landfills, such as methane gas, can create health risks for people in the surrounding areas. For example, methane and other gases emitted by landfills are carcinogenic, leading to long-term health problems.

Environmental injustice appears to be a global phenomenon. Ethnic minorities in Central Asia, Australia, Africa, and South America have all suffered acute and prolonged health problems caused by radiation tests, toxic waste from the petroleum industry, and many other hazardous materials (Bullard, 1993). In the US, several studies have found evidence of toxic waste materials being dumped near minority and/or low-income neighborhoods (Rowan, 1996).

More than 840 million people in the world suffer from hunger or are malnourished, and while hunger is certainly a problem in the US, most people facing hunger live in developing nations (Care.org, 2006). Millions of children suffer from hunger around the world, putting them at risk for developmental problems associated with malnutrition, such as stunted growth, susceptibility to disease, cognitive impairment, and early mortality rates. About 5 million children around the world die from problems related to malnutrition each year. In addition, hunger affects an individual's productivity, sense of hope, and overall well-being. There are many causes of world hunger, including the economic condition of countries and regions, land rights and ownership, inefficient agricultural practices, war, famine, drought, poor crop yields, and environmental problems.

As you can imagine, dealing with problems such as environmental injustice and world hunger is no easy task. At the very least, health communication scholars and other individuals can help to raise awareness about environmental problems and environmental injustice by conducting more studies that demonstrate the link between industry waste disposal practices and health problems, by interventions designed not only to raise awareness of these issues among people living in communities where these practices occur but also to give them the tools to promote change, and through health campaigns designed to change industry practices or that create new legislation that will end them.

While the world has the capacity to produce enough food for everyone, we are well short of achieving this goal. A variety of economic, political, educational, and cultural issues, such as the wealth of a region, rights to land, racism, and knowledge about agricultural practices, contribute to the inability of regions to produce and distribute food to everyone. Donating food as aid or charity in non-emergency situations is more or less a short-term solution to world hunger. While such donations can be crucial during emergency situations, the long-term solution to hunger may lie in economic, educational, and political reform efforts. Again, campaigns designed both to raise the awareness of those individuals who have the greatest needs and to improve economic and educational conditions are ways in which health communication scholars can help to make a long-term impact on hunger.

Pandemics

A pandemic is a global epidemic of a disease or health problem. The world is more vulnerable to pandemics than ever before due to increased travel around the world and immigration. The HIV/AIDS threat is the most prominent pandemic the world faces today. However, other diseases have the potential to become pandemics if efforts are not taken to contain them. We will focus on the impact of HIV/AIDS and the emergence of new threats, such as SARS and avian 'flu, and responses to these threats below.

HIV/AIDS More than 20 million people worldwide have died of AIDS since the beginning of the pandemic, and 38 million people were estimated to be living with HIV/AIDS by the end of 2003 (Joint United Nations Program on HIV/AIDS, 2004). Women now account for about half of the number of people with HIV worldwide. Young people (between the ages of 15 and 24) account for most of the new HIV infections worldwide.

Africa is the continent that has been hit the hardest by the HIV/AIDS pandemic, followed by South and Southeast Asia. Nearly 25 million individuals with HIV/AIDS live in African countries, while over 6 million live in Asian countries (Joint United Nations Program on HIV/AIDS, 2004). A large proportion of individuals living with HIV/AIDS are from low-income countries, such as many countries in sub-Saharan Africa and Asia, and lack access to antiviral medications that could prolong their lives. Even within higher-income countries, such as the US and a number of European countries, people who have reduced economic means typically lack access to these medications and are at greater risk for developing opportunistic infections associated with HIV/AIDS and dying from the disease sooner. The number of people with HIV/AIDS is expected to rise despite increased knowledge about prevention and treatment of the disease.

Patterns of infection vary among regions of the world. The populations that are at greatest risk for HIV/AIDS include pregnant women between 15 and 24 years in African countries (Joint United Nations Program on HIV/AIDS, 2004). In many Asian countries, injecting drug users, sex workers and their partners, and men who have sex with men are the most vulnerable to the disease (Steinfatt & Mielke, 1999). Within Europe and the US, injected drug use and sex between men are currently the greatest risk factors for contracting HIV. However, infection due to heterosexual sex is on the rise in the US, particularly among minority groups. These at-risk behaviors are associated with socioeconomic issues. Many people in Southeast Asian countries become sex workers because it is often a better economic alternative than other types of employment in economically depressed areas (Steinfatt & Mielke, 1999; Wenniger et al., 1991). In some cases, young women are forced by their family members to engage in sex work in order to financially support their family. Many people who inject heroin and other drugs often cannot afford clean needles, and so sharing needles (and the chance of contracting HIV) is more prevalent among low-income populations. In addition, lack of education about HIV/AIDS and low condom usage in many countries contribute to high incident rates.

Communicating about HIV/AIDS risks to vulnerable populations around the world has proven to be a difficult task. The risk factors for HIV/AIDS vary by region and culture around the world, and many at-risk behaviors are related to cultural beliefs and behavioral norms. These beliefs and behaviors are shaped by an array of complex social, economic, and political factors (Amaro, 1995), all of which health risk communicators need to take into consideration.

For example, Cameron, Witte, and Nzyuko (1999) found that the high prevalence of HIV infection in Kenya was related to the cultural practice of prostitution among young women and truck drivers on the Trans-Africa highway. Young women in this part of Kenya are often drawn to prostitution because of their economic situation. Cameron, Witte, and Nzyuko (1999) found that it was the cultural norm among male truck drivers in this culture to have sex with multiple partners, and they tended to have fatalistic beliefs about contracting HIV (e.g. the belief that everyone has to die of something, so what difference does HIV make?), and many held the belief that sex with a condom was not "real" sex. The women interviewed in this study said that they found it difficult to verbalize their desire to use condoms due to male/female power differentials in the culture (e.g. women are not typically assertive when interacting with men). In addition, economic and structural issues within the culture contributed to a shortage of available condoms or condoms that were damaged due to inadequate storage procedures.

In other parts of Africa and many cultures around the world, men are admired for having multiple sex partners, they often demand sex with females, or they forcibly engage in (unprotected) sexual intercourse with women (du Pré, 2005; Kamwendo & Kamowa, 1999). In China, knowledge about HIV/AIDS is related to the restricted control of media. In recent years the Chinese government has not perceived HIV/AIDS as a major health threat despite the fact that over a half-million people have been diagnosed with AIDS (Geist-Martin, Ray, & Sharf, 2003), and many people are unaware of the disease or lack basic information about how it is spread (Rosenthal, 2001).

SARS/avian flu

While few diseases have had the global impact of HIV/AIDS, there is always potential for the spread of disease worldwide. In February of 2003, we witnessed the advent of SARS, a viral respiratory illness that quickly spread from Asia to more than 24 countries in North and South America and Europe before it was contained. According to the World Health Organization (WHO), a total of 8,098 people worldwide became sick with SARS during the 2003 outbreak, and 774 people died from the disease (WHO, 2004). One of the frightening aspects of SARS was that rather than being spread by sexual contact or through the exchange of blood (such as HIV/AIDS), the disease could be contracted by casual human-to-human contact. People traveling to different countries were able to spread the disease to different continents relatively quickly. It is not difficult to imagine how similar types of viruses that are more lethal than SARS could spread around the world in the future.

More recently there has been growing concern over avian "bird" 'flu around the world. Avian 'flu caused numerous deaths among people who were in close contact with poultry or other types of birds. However, there is great concern among members of WHO that the virus may go through a series of genetic mutations in the future, causing the disease to spread from human-to-human contact. While the US was somewhat slow in responding to the avian 'flu threat, other countries, such as China, engaged in widespread campaigns to alert people about the potential threat of this virus and steps that could be taken to prevent it. Recently, when the first author of this book was in Hong Kong, he saw hundreds of posters in subways, billboards, and other public places warning individuals of this new threat.

Communication played a vital role in helping to contain the SARS outbreak of 2003 and avian 'flu. The CDC and WHO set up an Emergency Operations Center shortly after the SARS outbreak and avian 'flu were recognized. In addition, these organizations deployed medical officers, epidemiologists, and other specialists to assist with on-site investigations around the world. Information about the disease was communicated to clinicians who conducted extensive laboratory tests to identify the causes of the disease. Today, the CDC has developed recommendations and guidelines to help public health and healthcare officials plan for and respond quickly to the reappearance of SARS and avian 'flu. These guidelines are an example of a *crisis management plan*, which involves advanced planning and rehearsal for a health-related crisis. The CDC and WHO have a number of these plans in place to help prepare for other diseases and health risks. For example, WHO has developed the Global Outbreak Alert and Response Network (GOARN), which is a collaboration of health-related institutions and networks that pool human and technical resources for the rapid identification and confirmation of and response to outbreaks of international importance (WHO, 2004). However, in cases like SARS or avian 'flu where it is a new threat, communication between healthcare systems around the world can be challenging, especially given the availability and quality of health resources in different regions of the world. In the next section, we will examine how crisis management plans are also being used to prepare for terrorist attacks.

Terrorism

Over the past several decades, terrorism has emerged as a significant threat to the lives of people around the world. The US has witnessed relatively few terrorist attacks compared to other regions of the world. For example, terrorist attacks have occurred more frequently in African, Latin American, Asian, and Middle Eastern countries than in the US (US Department of State, 2001). Yet, as a nation, the US has become increasingly aware of domestic and foreign terrorist threats in recent years following the Oklahoma City bombing in 1995, the 9/11 attacks, and attacks by Al-Qaeda and other terrorist groups around the world (such as the many attacks on US troops in Iraq and the 2004 train bombing in Madrid, Spain). Scholars differ considerably in how they define terrorism. However, O'Hair and Heath (2005) provide a definition of terrorism based upon some of the most prevalent definitions in the terrorism literature:

> First, fear is the ultimate goal. Second, the violence only has to be threatened. Third, the victims are not always the ultimate targets. Fourth, primary audience members are those who observe the terrorist act. Fifth, political or social change are the primary objectives of terrorists. Terrorism, then, means deliberately exacting pain, suffering, and death on civilians for the purpose of accomplishing specific goals without regard for human rights and creating a climate of fear through violent means. (p. 12)

O'Hair and Heath (2005) argue that terrorism is essentially a communicative act in which terrorists send others a message designed to communicate fear in order to achieve their goals.

Besides the obvious threat to loss of life, terrorism affects health in many other ways. Prolonged periods of stress related to terrorist acts (or threats) can lead to negative stress-related health outcomes. Terrorist attacks are characterized by uncertainty and intense emotional responses (Sparks, 2005; Sparks, Kreps, Botan, & Rowan,

2005a, 2005b; Step, Finucane, & Horvath, 2002). In the months following the September 11 attacks, there was a reported increase in post-traumatic stress disorder (PTSD) and depression (Lacy & Benedek, 2003; MacGeorge *et al.*, 2007), particularly among people who were friends and relatives of those who died in the attacks and among people who lived in close geographic proximity to New York City and Washington, DC. Moreover, Ahern *et al.* (2002) found that heavy viewing of negative images of the 9/11 attacks in the mass media, such as people jumping out of the World Trade Center towers, was also associated with PTSD and depression.

In terms of threats to physical health, the US population has become more vulnerable to acts of bioterrorism, or the release of chemical, biological, or radiological hazards into the environment, in recent years due to the rise of domestic and foreign terrorist groups (Kreps *et al.*, 2005a, 2005b). For example, as with the use of chemical weapons (e.g. anthrax and sarin gas), diseases such as smallpox create serious threats to public health. A large-scale act of bioterrorism has the potential to severely challenge the available resources of our emergency response and healthcare systems.

At-Risk Communities within the United States

In addition to these large-scale threats, there are many different communities within the US where people are at significant risk for physical, psychological, and social health problems. Physical health problems include diseases and other threats to the body, while psychological health problems often consist of a variety of conditions, such as increased stress, anxiety, and low self-esteem. Social health problems include limited availability of social support or resources to help individuals cope with problems and feelings of social isolation. This section identifies several variables that are associated with being at risk in America and some of the groups that are most vulnerable to health threats in the US.

Risk factors

As we have seen, people who are at risk for poor health often face disparities in access to healthcare and the quality of care they receive due to their social status. In addition, they often live within communities that have limited social resources, such as social capital or human capital. These social factors often put members of such groups at higher risk for health problems such as environmental health threats, susceptibility to disease, substance abuse, mental illness, and depression (Aday, 2001; Wyshak & Modest, 1996). We will examine each of these risk factors and how they are related to health problems.

Social status Social status refers to disparities in political and personal power and access to resources in a society due to differences between people based on characteristics such as age, gender, race and ethnicity, and income. Moreover, social norms and institutions within a society reinforce power and access to resource differences between groups based on these characteristics. Social status is associated with health risks in the US. For example, infants, children, the elderly, single females who are living alone or as the head of a household, several racial and ethnic groups (primarily African Americans, Hispanics, Native Americans, and Asian Americans), and individuals who are unemployed or have lower incomes are at the most risk for health problems in the US. In addition, homeless individuals and many recent immigrants/refugees suffer from health problems due to their social status. These individuals often have difficulty affording or gaining access to healthcare, and they are often targets of discrimination due to the prevalence of ageist, sexist, and racist beliefs in our culture. Moreover, some groups such as illegal immigrants avoid seeking preventive care and/or help for many types of health problems because they fear facing legal action or deportation.

Members of these groups are often *marginalized*, or ignored, trivialized, unheard, perceived as inconsequential, or threatened due to processes within a society that privilege some groups over others based on their social status and negative societal perceptions of their status (Ford & Yep, 2003). When groups are marginalized, they are typically denied privileges, rights, and access to resources and the power to influence social structures in society, including access to adequate healthcare or the political process by which discriminatory practices in the healthcare system can be changed. According to Ford and Yep (2003), "individuals and groups that do not conform to the mythical norm, or 'the standards of normality' in society, are marginalized and devaluated, and their health concerns are treated differently than those in the dominant culture" (p. 244).

For example, in the early 1980s, during the first months of the HIV/AIDS epidemic in the US, gay men in California were the first group to encounter the disease. Because much of the US at that time held relatively negative attitudes about gay men and their lifestyles, early reports of HIV/AIDS were downplayed or ignored by the mainstream US media. Largely due to prejudices against gay men, the HIV/AIDS epidemic was trivialized in our culture as "the gay plague," and many people did not feel that the disease was something that they should be concerned about. Although health officials at that time were extremely concerned about the severity of the disease and how quickly it seemed to be spreading, much of mainstream America initially saw the epidemic as a problem within the gay community (if they thought about it all). It was not until the mid-1980s that the US media and mainstream America became concerned about HIV/AIDS. When stories began to break such as that of Ryan White, a child from Indiana who contracted the HIV virus, many people in the US started to pay attention to HIV/AIDS for the first time. Even then, children, hemophiliacs, and people who contracted the virus through blood transfusions were perceived as "innocent victims" of the disease while gay men were (and still largely are) seen as responsible for contracting the disease due to their own (undesirable) behaviors.

Of course, many groups of people, including gay men, continue to be marginalized in the US. Gay men still experience discrimination due to their lifestyle choices and in terms of healthcare coverage for their partners. Other groups of people are marginalized due to a wide variety of characteristics, including gender, race and ethnicity, social class, and disability (Ford & Yep, 2003). Political and legal issues can also lead to marginalization. For example, many illegal immigrants living in the US do not seek treatment for health problems for themselves or their family members because they fear deportation. As a result, many of the health concerns of this particular population go unnoticed by mainstream society.

Social capital Social capital can be defined as the quantity and quality of interpersonal ties among people within a community, and the resources that these network members make available to individuals (Aday, 2001; Dearing, 2003). Social capital often takes the form of informational, tangible, and social support. According to Dearing (2003), "availability of social capital is dependent on one's position within a network; network structure both enables and constrains one's opportunity to access and use resources" (p. 214).

People who have the most social capital within a community benefit physically, psychologically, and socially due to having greater availability of resources for coping with physical and psychological problems, and a greater sense of well-being and belonging. According to Aday (2001), individuals who have the least social capital include those who live alone, those who are not married or in committed relationships, individuals who do not belong to voluntary social organizations (e.g. interest groups, churches), and people who have a limited number of (or no) family or friends. People with limited social capital tend to be at greater risk for poor physical, psychological, and social health. Many populations or communities who are at risk for health problems have a high concentration of people with low social capital. For example, communities with a large number of people of lower socioeconomic status, people who are marginalized due to racial discrimination, and communities with people who may have few social connections, such as elderly people living alone or recent immigrants from other nations, often have less social capital than high-income communities or communities that have an infrastructure that better supports the development of social networks.

In terms of social capital, communities tend to benefit the most when their members are diverse, share similar social status, tie together organizations within the community, span other communities, and when individuals and organizations continue to create new network ties and bring resources to segments of the community that previously did not have them (Dearing, 2003; Flora, 1998). By contrast, communities with low social capital do not share these characteristics, and they tend to be much less organized, with fewer interrelationships among organizations and people, which typically often results in less overall access to resources. Homeless individuals often have few social support ties in their environment, and this may contribute to higher levels of stress and fewer tangible resources during times of need.

In addition, recent immigrants to the US often experience problems adjusting to life in a new culture. They may find few supportive ties in the communities where they reside to help buffer the stress of adjustment (which often takes years). Not surprisingly, there is a high prevalence of stress-related health problems among immigrants, including gastrointestinal disorders and greater susceptibility to illness due to suppressed immune systems (Kim & Grant, 1997). Some immigrants, such as the Hmong from Laos and people from Bosnia, are refugees who have had their lives disrupted by war and other political conflicts. Some individuals from these groups suffer from PTSD and depression (Ackerman, 1997; Wein *et al.*, 1995), and they may find relatively few sources of emotional support within their community (e.g. people who can identify with their situation).

Human capital Human capital refers to a community's investments in people's skills and capabilities (such as vocational training or public education) that enable them to act in new ways (such as mastering a trade) or enhance their ability to be productive members of society (Aday, 2001). Communities with higher unemployment rates, substandard schools or housing, and fewer opportunities for the creation of social ties among their members may be associated with lower human capital. In other words, some communities lack the resources or are otherwise unwilling or unable to invest in social structures that empower their members or enhance their quality of life. Lack of human capital may exacerbate problems such as homelessness, crime, and poverty.

A variety of issues may contribute to the lack of human capital in a community. In some communities, problems such as substandard housing, poor schools, and few employment opportunities often lead individuals to flee from the community in an effort to find better housing, schools, and employment elsewhere. In an attempt to find conditions that will better their lives, people living in communities with low human capital often move to nearby communities within a city or within the geographic area (Aday, 2001). Poor human capital conditions in a community can also contribute to an increase in crime, such as drug trafficking and gang violence, which in turn may motivate other citizens to leave who have the means to do so. Unfortunately, this may lead to even fewer job opportunities, worse school conditions, and more substandard housing as small business owners, teachers, and people who can invest in other types of human capital leave the community.

When this type of pattern occurs within a community, the members who are left behind typically have even fewer social resources to cope with problems, such as stress due to unemployment, higher crime rates, and other problems associated with the lack of human capital. People may cope with this stress in negative ways, such as drug and alcohol abuse, which can further exacerbate the community's problems. Higher stress levels coupled with fewer opportunities for social support may lead to psychological and physical health problems (see Chapter 4). Lower incomes associated with few job and educational opportunities limit the type and quality of healthcare community members can obtain. In addition, higher-quality hospitals, clinics, and other health services are often reluctant to stay in poorer communities or build new facilities there. Worse still, poorer communities can suffer from environmental injustice, such as when they become the dumping grounds for environmental waste, which can lead to other types of health problems (Rowan, 2004).

Communication Strategies for Addressing Health Risks

While finding solutions to health threats is challenging because of multiple economic, cultural, and political issues, in recent years researchers have become interested in addressing these problem at a variety of levels, including targeting communities, organizations, and individuals. This section briefly explores the use of such initiatives in the areas of HIV/AIDS, terrorism, community-based initiatives for marginalized at-risk populations within the US, and provider–patient interventions. While it is unrealistic to think that the approaches described in this section are capable of resolving all of the issues related to at-risk populations, they represent examples of responses to such threats by risk and crisis communication researchers.

Dealing with the threat of HIV/AIDS

Efforts to communicate about the risk of HIV/AIDS have had varying degrees of impact (Brinson & Brown, 1997; Siska, Jason, & Murdoch, 1992). Early interventions often focused on rational arguments for changing behaviors rather than considering emotional, social, and everyday life concerns of target audiences (Freimuth, Hammond, Edgar, & Monahan, 1990). Brinson and Brown (1997) suggest using culturally appropriate narratives when constructing HIV/AIDS campaign messages. In other words, based on narrative theory (Fisher, 1985), Brinson and Brown contend that campaign messages should convey a story to target audience members that is believable, relevant, well structured, and that provides culturally based "good reasons" for the audience to accept the campaign message. In many parts of the world and among a number of co-cultures in the US, storytelling is an important means for disseminating information (Airhihenbuwa, 1995), and thus it may be helpful in terms of raising awareness about HIV/AIDS and changing behaviors. However, more studies need to be conducted to assess the impact of campaigns using a narrative approach versus those that use more traditional types of persuasive messages.

Everett Rogers was a communication scholar who extensively researched HIV/AIDS in the US and other countries. He had some success using his *diffusion of innovations* model (Rogers, 1995) in HIV/AIDS campaigns (Dearing *et al.*, 1996). The diffusion of innovations model holds that innovations, including new information about HIV/AIDS prevention or medical technologies that can treat the disease, are spread through a serious of stages. According to Rogers' theory, *innovators* are those individuals who first acquire new knowledge. For example, when HIV/AIDS first appeared in the US, the researchers from the CDC who first discovered that the virus was being spread sexually were innovators in the HIV/AIDS epidemic. This information was then passed to *opinion leaders*, such as the news media, government officials, and other individuals who shared the responsibility for disseminating this information to the public. Those individuals who first received information about HIV/AIDS and acted on the public are known as the *early majority*, followed by the *late majority*, or people who learned about the disease (or acted upon this information) later. Finally, according to Rogers's theory, *laggards* were those individuals who were among the last to learn (or act on information) about HIV/AIDS.

Researchers learn new information about HIV/AIDS every day, but the problem is that it takes a great deal of time for such information to spread through the diffusion model. For example, in recent years, people with HIV have been able to prolong their lives by taking antiviral medication, especially if they were tested for HIV while the disease was in its early stages. Unfortunately, many people are still unaware of the advances that have been made in treating HIV, especially if they are in the late majority or are laggards in terms of exposure to this information, and they may avoid getting tested if they still perceive an HIV diagnosis as being equivalent to a death sentence.

It is important to have an understanding of where populations are in the diffusion process of information about HIV/AIDS. A number of at-risk populations within the US may be laggards in terms of awareness about how HIV/AIDS is spread. In addition, many places around the world lack access to new information about HIV/AIDS and/or to medications and medical advances that can treat it, and these regions are often in the beginning stages of the diffusion process as far as medical advances are concerned. This is especially true in countries where people do not have access to the mass media, or in cultures where interpersonal channels are more effective than the mass media in disseminating information due to literacy issues or cultural practices that privilege face-to-face communication over mediated channels (Airhihenbuwa, 1995), and in places that do not have a well-defined healthcare system infrastructure.

Dealing with the threat of terrorism

Communication and crisis management following a terrorist attack When a terrorist attack occurs anywhere in the world, communication plays a crucial role in responding to it (Seeger, Vennette, Ulmer, & Sellnow, 2002). Specifically, developing crisis management strategies can help to reduce the number of casualties, increase the effectiveness of first-response personnel, and contain certain threats so that they do not affect larger numbers of people. According to Coombs (2005), risk is a driving force behind crisis management. Crisis management includes measures to identify and reduce the threat of a risk and to prepare organizations for when a risk becomes a crisis.

Coombs contends that crisis management is a four-step process: prevention, preparation, response, and learning. *Prevention* includes actions organizations take to reduce risks and vulnerabilities to a crisis. *Preparation* involves creating a crisis management plan, forming and training a crisis management team, and rehearsing the crisis management plan. For example, following the 9/11 attacks many local and state government organizations developed crisis management plans to deal with a bioterrorist attack. Mock terrorist attacks were then staged in an attempt to rehearse and evaluate how well the plan might work if a real attack were to occur. Rehearsing for such terrorist attacks can help to reduce the impact of an attack when it occurs. Coombs argues that many more lives would have been lost on 9/11 if employees had not been planning and practicing evacuations following the bombing of the World Trade Center in the early 1990s. *Response* refers to the actual measures taken when a crisis occurs. *Learning* is a review of what went right and wrong in the crisis management effort in an attempt to understand how future plans can be improved. For example, after the 9/11 attacks, police and fire department officials examined the failure of two-way radio systems during the crisis and have since taken steps to improve these communication systems in the event of future attacks.

Within the US, significant steps have been taken since 9/11 to develop crisis management plans for a terrorist attack, most notably the creation of the Department of Homeland Security. The Department of Homeland Security has emphasized the need for industries that deal with chemicals, radioactive material, and other potential threats to the environment to develop emergency preparedness plans in the event of a terrorist attack. In addition, the Department of Homeland Security has required state and local governments to develop crisis management plans. According to Coombs (2005), the job of crisis managers is to identify and prioritize risks, which are then assessed in terms of the impact they can have on the organization and the likelihood of the risk occurring. Part of calculating the terrorist risk is the physical location of a facility, materials stored there, and the strategic importance of the facility. For example, many chemical facilities are located near densely populated areas in the US and other countries, and crisis managers should be involved in assessing the risk of terrorists attacking these facilities, the impact such an attack would have on the surrounding community, and emergency response plans if an attack should occur.

According to Scholl, Williams, and Olaniran (2005), the media, as the disseminators of important crisis-related information, play a significant role in the success or failure of crisis management, including management of a terrorist attack. The public often looks to the media as an important source of information about the effect of long-term hazards, significant disaster threats, and recommended actions in response to certain threats. According to Nacos (2003), the constant flow of information provided by print, radio, and television makes the public feel more involved with the unfolding events. In addition, the news media are a valuable resource in assisting crisis managers with communicating vital information during an attack. Finally, the dissemination of news provides individuals with public spaces where they can engage in discussions with experts and each other about the terrorist acts, their aftermath, and their implications.

Scholl, Williams, and Olaniran (2005) recommend the creation of crisis communication center (CCC) teams to help disseminate appropriate messages to the public in the event of a terrorist attack, to circumvent any aversive outcomes from news coverage, and to provide messages that can assist the community during crisis (Crelinsten, 1994). Ideally, a CCC team should consist of community and municipal members who have a working knowledge of industrial, technical, and agricultural elements of the community that might potentially become terrorist targets. The CCC team should establish and maintain a good relationship with the media, develop plans for getting important messages about risks and resources out quickly to the public through the media, and select a credible spokesperson to deliver these messages in the event of an attack.

Coping with the psychological effects of terrorism As we have seen, the threat of terrorism also impacts our psychological health by increasing our stress levels. Crisis communication researchers have examined a variety of strategies that may help to reduce stress following a terrorist attack or due to the threat of an attack. According to Becker (2005), supportive interpersonal communication can help people make sense of terrorist attacks and transform the meaning and significance of such events. Viewing television coverage of a terrorist attack appears to heighten individuals' emotional involvement with the televised content, which is related to a stronger need for interpersonal connections (Step, Finucane, & Horvath, 2002). Becker (2005) recommend increasing one's reliance on social support networks and viewing television with others as coping strategies to improve psychosocial health. As we saw in Chapter 4, social support networks can help us to buffer stress and facilitate positive forms of coping. In addition, as in other stressful periods, friends and family members can help us following a terrorist attack by elevating our mood and comforting us. MacGeorge *et al.* (2007) found that individuals who received higher levels of emotional support following the 9/11 attacks had lower levels of depression, perceived goal disruption, and physical symptoms associated with stress than people who experienced less emotional support. However, long-term significant stress and depression following a terrorist attack may need to be treated by a skilled mental health professional. Sparks (2005) suggests that it is the media that strengthen the impact of terrorism and aid in the creation and redefinition of individual and collective identities. She further argues that it is important to understand the powerful role played by the media, especially television and new media such as the Internet, in defining, redefining, negotiating, renegotiating, and creating such social identities, which are continually formed and shaped via conversations surrounding the events. Understanding how social support groups shape our social identities during such times of crisis is a key element in coping with the crisis (Sparks, 2005).

Community-Based Health Initiatives for At-Risk or Marginalized Populations

Efforts to communicate information to vulnerable communities about health risks started with the work of people in business, such as the nuclear power industry, and with public health researchers with scientific backgrounds who were interested raising awareness about risk levels for a variety of health issues (Scherer & Juanillo, 2003). In addition, according to Scherer and Juanillo (2003), early attempts to influence at-risk communities were somewhat elitist and paternalistic due to the fact that people in power (e.g. individuals from large corporations and government agencies) attempted to influence at-risk communities by providing them with scientific evidence regarding risk factors without considering the larger cultural beliefs, attitudes, and needs of the communities they were trying to influence. Early risk communication interventions largely relied upon providing communities with risk-related statistics or other scientific data, and researchers initially thought that this information would be persuasive enough to promote behavioral change. However, many people have a difficult time interpreting this type of information and understanding what the scientific data mean in terms of everyday behaviors (Tinker, 1996). Even after attempts to explain what the statistics meant to at-risk communities, many early risk communicators found that their strategies to promote health behavior change had only weak or moderate impact (Scherer & Juanillo, 2003).

These interventions rested on the assumption that individuals will behave rationally and change their behaviors when they are exposed to information about health risks. However, follow-up studies have found that many people often continue to smoke, eat high-fat foods, practice unsafe sex, and perform a host of other unhealthy behaviors despite being exposed to information about these health risks. People do not change their health behaviors simply by being exposed to more information about their risk for a health problem. Increasingly, risk communicators have come to recognize that health behavior change is influenced by a multitude of individual perceptions about health and health risks as well as by a variety of cultural and social influences. The failure of early risk communication campaigns has led to a growing appreciation of the critical role of psychosocial and cultural factors that influence the public's understanding and assessment of, as well as responses to, health risks (Scherer & Juanillo, 2003).

For example, layperson judgements of risk are often much different than expert judgements. People with low levels of education or who are unfamiliar with scientific methods may not understand the process by which risk factors are assessed through surveys and available data or how health risk statistics are calculated. Just saying that 33 percent of Latino adolescents in a certain suburb of Los Angeles are estimated to have HIV may not be sufficient to change risky behaviors within this community. Although this HIV prevalence rate would be considered high for a specific group of people within a relatively small geographic area, some adolescents may not see the relationship between their own behaviors and the risk, they may not believe that this statistic is credible, or the statistic may not be believed because it does not resonate with their personal experience (e.g. the majority of their friends and family do not have HIV).

In addition, risk factors may be linked to cultural beliefs and behavioral norms within a community. For example, drinking alcohol, eating certain types of food, and many other health-related behaviors are often linked to the culture of a group. Harwood and Sparks's (2003) research on social identity and health supports the notion that our health behaviors are often linked to our group identities (and vice versa). This research further argues that our group memberships with positive health behaviors (e.g. healthy diet and exercise) will likely lead to healthier and thus increased longevity, whereas our group memberships that carry out unhealthy behaviors (e.g. smoking, sunbathing without protection, poor diet, couch potato lifestyle, heavy alcohol consumption) will likely lead to decreased health across the life span. Some communities may not trust the motives of intervention researchers, or they may be resistant to persuasive attempts to change health behaviors (Guttman, 2000; Parrott & Steiner, 2003), especially marginalized groups, who may distrust federal, state, and local government sources of information due to past patterns of discrimination or neglect (Ford & Yep, 2003).

Several risk communication researchers have argued that risk communication efforts are most successful when people within at-risk communities are empowered by campaigns (Rowan, 1996, 2004), when they are involved in the risk communication campaign process (Ford & Yep, 2003), and when campaigns dealing with health risks are framed within the worldview of the individuals who constitute an at-risk community or population (Ford & Yep, 2003). In other words, these researchers argue that risk communication efforts need to move beyond simple dissemination of information, and risk communication campaigns work best when they empower people within a community and incorporate a community effort (e.g. involvement of community leaders and concerned citizens) toward promoting change.

Many scholars have found that community involvement is essential in influencing the health behaviors of marginalized groups (Airhihenbuwa, 1995; Ford & Yep, 2003). Ford and Yep (2003) suggest using community advisory boards, or a group of individuals from within the marginalized community who meet with health risk campaign promoters to discuss the health issue or issues facing the community on a regular basis. A community advisory board's involvement in the early stages of risk campaigns is essential to the risk communication process. Since the board consists of people who are members of the at-risk community, it can provide unique insights into the worldview of community members and the ways in which these cultural views shape perceptions of the health issue, responses to it, and how effective preventive efforts or health interventions can be developed from the standpoint of the community members.

In addition, a community forum, or a meeting where concerned citizens can interact with experts and informed laypersons from the community, can help risk communication campaigns and increase opportunities for dialogue between health promoters and members of the community. This type of interaction may help to merge scientific and community perceptions of health risk, and it may facilitate greater understanding and trust between the two parties. In addition, the use of lay health advisors, or members of the community who can provide insights into unique problems and barriers in the community, and who can be trained by risk communication specialists to help carry out the campaign, may improve the campaign's effectiveness.

Risk Communication Strategies at the Provider–Patient Level

There is a great need for health communication researchers to develop risk communication strategies at the provider–patient level. As trusted health authorities, providers are in an excellent position to motivate patients to reduce risky lifestyle behaviors and to engage in preventive screenings for diseases. As patients we are frequently encouraged to talk with our physicians about the risky choices we make in terms of our personal health (Rowan, Sparks, Pecchioni, & Villagran, 2003). While there exist lists of risk communication strategies (Covello & Allen, 1988) and disease risk communication guidelines (Arkin, 1999), these materials are not typically designed for physician–patient interaction. Instead, existing risk communication guidelines typically assume that communicators are speaking at a scientific meeting or press conference and that the principal communication goal is to explain the meaning of research findings as they pertain to groups or populations. This focus makes sense for press conferences and scientific meetings. It does not, however, reflect agendas that are typical in physician–patient consultations.

Moreover, advances in medical science often lead to new discoveries about health risks that can impact provider–patient communication. Consider, for example, the challenges endocrinologists, gynecologists, and internal medicine specialists faced when women on hormone replace therapy learned in July 2002 that there was a 26 percent increase in breast cancer among individuals taking this therapy as opposed to those in a control group (Rossouw *et al.*, 2002). The Women's Health Initiative was halted because the combination estrogen–progestin therapy was increasing, not decreasing, women's chances of both breast cancer and heart attack. These findings meant that many women wanted to consult with their physicians about their best course of action. But doctors' responses to these women varied. According to the *Washington Post*, some doctors rejected the findings of the Women's Health Initiative. Other physicians accepted these findings completely. Still others urged consideration of each woman's individual health history (Connelly, 2002).

In part, this range of varied responses reflects the difficulty of translating findings about population groups facing health risks into practical advice for individuals. Physicians need help in both translating population findings into advice for individuals and in determining how best to communicate cancer risk with patients. Books such as that by oncologist Daniel Rosenblum (1993) show that patients vary in terms of whether and when they want physicians mainly to listen and empathize with feelings, mainly to explain complexities, or mainly to make recommendations and support behavioral change (also see Dickson, Hargie, & Morrow, 1989; Jones, Kreps, & Phillips, 1995; Roter & Hall, 1992).

To help physicians meet challenges involved in communicating cancer risk during patient consultations, Rosenblum (1993) summarizes key findings on cancer risk communication and on physician–patient interaction. Specifically, his book presents a "cancer risk communication aid" that (i) draws from research to alert physicians to likely barriers associated with communicating about cancer risk; (ii) directs physicians to research-supported ways of overcoming these barriers through listening, empathizing, explaining, or persuading; and (iii) is packaged for easy recall during patient interaction.

Summary

People are vulnerable to many types of health threats both around the world and within the US. Health risk communicators attempt to raise awareness of these threats among the individuals who are most at risk as well as provide them with information or resources to avoid or reduce the impact of these threats. In all parts of the world, including the US, people who have fewer economic, educational, political, and social resources are often at the greatest risk for health threats. Many of these groups suffer from issues like racism or are marginalized for a variety of other reasons. Some health threats are global in nature, including environmental threats, HIV/AIDS, and terrorism. While these problems are challenging to address, health communicators can play a role in ameliorating them through interventions and other measures that help to raise awareness about the problems and provide resources for individuals.

References

Ackerman, L. K. (1997). Health problems of refugees. *Journal of the American Board of Family Practice, 10,* 337–348.

Aday, L. A. (2001). *At risk in America: The health and health care needs of vulnerable populations in the United States.* San Francisco, CA: Jossey-Bass.

Ahern, J., Galea, S., Resnick, H., Kilpatrick, D., Bucuvalas, M., Gold, J., & Vlahov, D. (2002). Television images and psychological symptoms after the September 11 terrorist attacks. *Psychiatry, 65*, 289–300.

Airhihenbuwa, C. O. (1995). *Health and culture: Beyond the Western paradigm*. Thousand Oaks, CA: Sage.

Amaro, H. (1995). Love, sex, and power: Considering women's realities in HIV prevention. *American Psychologist, 50*, 437–447.

Anderton, D. L., Anderson, A. B., Oakes, J. M., & Fraser, M. R. (1994). Environmental equity: The demographics of dumping. *Demography, 31*, 229–248.

Arkin, E. B. (1999). Cancer risk communication: What we know. *Journal of the National Cancer Institute Monographs, 25*, 182–185.

Becker, J. A. H. (2005). The intersection of terrorism, interpersonal communication, and health. In H. D. O'Hair, R. Heath, & G. Ledlow (Eds), *Communication preparedness and response to terrorism: Communication and the media* (pp. 47–64). Westport, CT: Praeger.

Brinson, S. L., & Brown, M. H. (1997). The AIDS risk narrative in the 1994 CDC campaign. *Journal of Health Communication, 2*, 101–112.

Bullard, R. D. (Ed.). (1993). *Confronting environmental racism: Voices from the grassroots*. Boston: South End Press.

Cameron, K. A., Witte, K., & Nzyuko, S. (1999). Perceptions of condoms and barriers to condom use along the Trans-Africa Highway in Kenya. In W. N. Elwood (Ed.), *Power in the blood: A handbook on AIDS, politics, and communication* (pp. 149–163). Mahwah, NJ: Lawrence Erlbaum.

Care.org. (2006). World hunger statistics. Retrieved October 25, 2006, from www.care.org.

Connelly, C. (2002, July 28). Doctors working to clear the fog of hormone study. *Washington Post*, pp. A-1, A-10.

Coombs, T. (2005). The terrorist threat: Shifts in crisis-management thinking and planning post-9/11. In H. D. O'Hair, R. Heath, & G. Ledlow (Eds), *Communication preparedness and response to terrorism: Communication and the media* (pp. 211–226). Westport, CT: Praeger.

Covello, V. T., & Allen, F. W. (1988). *Seven cardinal rules of risk communication*. Washington, DC: US Environmental Protection Agency, Office of Policy Analysis.

Crelinsten, R. D. (1994). The impact of television on terrorism and crisis situations: Implications for public policy. *Journal of Contingencies and Crisis Management, 2*(2), 61–72.

Dearing, J. W. (2003). The state of the art and the state of the science of community organizing. In T. L. Thompson, A. M. Dorsey, K. I. Miller, & R. Parrott (Eds), *Handbook of health communication* (pp. 207–220). Mahwah, NJ: Lawrence Erlbaum.

Dearing, J. W., Rogers, E. M., Meyer, G., Casey, M. K., Rao, N., Campo, S., & Henderson, G. M. (1996). Social marketing and diffusion-based strategies for communicating health with unique populations: HIV prevention in San Francisco. *Journal of Health Communication, 1*, 343–363.

Dickson, D. A., Hargie, O., & Morrow, N. C. (1989). *Communication skills training for health professionals*. New York: Chapman & Hall.

Du Pré, A. (2005). *Communicating about health: Current issues and perspectives* (2nd ed.). Boston: McGraw-Hill.

Fisher, W. R. (1985). The narrative paradigm: An elaboration. *Communication Monographs, 52*, 347–367.

Flora, J. L. (1998). Social capital and communities of place. *Rural Sociology, 63*, 481–506.

Ford, L. A., & Yep, G. A. (2003). Working along the margins: Developing community-based strategies for communicating about marginalized groups. In T. L. Thompson, A. M. Dorsey, K. I. Miller, & R. Parrott (Eds), *Handbook of health communication* (pp. 241–261). Mahwah, NJ: Lawrence Erlbaum.

Freimuth, V. S., Hammond, S. L., Edgar, T., & Monahan, J. L. (1990). Reaching those at risk: Content-analytic study of AIDS PSAs. *Communication Research, 17*, 775–791.

Geist-Martin, P., Ray, E. B., & Sharf, B. F. (2003). *Communicating health: Personal, cultural, and political complexities*. Belmont, CA: Wadsworth.

Guttman, N. (2000). *Public health communication interventions: Values and ethical dilemmas*. Thousand Oaks, CA: Sage.

Harwood, J., & Sparks, L. (2003). Social identity and health: An intergroup communication approach to cancer. *Health Communication, 15*, 145–170.

Joint United Nations Program on HIV/AIDS. (July, 2004). 2004 report on the global AIDS epidemic. Retrieved August 28, 2004, from www.unaids.org/.

Jones, A., Kreps, G., & Phillips, G. (1995). *Communicating with your doctor: Getting the most out of health care*. Cresskill, NJ: Hampton Press.

Kamwendo, G., & Kamowa, O. (1999). HIV/AIDS and a return to traditional cultural practices in Malawi. In K. R. Hope, Sr. (Ed.), *AIDS and development in Africa: A* social science perspective (pp. 165–184). New York: Haworth.

Kim, Y., & Grant, D. (1997). Immigration patterns, social support, and adaptation among Korean immigrant women and Korean American women. *Cultural Diversity and Mental Health, 3*, 235–245.

Kreps, G. L., Alibek, K., Bailey, C., Neuhauser, L., Rowan, K. E., & Sparks, L. (2005a). Emergency/risk communication to promote public health and respond to biological threats. In M. Haider (Ed.), *Global public health communication: Challenges, perspectives, and strategies* (pp. 349–362). Sudbury, MA: Jones & Bartlett.

Kreps, G. L., Alibek, K., Bailey, C., Neuhauser, L., Rowan, K. E., & Sparks, L. (2005b). The critical role of communication in preparing for biological threats: Prevention, mobilization, and response. In H. D. O'Hair, R. Heath, & G. Ledlow (Eds), *Community preparedness and response to terrorism: Communication and the media* (pp. 191–210). Westport, CT: Praeger.

Lacy, T. J., & Benedek, D. M. (2003). Terrorism and weapons of mass destruction: Managing the behavioral reaction in primary care. *Southern Medical Journal, 96*, 394–399.

Leiss, W., & Powell, D. H. (2004). *Mad cows and mother's milk: The perils of poor risk communication.* Montreal: McGill-Queen's University Press.

MacGeorge, E. L., Samter, W., Feng, B., Gillihan, S. J., Graves, A. R. (2007). After 9/11: Goals disruption, emotional support, and psychological health in a low exposure sample. *Health Communication, 21*, 11–22.

Nacos, B. L. (2003). Terrorism as breaking news: Attack on America. *Political Science Quarterly, 118*(1), 23.

O'Hair, H. D., & Heath, R. (2005). Conceptualizing communication and terrorism. In H. D. O'Hair, R. L. Heath, & G. R. Ledlow (Eds.), *Community preparedness and response to terrorism: Communication and the media.* Westport, CT: Praeger.

Parrott, R., & Steiner, C. (2003). Lessons learned about pubic health collaborations in the conduct of community-based research. In T. L. Thompson, A. M. Dorsey, K. I. Miller, & R. Parrott (Eds), *Handbook of health communication* (pp. 637–649). Mahwah, NJ: Lawrence Erlbaum.

Rogers, E. M. (1995). *Diffusion of innovations* (4th ed.). New York: Free Press.

Rosenblum, D. (1993). *A time to help, a time to hear: Listening to people with cancer.* New York: Free Press.

Rosenthal, E. (2001, December 30). With ignorance as fuel: AIDS speeds across China. *New York Times*, pp. A1, A8.

Rossouw, J. E., Anderson, G. L., Prentice, R. L., LaCroix, A. Z., Kooperberg, C., Stefanik, M. L., & Jackson, R. D. (2002). Risks and benefits of estrogen plus progestin in healthy postmenopausal women. *Journal of the American Medical Association, 288*(3). Retrieved online in the July 17 issue from www.jama.org.

Roter, D., & Hall, J. (1992). *Doctors talking with patients/patients talking with doctors: Improving communication in medical visits.* Westport, CT: Auburn House.

Rowan, F. (1996). The high stakes of risk communication. *Preventive Medicine, 25*, 26–29.

Rowan, K. E. (2004). *Risk and crisis communication: Earning trust and productive partnering with media and public during emergencies.* Washington, DC: Consortium of Social Science Associations.

Rowan, K. E., Sparks, L., Pecchioni, L., & Villagran, M. (2003). The "CAUSE" model: A research-supported guide for physicians communicating cancer risk. *Health Communication: Special Issue on Cancer Communication, 15*, 239–252.

Rowan, K. E., Kreps, G. L., Botan, C. H., Sparks, L., Samoilenko, S., & Bailey, C. L. (2008). Risk communication, crisis management, and the CAUSE model. In H. D. O'Hair, R. Heath, K. J. Ayotte, & G. Ledlow (Eds), *Terrorism: Communication and rhetorical perspectives.* Cresskill, NJ: Hampton Press.

Scherer, C. W., & Juanillo, N. K., Jr. (2003). The continuing challenge of community health risk management and communication. In. T. L. Thompson, A. M. Dorsey, K. I. Miller, & R. Parrott (Eds), *Handbook of health communication* (pp. 221–239). Mahwah, NJ: Lawrence Erlbaum.

Scholl, J., Williams, D., & Olaniran, B. (2005). Preparing for terrorism: A rationale for the crisis communication center. In H. D. O'Hair, R. Heath, & G. Ledlow (Eds), *Communication preparedness and response to terrorism: Communication and the media* (pp. 243–268). Westport, CT: Praeger.

Seeger, M. W., Vennette, S., Ulmer, R. R., & Sellnow, T. L. (2002). Media use, information seeking and reported needs in post crisis contexts. In B. S. Greenberg (Ed.), *Communication and terrorism* (pp. 53–63), Cresskill, NJ: Hampton Press.

Shrivasta, P. (1987). *Bhopal: Anatomy of a Crisis.* Cambridge, MA: Ballinger.

Siska, M., Jason, J., & Murdoch, P. (1992). Recall of AIDS public service announcements and their impact of ranking AIDS as a national problem. *American Journal of Public Health, 82*, 1029–1032.

Sparks, L. (2005). Social identity and perceptions of terrorist groups: How others see them and how they see themselves. In H. D. O'Hair, R. L. Heath, & G. R. Ledlow (Eds), *Community preparedness and response to terrorism: Communication and the media* (pp. 13–28). Westport, CT: Praeger.

Sparks, L., Kreps, G. L., Botan, C., & Rowan, K. (2005a). Responding to terrorism: Translating communication research into practice. *Communication Research Reports, 22*, 1–5.

Sparks, L., Kreps, G. L., Botan, C., & Rowan, K. (Eds). (2005b). Communication and terrorism [Special issue]. *Communication Research Reports, 22*(1).

Steinfatt, T. M., & Mielke, J. (1999). Communicating danger: The politics of AIDS in the Mekong region. In W. N. Elwood (Eds), *Power in the blood: A handbook on AIDS, politics, and communication* (pp. 385–402). Mahwah, NJ: Lawrence Erlbaum.

Step, M. M., Finucane, M. O., & Horvath, C. W. (2002). Emotional involvement in the attacks. In B. S. Greenberg (Ed), *Communication and terrorism: Public and media responses to 9/11* (pp. 261–274). Cresskill, NJ: Hampton Press.

Tinker, T. L. (1996). Recommendations to improve health risk communication: Lessons learned from the US Public Health Service. *Journal of Health Communication, 1*, 197–217.

Trumbo, C. W., & Rowan, K. E. (Eds). (2000). Global climate change and the public [Special issue]. *Public Understanding of Science, 9*(3).

US Department of State. (2001). Patterns of global terrorism. Retrieved August, 2, 2004, from www.state.gov/.

Wein, S. M., Becker, D. F., McGlashan, T. H., Laub, D., Lazrove, S., Vojvoda, D., & Hyman, L. (1995). Psychiatric consequences of "ethnic cleansing": Clinical assessments and trauma testimonies of newly resettled Bosnian refugees. *American Journal of Psychiatry, 152*, 536–542.

Wenniger, B. G., Limparkarnjanarat, K., Ungchusak, K., Thanprasertuk, S., Choopanya, K., Vanichseni, S., et al. (1991). The epidemiology of HIV infection and AIDS in Thailand. *AIDS, 5* (Supplement 2).

Whitford, F., Feinberg, R., Earl, R., Doering, O., Rowan, K., Neltner, T., & Mysz, A. (2002). Pesticides and risk communication: Interactions and dialogue with the public. In F. Whitford (Ed.), *The complete book of pesticide management: Science, regulation, stewardship, and communication* (pp. 710–748). New York: John Wiley.

World Health Organization (WHO) (2004). Severe Acute Respiratory Syndrome (SARS). Retrieved July 18, 2012, from www.who.int/csr/sars/en/.

Wyshak, G., & Modest, G. A. (1996). Violence, mental health, and substance abuse in patients who are seen in primary care settings. *Archives of Family Medicine, 5*, 441–447.

Chapter 10

Health Campaigns and Community Health Initiatives

"This is your brain on drugs," "Think before you drink," and "Just Say No to Drugs." Think about your favorite TV shows and videos and the powerful health messages and campaigns put forth to get you, the consumer, to think about your health behavior? the less obvious but just as powerful persuasive health messages we see in entertainment media in TV shows such as "Celebrity Rehab," "Scrubs," "House," "Law and Order," "Grey's Anatomy," "Breaking Bad," "Dexter," "90210," "Glee," or even "Modern Family" or "Mad Men"? Think about your favorite TV show, movie, or even one of your iTunes applications (apps) and no doubt at some point in your life you have seen, heard, or read an advertisement, game/application, or storyline attempting to get you to think about and/or change a health behavior. Just like there's an app for anything and everything, there's a health campaign stemming from just about anything and everything you are encountering in your daily life.

Imagine that you are charged with creating and developing a new iPhone app to change one thing in your community. What is one behavior you would you like to change in your university or community or neighborhood? Who would you target? What would you create to bring about that change? How would you do your homework on your target audience? How would your target audience be likely to respond to the app you created? How would they use it? Is the technology already embedded in their lives? Campaigners have a lot to think about when preparing to launch an effective health campaign!

Health campaigns are an essential part of health promotion, or efforts to enhance health and prevent disease on a large scale. Health campaigns can be defined as a systematic effort to change health behaviors (or attitudes and beliefs about health and/ or social and environmental conditions that mediate health behaviors) within a target population of people who are at risk for a health problem or problems (Bennett & Murphy, 1997; Salmon & Atkin, 2003).

Health Communication in the 21st Century, Second Edition. Kevin Bradley Wright, Lisa Sparks, and H. Dan O'Hair.
© 2013 John Wiley & Sons, Inc. Published 2013 by John Wiley & Sons, Inc.

Health campaigns have had a rich history in the US (Paisley, 2001). However, there is a great need to study how to make health campaigns more effective and one way is via an evidence-based approach to health campaigns. Although communication and public health researchers have learned more and more about how to effectively influence health behaviors in the past several decades, there is still much room for improvement. The literature on health campaigns suggests that the majority of campaigns conducted in recent years have had only limited success in changing targeted health behaviors (Kreps, 2001; Snyder, 2001; Snyder & Hamilton, 2002; Valente, 2002; Witte, Cameron, Lapinski, & Nzyuko, 1998). However, in many cases, researchers had unrealistic expectations in early health campaigns as well as poor implementation strategies. The 21st century health campaign is ever evolving, introducing innovative approaches that involve new technologies and target segmented populations utilizing such technologies such as Twitter, YouTube, Facebook, as well as the more traditional channels such as the Internet, TV, radio, and cinema. Nevertheless, changing any type of human behavior can be extremely difficult, and attempting to change health-related behaviors such as eating and exercise habits, alcohol and tobacco use, sexual practices, and compliance with recommended disease screenings can be particularly challenging.

Recall, the National Cancer Institute and the CDC define health communications as:

> The study and use of communication strategies to inform and influence individual and community decisions that enhance health.

Research and evaluation of ongoing health communication programs and related public health communication campaigns have affirmed the value of using specific communication strategies to promote health and prevent disease. Effective strategies combine theories, frameworks, and approaches from behavioral sciences, communication, social marketing, and health education. Increasingly, communication strategies involve mass and interpersonal communication activities both online and offline.

Public health campaigns can take many forms (e.g. written, verbal, and visual combinations, both in person and/or mediated by technologies). Essential to any effective health campaign effort is strategic planning. According to the CDC, strategic communication planning often involves the following steps:

- Identify the health problem and determine whether communication should be part of the intervention.
- Identify the audience for the communication program and determine the best ways to reach them.
- Develop and test communication concepts, messages, and materials with representatives of the target audiences.
- Implement the health communication program based on results of the testing.
- Assess how effectively the messages reached the target audience and modify the communication program if necessary.
- (see National Prevention Information Network, nd).

Large-scale health campaigns often require considerable financial resources in order to pay campaign workers, conduct target audience research, create effective messages, and purchase advertising space in the mass media (although smaller campaigns can sometimes be accomplished for relatively little cost). Government agencies such as the NIH and the CDC, university and medical researchers, and consumer advocacy groups are frequently involved in health campaigns.

Researchers who take a social scientific approach to health promotion draw from many disciplines when designing health campaigns, including public health, psychology, education, medical sociology, strategic business and social marketing, and communication. The communication discipline has played an instrumental role in the development of more effective health campaigns. Because health campaigns involve designing, disseminating, and evaluating messages about health, communication theory provides an evidence-based approach to health campaigns and plays an integral role in the process of conducting an effective and appropriate campaign to target audiences. This chapter explores various levels of the health campaign process. Toward that end, it focuses on campaign goals, theoretical frameworks for campaigns, and the process of designing, implementing, and evaluating a health campaign.

Campaign Goals

Determining what you want to accomplish with a health campaign is an important first step in the process of developing it. These goals also help to determine the *target audience*, or those individuals that campaign designers attempt to influence with the campaign message(s). This section focuses on common goals of two broad types of health campaigns: Health awareness and behavioral change campaigns and public policy campaigns.

Health awareness and behavioral change campaigns

The goal of many health campaigns is to not only raise awareness about a health issue or to change individual health behaviors, attitudes, and beliefs, but to also enact behavioral change. As we have seen in other chapters of this book, many diseases and health problems are linked to lifestyle choices, such as diet and exercise, and to other health problems that can be prevented through early screening efforts. A large number of health campaigns target the behaviors, attitudes, and beliefs that surround these areas. Campaigns dealing with smoking, diet, alcohol consumption, exercise, and sexual behaviors are common examples.

Public policy approaches

Other campaigns attempt to educate people about societal conditions or situations that promote health or healthcare inequities among marginalized groups in an effort to spur new legislation or grassroots efforts to improve healthcare, an area that is often referred to as health disparities in the research literature. For instance, as we have seen, people from certain ethnic groups and income levels are often at greater risk for health problems because of inadequate access to healthcare due to financial reasons or discrimination. Examples of this type of campaign are those that deal with improving social inequities in healthcare or with changing societal or institutional practices that disadvantage certain groups on account of race/ethnicity, economic status, gender, and age.

Theoretical Approaches to Health Campaigns

Prior to discussing the specifics of health campaign design and implementation, it is important to examine theories about how individuals' attitudes and behaviors can be influenced. Health communication researchers have found the theoretical frameworks discussed in this section to be important for understanding why some people are influenced by campaign messages while others are not. In addition, these theories help to provide crucial explanations for the links between cognitive processes, such as knowledge about a health problem and perceptions of health risk, and changes in health behaviors. For a comprehensive review of health communication campaigns and recommended theories and processes see Noar (2006).

Social cognitive theory

Some health campaign researchers have attempted to understand how people learn about health-related issues, how they process health information, and how this information is linked to specific health-related behaviors. *Social cognitive theory* (Bandura, 1977, 1986) assumes that behavior is the outcome of interaction between cognitive processes and environmental events. In other words, health-related behaviors are ultimately the result of a combination of an individual's thought processes and influences from his or her social network and life situation. This section explores these aspects of social cognitive theory.

According to social cognitive theory, a number of cognitive processes, such as expectations, self-efficacy, attitudes, beliefs, and values, influence various health-related behaviors. It is important to remember that these cognitive processes are triggered by stimuli from a person's environment (discussed below). For example, we learn many attitudes about health by listening to our friends and family members as well as from what we see and hear through the mass media.

A person's beliefs and expectations can have considerable influence over his or her behavior. However, human beings vary considerably in their beliefs and expectations. Beliefs can be accurate or inaccurate, and expectations can be realistic or unrealistic. Social cognitive theory posits that behaviors are guided by two sets of expectations: (i) *the expectation that an action will lead to a particular outcome* and (ii) *the expectation a person has about his or her ability to perform this action*. In terms of the first expectation, suppose a male geriatric patient does not believe that engaging in vigorous physical exercise three times a week will reduce his risk for heart disease. Based upon this expectation, it is unlikely that he will follow such a recommendation in a health campaign.

Second, a person's expectation that she is capable of performing an action that will lead to a particular outcome influences whether or not she will ultimately change her behavior. This expectation is influenced by an individual's *self-efficacy*, or the belief in one's ability to exert personal control over a situation (Bandura, 1977). In terms of health behaviors, researchers have found that self-efficacy is an important determinant of health information-seeking practices (Rimal, 2001), health behavior change (Bagozzi & Warshaw, 1990; Schwarzer, 1994), and health maintenance behaviors. Self-efficacy can range from generalized beliefs about one's own ability to perform health-related behaviors (e.g. "I can avoid getting sick most of the time") to beliefs about one's ability to perform very specific health-related behaviors (e.g. "I can remember to get a mammogram once a year"). Health self-efficacy beliefs are often better predictors of behavior than more generalized self-efficacy beliefs. Therefore, it is crucial for health campaign designers to consider the specific health self-efficacy beliefs that members of a target audience have about a course of action when recommending it during a campaign.

Bandura's social cognitive theory or social learning theory has been used extensively for interventions and evaluation efforts. The Stanford 5-Cities project used social cognitive theory to prevent heart disease. Social cognitive theory has also been used in a number of AIDS-prevention projects. The thrust of the theory focuses on perceived self-efficacy.

In short, according to social cognitive theory, a person can believe that certain actions lead to a particular outcome, but this individual may doubt his or her ability to perform the action. According to Bandura (1977), only when efficacy expectations are high will people perform certain behaviors. Efficacy expectations can vary on dimensions of magnitude (level of difficulty of task; people may have different efficacy expectations for simple tasks than for difficult tasks), generality (specific to general), and strength (weak to strong; Bandura, 1977).

For example, if a health campaign designer is interested in reducing the incident rates of HIV infection among high school students by informing them about risk factors for the disease and the use of condoms as a preventive measure, it is possible that self-efficacy beliefs about condom use might be more important in influencing behavior than other beliefs about HIV. A high school student may be aware that unsafe sex can increase the risk of contracting HIV/AIDS, and he may believe that condoms can reduce the risk of HIV/AIDS. However, if this student does not believe that he is capable of using a condom every time he has sex (e.g. due to not being able to plan when opportunities for sexual intercourse might occur), then this belief will most likely be more important than other beliefs in terms of whether or not he ultimately practices safe sex.

Attitudes and values can also influence health behaviors. While social cognitive theory recognizes the influence of attitudes on behaviors, it does not provide a detailed explanation of this relationship. Values can influence health behaviors in a variety of ways. For example, when exposed to messages designed to change health-related behaviors, individuals make value judgements about outcomes related to the proposed behavioral changes. Good health is generally a long-term value for most people. However, long-term health values often compete with many short-term values, such as pleasure, excitement, and wanting to "fit in" with others. These short-term values may cause people to lose sight of long-term health values. For example, while most people do not want to be obese or suffer from weight-related problems such as diabetes or heart disease in the future, short-term values such as the pleasure that comes from eating rich foods or the convenience of unhealthy fast food may override the long-term value of being healthy.

Human beings learn how to behave in various life contexts by observing and modeling the behavior of others, typically family members, peers, and what we see and hear through the mass media. Behaviors are also associated with social norms or rules for following behavior. People tend to be rewarded or punished socially for adhering to (or ignoring) these rules in social situations. Social rewards may take the form of approval and inclusion, and punishments may involve anger, disapproval, and exclusion from social circles. In general, individuals typically behave in ways that maximize rewards and minimize costs. For example, if a teenager wants to fit in with her peers (who are perceived as having a high social status due to the social rewards and punishments they can provide), and smoking cigarettes is important to the peer group, then these sources of information about how to behave may be more likely to influence her behaviors than lower-status sources (e.g. a teacher or younger sibling).

Theory of reasoned action

The theory of reasoned action (Ajzen & Fishbein, 1980) states that the primary predictor of a behavior is an intention to engage in that behavior. This theory posits that *behavioral intentions* can be predicted by two parallel cognitive processes: (i) a person's attitude toward the behavior under consideration and (ii) his or her appraisal of relevant social norms. An individual's attitudes about a behavior (i.e. evaluation of the behavior as positive, negative, or neutral) are influenced by his or her beliefs about the behavior. For example, if you believe that eating a low carbohydrate diet is an effective way to lose weight, then it is likely that you will have a more positive attitude about someone suggesting a "low carb" item on a restaurant menu than someone who does not believe that this type of diet is effective.

In addition, the theory of reasoned action takes into account social norms, such as the approval of friends and family members, surrounding the behavior under consideration. While a woman may have a positive attitude toward the idea of eating better and exercising more in an effort to lose weight, her husband may enjoy sedentary or unhealthy activities such as watching television or eating fried foods. If the husband sees his wife's interest in eating more healthily and exercising as an attempt to get him to change his behaviors, he may be unsupportive of her engaging in a diet and exercise program. Depending upon the husband's approval or disapproval of his wife's proposed lifestyle changes and the wife's motivation to comply with her husband's wishes, this may outweigh the positive attitude the wife has about dieting and exercise and ultimately influence her behavioral intentions.

The theory of reasoned action also takes into account an individual's resources, skills, self-efficacy, opportunities, and ability to engage in the proposed behavior. Some of these factors may be internal (e.g. skills) or external to the person (e.g. opportunities to change behavior), and they can either inhibit or facilitate a person's perceived control over the proposed behavior (Ajzen & Fishbein, 1980). According to the theory, all of these factors need to be considered when predicting a person's intentions to perform a behavior. Health campaign designers often assess these variables when analyzing a target audience in order to get a better idea of what might lead a person to ultimately engage in a health-related behavior. However, although behavioral intentions are often predictive of actual behaviors, there is no guarantee that behavioral intentions will ultimately lead to behavioral changes.

The health belief model (Becker, 1974) focuses on individuals' perceived threat of illness and their behavioral response to that threat. When confronted with information about a disease or illness, people generally assess their perceived susceptibility to the threat and attempt to gauge the severity of the threat were it to affect them. In addition, individuals assess threats to their health vis-à-vis the costs and benefits of changing their behaviors and make appraisals of their environment and resources when making decisions about how to avoid or manage the threat. Each of these factors combines in unique ways to influence decision-making about health issues, depending upon the health issue and the target audience.

For example, a campaign designed to promote preventive screenings for prostate cancer among men between the ages of 45 and 60 would need to take a number of issues into consideration. In terms of perceived threat, a target audience member would assess how likely he would be to develop prostate cancer. Younger audience members may perceive that prostate cancer is an "older man's disease," and they may not see it as particularly threatening despite the fact that early detection of risk factors (such as an enlarged prostate or high prostate-specific antigen (PSA) levels) can prevent prostate cancer. In terms of perceptions of severity, target audience members may or may not assess the symptoms of prostate cancer to be severe. Many people perceive prostate cancer as a more manageable type of cancer than other types (e.g. pancreatic cancer or breast cancer), even though prostate cancer has a high morbidity rate compared to other cancers in the US. In terms of behavioral responses to the threat, perceptions such as whether or not a person believes that screenings can prevent prostate cancer, perceptions of the prostate exam as an unpleasant experience, and assessments of the costs versus the benefits of taking the time to have a prostate exam may motivate or hinder a person from getting screened for prostate cancer. Resources, such as access to adequate healthcare, and environmental influences, such as the support of family or peers in terms of getting the exam, also might factor into a person's decision to participate in a preventive screening for the disease.

An important contribution of this theory is the concept of *cues to action*, or message features that prompt individuals to pay attention to the content of messages (Murray-Johnson & Witte, 2003). According to Murray-Johnson and Witte (2003), cues to action are important in triggering an individual's motivation to make assessments of his or her available resources when acting on campaign messages. In order to effectively motivate target audience members to change health behaviors, campaign designers need to incorporate cues to action within campaign messages. In addition, Murray-Johnson and Witte state that cues to action can be *internal*, meaning that they emerge from within the individual, such as if a person starts an exercise program because of feeling bloated or unenergetic from living a sedentary lifestyle, or they can be *external*, such as pressure from peer group members to exercise or celebrity testimonials on television about the positive effects of an exercise program (e.g. an advertisement saying, "Oprah Winfrey lost 25 pounds using our aerobics video"). Identifying appropriate internal and external cues to action for a target audience can be a challenging aspect of campaign design, but it can be accomplished through careful audience analysis (discussed later in this chapter).

Extended parallel process model

Witte's (1992) *extended parallel process model* examines fear appeals as a motivation for health behavior change. Undoubtedly you have been exposed to a health campaign that attempted to use fear to get you to think about HIV/AIDS, the dangers of drug use, or other risky practices (e.g. not wearing a seatbelt or drunk driving). According to Murray-Johnson and Witte (2003), motivation is central to how a message is processed and acted upon, and fear has been used as a prominent motivating force in a variety of health-related campaigns because it is a common human emotion. According to the extended parallel process model, individuals exposed to a fear message engage in two sets of parallel cognitive processing (see Figure 10.1). First, *danger control* refers to the appraisal of a threat and how it should be dealt with. Second, *fear control* involves an assessment of how to cope with the emotional reaction to a threat. Similar to other theories we have examined, individuals' self-efficacy and appraisals of their

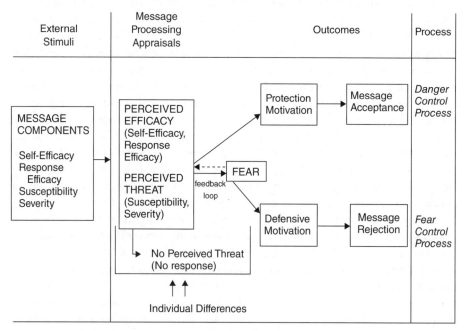

Figure 10.1   Extended parallel processing model.
Source: Witte, 1992.

resources and environment play an important role in the process of thinking about how to cope with a threatening situation. Emotional responses to fear often involve increased anxiety and physiological responses, such as increased heart rate and perspiration. Both sets of processing lead to a behavioral response to the threat. Fear appeals are defined as persuasive messages that attempt to frighten an audience into implementing a recommended response and are used frequently by politicians, advertisers, etc. Fear appeal research is used in studying effective risk messages often focusing on health, physical, or social risks. For example, after the terrorist attacks on September 11, 2001 and the deaths resulting from anthrax mailed to various people in the following months, many Americans became concerned about the threat of bioterrorism. In terms of danger control, some people, particularly those living in big cities, saw bioterrorism as a large threat whereas many people in rural parts of the US felt it was less of a threat. Some people decided to deal with these threats by purchasing gas masks and other supplies that would be helpful in case of a bioterrorist act, while others did not see this threat as problematic enough to change their behaviors. These events also create a strong emotional impact. Some people attempted to control their emotional response to this threat through activities such as diversion (e.g. spending more time with family or engaging in pleasant activities), while others tried to reduce their fear by learning how to better prepare for such an attack in the future.

In terms of health campaigns, fear appeals need to be used with some degree of caution. Too much fear can lead to such intense emotional reactions that people become too preoccupied with their fear to think rationally about steps they can take to avoid the threat (Dillard & Peck, 2000; Dillard *et al.*, 1996; Stephenson & Witte, 2001). For example, a HIV/AIDS campaign that emphasizes death might produce such strong emotional reactions that individuals avoid thinking about the issue as a fear control response. This may prevent them from also thinking about ways in which they can reduce their susceptibility to the disease. Murray-Johnson and Witte (2003) advocate using high fear appeals only in cases where target audience members possess response efficacy, or the perceived ability to easily perform the recommended response behaviors promoted in the campaign. In addition, high fear appeals should be avoided with audiences who are already fearful of a threat since it can lead them to think less about the threat as a coping mechanism. In other cases the use of moderate fear appeals may be more appropriate to an audience (Hale & Dillard, 1995; Stephenson & Witte, 2001). Careful target audience analysis is needed to assess which type of fear appeal may be most effective for a specific population.

Stages of change models

Some researchers have developed theories of behavior change that take into account various stages of readiness that individuals pass through over time toward behavior change (Lippke & Ziegelmann, 2006; Prochaska & DiClemente, 1984; Schwarzer, 1992). The advantage of this approach is that it assumes people may be in different stages when it comes to changing their health behaviors. A prominent stage theory is the *transtheoretical model* (Prochaska & DiClemente, 1984), which describes five stages of behavioral change: precontemplation, contemplation, preparation, action, and maintenance/relapse. The HIV/AIDS pandemic is a helpful issue to illustrate this particular model, and examples from this crisis will be used to help explain it.

In the *precontemplation stage*, individuals are unaware of a health issue and subsequently do not think about making a behavioral change. For example, in the early 1980s many Americans were unaware of the looming threat of HIV/AIDS because it was not being widely discussed in the mass media, and consequently, most people did not consider changing their sexual behaviors. In the *contemplation stage*, people are aware of a health issue but may still be weighing the pros and cons of adopting some type of behavioral change. Once stories about HIV/AIDS and its relationship to safe sex gained prominence in the mid- to late 1980s, many people began to examine their own sexual behaviors. However, many heterosexual people still questioned whether they were really at risk for the disease since HIV/AIDS was first seen within the gay community and among intravenous drug users. Even though people were thinking about the disease, many people continued to practice unsafe sex. In the *preparation stage*, individuals actively begin planning to change their behavior. As more and more reports of heterosexual people and non-intravenous drug users began to surface in the media, many Americans felt they were ready to begin practicing safe sex. In the *action stage*, behavioral change actually occurs, such as when people started using condoms when having sex. Finally, the *maintenance/relapse* stage refers to whether people stick with their behavior change or relapse into one of the previous stages. Since the 1980s many people have continued to practice safe sex in an effort to prevent the spread of HIV/AIDS.

Lippke and Ziegelmann (2006) have proposed the multi-stage model of health behavior change (MSM), which extends the number of stages in the transtheoretical model (see Figure 10.2). Lippke and Ziegelmann distinguish between nonintentional inactive stages (precontemplation and contemplation) and the intentional (but still inactive) stages by adding the *disposition* stage, in which individuals implement certain goals for behavioral change, and the *preaction* stage, where people detail their plans for action. In addition, these researchers take into account the degree to which people

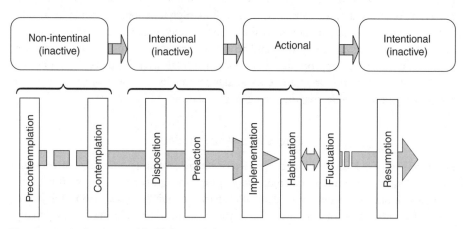

Figure 10.2   Multi-stage model of behavioral change.
Source: Lippke & Ziegelmann, 2006.

stick to their behavioral changes (habituation), fluctuate, and resume behavioral changes following the decision to take action. When using stages of change models to plan a health campaign, campaign designers need to assess the various stages at which individuals within a target population may be in regarding the campaign health issue. For example, different types of messages need to be constructed for people in the precontemplative stage versus the maintenance/relapse stage. For people who are in the precontemplative stage, campaign messages should be directed toward raising awareness of the health issue and influencing perceptions of susceptibility to it. By contrast, audience members who are in the maintenance/relapse stage should be encouraged through campaign messages to continue engaging in preventive behaviors and warned against the threat of relapse.

The SOC model is useful to campaign designers for several reasons. First, individuals in different stages exhibit distinct behavioral characteristics. Thus, researchers can effectively analyze and segment a target audience according to their different stages of change. Then, practitioners can strategically design messages to move individuals through the stages. For example, if campaigners wish to design a campaign to promote a new service, and they determine that the majority of the members of the target population are in the contemplation stage, they can design messages to systematically move audience members through the preparation, action, and maintenance stages. Similarly, if the majority of the target audience is in the maintenance stage, educators can provide messages, which reinforce and support the desired behavior. This model has been empirically tested with numerous health topics, including cancer prevention behaviors, smoking cessation, sunscreen use, addictive behaviors, pregnancy prevention, and risky sexual behaviors.

Diffusion of innovations

Rogers' (2003) diffusion of innovations theory targets adoption of health innovations (i.e. an idea, behavior, technology, etc.) by defining characteristics of innovations that impact an individual's decision to reject or adopt the innovation or behavior. If the health campaign is recommending the audience to adopt a new diet or getting a H1N1 flu shot, the message campaign would do well to incorporate what we have learned about the diffusion of innovations process. Specifically a health campaign must consider the following innovation attributes:

1. Relative advantage: the health innovation must be perceived as an improvement to the previous idea.
2. Compatibility: the health innovation must be consistent and assimilated into an individual's life.
3. Complexity or simplicity: the health innovation must be simple to use or people will not adopt it.
4. Trialability: a health campaign must be able to be experimented with as it is being considered for adoption.
5. Observability: the extent that an innovation is visible to others will help with adoption.

The Process of Conducting a Health Campaign

As we have seen, changing attitudes and beliefs about health and health-related behaviors can be extremely complex. Designing appropriate and effective messages that can lead to these goals in a health campaign requires a great deal of thought and planning. As we will discuss in more detail later in this chapter, the persuasion process greatly impacts what we should do in a health communication campaign. The first step in this process is to recognize that persuasion is a somewhat puzzling and often random process. However, for a message to be effective, a considerable number of events, thoughts, and behaviors must occur. For instance, the individual must be:

1. Exposed to the message: the audience member must be exposed to the public service announcement.
2. Attend to the message: the audience member must be in a position to notice the message.
3. Comprehend the message: the audience member must be able to understand the message.
4. Retain the message: the audience member must be able to recall the message.

Obviously message failure at any point along these instances can result in failed behavioral outcomes. Therefore, a message campaign or a message strategy must be sure to address these issues. This section further explores some of the key steps and considerations when conducting a health campaign.

Audience analysis

As with any attempt to inform or persuade a large group of people, health campaigns require a careful analysis of target audience characteristics. Having a thorough understanding of audience characteristics such as demographics, attitudes and beliefs, current behaviors, and reasons for current behaviors allows health campaign designers to appropriately segment audiences into smaller groups in order to produce messages that are appropriate to the characteristics of these subgroups within a target audience. As we will see, the greater the extent to which messages can be tailored to the characteristics of audience members, the more likely they will be to successfully influence attitudes, beliefs, and behaviors.

Conducting audience analysis research Once a health campaign designer has decided upon a target audience for the campaign, he or she needs to conduct an *audience analysis*, or an assessment of a variety of characteristics of the audience members that are related to the campaign health issue, in order to gain a better understanding of how to influence them (Atkin & Freimuth, 2001). Analyzing a target audience typically requires research method skills, and while this topic is beyond the scope of this book, this section provides an overview of common ways in which campaign designers conduct target audience research. When conducting an audience analysis, campaign designers attempt to understand audience characteristics in a systematic way. The most common types of research methods for audience analysis are using available data, surveys, and interviews and focus groups. Each of these research methods is discussed below.

Using available data In many cases information about target audience members already exists in the form of databases (Atkin & Freimuth, 2001). For instance, hospitals keep patient records, local and state governments compile health-related statistics about their regions, organizations keep employee records, and the federal government has databases about health-related variables through information provided on the US Census and through research efforts by organizations such as the CDC and the NIH. These databases allow campaign designers to examine characteristics of some target audiences without having to conduct primary research themselves. They can thus save campaign designers a great deal of time and money, since both are required to carry out interviews, focus groups, and surveys. However, these databases rarely contain all of the target audience characteristics that may be of interest to campaign designers. In addition, information gained from some databases can be dated (e.g. US Census data), and the information may no longer apply to the current target audience.

Surveys Surveys are useful for collecting new information about a relatively large target audience through the use of questionnaires. Audience analysis surveys typically ask a variety of questions about audience demographics (e.g. age, gender, ethnicity, income), current health-related behaviors, attitudes and beliefs about health, efficacies and skills, and a variety of other questions that may help the campaign designer to better understand what will meet audience members' health needs and motivate them toward achieving the campaign goals (Atkin & Freimuth, 2001). Survey researchers rarely disseminate questionnaires to an entire target population because most populations are either too large or difficult to reach. Instead, audience researchers conduct surveys using a *sample* of individuals who are representative of the larger population, and they make inferences about the larger population based upon the findings from the sample.

A key aspect of samples is that they should be *representative* of the larger target population as much as possible. One way to be more confident about how representative a sample is of a population is to use a *probability sample*. *Sampling* is the process of obtaining a sample for a survey, and *probability sampling* involves randomly selecting participants for a sample from a *sample frame*, or list of population members. Each population member is given a number, and researchers use random number tables or random numbers generated by a computer to select certain numbers (and subsequently people) into the sample. It can be very difficult to find a sampling frame for many larger populations.

In many cases probability sampling is too difficult to accomplish, and researchers have to engage in *nonprobability sampling*, such as convenience samples (e.g. finding anyone who is willing to participate in the survey). When using a nonprobability sample, campaign designers need to be careful when segmenting the target audience based upon sample data results. However, in these cases, using a nonprobability sample is better than not conducting an audience analysis at all.

Interviews and focus groups. Interviews and focus groups are excellent methods for gaining a thorough understanding of target audiences' perceptions of a health issue and their health-related needs (Slater, 1995). Interviews and focus groups involve talking to a sample of target audience members and asking them various questions about their thought processes and behaviors relating to the campaign health issue. Interviews involve talking to individual audience members, whereas focus groups are group interviews with typically eight to ten people. When conducting interviews with individuals or within focus groups, it is important to try to make participants feel relaxed. The researcher should obtain informed consent, or permission from the participants after they have been informed about the purposes and potential risks of the study, prior to starting an interview or focus group. Focus groups should occur in comfortable surroundings, and the facilitator of the focus group should be skilled at getting people to express their opinions.

One advantage of focus groups over interviews is that one person's responses during a focus group can remind another participant of similar experiences or feelings with a health issue, and this can add to the richness of the data by allowing researchers to obtain multiple viewpoints on the subject. However, some individuals are more apprehensive about speaking up in a focus group compared to a one-on-one interview because they may feel that others in the group will judge them if they express a viewpoint. In addition, some individuals in groups tend to dominate the discussion, and this may take time away from other participants who are more reticent. Focus group facilitators should attempt to intervene in such situations and try to get all members of the group to talk if possible.

In addition, the researcher should ask participants' permission to tape record or videotape the interview or focus group. This will provide a record of the participant responses for data analysis. Videotape offers researchers the advantage of being able to assess nonverbal cues from participants that can give insights into how people feel about certain topics being discussed. Videotaping can be even more valuable for recording interactions during focus groups because it is often difficult to distinguish one participant from another on an audiotape. However, the researcher should protect the anonymity of all participants by using pseudonyms during the interview or focus group and when transcribing content from audio and videotape recordings, and the tapes should be stored in a locked facility so that people other than the researcher and his or her associates cannot access them.

Audience segmentation

Audience segmentation is the process of dividing the larger target audience population into smaller subgroups of individuals based upon some meaningful criteria (Rimal & Adkins, 2003; Slater, 1995), usually the demographic, psychological, and behavioral characteristics that were assessed during the audience analysis. Because people often differ considerably on these characteristics, it is difficult to design campaign messages that will influence an entire target population. Thus, the purpose of audience segmentation is to help maximize the impact of campaign messages. Generic health campaign messages (messages that apply to the majority of the population) tend to have limited impact on target audiences (Atkin & Freimuth, 2001), but more specific messages (i.e. messages tailored to unique characteristics of subgroups of the target population) tend to be much more effective in influencing attitudes, beliefs, and behaviors (Rimal & Adkins, 2003).

For example, communication researchers at the University of Kentucky have had a great deal of success segmenting audiences based on a psychological variable known as sensation seeking (Everett & Palmgreen, 1995; Palmgreen & Donohew, 2003; Palmgreen, Donohew, & Harrington, 2001). High sensation seekers are individuals who enjoy taking risks as well as vivid, exciting, and novel experiences, for example, people who like to bungee jump, sample exotic foods, and those who "like to live dangerously." In contrast, low sensation seekers tend to prefer mundane, everyday types of experiences, and they often feel more comfortable "playing it safe." According to Palmgreen, Donohew, & Harrington (2001), "high sensation seekers (HSSs) also have distinct and consistent preferences for particular kinds of messages based on their needs for the novel, the unusual, and the intense" (p. 301). For example, high sensation seekers like messages that are fast-paced and exciting, use close-up shots and music, and advertisements that employ rapid cutting. Using the SENTAR approach (a campaign approach based upon sensation-seeking tendencies), Palmgreen and associates have been successful in designing antidrug messages that appeal to high sensation seekers (who tend to be at high risk for drug abuse, risky sexual practices, and other negative health-related behaviors) and that have led to reductions in self-reported drug use.

Of course, sensation seeking is just one of many variables that can be used to segment target audiences. Other variables that can be used include (i) demographics (e.g. sex, race, socioeconomic status); (ii) psychological variables (e.g. health beliefs, psychological tendencies, attitudes, values); and (iii) health-related skills. Audience analysis and health-related theories play a crucial role in determining key variables that can be used to segment subgroups of target audiences. Segmentation helps campaign designers to maximize the potential of a campaign to influence positive health outcomes and to gain a careful understanding of important variables that can be used to improve the impact of future health campaigns.

Creating message content

Much of what appears in the specific content of messages during a health campaign is influenced by the characteristics of the target audience and the health issue itself. However, there are variables and considerations common to message content design in most campaigns that campaign designers should be familiar with. According to Salmon and Atkin (2003), "campaigns utilize three general communication processes to move a target audience toward a desired response: awareness, instruction, and persuasion" (p. 455). This section explores these aspects of message design and other important message content features, including gaining audience members' attention, variables associated with motivating audience members to action, and variables associated with the perceived personal and social resources for changing attitudes, beliefs, and behaviors among target audience members.

Gaining audience members' attention and motivating them to action Health campaign message designers have to compete with many other types of messages in society, including advertisements, news, and entertainment (Murray-Johnson & Witte, 2003; Parrott, 1995; Salmon, 1989). Through the use of theoretical models of changing health-related cognitions and behaviors and a careful audience analysis, campaign designers can often identify key variables that have a high probability of motivating their target audience. Drawing on the health belief model, Murray-Johnson and Witte (2003) argue that campaign messages should contain cues to action, or message features that prompt individuals to pay attention to the content of messages. Recall from earlier in the chapter that cues to action are needed to trigger motivation, and they can be developed from sources internal to audience members, such as guilt or fear, or external sources, such as using credible spokespersons (e.g. the Surgeon General) to motivate change. During the audience analysis, campaign designers can assess the *salience* of certain types of messages, or the perceived importance of messages to audience members. Variables such as the perceived severity of a health threat, perceived susceptibility, and attitudes, beliefs, values, and perceived resources surrounding a health issue all influence the salience of messages.

Vividness, repetition, and how messages are placed in the media are also important factors in message design (Murray-Johnson & Witte, 2003). *Vivid messages*, such as messages that contain more exciting, colorful, or detailed images and/or audio cues, may motivate change because they are more memorable than less vivid messages. In addition, campaign messages that are novel or unexpected tend to motivate audience member involvement (Parrott, 1995). *Repetition of messages* can also stimulate motivation, and campaign designers should consider repeating key messages several times within campaign materials. Ideal placement of campaign messages should also be assessed during campaigns. Campaign designers can assess how target audience members respond to messages that vary in terms of vividness and repetition during the audience analysis phase of the campaign. *Placement* deals with where target audience members are most likely to see the message, and assessing ideal placement during the audience analysis phase helps campaign designers decide which media are best suited for disseminating the campaign messages.

Persuasive message appeals There are a number of issues that campaign designers need to consider when constructing persuasive appeals for a health campaign. Individuals vary considerably in terms of the types of messages that influence their cognitions and behaviors.

Some individuals are influenced by messages emphasizing *credibility*, or the extent to which message content is believed to be accurate, and it is typically conveyed by the trustworthiness and competence of the person delivering the campaign message and through convincing evidence for a persuasive argument (Salmon & Atkin, 2003). According to Salmon and Atkin (2003), the *campaign messenger*, or the person who provides information and testimonials or demonstrates appropriate behaviors during a health campaign, is crucial in enhancing the message's credibility. Salmon and Atkin contend that when selecting a campaign messenger, he or she will be more credible and attractive (and subsequently more persuasive) to a target audience if he or she exhibits expertise, trustworthiness, familiarity, interpersonal attractiveness, and similarity to the target audience.

The messenger can be any person capable of conveying these characteristics to the target audience and does not necessarily need to be a celebrity, although for certain target audiences a celebrity such as Magic Johnson speaking about HIV/AIDS might embody these characteristics. Celebrity messengers can sometimes produce negative effects for a campaign, especially when stories emerge within popular media about their lifestyles or other controversial information that can undermine the campaign message. However, physicians, specialists, cancer survivors, and many other types of individuals may be good candidates for a campaign messenger. In addition to the campaign messenger, the credibility of a campaign can be enhanced by using evidence for cognitive and/or behavioral change that comes from credible sources, such as studies from established scientific journals (e.g. *Journal of the American Medical Association*) or trusted government sources (e.g. the CDC).

Other audiences are influenced by *logical appeals*, or persuasive messages that provide logical and convincing evidence for change, while others are influenced by *emotional appeals*, such as messages that emphasize strong emotions such as fear. Some researchers have found that messages that influence positive emotions in health campaigns, such as positive imagery and mood, tend to increase attention to messages, recall, positive attitudes, and compliance to recommended behaviors (Monahan, 1995). Less is known about other types of positive affect strategies in health campaigns, such as the use of humor. However, it appears that positive affect appeals tend to reduce psychological reactance, or the tendency of people to disregard messages that they find threatening or offensive.

When constructing campaign messages using these appeals, designers again need to consider many characteristics of the target audience that are found to be relevant during formative research and audience analysis procedures. For example, highly educated audiences may be more persuaded than less educated audiences by statistics or certain types of logical argument. For more educated audiences, *two-sided persuasive messages*, or messages that contain and refute counterarguments for the proposed behavioral change, may be more influential than one-sided messages (Salmon & Atkin, 2003). Depending upon the audience, emphasizing positive (e.g. health benefits) and/or negative (e.g. symptoms of a disease) incentives for change may be equally effective. One approach that draws upon presenting multiple arguments within a health campaign message is *inoculation theory* (McGuire, 1970; Pfau, 1995). Essentially, inoculation involves presenting audience members with weak arguments that are contrary to the goals of the campaign (e.g. reasons for drinking in an anti-drinking campaign) along with information that refutes these arguments. When these types of efforts are successful, target audience members are said to be inoculated to the influence of messages that run counter to the goals of the campaign. For example, a college student who has been exposed to a variety of arguments against binge drinking may be more likely to resist attempts by peers to engage in such behaviors.

In recent years, health communication scholars and health practitioners have utilized *prospect theory* by using message framing as a way to understand the communication involved in risky decisions (see, e.g. Kahneman & Tversky, 1979, 2000; Sparks,

2012; Sparks & Turner, 2008; Tversky & Kahneman, 1981). The landmark essays of Amos Tversky and Daniel Kahneman resulted in prospect theory, which suggests that individuals will react differently to information presented as gains or losses. People encode information relevant to choice options in terms of potential gains or potential losses. Thus, factually equivalent information can be presented to people differently so that they encode it as either a gain or a loss (framing). A framing effect is demonstrated by constructing two transparently equivalent versions of a given problem, which nevertheless yield predictably different choices. The standard example of a framing problem, which was developed quite early, is the "lives saved, lives lost" question, which offers a choice between two public health programs proposed to deal with an epidemic that is threatening 600 lives: one program will save 200 lives, the other has a 1/3 chance of saving all 600 lives and a 2/3 chance of saving none. In this version, people prefer the program that will save 200 lives for sure. In the second version, one program will result in 400 deaths, the other has a 2/3 chance of 600 deaths and a 1/3 chance of no deaths. In this formulation most people prefer the gamble. Of course, these formulations present identical situations. The only difference is that in the first formulation the problem is framed in terms of lives saved, and in the second the situation is framed as a matter of lives lost. Thus, the message frame that a decision-maker adopts is controlled partly by the *formulation of the problem* and partly by the norms, habits, and personal characteristics of the decision-maker (Tversky & Kahneman, 1981, p. 453). Nearly all health-related information can be construed in terms of either gains (benefits) or losses (costs). For example, a gain-framed message would say that obtaining a mammogram allows tumors to be detected early, which maximizes treatment options. In contrast, the same message framed as a loss would say that if you do not obtain a mammogram, tumors cannot be detected early, which minimizes your treatment options. Thus, which frame works better?

The answer depends on whether the target health behavior is an illness detection behavior or an illness protection behavior (Rothman & Salovey, 1997). Detection behaviors (e.g. prostate exam) involve uncertainty—that is, you may find a problem! Protection behaviors (e.g. using sunscreen) typically lead to relatively certain outcomes—that is, you maintain your current healthy status.

The message-framing component of prospect theory has been utilized in health risk studies dealing with the uncertainty and risks involved in disease detection (Sparks, 2012). Prospect theory predicts that loss-framed information leads to preference for uncertainty, whereas gain-framed information leads to preference for certainty. Research findings indicate that loss-framed messages were effective in promoting mammography, breast self-examinations, and HIV testing. Gain-framed messages were effective in promoting infant car restraints, physical exercise, smoking cessation, and sunscreen.

Other message considerations Snyder and Hamilton (2002) examined the impact of several message characteristics in a wide variety of health-related campaigns. These researchers found that for some types of campaigns, especially health-related issues that have legal ramifications, such as driving under the influence, abuse of controlled substances like Oxycontin, and seat belt usage, *enforcement messages*, or messages that emphasize negative repercussions (e.g. fines, arrests) to target audience members as a result of not following laws, may be effective in motivating behavioral change. Snyder and Hamilton found that campaigns using enforcement messages influenced target audience members more than campaigns that did not include these types of messages. In addition, campaigns using messages that give audiences *new reasons to change* their behavior (e.g. new information about the importance of getting a mammogram) were more influential in terms of behavioral change than campaigns that relied on older information about a health topic.

Channels and message dissemination processes

One important consideration in designing a health campaign is the type of channel that will be used to disseminate the campaign message(s). Traditionally, health campaign designers have relied on traditional mass media when delivering campaign messages, such as television, radio, and print material (Atkin, 2001). In recent years researchers have started to investigate the efficacy of new media for disseminating health campaign messages, such as cell phones and the Internet. This section examines a number of different channel characteristics that have important implications for health campaign design.

Targeting is the process of selecting the best communication channel for disseminating a message (Rimal & Adkins, 2003). Again using information from the audience analysis, campaign designers need to make decisions about which channel or channels are appropriate for reaching and influencing the target audience. For example, campaign designers need to consider where target audience members are most likely to see campaign messages, the type of media they use, the ability of a channel to support specific types of messages, audience literacy levels, and the potential impact of various channels.

Some target audiences may be more likely to see television or radio messages, while other audiences are more likely to be exposed to a message when it comes to them through billboards, Internet advertisements, or interpersonal channels (e.g. peer group members). Among low literacy audiences, radio and television campaigns may be more influential than printed materials because radio and television can transcend the written word through audio messages and/or images that convey a message without words. Snyder and Hamilton (2002) found that campaigns with greater *reach*, or a higher percentage of people being exposed to the campaign message, were more influential in changing target audience behaviors than campaigns with a more limited reach. Messages on television and radio tend to have greater reach than messages disseminated through other channels. However, television and radio messages are typically more generic than printed materials or messages delivered in person (which are less expensive to produce and can be changed more easily for different segments of the target audience).

As we have seen, tailored messages tend to have greater impact than generic messages in campaigns. This aspect has to do with *specification*, or the ability of a channel to influence certain subgroups within the population (Atkin, 2001). In addition, using channels such as the Internet or a dialogue between a community spokesperson and target audience members in a face-to-face meeting invites greater audience participation and involvement than radio or television advertisements. All of these features of channels, as well as the cost and efficiency of the channel, need to be assessed by campaign designers (Salmon & Atkin, 2003).

However, researchers have recently been paying more attention to multi-pronged approaches to health campaigns. These advocate an interpersonal theory-based approach to changing health behaviors when it is appropriate and possible to implement (Rogers, 2003; Sparks, 2012), particularly with specialized populations that do not use mediated sources, such as older adults and those from cultural and socioeconomic backgrounds with little access to technologies (Sparks & McPherson, 2007; Sparks & Turner, 2008). Health behavior and health communication scholars study messages and interventions that encourage patients to be active participants in health communication contexts. In addition to designing mediated health messages, researchers are also focusing on effective interpersonal message strategies that will prove effective given the unique complexities and barriers patients and their family members often face (see, e.g. Sparks, 2007). Researchers can no longer ignore the unique cognitive and emotional processes different populations often experience. Interpersonal messages are more likely to reach such specific populations, one patient and one family at a time (Sparks, 2007, 2008).

As we have seen, while it is always possible to create a more generalized or generic message that will be communicated to an audience, generalized messages often lack the impact of more specific messages. Traditionally, health campaign materials have been generic, and the creators of campaign messages have attempted to provide as much information as possible within a single communication without considering the specific characteristics of an audience (Kreuter & Wray, 2003; Kreuter, Farrell, Olevitch, & Brennan, 2000; Strecher, Rimer, & Monaco, 1989). However, *tailored* health messages, or messages designed to influence specific subgroups of a target audience based on individual member characteristics (Rimal & Adkins, 2003), tend to be more effective than generic messages in influencing cognitive and behavioral changes in target audiences (Davis *et al.*, 1992; Kreuter, Oswald, Bull & Clark, 2000; Rimal & Adkins, 2003; Rosen, 2000; Sparks & Turner, 2008).

According to Salmon and Atkin (2003), "a typical health campaign might subdivide the population on a dozen dimensions (e.g. age, ethnicity, stage of change, susceptibility, self-efficacy, values, personality characteristics, and social context), each with multiple levels" (p. 453). In many cases, while it is possible to segment target audiences into literally thousands of subgroups, the majority of health campaigns create substantially fewer groups, due to financial and logistical constraints. Yet, even segmenting audiences into relatively few small subgroups can increase the precision of messages over generic messages.

It is now possible to create *personalized* messages in a health campaign through the use of computer programs (Kreuter, Farrell *et al.*, 2000) that use algorithms to match the characteristics of *each* individual in a target audience to a specific, individually tailored message. However, this method can increase the complexity and cost of a campaign. In addition, according to Schooler, Chaffee, Flora, and Roser (1998), there is always a tradeoff between the specificity of a health message and its reach. In other words, generic messages tend to have greater reach than tailored messages, which means that because the message is more generalized it can appeal to greater numbers of individuals who are exposed to it than tailored messages. Tailored messages, on the other hand, provide more specific information, but they may have limited reach because they are so specialized.

Atkin (2001) pinpoints a variety of other channel considerations when designing health campaigns. These include *accessibility* of the channel for the target audience (e.g. some individuals may have limited access to the Internet), *depth*, or the ability of the channel to convey complex information, *economy*, or the cost of using a particular channel, and *efficiency*, or the amount and quality of information a channel can deliver vis-à-vis the cost of using it. As you can see, there are many decisions a health campaign designer needs to make regarding the most appropriate and useful channel for the target audience.

Formative Campaign Evaluation

As we have seen, the process of creating a health campaign can be complex, especially when dealing with certain health issues and hard-to-influence audiences, and this may lead to many things that can potentially go wrong with a campaign. Larger campaigns can be quite expensive given the amount of time that is needed to analyze the audience, the cost of creating campaign materials, and the cost of using different media. Therefore, it is important for campaign designers to take measures to minimize possible campaign shortcomings. One way to identify and potentially minimize problems prior to launching a campaign is to engage in formative campaign evaluation (Atkin & Freimuth, 2001; Valente, 2002). Formative campaign evaluation research refers to the activities conducted prior to the start of a campaign. Valente (2002) outlines the objectives and the specific research activities that are important during the formative evaluation stage. Objectives in this stage include (i) understanding the target audience's barriers to action; (ii) learning the appropriate language to develop messages; and (iii) developing a conceptual model. Specifically, focus group discussions and/or in-depth interviews are conducted to determine knowledge, attitudes, and behaviors of the target population. This is particularly important prior to message development because evaluation data are useful in identifying target audience characteristics and predispositions, specifying intermediate response variables and behavioral outcomes, assessing channel exposure patterns, and determining receptivity to potential message components (Atkin & Marshall, 1996).

There are many ways that health campaigns can be evaluated, including some of the research methods that are mentioned in the section on audience analysis procedures in this chapter. Available data, interviews, focus groups, and surveys can all be used to assess the degree to which campaign goals were met, although these methods are not without limitations.

Pilot testing

By using a sample of the target population, campaign designers can gauge what aspects of the campaign work and do not work with a group of people who are similar to the larger population. When obtaining feedback about the campaign from the pilot sample, campaign designers should measure the degree to which the campaign messages led to cognitive and/or behavioral changes in the group, and potential problems with the campaign, such as determining whether messages were noticed, salient, or understandable to the audience, reasons why some people may not have been influenced by the messages, and the appropriateness of the spokesperson, medium, and message content.

Launching the campaign, process evaluation, and outcome evaluation

After making additional adjustments to campaign messages following formative evaluation and pilot testing, campaign designers are then ready to launch the campaign. The length of a health campaign will largely depend upon the goals of the campaign, such as if the campaign is targeting awareness about a health issue or behavioral outcomes related to it, the budget and resources available to the campaign designers, and other pragmatic issues, such as the amount of time that campaign designers can devote to it.

Determining whether or not a campaign is successful can be assessed by conducting outcome evaluation research. However, the question of why a campaign was or was not successful requires process evaluation research. Evaluation is widely understood to be conducted as a set of stages that require the systematic application of research procedures to assess the conceptualization, design, implementation, and utility of intervention programs (Rossi & Freeman, 1993; Shadish, Cook, & Leviton, 1991; Valente, 2002). Health campaign planners and researchers can rely on program evaluation strategies for assessment and improvement to inform future campaigns. In addition, evaluations serve as a means by which campaign planners and funding agencies can determine the effectiveness of a health campaign's promotion activities or treatments. Process evaluations tend to be easier to design and conduct when the campaign approach is derived from a strong theoretical framework. According to Valente (2002), "theory specifies how these factors relate to one another by constructing a conceptual model of the process of behavioral change" (p. 30). Ideally, campaign designers should integrate formative, process, and outcome evaluations into the campaign design (see Figure 10.3).

However, there are a number of pragmatic barriers to conducting campaign evaluations within everyday types of health campaigns. For example, conducting additional research within a campaign for the purposes of evaluation can be costly and time consuming. In addition, some campaign planners believe that evaluation activities detract attention away from the actual campaign. While these barriers are certainly understandable from a practical standpoint, thorough process and outcome evaluations within campaigns help researchers gain a better understanding of whether or not a certain campaign approach works and why.

Figure 10.3 Integrative social marketing research model.
Source: Weinreich, 2010.

Measuring behavioral changes within a target audience can take much more time than assessing awareness of the campaign messages. Campaign evaluators need to be aware of problems such as the *sleeper effect*, or when behavioral change due to being exposed to a campaign message occurs slowly. In some cases change may not occur for several months after a campaign, so it is often difficult for evaluators to find the optimal time to engage in an assessment of target audience change. When measuring awareness, campaign evaluators should ask for specific examples of what people saw, read, or heard about the campaign health issue during the period of the campaign, and what they remember about the issue. Of course, memory problems, leading questions by campaign evaluators in interviews or surveys, and other methodological issues can potentially create biases in terms of understanding actual awareness change.

Summary

Designing, implementing, and evaluating the effectiveness of a health campaign is a complex process, and campaign designers have to make numerous decisions that can ultimately lead to the success or failure of the campaign. Clear and realistic goals for a campaign are an important first step. Researchers have developed a number of theories about how to influence health attitudes, beliefs, and behaviors, and campaign designers can draw upon these theories when developing a campaign. After conducting a thorough audience analysis, campaign designers have numerous decisions to make about message design and message dissemination. Finally, campaigns should be pilot tested prior to implementation to assess any potential problems, and campaign designers need to conduct an evaluation of campaign processes and outcomes so that this information can be used to inform future campaigns.

References

Ajzen, I., & Fishbein, M. (1980). *Understanding attitudes and predicting social behavior*. Englewood Cliffs, NJ: Prentice-Hall.

Atkin, C. (2001). Theory and principles of media health campaigns. In R. E. Rice & C. K. Atkin (Eds), *Public communication campaigns* (3rd ed., pp. 49–68). Thousand Oaks, CA: Sage.

Atkin, C., & Freimuth, V. S. (2001). Formative evaluation research in campaign design. In R. E. Rice & C. K. Atkin (Eds), *Public communication campaigns* (3rd ed., pp. 125–145). Thousand Oaks, CA: Sage.

Atkin, C., & Marshall, A. (1996). Health communication. In W. Stacks & M. B. Salwen (Eds), *An integrated approach to communication theory and research* (pp. 479–495). Newbury Park, CA: Sage.

Bagozzi, R. P., & Warshaw, P. R. (1990). Trying to consume. *Journal of Consumer Research, 17,* 127–140.

Bandura, A. (1977). Self-efficacy: Toward a unifying theory of behavioral change. *Psychological Review, 84,* 191–215.

Bandura, A. (1986). *Social foundations of thought and action: A social cognitive theory*. Englewood Cliffs, NJ: Prentice-Hall.

Becker, M. H. (1974). The health belief model and personal health behavior. *Health Education Monographs, 2,* 324–508.

Bennett, P., & Murphy, S. (1997). *Psychology and health promotion*. Buckingham: Open University Press.

Davis, S. W., Cummings, K. M., Rimer, B. K., Sciandra, R., & Stone, J. C. (1992). The impact of tailored self-help smoking cessation guides on young mothers. *Health Education Quarterly, 19,* 495–504.

Dillard, J. P., & Peck, E. (2000). Affect and persuasion: Emotional responses to public service announcements. *Communication Research, 27,* 461–495.

Dillard, J. P., Plotnick, C. A., Godbold, L. C., Freimuth, V. S., & Edgar, T. (1996). The multiple affective outcomes of AIDS PSAs: Fear appeals do more than scare people. *Communication Research, 23,* 44–72.

Everett, M. W., & Palmgreen, P. (1995). Influences of sensation seeking, message sensation value, and program context on effectiveness of anticocaine public service announcements. *Health Communication, 7,* 225–248.

Hale, J., & Dillard, J. (1995). Fear appeals in health promotion: Too much, too little, or just right? In E. Maibach & R. Parrott (Eds), *Designing health messages: Approaches from communication theory and public health practice* (pp. 65–80). Newbury Park, CA: Sage.

Kahneman, D., & Tversky, A. (1979). "Prospect theory": An analysis of decision under risk. *Econometrica, 47,* 263–291.

Kahneman, D., & Tversky, A. (2000). *Choices, values, and frames*. Cambridge: Cambridge University Press.

Kreps, G. L. (2001). The evolution and advancement of health communication inquiry. In W. B. Gudykunst (Ed.), *Communication yearbook 24* (pp. 232–254). Newbury Park, CA: Sage.

Kreuter, M., & Wray, R. (2003). Tailored and targeted health communication: Strategies for enhancing information relevance. *American Journal of Health Behavior, 27* (Supplement 3), S227–S232.

Kreuter, M., Farrell, D., Olevitch, L., & Brennan, L. (2000). *Tailoring health messages: Customizing communication with computer technology.* Mahwah, NJ: Lawrence Erlbaum.

Kreuter, M., Oswald, D. L., Bull, F. C., & Clark, E. M. (2000). Are tailored health education materials always more effective than non-tailored materials? *Health Education Research, 15,* 305–315.

Lippke, S., & Ziegelmann, J. P. (2006). Understanding and modeling health behavior: The multi-stage model of health behavior change. *Journal of Health Psychology, 11,* 37–50.

McGuire, W. J. (1970, February). A vaccine for brainwash. *Psychology Today, 3,* 36–39, 63–64.

Monahan, J. (1995). Thinking positively: Using positive affect when designing health messages. In E. Maibach & R. L. Parrott (Eds), *Designing health messages: Approaches from communication theory and public health practice* (pp. 81–98). Thousand Oaks, CA: Sage.

Murray-Johnson, L., & Witte, K. (2003). Looking toward the future: Health message design strategies. In T. L. Thompson, A. M. Dorsey, K. I. Miller, & R. Parrott (Eds), *Handbook of health communication* (pp. 473–495). Mahwah, NJ: Lawrence Erlbaum.

National Prevention Information Network. (nd). Health communication strategies. Retrieved July 23, 2012, from http://cdcnpin.org/scripts/campaign/strategy.asp.

Noar, S. (2006). A 10-year retrospective of research in health mass media campaigns: Where do we go from here? *Journal of Health Communication, 11,* 21–42.

Paisley, W. J. (2001). Public communication campaigns: The American experience. In R. E. Rice & C. K. Atkin (Eds), *Public communication campaigns* (3rd ed., pp. 3–21). Thousand Oaks, CA: Sage.

Palmgreen, P., & Donohew, L. (2003). Effective mass media strategies for drug abuse prevention campaigns. In Z. Slobada & W. J. Bukoski (Eds), *Handbook of drug abuse prevention: Theory, science, and practice* (pp. 27–43). New York: Plenum.

Palmgreen, P., Donohew, L., & Harrington, N. G. (2001). Sensation seeking in antidrug campaign and message design. In R. E. Rice & C. K. Atkin (Eds), *Public communication campaigns* (3rd ed., pp. 300–304). Thousand Oaks, CA: Sage.

Parrott, R. L. (1995). Motivation to attend to health messages: Presentation of content and linguistic considerations. In E. Maibach & R. L. Parrott (Eds), *Designing health messages: Approaches from communication theory and public health practice* (pp. 7–23). Thousand Oaks, CA: Sage.

Pfau, M. (1995). Designing messages for behavioral inoculation. In E. Maibach & R. L. Parrott (Eds), *Designing health messages: Approaches from communication theory and public health practice* (pp. 99–113). Thousand Oaks, CA: Sage.

Prochaska, J. O., & DiClemente, C. C. (1984). *The transtheoretical approach: Crossing the traditional boundaries of therapy.* Homewood, IL: Dow Jones/Irvin.

Rimal, R. N. (2001). Perceived risk and self-efficacy as motivators: Understanding individuals' long-term use of health information. *Journal of Communication, 51,* 633–654.

Rimal, R. N., & Adkins, A. D. (2003). Using computers to narrowcast health messages: The role of audience segmentation, targeting, and tailoring in health promotion. In T. L. Thompson, A. M. Dorsey, K. I. Miller, & R. Parrott (Eds), *Handbook of health communication* (pp. 497–513). Mahwah, NJ: Lawrence Erlbaum.

Rogers, E. V. (2003). *Diffusion of innovations* (5th ed.). New York: Free Press.

Rosen, C. S. (2000). Intergrating stage and continuum models to explain processing of exercise messages and exercise initiation among sedentary college students. *Health Psychology, 19,* 172–180.

Rossi, P. H., & Freeman, H. E. (1993). *Evaluation: A systematic approach.* Newbury Park, CA: Sage.

Rothman, A. J., & Salovey, P. (1997). Shaping perceptions to motivate healthy behavior: The role of message framing. *Psychological Bulletin, 12,* 3–19.

Salmon, C. (1989). Campaigns for social "improvement": An overview of values, rationales, and impacts. In C. Salmon (Ed.), *Information campaigns: Balancing social values and social change.* Newbury Park, CA: Sage.

Salmon, C., & Atkin, C. (2003). Using media campaigns for health promotion. In T. L. Thompson, A. M. Dorsey, K. I. Miller, & R. Parrott (Eds), *Handbook of health communication* (pp. 449–472). Mahwah, NJ: Lawrence Erlbaum.

Schooler, C., Chaffee, S. H., Flora, J. A., & Roser, C. (1998). Health campaign channels: Tradeoffs among reach, specificity, and impact. *Human Communication Research, 24,* 410–432.

Schwarzer, R. (1992). Self-efficacy in the adoption and maintenance of health behaviors: Theoretical approaches and a new model. In R. Schwarzer (Ed.), *Self-efficacy: Thought control of action* (pp. 217–243). Washington, DC: Hemisphere.

Schwarzer, R. (1994). Optimism, vulnerability, and self-beliefs as health-related cognitions: A systematic overview. *Psychology and Health, 9,* 161–180.

Shadish, W. R., Cook, T. D., & Leviton, L. C. (1991). *Foundations of program evaluation: Theories and practice.* Newbury Park, CA: Sage.

Slater, M. D. (1995). Choosing audience segmentation strategies and methods for health communication. In E. Maibach & R. L. Parrott (Eds), *Designing health messages: Approaches from communication theory and public health practice* (pp. 186–198). Thousand Oaks, CA: Sage.

Snyder, L. B. (2001). How effective are mediated health campaigns? In R. E. Rice & C. K. Atkin (Eds), *Public communication campaigns* (3rd ed., pp. 181–190). Thousand Oaks, CA: Sage.

Snyder, L. B., & Hamilton, M. A. (2002). A meta-analysis of US health campaign effects on behavior: Emphasizing enforcement, exposure, and new information, and beware the secular trend. In R. C. Hornik (Ed.), *Public health communication: Evidence for behavior change* (pp. 357–383). Mahwah, NJ: Lawrence Erlbaum.

Sparks, L. (2012). Health communication and caregiving research, policy, and practice: A health literacy approach to reducing health disparities. *Reducing health disparities: Communication interventions.* New York and Berlin: Peter Lang.

Sparks, L. (2008). Family decision-making. In W. Donsbach (Ed.) *The international encyclopedia of communication, 4,* (pp. 1729–1733). Oxford, UK and Malden, MA: Wiley-Blackwell.

Sparks, L. (2007). Cancer care and the aging patient: Complexities of age-related communication barriers. In H. D. O'Hair, G. L. Kreps & L. Sparks (Eds), *Handbook of communication and cancer care* (pp. 233–249). Cresskill, NJ: Hampton Press.

Sparks, L., & McPherson, J. (2007). Cross-cultural differences in choices of health information by older cancer patients and their family caregivers. In K. B. Wright & S. D. Moore (Eds), *Applied health communication* (pp. 179–205). Cresskill, NJ: Hampton Press.

Sparks, L., & Turner, M. M. (2008). Cognitive and emotional processing of cancer messages and information seeking with older adults. In L. Sparks, H. D. O'Hair, & G. L. Kreps (Eds), *Cancer communication and aging* (pp. 17–45). Cresskill, NJ: Hampton Press.

Stephenson, M. T., & Witte, K. (2001). Creating fear in a risky world. In R. E. Rice & C. K. Atkin (Eds), *Public communication campaigns* (3rd ed., pp. 88–102). Thousand Oaks, CA: Sage.

Strecher, V. J., Rimer, B. K., & Monaco, K. D. (1989). Development of a new self-help guide: Freedom from smoking for you and your family. *Health Education Quarterly, 16,* 101–112.

Tversky, A., & Kahneman, D. (1980). Causal schemata in judgments under uncertainty. In M. Fishbein (Ed.), *Progress in social psychology* (pp. 49–72). Hillsdale, NJ: Lawrence Erlbaum.

Tversky, A., & Kahneman, D. (1981). The framing of decisions and the psychology of choice. *Science, 211,* 453–458.

Valente, T. W. (2002). *Evaluating health promotion programs.* New York: Oxford University Press.

Witte, K. (1992). Putting fear back into fear appeals: The extended parallel process model. *Communication Monographs, 59,* 329–349.

Witte, K., Cameron, K. A., Lapinski, M. K., & Nzyuko, S. (1998). A theoretically based evaluation of HIV/AIDS prevention campaigns along the Trans-Africa Highway in Kenya. *Journal of Health Communication, 3,* 345–363.

Chapter 11

Interdisciplinary Healthcare Teams

Depictions of healthcare teams in movies and television shows dramatize many of the key elements involved in case management regardless of success or failure. Invariably, team-based communication is at the root of the situation. You may have noticed that you can often accomplish more with a group of people when you are working on a project than when you work on it by yourself. For example, in one of your classes, a professor may have required you to participate in a group assignment, such as a research paper or presentation. Many students like group assignments because they can share the workload and each group member can concentrate on a specific part of the assignment. This allows them to research different facets of a topic in much greater detail than if it were an individual assignment. As you may have experienced, sometimes a group effort such as this can lead to a better-quality assignment when each group member contributes a substantial amount. However, when some group members do not pull their weight, if group members do not recognize the contributions of others, or if members do not understand a part of the assignment that another member focused on, then problems can occur that may lead to an unsatisfactory outcome. Group assignments such as these can give you an idea of what it is like to be a member of an interdisciplinary healthcare team. While there are many types of groups and teams within healthcare organizations, this chapter focuses on interdisciplinary teams, or what we will eventually term synergistic teams, or sometimes known as team science (or the collaborative and cross-disciplinary pursuit of solving healthcare problems (Bennett, Gadlin, & Levine-Finley, 2010).

Diversity of Healthcare Professionals

Healthcare has become increasingly complex due to the specialized nature of the various disciplines that are part of the delivery system. As each discipline advances its

Health Communication in the 21st Century, Second Edition. Kevin Bradley Wright, Lisa Sparks, and H. Dan O'Hair.

art of caring based on increasingly evidence-based science, new opportunities for improved care are possible. Concomitant with the advancement in these disciplines is a renewed pride in itself that each discipline thinks is intrinsic to the care of patients. The increase in specialties creates a larger number of roles and players in the equation of care delivery. Examine just a *sampling* of healthcare disciplines represented in the following list.

administrators
clergy
dentists
families
health educators
interpreters
mental health providers
nutritionists
occupational therapists
patient care assistants
pharmacists
physical therapists
physician assistants
physicians
psychologists
registered nurses
social workers
vocational nurses

With specialization comes the challenge of coordinating and managing the multiple roles that professionals deliver to the context. Team science or team-based processes have emerged as solutions for ensuring that all parties contributing to the care of the patient act in a nonduplicative, error-free manner.

Importance of Interdisciplinary Teams

Interdisciplinary teamwork has become central to modern healthcare organizations (Hall *et al.*, 2008), largely because of the growing belief within such organizations that no one person or discipline can have expertise in all the areas of specialty knowledge needed for the high-quality care of clients with complex conditions. According to Coopman (2001), "the very nature of health care is bringing providers from numerous disciplines together to address health care problems" (p. 262).

Interdisciplinary health teams capitalize on provider diversity within a healthcare organization by drawing together the unique perspectives of providers from a range of health-related disciplines. The perspective of each team member is influenced by the culture of the health-related discipline in which he or she was trained, and this often leads to very different perceptions about a patient and his or her health situation.

Members of a team can often work more effectively with others rather than separately, and interdisciplinary teams can often draw upon the collective strength of team members' unique experiences and diverse perspectives on a health problem. Not all healthcare teams are interdisciplinary, but are rather a collection of individuals from different disciplines. In order for a healthcare team to be truly interdisciplinary, each team member must have some training in or some understanding of the other disciplines of other team members (Hall *et al.*, 2008; Poole & Real, 2003). In other words, quality team members and effective team communication are important to the success of interdisciplinary teams, and just bringing people together from different disciplines does not necessarily guarantee successful outcomes for the patient (Rees, Edmunds, & Huby, 2005).

Interdisciplinary collaboration and teamwork offer a number of advantages in addressing the complexities of patient care, especially among patients with chronic multiple health problems (Hall *et al.*, 2008). For example, diverse interdisciplinary teams can target a patient's physical, psychosocial, and in some cases spiritual concerns with the goal of providing more comprehensive care. Targeting the multiple health issues and concerns of patients may lead to better outcomes than any single course of treatment, although successful outcomes are also influenced by the expertise of team members and the quality of group interaction (Poole & Real, 2003). There are many other reasons that favor effective teamwork over individual action or poorly executed teamwork, including a reduction in mortality due to fewer medical errors (Bleakley *et al.*, 2006; Catchpole, Mishra, Handa, & McCulloch, 2008). Teams also contribute to overall better care (Cooke, 1997), improved management of patient care (McHugh *et al.*, 1996), help to reduce the length of hospitalizations (Wieland, Kramer, Waite, & Rubenstein 1996), and encourage prevention of illness (Mills, Neily & Dunn, 2008). Teams also have a tendency to involve patients more in their own care, creating greater empowerment on the part of the care receiver (Grant & Finocchio, 1995). From a healthcare profession's perspective, teams create greater learning opportunities (Edwards & Smith, 1998) and foster greater job satisfaction for the team members involved (Gage, 1998).

Just as team members must be ideally suited to address one or more of a patient's problems, the team should be able to work together well and have realistic goals for team meetings in order for it to be successful. Decision-making is central to interdisciplinary healthcare teams, and effective communication plays a crucial role in the decision-making process (Apker, Propp, & Ford, 2009; Lefley, 1998). Team members often require training in group communication and decision-making skills, especially since these skills are not always taught within the curriculum of some healthcare disciplines. Greater equality in decision-making during team meetings often leads to better patient care (Apker, Propp, & Ford, 2009; Kirkmann-Liff, 1999). In other words, when each team member has the opportunity to participate equally in making decisions about the patient, then the diversity of team member viewpoints often leads to better decisions. However, other factors, such as the type and severity of the patient's health problems, available treatments, and organizational issues (e.g. managed care), also play an important part in the success of the team. In addition, interdisciplinary healthcare team members often vary in terms of their degree of involvement with the team. Some members are core members (usually a physician and a nurse), while other providers may be peripheral members, attending meetings only when necessary.

Determined and sustained efforts toward effective teamwork are unlikely to occur on their own. Fragmented, sporadic, and uncoordinated actions by diverse healthcare professionals are an inherent part of the status quo. Team-based medical care requires not only effort but training as well. That is why a number of policy and regulatory bodies (the Institute of Medicine, PEW Health Professions Commission, the Joint Commission on Accreditation of Healthcare Organizations) have recommended or stipulated systematic training in team-based, interdisciplinary collaborative practices (Bokhour, 2006; Ladden, Bednash, Stevens, & Moore, 2006). A primary goal of this chapter is to propose a model that facilitates team-based communication for healthcare professionals.

Continuum of Healthcare Teams

Multiple models of healthcare teams have been designed and used in healthcare organizations for decades. A typical model is one where a healthcare professional, usually a physician, makes all decisions about patient care and communicates those decisions in a top-down communication mode (giving orders and directives to nurses, pharmacists, etc.). A completely opposite perspective is one in which all members of the healthcare context come together in a shared decision-making team where communication is multilateral, uninhibited, and interactive. These very different models of patient care can be placed on opposite sides of a continuum to better understand the various communication options during healthcare delivery. Based on previous research (Ellingson, 2003; Grant & Finocchio, 1995; Hall *et al.*, 2008; Jones, 1997; Wieland *et al.*, 1996), we can construct a continuum that allows us to understand the motives and operations of healthcare professionals as they come together to deliver care (see Figure 11.1).

At the extreme left of the continuum is the model we mentioned above that views healthcare delivery from a *unidimensional* perspective. Physicians make decisions, tell others what their roles and duties are, and expect orders to be carried out without exception. As a more traditional model of care, this is often observed in physicians' offices where other members of the team are direct employees of the team leader (physician). Communication is often one-way and any sharing of decision-making is operationalized by the physician asking questions about conditions, lab results, or medication protocols.

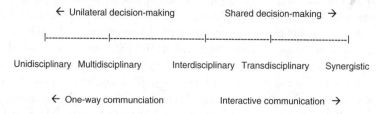

Figure 11.1   Continuum of healthcare teams.
Source: Based on research from Ellingson, 2003; Grant & Finocchio, 1995; Jones, 1997; Pike, 1991; Wieland *et al.*, 1996.

A *multidisciplinary* approach to healthcare takes into consideration the expertise and experience of several healthcare professionals with an understanding that multiple viewpoints are possible. With this model it is still very likely that one individual, again usually a physician, makes most of the decisions and communicates her desires to other members of the team. Unlike the unidisciplinary model where the physician assumes an omnipotent role, input from other team members is likely to occur with some regularity. The extent to which the physician acts on such information and acknowledges it as a valuable contribution still remains her prerogative.

A third option is the popular *interdisciplinary* team model. Occupying the middle part of the continuum, the interdisciplinary team approach stresses the importance of each team member's contribution and strives to develop coordination and harmony among the diverse members of the team. The notion of coming together for the good of the patient is an important one to the interdisciplinary team, although ensuring the implementation of multiple approaches to care based on different medical disciplines can be challenging, if not problematic, with this approach. In some instances such teams find themselves in competition for the medical plan designed for the patient. Elements of negotiation and emergent leadership are observed. Ultimately, if the team experiences indecisiveness, a physician or charge nurse will intervene to make a unilateral decision on behalf of the patient.

Transdisciplinary teams are different from interdisciplinary teams in that they adopt more of an amalgamation model, where medical care emphasizes not so much the delivery of nursing, medicine, therapy, or other healthcare professional discipline as a blended approach that identifies the needs of the patient from a consultative and problem-solving perspective. Interdisciplinary teams evolve into transdisciplinary forms when team members develop trust among their colleagues and begin to share authority, responsibility, and expertise with other members (Wieland *et al.*, 1996). In essence, the interdisciplinary effort becomes transformed into an integrated team working for the good of the patient rather than insisting on strict disciplinary influence. Clearly, effective and responsive communication is a key determinant for moving healthcare professionals into this transformative state.

At the other end of the continuum is the *synergistic* team. Like the transdisciplinary team that assumes a shared decision profile, this team model makes every effort to ensure that decisions not only involve the participation of all members of the team but that they are patient-centered. A synergistic team approach is not a common model for healthcare organizations, yet it offers the greatest opportunity for patient health and safety (Lee, 2010). In the next section we explore what a synergistic team is like and how it can succeed in highly complex healthcare organizations.

Model of Synergistic Healthcare Teams

Synergistic healthcare teams offer the greatest potential for improving patient outcomes and elevating organizational and system efficiency (Farr & Ames, 2008). Synergistic healthcare teams have three essential elements: (i) *instilling a sense of ownership*; (ii) *becoming performance based*; and (iii) *developing team synergy*. Marginalizing any

Figure 11.2   Model of synergistic healthcare teams.

one of these elements will limit the effectiveness of the team effort (see Figure 11.2). Let us look at each of these elements in turn.

Instilling a sense of ownership

Rosabeth Moss Kanter suggests in her book *Evolve!* (2001) that effective teams distinguish themselves from ineffectual ones through a feeling for and commitment to the greater good. Effective teams are those that take on a sense of ownership for the things they do, the decisions they make, and the ways that they feel. Medical teams are often under enormous pressure and find intrinsic fulfillment from personal accomplishments in delivering care. Personal achievement is critical to building confidence in oneself. However, the key to building effective, synergistic teams is inculcating a sense that what one does is part of a greater purpose that integrates personal goals into the good of the team and the patient. Accomplishing three goals instills this sense of team ownership: building and maintaining trust, building commitment to team and mission, and realizing a sense of accomplishment.

Building and maintaining trust Drawing together a collection of healthcare professionals does not ensure a sense of devotion to the team or the care it delivers. This is especially true when team members hail from diverse backgrounds, groups, and locations (Rees, Edmunds, & Huby, 2005). Having confidence in each member of the team is a challenging but necessary component of synergy. *Trust* is a key ingredient in developing ownership of the team (Smith & Cole, 2008). Trust comes in multiple forms. Trust in the group is the hope, belief, and confidence of team members that what is said and done in the group is both meaningful and appropriate. Team members expect that their efforts count for something. Trust in team colleagues comes from a history of communication that is open, sincere, and consistent. Team members trust those who are willing to say what they mean, have something valuable to say, and understand that what is said is honest and forthright. Team communication must ensure high levels of trust throughout the team process.

Trust can also be facilitated by:

- demonstrating that you do what you say and mean what you say;
- acting consistently;
- a willingness to listen to others and defer to their judgement;
- sharing information and asking for help;
- avoiding favoritism;
- disclosing personal things about self;
- acknowledging others' skills and talents (Kinlaw, 1991).

From these processes comes a greater sense of mutual respect for one another that promotes trust in teams, a key ingredient in acting on the patient's behalf in the absence of direct evidence. Teams must understand one another and develop mutual respect (O'Brien, Martin, Heyworth & Meyer, 2009). For example, if a charge nurse on a midnight shift reads a patient chart indicating the removal of oxygen therapy after two hours, she must have trust in the respiratory therapist in order to comply if her experience tells her to leave the oxygen in place.

Building commitment to team and mission (vision) It is entirely possible that team members trust one another and still lack a strong commitment to the team and mission of the healthcare organization. Teams that exist primarily for social reasons are a good example of this phenomenon. To instill ownership in a healthcare team, *commitment* to the team and mission must also be present. Commitment is a state that reflects team members' willingness to care personally for the team and its members and to maintain a dogged determination to help the team succeed. This type of commitment is developed primarily through explicit clarification of the vision and mission entrusted to the team (O'Hair & Wiemann, 2012). Communication skills must include persuasive efforts to convince team members of the importance of the mission and vision, and providing feedback about how their efforts are making a difference within the larger organization. From this communication, team members come to assume a greater sense of identity with the team which can often become the focal point of their behaviors. Commitment can additionally be demonstrated by:

- caring personally about the team and its success;
- loyalty to the team, its members, and their mission;
- remaining focused on the team's mission and goals of patient care;
- maintaining high intensity levels for the team's efforts;
- demonstrating to others positive attitudes about the patient, organization, and healthcare in general;
- asking for commitment from other members of the healthcare team;
- taking pride in being part of the well-being of the patient (Kinlaw, 1991).

Once in place, commitment becomes easier to maintain because it is self-perpetuating through the sharing of common goals and a sense of needing one another to ensure positive health outcomes.

Sense of accomplishment Healthcare professionals choose their profession for a multitude of reasons, but seeking a sense of accomplishment is an important goal. The feeling of contributing to the well-being of patients is more than a cliché. It is a sensation that rewards and motivates team members to assume ownership of the healthcare team. Not unlike sports teams who reach beyond normal expectations, healthcare teams take great pride in their accomplishments, whether large or small. It should be noted that team members can experience satisfaction with their own individual efforts as a team excels. It is that type of self-efficacy that causes healthcare professionals to seek additional experiences. However, experiencing a sense of team accomplishment can transcend even personal triumph precisely for the reasons teams exist—accomplishing more than individuals can. Taking ownership of team accomplishment feeds on itself and becomes a symbiotic experience for all involved Zismer, 2011). Inculcating a sense of accomplishment in team members can be achieved through:

- identifying and celebrating positive patient outcomes;
- demonstrating how the team is improving the healthcare organization;
- recognizing individual achievement within the context of team success;
- collective responsibility—holding the entire team accountable for its level of success.

It is through these levels of accomplishment that team members are able to address lingering uncertainties facing them during stressful times and understand that the team stands ready to offer encouragement and facilitation when the occasion arises.

Becoming performance based

Effective healthcare teams are those with an understanding that their performance counts and will be measured and rewarded accordingly. Not all rewards come in tangible ways, and teams do not necessarily anticipate that to be the case. However, what teams should expect is that their performance contributes to patient care and can be measured according to some acceptable standard (Zismer, 2011). Three key factors are essential to instilling a performance-based team-building structure in healthcare organizations: prioritizing and setting goals, measuring results, and instilling strong decision-making procedures.

Prioritizing and setting goals A first rule of thumb for basing a team's effort on its performance is through a process of goal setting. Teams must be allowed to take their charge from the office, clinic, or hospital and then prioritize and develop goals that are tangible, meaningful, and performance based. Some hospitals institute team-based structures to facilitate the collective management of patient care. Some of these contexts are more successful than others in developing the types of goals and the needed support to accomplish these goals. Besides setting the benchmark for success, goal setting/prioritization serves to focus team members' efforts on specific patient or organizational objectives, gives them a sense of direction, and helps them persist in their labors. One of the greatest concerns of hospitals, clinics, and long-term care facilities is patient safety. A mantra in healthcare, especially the facilities in which patients are cared for, is that they should do no harm to patients. Unfortunately, thousands of patients die each year in healthcare settings due to medical errors, poor safety practices, and ineffective coordination of patient care. For that reason healthcare organizations ask their teams to include patient safety in their goals for overall patient care.

Research has demonstrated that performance is enhanced when goals are specific, exciting, lofty, and prioritized (O'Hair, Friedrich, & Dixon, 2011). It is also important for teams to develop goals that allow some acceptable level of flexibility in their implementation and measurement, allowing for contingencies. Other strategies to keep in mind, according to O'Hair, Friedrich, & Dixon (2011), include the following:

- Goals should be problem based, not value based. Values are important, especially ethical values, but they must be practical and relevant and should explicitly state how they can be incorporated into immediate patient care.
- Teams should set performance standards. How will the team know that it succeeded? Is length of hospital stay a good criterion? Is the control of pain a preeminent concern over a persistent physical therapy routine? Teams have to come to terms with diverse patient priorities.
- Resources needed to accomplish goals (time, space, funds, etc.) should be identified. Generally, healthcare organizations are not going to volunteer resources without some driving impetus. Teams have to be ready to make credible requests for resources in order to accomplish their goals.
- Teams will always need to recognize contingencies as they arise. Patients in critical care units will require adaptive plans for their care. Do all members of the team

understand and interpret the goals and plans for the patient in a way where adjustments can be made with immediate notice?

Measuring results Teams have a professional obligation to monitor and report their progress. Teams are in constant need of valid and consistent information flows to effectively manage patient care (Demiris, Washington, Oliver, & Wittenberg-Lyles, 2008). Here we are not focusing on patient progress per se. That is accomplished through discharge reports and review committees. Instead, members must gauge their own performance as a team and how the activities of the team have contributed to positive outcomes. Therefore, teams must systematically assess their goals. It should be left up to the team how their results are measured, so long as they are accountable to the organization and the mission and vision of the team (Lee, 2010). Unfortunately, this is not always promoted in some healthcare organizations. Regardless, measurement or assessment techniques will vary according to the goals prioritized by the team, but should certainly include many of the standard criteria used for assessing performance. The key issue is that team members understand and appreciate the fact that their efforts are being measured on a systematic basis. The following guidelines are important:

- Results should be understood and accepted by the team.
- Results should be measured against the goals set by the team. Should goals be revised?
- Results should be compared to the mission of the organization.
- Results could be compared against other teams in the organization.
- How does the team feel about the results? Does it have a sense of accomplishment?
- How does the team feel about its level of commitment to the team and the mission?
- Were expectations set at the appropriate level? Were expectations violated?
- Do team members have confidence in themselves?
- Do team members seem to care about each other?
- Were facilitation efforts effective?
- How effective was the creative problem-solving process?
- How efficient was the group during its deliberations?

Decision-making procedures Developing, understanding, and adhering to a set of rules for making decisions on patients' behalf comes under intense scrutiny from various sources within the organization. As an end point for just about everything that comes before it (analysis, assessment, evaluation, judgement), decision-making is influenced at every conceivable level (Koopman, 1998). Disciplinary norms influence how professionals make decisions, as do legal statutes and normative standards set by courts. The healthcare delivery system itself may weigh in on how decisions should be made in certain contexts ("do no harm," "do not over-medicate"). The healthcare organization where professionals practice no doubt has stipulations regarding certain decision-making rules and the team itself may impose decision-making rules that apply to its own activities. Figure 11.3 offers a simplified glimpse into how involved and potentially

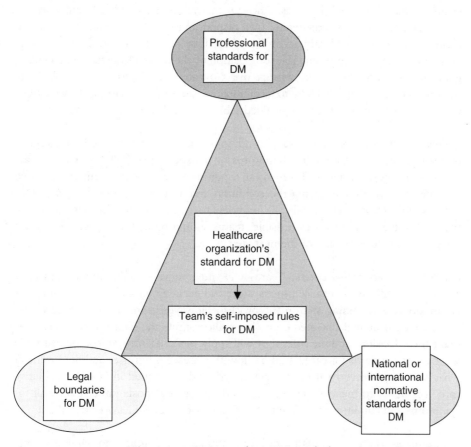

Figure 11.3 Decision-making (DM) standards.

complicated decision-making procedures and stipulations can permeate the actions taken by healthcare teams. Taken together, this system or culture of rules for decision-making offers important implications for team members, especially when decision rules appear to conflict.

Similar to other organizations, healthcare facilities have a tendency to influence decisions on lower units such as teams. A key reason behind this influence involves the focus on liability and litigation. As members of an organization, teams are afforded a reasonable degree of protection from legal implications through protection from their healthcare organization and from their own personal malpractice insurance. Hospitals may carry their own insurance or choose to self-insure, but regardless of their preferences they have a great deal at stake in how decisions are reached by healthcare teams. Therefore, healthcare organizations have a role in the process that becomes manifested through decision rules that protect them from negligence. Like teams, organizations develop a strong sense of normative standards for decisions through environmental scanning (Sutcliffe, 2001) in order to avoid exposure to litigation claims based on unusual practices. Once normative and standardized guidelines are put in place for teams, it is the teams' own responsibility to develop rules for decision-making. These rules will vary according to the type of care they are delivering (e.g. acute, long-term palliative) and the composition of the team. However, some general guidelines based on the *functional perspective* (Gouran & Hirokawa, 1996; Hirokawa & Salazar, 1999) can be offered here to facilitate how teams make decisions (Dewey, 1933; Gouran & Hirokawa, 1999; O'Hair, Friedrich, & Dixon, 2011).

Problem identification Not all medical conditions confronted by the medical team can be readily surmised. Unfamiliar symptoms or unexpected complications can create doubt about how to define the medical condition of a patient. Teams have much at stake in correctly identifying the condition and agreeing upon its etiology. Discussion and analysis will usually be required to make any conclusions about the medical problem. As much as possible, teams should be in solid agreement about the problem before moving to the next step.

Clarifying parameters and criteria Teams will often move to subsequent steps after problem identification because time is short and deciding on a treatment regimen is an important intervening step in the process. However, teams need to ensure that they have adequately deliberated over what will constitute the standards by which they judge their decisions and the rules they will apply. In a cancer diagnosis, the team will want to set standards for care based on how the disease progresses and determine at what point aggressive treatment is continued or discontinued in favor of palliative care. It is better to make these decisions early on as guideposts rather than wait for symptoms and conditions to present, creating emotional conflict over treatment.

Generating alternatives Teams have the advantage of being able to generate some creative options for medical care. Sometime known as "risky shift" or group polarization (Myers & Lamm, 1976; West, 1998), teams have a tendency to move away from neutral, normal, or expected alternatives toward decisions that are more extreme or unusual. Teams generate a sense of confidence that reduces their inhibitions to try something new. This can be good or bad. Innovative treatment options can save lives and reduce suffering for patients—when they work. Alternative treatment options that steer too far from the normal should probably come under the scrutiny of an outside party before moving forward (see the next phase). The point here is that as the touchstone phase for team decision-making, groups need to consider the opinions of all team members (including the patient) and to avoid being reticent in advancing strong and creative alternatives (Lee, 2010).

Evaluating alternatives As an equally important step, team members must be ready to step up and offer their considered opinion about all of the alternatives generated by the prior step. It is within this phase that the ingenuity, care, and safety of the alternatives are carefully analyzed. Advantages and contraindications of all treatment alternatives should be exposed and weighed, and it is in this step that a diversity of team members can bring critical knowledge to bear on the options being tested. The best available evidence (referred to as evidenced-based medicine) should be applied to the alternatives and tested for strength. For example, a young patient with a protrusion on his midriff is being examined for the possibility of a tumor. Imaging has not reached a conclusion about the mass and two team members argue for the normal protocol of outpatient but invasive surgery to determine if the mass is malignant. Another team member argues that, based on the patient's age, it would be better to conduct a positron emission tomography (PET) scan to determine if the growth is more cyst-like. A previous research article this team member read argues for the likelihood of such a mass and that further imaging would be less risky than surgery at this point.

Selecting the best option In the previous case, a consensus may not be achieved among all team members. It is important that sufficient analysis and deliberation be pursued before reaching a final decision. Obviously, some medical conditions require a more rapid decision, such as in emergencies. In cases such as these it is likely that the physician will consider as much information and as many perspectives from the team as possible and then make a unilateral decision for care. When more time is available, generating as much agreement as possible for the treatment protocol is critical for several reasons. First, the evidence and experience that can be brought to bear in the case, the more likely it is that an option will be more valid. Second, team members want to know that what they are doing for the patient was a result of their input; they feel more invested in the decisions derived for the patient and develop that sense of ownership discussed earlier. Ultimately, a decision is usually made by the team leader based on due deliberation. Seldom do teams vote on a treatment option; a consensus is preferred when time allows.

Implementing the option Putting the treatment option in place is much easier and teams have more confidence when all of the previous steps to decision-making have been followed. Many of the details and loose ends associated with treatment have been previously considered and steps for successful treatment have been laid out. The team will want to consider the most efficient pathways for care and develop a plan for implementation. As with any team-based decision involving complex processes, alternative options considered as part of the decision-making process must be kept in the background for handy reference should the original option fail the team. That is one of the more important reasons for arriving at medical decisions through a team-based format. Second- and third-place choices suggested by the team can be moved into place with confidence.

Evaluating the results Teams can learn as much from their failures as they can from their successes. One of the hallmarks of effective team deliberation is taking advantage of hindsight as a learning tool. Known by many labels (after-action reviews, patient outcome reports, etc.), the process of understanding what worked and what didn't is invaluable to healthcare team members. Questions can be directed toward the evidence-based process of diagnosis and generation of alternatives. Did the systematic process of problem-solving work? Were some steps weaker than others? Was there a disconnect between the decisions reached by the team and the manner in which the treatment was implemented? How could the process have been improved? Teams have a functional and professional responsibility to bridge the gap between what occurred and what could have been better accomplished.

Developing team synergy

Group synergy is the phenomenon of groups performing in ways that reach beyond the collective efforts of individuals. "The whole is greater than the sum of its parts" is the typical phrase used to characterize group synergy. Group synergy is composed of role congruence, competent listening, participation and empowerment, conflict management, consensus building, and being patient centered.

Role congruence Other problems within the team can lead to unsatisfactory outcomes. Role confusion as well as overlapping tasks and responsibilities can also inhibit interdisciplinary teamwork (Apker, Propp, & Ford, 2005; Berteotti & Seibold, 1994). Role congruence is important in terms of clarifying each team member's role, tasks, and responsibilities, and these should be clearly discussed during initial team meetings. What is well to remember is that while healthcare team members retain and promote their disciplinary professional roles (occupational therapistss, nurses, pharmacists, etc.), they are also very likely to take on team-based roles as well. Who is expected to set up meetings as needed? Who will act as the facilitator of the meetings? Who will be responsible for recording the deliberation of teams? Who will be in charge of communicating decisions to other organizational personnel? Who is responsible for follow-up through the treatment regimen? Responses to these questions provide essential substance for ensuring that team-based decisions and actions are efficient and complete.

Role congruence also involves the ability of members to suspend their personal inclinations for the good of the team. Roles are powerful forces in promoting an individual's identity in a professional organization. Identity is a key motivating force for why people behave in certain ways, and identity is all too often wrapped up in the specific roles medical professionals expect themselves to play (Lingard *et al.*, 2006). When team members consider that their knowledge and expertise are intrinsically valuable to the patient and the team while at the same time perceiving that what they bring to the table is an integrated piece of the puzzle, it is easier to move toward role congruence that emulates synergy rather than unidisciplinary efforts (Lee, 2010).

Competent listening Teams will succeed or fail based on their communication skills. In a way, all of the components of group synergy are communication based (Norris *et al.*, 2005). However, championing the use of competent listening skills is clearly key. Listening is one of the most overlooked skills of team members and facilitators. As Stephen Covey said in his *Seven Habits* book (1986), seek to understand before you attempt to be understood. Make the effort to understand not only what a person is saying, but also why they are saying it (what are their true intent and motivation?). Try to understand their feelings. Determine whether they are communicating from a professional or a team-based role. Ask questions if you are unsure ("I am not sure I understand . . ."). Increase your tolerance for listening to others. Respect their input to the group. Give responsive nonverbal feedback when you are listening (nodding, eye contact, forward lean, etc.) (O'Hair, Friedrich, & Dixon, 2011).

Approachability gives team members the impression that you are open and accessible to their ideas and opinions. Effective listening is one way to demonstrate approachability, as is an accessible nonverbal demeanor (smiling, eye contact, open body orientation, etc.) (Romig, 1996). Approachability can also be established by asking for opinions, commenting on ideas, and expressing positive regard for groups or team members.

Participation and empowerment Medical teams do not automatically enjoy engaged, active, and creative participation. It takes clever facilitation skills to keep the team going and on track. Beyond the normal questioning and responding, team members must probe, nurture, and encourage one another. In addition, it is important to stand ready to handle various dysfunctional roles that team members have a tendency to adopt.

Asking questions. Nothing is more important for team functioning than asking good questions. The following constitute some good rules for asking effective questions (O'Hair, Friedrich, & Dixon, 2011):

- Begin questions with "Who," "What," "Where," "When," and "How."
- Avoid questions requiring a yes or no answer.
- Ask questions that focus the medical team on the issues at hand (goals, mission).
- Phrase questions positively. Try not to be confrontational.
- Use secondary questions for elaboration or clarification.

Responding/feedback. One of the most effective ways to keep the discussion going is through effective responses or feedback. Responding is best accomplished through the following strategies:

- Paraphrasing: translating responses through summarizing, recapping in your own words.
- Evaluating: judging the effectiveness and appropriateness of responses in a constructive manner.
- Supporting: reassuring, encouraging, and sustaining responses of others.
- Probing: seeking additional information, provoking additional discussion.
- Interpreting: offering your own meaning (interpretation) for what someone has said.

Managing participation styles. Team members will not come to the table with similar inclinations and skills. Participation styles can be managed through effective facilitation skills (O'Hair, Friedrich, Wiemann, & Wiemann, in press). Examine the team communication styles that facilitate participation in Table 11.1.

Conflict management All teams will experience some level of conflict, and the success of interdisciplinary healthcare teams can be undermined by conflicts between different

Table 11.1   Team communication styles that facilitate participation

Style	Description	Facilitation
Rambling	Much discussion except on the subject. Loses the point.	Raise hand slightly, get floor, refocus attention on the issue. Glance at watch.
Verbose	Excessive talkativeness, anxious to show off, very wordy.	Ask difficult questions to slow them down. Ask others to interpret the meaning. Ask for additional input.
Inarticulate	Can't put thoughts into a coherent form. Can't express themselves.	Paraphrase their comments. Ask others if they feel the same way.
Sidebar conversations	Two people talking privately during team discussion.	Call one by name and ask for their feelings on the discussion.
Avoiding	Noninvolvement, little participation.	Call on them by name. Ask for opinion.
Blocking	Indulges in negative or disagreeable comments.	Ask *why* they feel that way. Have them compare their view to the others.

team members. Within any healthcare team, members will vary in terms of their social status and power. For example, physicians tend to have a higher social status and more power within healthcare organizations than nurses or social workers. Power differences may lead team members with less power to become apprehensive and contribute less to the group discussion. When this happens, ideas that may be beneficial in terms of treating the patient or meeting his or her needs may be lost. Power disparities can also lead to resentment among team members and impede successful collaboration (Abramson & Mizrahi, 1996).

Conflict between team members can arise in interdisciplinary teams for a variety of reasons, such as when people are not satisfied with the team discussion, if they feel that their viewpoint is being disregarded by other members, or because of personality differences (Bennett, Gadlin, & Levine-Finley, 2010). Conflict can also be productive or unproductive. Conflict can lead to differing viewpoints about the nature of a problem, a healthy discussion of competing options for treating a patient, better-informed decisions, and reduction of oversights and redundancies that can be costly to the patient's health or the healthcare organization. Sometimes interpersonal conflict occurs due to personality differences and sometimes it is content oriented. Regardless, here are five steps to take to management conflict productively: (i) openly state the cause of the conflict (is it personality based or differences of opinion?); (ii) discuss the goals of those in conflict; (iii) probe for areas of agreement; (iv) discuss means of resolving conflict through consensus; (v) make a decision (O'Hair & Wiemann, 2012).

Consensus building Diversity of interests and styles in the team is a strength. Without diversity, there is no reason to form teams and individuals can be left to make decisions. Bringing diverse ideas to a consensual decision, however, is a challenge. One method of consensus building is through the process of normalizing norms. All groups will develop norms (regularized practices, behaviors) over time. Some are effective and others are not. Most experts agree that it is best to establish certain norms from the beginning of the group's existence. In this way, groups understand early on the ground rules for their deliberations. As a facilitation strategy, the first few sessions can begin by stating and agreeing on appropriate norms (e.g. being on time, turn-taking, no excessive speeches, no hostile remarks, active participation).

Coordination and collaboration among team members is also an ideal way to build consensus. Building upon one another's ideas, being supportive of the creative process, and engaging in reasoned skepticism contribute to consensus building. In addition, the following steps can be taken to reach consensual decisions in teams (O'Hair, Friedrich, & Dixon, 2011):

- Encourage team members to concede their personal positions when they are illogical or unworkable.
- Maintain an open mind about constructive conflict. Conflict can lead to better decisions when handled professionally. Use conflict to guide the team to a few remaining positions.
- Unless pressed for time, avoid voting or averaging as a means for decision-making.
- During stalemates, identify issues common to all positions and combine them into one integrated idea (decision)—known as the *common-denominator rule*.

For many people, team efficiency is a top priority among their "issues" concerning groups. Teamwork is often perceived as busy work or lost time, especially when team members have other responsibilities in the organization. Facilitation efforts that maintain an efficient team process are highly valued and contribute to consensus building. Consider the following steps to increasing efficiency in teams.

- Set an agenda and stick to it. Effective agendas are time bound (each item has a deadline associated with it).
- Employ a time monitor (timekeeper) to keep the group on track.
- Consider rules for participation (no speeches, comments to be one minute or less, etc.).
- Build in a reward system for maintaining efficiency.
- Do not hesitate to confront and challenge members when instances of inefficiency are observed.
- Demonstrate an energized level of communication as a model for efficient teamwork.

Patient-centered focus Patients can also play a role in a synergistic team approach to healthcare, and many teams include the patient and/or his or her significant other(s) as team members (Poole & Real, 2003). Rather than being passive recipients of instructions and medications from their providers, healthcare teams should educate patients about the biological and psychological implications of their health issues and the various treatment options available to them (Coopman, 2001). As a form of patient agency (O'Hair *et al.*, 2003), including patients in the process of decision-making can go a long way toward enriching the alternatives generated for care and investing the patient in the treatment regimen. As we have seen, allowing patients to become active and informed participants in their own wellness process maximizes the potential for successful treatment outcomes and patient satisfaction (Howe, 2006).

Tips for Building a Team

Healthcare contexts do not always allow members to choose their own team members. Members are often assigned to a team without consultation. That is the purpose of going into detail for how teams can be effective. Sometimes, however, teams can be formed voluntarily and the National institutes of Health (Bennett, Gadlin, & Levine-Finley, 2010) suggest the follow tips for developing strong and effective teams:

- Bring together members with diverse backgrounds and experiences to promote mutual learning.
- Make sure each person understands his or her roles, responsibilities, and contributions to the team's goals.
- As a leader, establish expectations for working together; as a participant, understand your contribution to the end goal.
- Recognize that discussing team goals openly and honestly will be a dynamic process and will evolve over time.
- Be prepared for disagreements and even conflicts, especially in the early stages of team formation.
- Agree on processes for sharing data, establishing and sharing credit, and managing authorship immediately and over the course of the project.
- Regularly consider new scientific perspectives and ideas related to the research.

Summary

Healthcare teams are an indispensable part of the delivery system. Healthcare organizations that design and structure teams enjoy advantages over organizations that foster more unidisciplinary efforts toward patient care. These advantages come in the form of improved patient care and organizational efficiency, to name just a few. Healthcare teams do not happen on their own. Great efforts are necessary to instill the type of communication processes necessary for effective team-based care. The sheer number of healthcare professionals involved in care is a salient issue. Also, developing healthcare teams that suspend their own professional expectations for the good of the team and the patient presents a number of challenges, not the least of which is the tendency for professionals to promote their own knowledge and expertise over others. We argue that healthcare teams need to move to a perspective of care that takes advantage of the interdisciplinary strength represented by organizational members, a process we term synergistic healthcare teams that promote team science.

The model for synergistic healthcare teams can be used by any healthcare organization hoping to improve the effectiveness and efficiency of its diverse interdisciplinary teams. The essential components of facilitation include instilling a sense of ownership, becoming performance based, and developing team synergy.

Team members can gain a sense of team ownership by developing trust with one another and with the team process. Trust leads to developing a commitment to the team and to the mission of the organization (Heath & O'Hair, 2009). Ownership is also assumed when team members gain a sense of accomplishment from their teamwork.

Medical team members can become performance based when they appropriately prioritize and set goals for themselves. These goals then lead to a process of creative problem solving where team members engage in innovative and critical thinking that leads to breakthrough results. These results are then measured to ensure that the team is on track and responsive to its mission. Recognizing and celebrating these results obviously contributes to instilling that sense of accomplishment mentioned earlier.

Group synergy is a result of ensuring that team members are employing competent communication skills. Group synergy is also a result of effective participation and empowerment of group members. These processes lead to consensus building which is so important to making team members feel like a "team." Finally, group synergy is maintained through efficient team processes, including a focus on patients as they become part of the synergistic team.

References

Abramson, J. S., & Mizrahi, T. (1996). When social workers and physicians collaborate: Positive and negative interdisciplinary experiences. *Social Work, 41*, 270–281.

Apker, J., Propp, K. M., & Ford, W. S. Z. (2009). Investigating the effect of nurse-team communication on nurse turnover: Relationships among communication processes, identification, and intent to leave. *Health Communication, 24*, 106–114.

Apker, J., Propp, K. M., & Ford, W. S. Z. (2005). Negotiating status and identity tensions in healthcare team interactions: An exploration of nurse role dialectics. *Journal of Applied Communication Research, 33*, 93–115.

Bennett, L. M., Gadlin, H., & Levine-Finley, S., (2010). *Collaboration and team science: A field guide*. Rockville, MD: National Institutes of Health.

Berteotti, C. R., & Seibold, D. R. (1994). Coordination and role-definition problems in health-care teams: A hospice case study. In L. R. Frey (Ed.), *Group communication in context: Studies of natural groups* (pp. 107–131). Hillsdale, NJ: Lawrence Erlbaum.

Bleakley, A., Boyden, J., Hobbs, A., Walsh, L., & Allard, J. (2006). Improving teamwork climate in operating theaters: The shift from multiprofessionalism to interprofessionalism. *Journal of Interprofessional care, 20*, 461–470.

Bokhour, B. (2006). Communication in interdisciplinary team meetings: What are we talking about? *Journal of Interprofessional Care, 20,* 349–363.

Catchpole, K., Mishra, A., Handa, A., & McCulloch, P. (2008). Teamwork and error in the operating room analysis of skills and roles. *Annals of Surgery, 247,* 699–706.

Cooke, C. (1997). Reflections on the healthcare team: My experiences in an interdisciplinary program. *Journal of the American Medical Association, 277,* 1091–1092.

Coopman, S. J. (2001). Democracy, performance, and outcomes in interdisciplinary health care teams. *Journal of Business Communication, 38,* 261–284.

Covey, S. (1986). *Seven Habits Of Highly Effective People.* New York: McGraw-Hill.

Demiris, G., Washington, K., Oliver, D. P., Wittenberg-Lyles, E. (2008). A study of information flow in hospice interdisciplinary team meetings. *Journal of Interprofessional Care, 22,* 621–629.

Dewey, J. (1933). *How we think.* Lexington, MA: D. C. Heath.

Edwards, J., & Smith, P. (1998). Impact of interdisciplinary education in underserved areas: Health professions collaboration in Tennessee. *Journal of Professional Nursing, 14,* 144–149.

Ellingson, L. L. (2003). Interdisciplinary health care teamwork in the clinical backstage. *Journal of Applied Communication Research, 31,* 93–117.

Farr, A. C., & Ames, N. (2008). Using diffusion of innovation theory to encourage the development of a children's health collaborative: A formative evaluation. *Journal of Health Communication, 13,* 375–388.

Gage, M. (1998). From independence to interdependence: Creating synergistic healthcare teams. *Journal of Nursing Administration, 28*(4), 17–26.

Gouran, D. S., & Hirokawa, R. Y. (1996). Functional theory and communication in decision-making and problem solving groups. An expanded view. In R. Y. Hirokawa & M. S. Poole (Eds), *Communication and group decision making* (2nd ed., pp. 55–80). Thousand Oaks, CA: Sage.

Grant, R. W., & Finocchio, L. J. (1995). California primary care consortium subcommittee on interdisciplinary collaboration. *Interdisciplinary collaborative teams in primary care: A model curriculum and resource guide.* San Francisco, CA: Pew Health Professions Commission.

Hall, K. l., Feng, A., Moser, R., Stokols, D., & Taylor, B. (2008). Moving the science of team science forward. *American Journal of Preventive Medicine, 35,* 243–249.

Heath, R. L., & O'Hair, H. D. (2009). The significance of risk and crisis communication. In R. Heath & H. D. O'Hair (Eds), *Handbook of risk and crisis communication* (pp. 5–30). New York: Routledge.

Hirokawa, R. Y., & Salazar, A. J. (1999). Task-group communication and decision-making performance. In L. Frey (Ed.), *Handbook of group communication theory and research* (pp. 167–191). Thousand Oaks, CA: Sage.

Howe, A. (2006). Can the patient be on our team? An operational approach to patient involvement in interprofessional approaches to safe care. *Journal of Interprofessional Care, 20,* 527–534.

Jones, R. A. P. (1997). Multidisciplinary collaboration: Conceptual development as a foundation for patient-focused care. *Holistic Nursing Practice, 11*(3), 8–16.

Kanter, R. K. (2001). *Evolve!* Boston, MA: Harvard Business School Press.

Kinlaw, D. C. (1991). *Developing superior work teams.* San Diego, CA: Lexington Books.

Kirkman-Liff, B. (1999). Medicare managed care and primary care of elderly people. In F. Netting & F. Williams (Eds), *Enhancing primary care of elderly people* (pp. 3–23). New York: Garland.

Koopman, P. (1998). Decision making. In N. Nicholson (Ed.), *Encyclopedic dictionary of organizational behavior* (pp. 128–133). Malden, MA: Blackwell.

Ladden, M. D., Bednash, G., Stevens, D. P., & Moore, G. T. (2006). Educating interprofessional learners for quality, safety and systems improvement. *Journal of Interprofessional Care, 20,* 497–505.

Lee, T. H. (2010). Turning doctors into leaders. *Harvard Business Review,* April, 50–58.

Lefley, H. (1998). Training professionals for rehabilitation teams. In P. Corrigan & D. Giffort (Eds), *Building teams and programs for effective psychiatric rehabilitation* (pp. 13–23). San Francisco: Jossey-Bass.

Lingard, L., Whyte, S., Espin, S., Baker, G. R., Orser, B., & Doran, D. (2006). Towards safer interprofessional communication: Constructing a model of "utility" from preoperative team briefings. *Journal of Interprofessional Care, 20,* 471–483.

McHugh, M., West, P., Assatly, C., Duprat, L., Niloff, J., Waldo, K. *et al.* (1996). Establishing an interdisciplinary patient care team: Collaboration at the bedside and beyond. *Journal of Nursing Administration, 26*(4), 21–27.

Mills, P., Neily, J., & Dunn, E. (2008). Teamwork and communication in surgical teams: Implications for patient safety. *Journal of American College of Surgeons, 206,* 107–112.

Myers, D. G., & Lamm, H. (1976). The group polarization phenomenon. *Psychological Bulletin, 83,* 602–627.

Norris, E., Alexander, H., Livingston, M., Woods, K., Fischbacher, M., & Macdonald, E. (2005). Multidisciplinary perspectives on core networking skills. A study of skills and associated training needs for professionals working in managed clinical networks. *Journal of Interprofessional Care, 19,* 156–163.

O'Brien, J. L., Martin, D. R., Heyworth, J. A., & Meyer, N. R. (2009). A phenomenological perspective on advanced practice nurse–physician collaboration within an interdisciplinary healthcare team. *Journal of the American Academy of Nurse Practitioners, 21,* 444–453.

O'Hair, H. D., Friedrich, G., & Dixon, L. (2011). *Strategic communication for business and the professions* (7th ed.). Boston, MA: Houghton Mifflin.

O'Hair, H. D., & Wiemann, M. (2012). *Real communication* (2nd ed.). New York: Bedford St. Martin's Press.

O'Hair, H. D., Villagran, M., Wittenberg, E., Brown, K., Hall, T., Ferguson, M., & Doty, T. (2003). Cancer survivorship and agency model (CSAM): Implications for patient choice, decision making, and influence. *Health Communication, 15,* 193–202.

Pike, A. W. (1991). Moral outrage and moral discourse in nurse–physician collaboration. *Journal of Professional Nursing, 7,* 351–363.

Poole, M. S., & Real, K. (2003). Groups and teams in health care: Communication and effectiveness. In T. L. Thompson, A. M. Dorsey, K. I. Miller, & R. Parrott (Eds), *Handbook of health communication* (pp. 369–402). Mahwah, NJ: Lawrence Erlbaum.

Rees, G., Edmunds, S., & Huby, G. (2005). Evaluation and development of integrated teams: The use of Significant Event Analysis. *Journal of Interprofessional Care, 19,* 125–136.

Romig, D. A. (1996). *Breakthrough teamwork: Outstanding results using structured teamwork.* Chicago: Irwin.

Smith, J. R., & Cole, F. S. (2008). Patient safety: Effective interdisciplinary teamwork through simulation and debriefing in the neonatal ICU. *Critical Care Nurse Clinical North America, 21,* 163–179.

Sutcliffe, K. M. (2001). Organizational environments and organizational information processing. In F. Jablin & L. Putnam (Eds), *The new handbook of organizational communication* (pp. 197–230). Thousand Oaks, CA: Sage.

West, M. A. (1998). Risky shift/group polarization. In N. Nicholson (Ed.), *Encyclopedic dictionary of organizational behavior* (pp. 493–494). Malden, MA: Blackwell.

Wieland, D., Kramer, B. J., Waite, M. S., & Rubenstein, L. Z. (1996). The interdisciplinary team in geriatric care. *American Behavioral Scientist, 39,* 655–664.

Zismer, D. K. (2011). The psychology of organizational structure in integrated health systems. *Physician Executive, 37,* 36–43.

Part VI

Contexts, Challenges, and Choices

Chapter 12

Political Issues and Health Communication

"You lie!" This shout out from Representative Joe Wilson during President Obama's State of the Union speech immediately got the nation's attention as well as an instant barrage of press coverage. Rep. Wilson was referring to the President's contention that illegal immigrants would not be covered by the proposed healthcare reform legislation. The culmination of intense rhetoric that had characterized the debate over reforming healthcare in the US resulted in this eruption of emotion and intensity. Supporters and opponents of the legislation had attempted to garner support through framing the debate in their favor.

Dan Nimmo, often referred to as the father of political communication, along with counterpart, Lynda Lee Kaid, often referred to as the mother of political communication both frequently stated that *all* communication is political. Although not all communication scholars agree, certainly the lens of political communication and health policy influences health communication in significant ways that we do not completely understand.

The Patient Protection and Affordable Care Act of 2010 (PPACA) that was passed in March 2010 very quickly started to change our healthcare system. PPACA, or healthcare reform, has caused much controversy and debate among citizens and policy-makers and will likely contribute greatly to transformation of the US healthcare system (Bevan *et al.*, 2012).

Healthcare reform will impact almost every single American by changing legislation, regulating insurance laws and employee benefits, and covering an additional 32 million individuals (The Commonwealth Fund, 2010). Though there is continued debate about healthcare reform and the impact it will have on the health industry as well as the economy (Doherty, 2010), there is little systematic knowledge regarding how the public is acquiring information about healthcare reform and the public's perceptions and understanding of healthcare reform itself (Bevan *et al.*, 2012)

Health Communication in the 21st Century, Second Edition. Kevin Bradley Wright, Lisa Sparks, and H. Dan O'Hair.
© 2013 John Wiley & Sons, Inc. Published 2013 by John Wiley & Sons, Inc.

As an emerging health policy context, the changes that healthcare reform will bring are increasingly relevant to health communication researchers for several reasons (e.g. Bevan *et al.*, 2012). Healthcare reform will have a direct impact on those who are sick, but also on those without health issues and problems . . . the healthy ones! Further, healthcare reform information also includes aspects of prevention, diagnosis, treatment, and intervention based on individuals' current health status. Due to the politics and policy implications of healthcare reform as well as its partisan nature, public perceptions and understandings of it could be significantly impacted by the one-sided, divisive perspectives of the political entities and organizations that have a considerable stake in the success or failure of the legislation. Thus, determining how and where the public is acquiring healthcare reform information is of utmost importance for beginning to recognize public perceptions and understandings of the legislation (Bevan *et al.*, 2012).

The debate over reforming healthcare from the earliest promises made during the presidential campaign of 2008 to the tea parties, protests, and town hall meetings that characterized the first half of Obama's term could result in the most expensive advertising war ever fought over a piece of legislation. The back and forth of speeches on the House and Senate Floor, and the arguments from the White House as the Obama administration sought to regain control over the terms of the debate are still unfolding. The story of healthcare reform is, at its root, the story of how health messages (rhetoric) shaped the debate over what was desirable or even possible and ultimately the content of the law itself. Perhaps Drs Nimmo and Kaid were onto something!

The ways by which Americans received and processed the healthcare reform messages from elites, the media and even the town hall meetings and protests in which many American participated, we would argue are grounded in health and media literacy. It is an empirical question just how the public came to understand or misunderstand the most significant piece of healthcare legislation since the creation of Medicare and Medicaid nearly a half century ago.

But, the story does not end with the President signing the PPACA into law. The White House then faced the overwhelming and difficult task of selling the new law to the public. Interest groups engaged in outreach, educational, and advocacy efforts. For example, the AARP began what many consider the most costly campaign in the group's history to explain the new law to its informed and active members. Despite these types of efforts, many Americans remained uninformed or misinformed. Why are so many Americans still uninformed on the most significant legislation to be passed in a generation? Likely because we have not given much thought to the merging of health and politics, but perhaps it is time to think differently, think critically, think mindfully about the intersection of health, politics, public policy, and the significant role health communication plays in our understanding of these often complicated issues affecting our daily lives.

Many people may not think of health and political issues as being interrelated at first glance. However, again, when you stop and consider many of the recent (and often heated) political debates regarding President Obama's national healthcare law, debates about the legalization of marijuana for medical purposes, arguments among political figures for and against stem cell research, discussions about the corporate greed and the pharmaceutical industry, and the rights of marginalized groups in our society to have access to healthcare services, you can see that health and politics are frequently intertwined in interesting and complex ways.

As we saw in Chapter 8, the media play an important role in terms of influencing our knowledge, beliefs, and attitudes toward a variety of health-related concerns, and this is certainly the case when it comes to political issues. As a society, we are constantly exposed to television and radio news stories, political debates, websites, blogs, and even documentaries such as Michael Moore's "Sicko" (2007), Morgan Spurlock's (2004) film "Supersize Me," Lee Fulkerson and Brian Wendel's "Forks Over Knives" (2011), or Michael Pollan's "Food, Inc." (2008). These media sources provide us with a relatively wide spectrum of political viewpoints regarding health and healthcare, and many people gravitate toward media sources that present health information that is consistent with their existing political views. In addition, political/health issues intersect with communication in many other ways, such as individuals seeking medical and public legitimacy for diseases that the mainstream public may be relatively unfamiliar with, such as actor Michael J. Fox's television efforts to raise awareness about Parkinson's disease or people suffering from chronic fatigue syndrome, cancer, or diabetes using social networking sites to inform others about this condition. Moreover, when marginalized groups or people who lack access to adequate healthcare due to racial discrimination or low levels of income organize at the grassroots level to better their situation, or when concerned citizens create campaigns to change environmental policies, such as removing toxic waste sites from their neighborhoods in an effort to reduce exposure to carcinogens, communication is central in terms of creating social and political change.

This chapter explores the role of communication as it pertains to a variety of current political issues surrounding health and healthcare. We begin by providing an overview of politics and health communication and some background on the recent healthcare legislation, followed by a section on current political issues surrounding health and healthcare including a discussion of message framing and political communication, the impact of health disparities, disadvantaged groups, and access to healthcare and related policy issues, followed by a discussion of healthcare system problems, and medical tourism as a response to medical access problems, political issues surrounding death and dying, nutrition, and international health and policy issues.

Politics and Health Communication

No matter whether you are a democrat, republican, independent, or libertarian, or consider yourself fiscally conservative and/or socially liberal, health is an important issue for everyone. Consider for a moment the history of healthcare and healthcare reform in the US, from placing the new healthcare reform law into context with landmark legislation in 1935 that created Social Security and the legislation in 1965 that enacted Medicare and Medicaid. The landmark PPACA and the Health Care and Education Reconciliation Act of 2010, which comprised the healthcare reform legislation in

2010 are real and impacting our healthcare delivery systems and patient care in unique, complex, even radical ways that we have yet to fully understand.

A New York Times report on July 29, 2012 summarized that in March 2010, Congress passed the healthcare bill put forth by President Obama. The law put in motion the creation of a nationwide insurance system that would provide most Americans with basic healthcare coverage, a goal that had been on the Democratic agenda for 75 years. In 2012, the Supreme Court in a 5–4 vote, largely upheld it after considering a several challenges to much of the law's key provisions. The healthcare law seeks to extend insurance to more than 30 million people, primarily by expanding Medicaid and providing federal subsidies to help lower- and middle-income Americans to purchase private coverage. It will create insurance exchanges for those buying individual policies and prohibit insurers from denying coverage on the basis of pre-existing conditions. To reduce the increasing cost of Medicare, it puts together a panel of experts to limit government reimbursement to only those treatments shown to be effective, and creates incentives for providers to package services rather than charge by individual procedure.

The Congressional Budget Office claims that the law will cost the government about $938 billion over 10 years, and also estimates that it will reduce the federal deficit by $138 billion over a decade (see Crowley 2012).

This legislation is not without controversy, as it has components involving significant disagreement among politicians, corporate stakeholders, physicians, citizens, and the insurance industry. If you have not paid much attention to healthcare in America, it is time to do so because it will very likely impact you and your loved ones in the future.

Bevan *et al.*'s (2012) exploration of healthcare reform information sources in relation to information quality, information seeking, and uncertainty found that magazines are the preferred source for such quality information and decreased uncertainty.

In particular, when magazines were employed as a source of healthcare reform information, individuals employed information seeking, and revealed that this information was satisfying and easier to obtain, and were more certain about their understanding of healthcare reform (Bevan *et al.*, 2012). Further, when newspapers were rated the most important healthcare reform information source, participants sought more information. These findings are particularly consistent with Dutta-Bergman's (2004) research, which found that those who obtained health information from newspapers or magazines were more health-oriented than individuals who did not.

Both newspapers and magazines can provide active, cognitively involved, in-depth coverage of a health issue and can also be archived for future information-seeking (Bevan *et al.*, 2012). These qualities may make magazines, and to a lesser extent, newspapers, particularly appealing as an information source to individuals who are learning about healthcare reform and may thus explain this pattern of findings. The growth of magazines as a health information source (Gill & Babrow, 2007) means that this media channel has the potential to be an invaluable resource for individuals seeking healthcare reform information (Bevan *et al.*, 2012).

When healthcare reform information was obtained from interpersonal sources such as family or friends, participants felt that knowledge was less satisfying, more difficult to obtain, and felt more uncertain about healthcare reform than those who did not. This pattern aligns with Pecchioni and Sparks' (2007) health information sources research on family caregivers who reported more satisfaction with Internet sources of health information, but differs from their findings related to patient satisfaction and preferences for interpersonal-based health information sources (i.e. doctors and nurses). In addition, when family or friends were selected as the most important healthcare reform information source, less information seeking occurred. However, the authors suggest that the Internet is still a frequently used and important source of healthcare reform information, and should also be considered by those who are invested in the continuation and success of the healthcare reform legislation.

Debates about health and healthcare policies are frequent topics on television and in other media. While most people would probably agree that health is an important attribute that is essential to happy life, differences quickly appear when the discussion turns to issues such as how to best fund healthcare, questions regarding where life begins and ends, what is considered to be a legitimate treatment for a health issue, and even debates over what types of food are considered healthy and unhealthy. In short, health issues are often political and complex, and it important for people who are interested in health communication to try to understand political issues surrounding heath and how communication plays a role in terms of helping people to share their political beliefs with others as well as how political messages about health affect individuals attitudes, beliefs, and behaviors.

Message Framing Theory and Political Communication

A great deal of health communication research has examined the framing of health messages in the mass media. While theories of message framing do not always deal with political issues, they can be a helpful framework to better understand politicized health messages within the mass media. Entman (1991) argued that to frame is to select some aspect of an issue and make it more salient in a message, in such a way as to promote a particular definition, viewpoint, interpretation, moral evaluation, and/or treatment recommendation. Message framing has had a long history in media effects research within the communication discipline (Price & Tewksbury, 1997). When examining the media, framing effects are important to consider because the manner in which information is presented may ultimately decisions and judgements toward issues (see Levin & Gaeth, 1998), including health issues.

A great deal of message framing research is focused on the way in which information is presented in gain- versus loss-framed scenarios, and how this affects people's cognitions, intentions, and dispositions toward issues (Block & Keller, 1995; Rothman *et al.*, 1999). Gain-framed messages emphasize the advantages or benefits of certain behaviors or the potential of adopting such behaviors, while loss-framed messages highlight the disadvantages or costs associated with engaging in certain behaviors. For example, as we will see later in the chapter, people who are for medical marijuana usage will often use gain-framed messages, such as emphasizing how marijuana causes cancer patients going through chemotherapy to feel less nauseous, while people who are against medical marijuana usage will typically use loss-framed messages, such as emphasizing the link between smoking marijuana and lung cancer or the distortion of spatial perception resulting from being under the influence of marijuana and how this might lead to more accidents (i.e. if a medical marijuana patient is driving under the influence of the drug). See also, Sparks (2011).

As you can imagine, an individual's or group's political beliefs can influence the way health-related messages are framed within the media. In short, people who are for an issue are more likely to emphasize positive aspects of their position on an issue while downplaying the negative elements than individuals who are against the same issue. You have probably noticed that you can hear radically different viewpoints on the same political issue depending upon whether you are watching Fox News or the Daily Show on Comedy Central.

Some researchers have found that loss frames tend to be more influential in terms of influencing people's attitudes, beliefs, and behaviors (Hale & Dillard, 1995; Meyerowitz & Chaiken, 1987) while others have found gain-framed messages to be more effective in persuading people to change health-related cognitions and behaviors (Rothman, Bartels, Wlaschin, & Salovey, 2006). However, both types of messages have been found to persuade audiences, although many other variables, such as the perceived credibility of the message source and people's cognitive processing abilities, complicate things. As we discuss a variety of political issues related to health in this chapter, think of how you have seen these issues framed in the media by different sources or people/groups with differing political viewpoints.

Current Political Issues Surrounding Health and Healthcare

In this section, we highlight a number of current political issues associated with health and healthcare in the US and, in some cases, how they relate to more global healthcare issues. Toward that end, we focus on the central role of communication plays within these issues, with a particular focus on how health-related political issues are framed within the media.

Health disparities, disadvantaged groups, and access to healthcare issues

Health disparities Unfortunately, who we are, where we live, and how much money we make directly influence our access to quality healthcare and our political power to make changes to the healthcare system. Over a decade ago, the US government set a number of goals for reducing health disparities within the US through a program entitled Healthy People 2010. Despite considerable research, efforts to change health-related policies and legislation, and initiatives to improve the quality of healthcare and provide greater access to traditionally marginalized groups across the country, many of the goals of this program are far from being met. Access to quality healthcare remains inaccessible to disadvantaged populations in the US, including low income people from minority groups, such as African Americans and Latinos, people living in rural areas of the country, and low income older adults, women, and children.

Discrimination and health disparities has also been linked to sexual orientation, with gay, lesbian, and transgendered individuals facing higher levels of depression and substance abuse (Archer, Hoff, & Snook, 2009). For example, African Americans have the highest rates of heart disease, diabetes, and cancer (CDC, 2005). People living in rural areas of the country are less likely than people in urban areas to use recommended preventive screenings for disease, receive treatment for cancer, and visit health providers on a regular basis (Ndiaye *et al.*, 2008). These groups often have lower levels of health literacy and education than more privileged groups in society, and this adds to the difficulty of helping these individuals understand the impact of lifestyle and preventive behaviors on their health. Literacy is related to political power, and it likely influences a person's ability to change their health situation, such as influencing politicians or organizing at a grassroots level.

Many of these disadvantaged populations are marginalized due to factors such as racism, discrimination, inadequacies in government health programs, such as Medicaid and Medicare, and economic policies and practices that favor urban over rural residents in terms of access to adequate healthcare (e.g. it is more economically viable to build a technologically cutting-edge hospital in a large city than in an isolated small town). Individuals from marginalized racial/ethnic groups report dissatisfaction with the US mainstream healthcare system (Ford & Yep, 2008). Studies of African American, Asian American, and Hispanic patients have found that members of these groups frequently report low levels of cultural sensitivity, discrimination, and unsatisfactory treatment from providers (Ford & Yep, 2008; Merrill & Allen, 2003; Saha, Arbelaez, & Cooper, 2003). Lower income individuals and older adults have also been found to encounter negative stereotyping or inadequate treatment by healthcare providers (Becker & Newsom, 2003; Greene & Adelman, 2002). Individuals from rural areas also have been found to face negative stereotypes and discrimination from healthcare providers (Krieger, Moreland, & Sabo, 2010) and often lack adequate access to healthcare due to shortages of providers (especially specialists) in rural areas (Gamm, Castillo, & Pittman, 2003). Discrimination based on race/ethnicity, age, and sexual orientation has been linked to higher levels of substance abuse (Kam & Cleveland, 2011).

Further, large disparities exist between individuals and basic healthcare knowledge, resulting in generally low health literacy levels. While this general lack of health literacy is prominent in many sectors of the population, it is particularly disproportionate among certain demographic groups, showing that certain populations are marginalized under current health education practices. Those who are more vulnerable to health risks, due to lower levels of health literacy, include ethnic minorities, recent immigrants, the elderly, those who suffer from a limited formal education, are socio-economically deprived and have poor access to relevant healthcare information (Kreps, 1986; Kreps & Sparks, 2008; Sparks & Nussbaum, 2008). This also gives evidence that opportunities to increase health literacy may provide a way to lessen inequities in health concerns. Considering healthcare is a public and personal issue, discrepancies over health literacy in terms of patient treatment may also translate into discrepancies over knowledge of the public healthcare system, healthcare reform law, and healthcare decision-making (Sparks, 2008).

For example, the recently passed healthcare legislation is over 2000 pages of complex, legal language. With some 25 percent of the US population being functionally illiterate, it may be assumed that those who receive a limited formal education may have increased difficulty in information acquisition, having to navigate a complex system of healthcare reform law. Therefore these groups may fall into a perpetual cycle of inequity with low health literacy levels and therefore increased vulnerability to personal health risks and confusion in a complex healthcare system. Health literacy has vast implications for health communication researchers and practitioners interested in health information delivery, comprehension, and subsequent medical adherence issues that may arise.

Politicians, government officials, healthcare administrators, physicians, and a variety of interest groups who have economic interests in the healthcare system are also the same individuals who tend to have more political power than those people facing health disparities. Therefore, despite widespread interest in reforming the healthcare system, the individuals with the greatest disparities do not have the political and economic resources to make changes to healthcare that are in their best interest.

Healthcare system problems Despite frequent claims in the media that the US has the best healthcare system in the world, the US actually ranks 37th in the world in terms of healthcare performance ranking. Yet, as a country, we spend more money on healthcare than any other country in the world, and a large number (find percentage) of individuals in the US lack access to adequate healthcare. Even for those individuals who do have some type of health insurance, out-of-pocket expenses related to medical services create a financial burden that many families cannot afford. Recently, one of the authors of this textbook broke his hand and paid more than $5000 for services not covered by his health insurance, including certain physician fees, lab fees, and physical therapy costs. As you can imagine, such a financial burden would be difficult for someone who makes far less money than a university professor (and most likely has less health insurance coverage). The healthcare reform law spearheaded by President Obama is one response to the healthcare crisis. However, as you have likely seen and heard, members of the Tea Party and other groups who oppose what is often referred to as "Obama-care" are frequently seen presenting their arguments against this law in the media. However, in many ways, it may be too early to judge the positive and negative impact of this law since it will take time to assess the degree to which it might help to reduce healthcare costs in the long run. This issue is not going away anytime soon. It will be a crucial and important political health issue to follow all the way to the Supreme Court.

Medical tourism as a response to medical access problems As the cost of healthcare services in the US has steadily increased in recent years along with a the proportion of individuals who are uninsured or underinsured, more and more people are seeking healthcare services that are offered at much cheaper rates in other countries. This practice is known as medical tourism, or travel to foreign countries to obtain cheaper health services. More than 500 000 Americans travel abroad for medical treatment each year to obtain more affordable medical procedures or services (Go, 2008), and it is projected to be a $100 billion industry worldwide by 2012 (Al-Bawaba, 2008). The types of medical services offered in other countries range from cheaply and easily obtaining pharmaceutical products that are tightly controlled in the US (such as Oxycodone or Valium) to relatively minor cosmetic surgeries to complex procedures such as heart valve operations. Yet, the cost of the procedures is considerably less outside the US. For example, a heart bypass operation in the US typically costs more than $130 000 whereas it only costs $11 000 in Thailand. The US loses millions of dollars in medical revenue to other countries around the world. This has led to an increase in web-based advertising for services outside of the US since the Internet allows foreign medical services to circumvent the traditional mass media in the US. Mason & Wright (2011) analyzed medical tourism websites from a number of different countries and found that they largely promote the cost benefits of the medical procedures vis-à-vis having them done in the US as well as the exotic location of the medical facility (e.g. near a beautiful beach in Thailand) while significantly downplaying the risks of obtaining medical services abroad, such as poor postoperative care, questionable credibility of healthcare providers, and legal rights if a person is dissatisfied with services. Consumers should be aware of such biases in web advertisements to avoid dangerous or potentially even more costly medical procedures. However, the political and economic issues associated with access to affordable healthcare in the US may continue to influence people's decisions to opt for medical care abroad, particularly when the cost attractiveness (and the experience of travelling to another country) appears to override the risks involved. For some individuals, the ability to obtain fertility treatments, gender reassignments, and other elective treatments that are not covered within traditional insurance provisions in the US may lure individuals to seek these health services in other countries.

Health Literacy

Health disparities are also related to health literacy. Health literacy is defined by the US DHHS as the capacity to obtain, process, and understand basic health information and services needed to make appropriate health decisions. It is rapidly becoming an important health communication topic and has received national and international attention in the last few years (see www.health.gov/communication/literacy/).

Health literacy is increasingly recognized as a crucial issue affecting communication across the continuum of healthcare (Davis *et al.*, 2002). Recent research shows that on receiving diagnoses of illnesses such as cancer and Alzheimer's disease, patients and their families often face decisions for which they are usually unprepared. Surprisingly, healthcare providers and the medical establishment are often equally unprepared to help patients and their families make decisions that are right for them. In other words, health literacy is an issue for both patients and providers. Treatment choices are often made in an environment of uncertainty, ambiguity, misinformation, high emotion, and anguish, and the outcome ends up being less favorable than recent medical advances could allow (O'Hair, Kreps, & Sparks, 2007 Pecchioni & Sparks, 2007; Sparks, 2003a, 2003b; Sparks, O'Hair, & Kreps, 2007).

Health literacy has been found to affect the health outcomes of individuals. While there is no consensus about the most appropriate way to measure health literacy, it typically deals with four important aspects: (i) cultural and conceptual knowledge; (ii) listening and speaking (oral literacy); (iii) writing and reading (print literacy); and (iv) numeracy (knowledge of statistics and other numeric data used in healthcare). As Merriman, Ades, and Seffrin (2002) point out, most formulae for literacy base their results on sentence length and word difficulty, while word difficulty typically translates to word length. In other words (no pun intended), words of over two syllables are viewed as more difficult than those with fewer syllables. The results are usually expressed as a reading grade level (RGL), sometimes as a decimal or fraction (e.g. "8th RGL" or "12.5 RGL"). The authors further note that there is usually no correspondence between the highest grade level completed and the literacy skills of an individual. Although most adults in the US have completed high school, the average reading grade level is eighth to ninth grade, which is the level of reading most newspapers and television news broadcasts attempt to write at. Of course, similar to many other skills, reading skills atrophy if not used regularly, so people who are not reading consistently after they finish school will have correspondingly lower reading levels (Merriman, Ades, & Seffrin, 2002).

Patients with poor health literacy have a complex array of difficulties with written and oral communication that may limit their understanding of preventive screening and symptoms of diseases like cancer, adversely affecting their stage at diagnosis (Davis *et al.*, 2002). In addition, these barriers impair communication and discussion about risks and benefits of treatment options, as well as patient understanding of informed consent for routine procedures and clinical trials. More research is needed to identify successful methods for educating and communicating with patients who have limited health literacy.

Health-literate physicians tend to be better at communicating with patients. Patients increasingly desire to know more about the state of their health and related diagnoses, and a provider's ability to deliver health information in an appropriate way is now considered a crucial skill (Gillotti & Applegate, 1999; Sparks, 2003a, 2003b). Unfortunately, physicians often still take a routine approach to medicine and patients rather than using an approach tailored to each individual case and patient needs.

Yet, it is important to realize that health literacy is not a one-way street (i.e. the responsibility of healthcare providers). Patients must learn how to gather credible health information from a variety of providers. Consumer health literacy can be quite confusing and daunting. Patients must come to healthcare situations prepared with as much credible information as possible. The healthcare system can be a maze of misinformation. It is the health consumer's job to acquire as much information as possible. When reading health information or talking to health authorities, it is important to understand that statistics about your particular health issue may not necessarily apply to your particular case. Each individual patient has different characteristics that may result in a stronger health outcome (e.g. overall physical health status, genetic predispositions, tolerance for certain medications and treatments). However, it is not surprising that people who simply look at the numbers associated with a certain disease often lose hope, give up, and die without any real knowledge about how they might have responded to certain treatment options that may have resulted in gaining several years or more. Because health literacy is such a complex issue for patients, a variety of patient and caregiver advocacy groups have been formed in recent years (see, e.g. www.pancan.org) in an effort to raise awareness about particular diseases.

Health interventions and disadvantaged populations

Those who are more vulnerable to health risks, are often due to lower levels of health literacy (Sparks, in press). Such at risk groups often consist of ethnic minorities, recent immigrants, the elderly, those who suffer from a limited formal education, those who are socio-economically deprived, and those who have poor access to relevant healthcare information (Kreps, 1986; Kreps & Sparks, 2008; Sparks, in press; Sparks & Nussbaum, 2008; Sparks & Villagran, 2010).

Aside from healthcare legislation, other important mechanisms for reducing health disparities are health campaigns in the media which focus on prevention and treatment of health conditions that have the greatest negative impact on those with health disparities, including heart disease, diabetes, and cancer. These diseases are costly because they are chronic in nature, and they are expense to treat over long periods of time. However, these diseases have been largely linked to lifestyle choices, such as diet and exercise, smoking, and consumption of alcoholic beverages. Moreover, they can often be prevented by early screening practices. Health campaigns targeting disadvantaged groups within the US often emphasize positive lifestyle behavioral changes, education about preventive screenings, and overcoming cultural barriers to changing health behaviors. Such efforts work best when health campaigns also emphasize simple steps people can take to make lifestyle changes and ways that they can access preventive screenings and health services cheaply or at no cost (such as volunteer clinics). Unfortunately, such efforts are often at odds with our profit-based healthcare system, and people with healthcare disparities often mistrust the spokespeople or sources of these campaigns when they are seen as coming from the same groups of people who have exhibited prejudices and discrimination in the past. Cultural misunderstandings and stereotypes about disadvantaged groups can lead to a situation where health campaigns do more harm than good when campaign messages are poorly designed or inadvertently stigmatize members of the target population. For example, African Americans often make healthcare decisions based upon peer and family networks and may not be influenced by a campaign message using a physician as a spokesperson. In such cases, health campaigns that target social settings within African American communities or that use peers, family members, or trusted community leaders may be more effective in terms of changing behaviors (Ndiaye *et al.*, 2011).

In addition, interventions that are designed to enhance provider–patient communication may help to reduce health disparities (Ndiaye *et al.*, 2011). Since provider stereotypes of minority groups have been found to influence the quality of healthcare, interventions should be designed to educate providers about important cultural differences and should teach competent communication strategies for interacting with patients who are members of marginalized groups.

One important health communication research goal, especially of the National Network of Libraries of Medicine (NN/LM), has centered on improving healthcare provider access to health information, especially in rural, underserved, and minority communities (see Sparks, in press; Witte, 1998). Research has generated increasing understanding of how to stimulate desired health behaviors via communication (see Sparks, in press; Sparks & Villagran, 2010).

As Kreps and Sparks (2008) point out, immigrant populations are among the most vulnerable members of American society in terms of experiencing cancer-related health disparities. Similar problems with high levels of cancer morbidity and mortality exist for poor and immigrant populations across the globe, particularly in low and middle income countries. Unfortunately, current efforts are sorely insufficient to provide immigrant populations with relevant health information to empower them to make informed decisions about their best healthcare choices. Health communication can contribute to all aspects of disease prevention and health promotion and is relevant in a number of contexts, including health professional–patient relations, individuals' exposure to, search for, and use of health information, individuals' adherence to clinical recommendations and regimens, the construction of public health messages and campaigns, the dissemination of individual and population health risk information, images of health in the mass media and the culture at large, and the education of consumers about how to gain access to the public health and healthcare systems.

The need for effective communication about health risks and benefits is crucial, yet complex in terms of reaching immigrant populations in the US. Immigrants are often the most vulnerable healthcare consumer populations who are at the greatest risk and experience significantly higher levels of morbidity and mortality than other segments of the population (Kreps & Sparks, 2008), next to older adults (Sparks & Nussbaum, 2008). Vulnerable populations often have significant health literacy barriers and are challenged by cultural barriers to effective communication with their providers as well as difficulties with accessing and making sense of relevant health information (Gazmararian, Williams, Peel, & Baker, 2003). These consumers are often confused and misinformed about healthcare services, early detection guidelines, disease prevention practices, treatment strategies, and the correct use of prescription drugs, which can lead to serious errors and health problems (IOM, 2002).

Moreover, interventions that focus on helping individuals with health disparities utilize family and peer social support to reinforce positive lifestyle changes and to influence preventive screenings may also help to reduce health disparities.

Health Stigma, Discrimination, and Politics

Many health conditions, such as HIV/AIDS, eating disorders, and mental illness are often associated with a stigma, or negative stereotype about the disease. Stigmas about health conditions influence devaluation, discrimination, and denial of access to adequate healthcare treatment (McCarthy, Koval, & MacDonald, 1999). In addition, stigmatized health conditions can become politicized when certain behaviors associated with them are demonized by people holding certain political viewpoints. For example, people with HIV/AIDS have often been blamed by politically conservative groups who denounce such behaviors as sexual relationships between gay men, intravenous drug use, and other behaviors that are seen as morally reprehensible. Even diseases such as lung cancer and liver disease may be politicized if risky behaviors (such as smoking and drinking) are seen as moral issues or resulting from irresponsibility. In such cases, this may lead to "blaming the victim" when encountering a person who is living with a stigmatized illness. Smith (2011) contends that people living with a stigmatized health condition may benefit from understanding how stigma is communicated within society and how people's beliefs about stigmatized health conditions can ultimately pose threats to the stigmatized group's access to rights and access to healthcare resources. In addition, stigmas can influence stigmatized individuals to experience greater levels of stress and limited social support, and social withdrawal.

For example, individuals who are HIV positive are often stigmatized due to their health condition, and this may influence their decision to withdraw from others (rather than seek social support) that may, in turn, lead to greater levels of depression. Depression among people living with HIV has been linked to faster CD4 decline, progression to AIDS, and higher mortality rates (Ickovics *et al.*, 2001; Lesserman, 2003).

Further, recently more attention is being given to reducing stigma and discrimination surrounding mental health (see e.g. Rusch, Angermeyer, & Corrigan, 2005). Individuals struggling with mental health issues often have to struggle with multiple problems. Such individuals, and often their family members, must not only cope with the symptoms of the disease itself, but also may have problems such as recurrent hallucinations, delusions, anxiety, or alterations in mood. These symptoms can make it difficult for someone with a mental illness to work, or to maintain a good quality of daily life. Second, society often stigmatizes and discriminates against such individuals due to a lack of understanding and limited knowledge about mental illnesses (some persons who manage their mental illness well enough to work still have tremendous difficulties finding a job because employers discriminate against them). Thus, mental illness results not only in the difficulties arising from the symptoms of the disease but also in disadvantages through society's reactions. As a further complication, some people with mental illness may accept the common prejudices about mental illness, turn them against themselves, and lose self-confidence.

As Sparks and Villagran (2010) contend, communication is essential to the diagnosis and treatment of an individual's mental health because the symptoms often arise based on what is considered non-normative or atypical behavior. Mental health frequently impacts family, friends, and social support networks months or even years before the person experiencing a mental illness ever sets foot into a doctor's office. The history of interactions that emerge before diagnosis can greatly impact how we view ourselves as well as the way we orient to those around us via communication, which creates our social identities across the life span (Sparks *et al.*, 2010). The mental health continuum from the most severe cases to the more simplistic has communicative and behavioral characteristics that make it distinctively tied to our social identities. Such stigma creates barriers to open communication about mental health with family members and other traditional sources of social support, making patient provider interactions especially important (Sparks *et al.*, 2010).

However, stigmatized groups (and their caregivers) can alter public perceptions surrounding their health condition by organizing communities (both face-to-face and virtual) where individuals can support each other, put pressure on government agencies and healthcare organizations, and through launching communication interventions that utilize educational campaigns focused on changing attitudes and beliefs about stigmatized health conditions (Smith, 2011). In particular, Smith (2011) advocates campaigns that increase interaction between stigmatized and nonstigmatized people. Such campaigns can help to shatter stereotypes and increase empathy for people who are living with stigmatized health issues.

The Medical Marijuana Debate

Television shows like Showtime's "Weeds" and the 2007 film "Super High Me" have poked fun at the medical marijuana usage laws in California. Proposition 215 and Senate Bill 420 in California have made it legal for individuals who possess the proper medical card to access marijuana dispensaries in the state of California. The act has also removed state-level criminal penalties on the use, possession, and cultivation of marijuana by patients who possess a recommendation from their physicians that he or she has a health condition that would benefit from the use of medical marijuana. This law has sparked a great deal of controversy in terms of the risks vs. benefits of using marijuana to treat symptoms of some diseases/health conditions, such as symptoms resulting from AIDS, anorexia, chronic pain, and glaucoma.

Since the passing of the California laws, medical marijuana advocates in other states have sought similar legislation. However, opponents of these laws have used the media as a channel to denounce the laws as immoral, unsafe, and so on. The federal government may ultimately pass legislation that limits or ultimately undermines the California state laws regarding medical marijuana.

Many individuals object to the use of marijuana for medical uses on the grounds that it is a dangerous drug. However, proponents of the medical marijuana point to the benefits marijuana provides individuals living with certain health conditions. While many legal substances, such as alcohol and some prescription medications, can cause much worse health problems than marijuana (especially when they are abused), marijuana usage has traditionally been stigmatized in the US, and it has been portrayed as a dangerous, addictive drug in the media. In other countries, such as the Netherlands, marijuana usage carries less of a stigma, and customers can purchase small quantities of the drug in "coffee shops" in cities like Amsterdam for recreational purposes. Similar to California laws, marijuana possession has been decriminalized in the Netherlands, and the toleration of marijuana usage has not led to increased crime or health problems in that country (Netherlands Ministry of Justice, 2009).

While marijuana certainly has some negative side effects, such as intoxication (similar to alcohol and other drugs) and greater risk for lung cancer among heavy smokers, marijuana does not appear to be a highly addictive or dangerous drug.

However, like alcohol and other controlled substances, most supporters of medical marijuana feel that safeguards should be in place to guard against access by children or driving under the influence. Some medical marijuana users ingest the marijuana in the form of baked goods or candy (also sold at medical marijuana dispensaries) in an effort to avoid possible damage to the lungs (from smoking marijuana). However, a recent decision by the US Justice Department and a report from the Obama administration concluded that marijuana is a dangerous drug that should be classified along with heroin (Goodwin, 2011). Moreover, the Obama administration report came out against decriminalization of marijuana usage and possession as well as denouncing any potential economic benefits of the drug. While the US Justice Department decision and the Obama administration report were not scientific studies of the effects of marijuana (the drug has yet to be evaluated by the Food and Drug Administration), they do reflect the current government trend to be more conservative when considering the use of medical marijuana.

Medical marijuana usage has been portrayed negatively in the media by some political groups (e.g. causing widespread addiction, criminal activity, etc.). The stigma of marijuana being associated with illegal drug use in the US, and spurred by decades of initiatives such as the "War on Drugs," has made it difficult for many individuals to see marijuana use in a positive light. Portrayals of marijuana use in US films and television programs have traditionally exaggerated the effects of using marijuana or they have shown people behaving in mentally unstable ways. In some cases, marijuana users have been seen as going crazy or its use as leading to suicide or fatalities. Even the 1930s film "Reefer Madness" showed people losing their minds and engaging in criminal activities after smoking one joint. These media influences have likely had an effect on the negative stigma of marijuana usage despite scientific evidence pointing to some positive medicinal effects for people with certain health problems. The political fight over medical marijuana use will probably continue to be a frequent issue in the media for years to come.

The Politics of Life and Death

Several political issues surrounding life and death issues have been prominent in the media in recent years. The ways in which these issues are framed in the media (both from media sources that are politically conservative and politically liberal) often frame news stories in ways that are consistent with political beliefs. Two prominent life and death issues that we focus on in this section are right to live/die issues and stem cell research. In this section, we examine both of these issues and how they have been communicated in the media in greater depth.

Right to Life Issues in the Media

In 2005, the media, including television and the Internet, focused its attention for several weeks on the sad and difficult story of Terri Schiavo, a woman who had been kept on life support in a persistent vegetative state. The story soon gained national attention as what started as a private disagreement between her parents and her husband over whether or not to continue life-sustaining treatments elevated into a large-scale debate between individuals who value a "life-at-all-costs" perspective in this situation and people who believe that family members have the right to decide when it is appropriate to remove life support from a loved one who has little chance of returning to a normal life. This obviously was, is, and always will be a delicate political health issue about the ways we view decision-making surrounding life and death, whether from the beginning of life and concerns about when life begins in the womb to concerns about awareness and ways of living near the end-of-life. In the case of Terri Schiavo not only were representatives from political groups from both sides of the issue regularly featured on the news, but talk show hosts, political pundits, blogs, and even Comedy Central's "South Park" were drawn into the controversy, which seemed to escalate to the point where it moved far beyond Terri Schiavo and her family. The escalations likely emerged due to varied political views regarding life, ways of living at points across the lifespan from beginning to end, as well as death and difficult choices regarding end-of-life. Interestingly, the discussions moved quickly from interpersonal and family discussions about how or when or if Terri Schiavo should continue on life support or not and rapidly moved into the greater public sphere. Interpersonal and family decision-making surrounding health decisions is most certainly a different private context than health public policy or media coverage regarding such complex health choices. As consumers, we must cast a critical eye on such differences and the ways they are presented or depicted in the public arena.

This particular incident is just one of many exemplars of on-going debates between individuals who differ politically in terms of the desire to protect life at all costs versus the protection of individual and situational rights when it comes to decisions about when life begins, how it should end, and beyond. These values have become intertwined with larger political views in recent years, and unfortunately this has led to extremely polarized views of life (often associated with partisan politics). It is likely you have seen many debates between groups in America holding different political views in the media in recent years, and they are often centered on issues such as assisted suicide, abortion rights, and even stem cell research. Global views are also very interesting to consider as these debates are carried out in America. For instance, assisted suicide is viewed differently in countries throughout the world (see e.g. BBC, 2011, or assistedsuicide.org).

The Politics of Nutrition

Proper nutrition is an essential part of health, and the food that we eat everyday seems as far away from a political topic as you can get. However, the decisions we make about where our food comes from, the types of food we eat, what big business and advertising tell us to eat, and even government dietary recommendations are often surrounded by politics. You have probably read about animal rights activists and environmentalists protesting fast food restaurant chains like McDonalds in an effort to bring attention to the mistreatment of animals in factory farms or the destruction of the rain forest to create cattle grazing land to ensure that we have a steady supply of Big Macs. The restaurant and food industry in general tends to promote products through the mass media that are often low in nutritional value, highly processed, full of heavily government-subsidized high fructose corn syrup, hormones, and a host of other (often unhealthy) chemicals used in the food preservation process as opposed to healthier, organically grown raw foods that are more nutritional. Fast foods and "junk" foods found at our local grocery stores are often high in calories and fat, and eating such foods over long periods of time has been linked to obesity, diabetes, heart disease, cancer, and a host of other medical problems. The meat and dairy industries have heavily lobbied congress and government agencies to promote their products, despite substantial evidence that a diet that consists of large amounts of meat and dairy is associated with heart disease and cancer.

Over 50 percent of the most devastating diseases in the US have been linked to dietary choices and lack of exercise (Neuhauser & Kreps, 2003). Increased consumption of low-nutrient calorie-dense foods and reduced levels of exercise both contribute to this problem. While we hear quite a bit about the need for exercise in the mass media as a way to ward off obesity, we tend to hear less about the high caloric and fat properties of foods that we eat every day. While exercise is certainly beneficial to guard against obesity, diabetes, and so on, even three hours on the treadmill will do little if you eat a steady diet of cheeseburgers, Coke, candy bars, and Kraft instant macaroni and cheese dinners. Of course, this problem is difficult to battle, considering the economic implications of supporting fast food restaurants and purchasing everyday "convenience" products at the supermarket. Many of the major restaurant chains and companies like Kraft are among the largest corporations in the US, bringing in billions of dollars in revenues and employing large numbers of people. Similar to battles with big tobacco companies in the last 30 years, many activist groups have turned their attention to the food industry in recent years, and they have put increasing pressure on them to discontinue environmentally damaging practices, to reduce the fat and sugar content of foods, and to consider offering the public healthier nutritious food alternatives.

Dr T. Colin Campbell, in his book *The China Study*, describes the impact of the American mainstream diet on our health, and his research has some interesting implications for considering the politics of nutrition and health and how information is conveyed to us through the popular media. During the 1970s, Campbell and his colleagues engaged in several studies in rural China that examined the link between diet and disease. Campbell found high correlations between areas in China where people's diets were heavy in animal protein (meat and dairy) and incidence of colon, breast, stomach, and liver cancer, diabetes, and coronary heart disease. Conversely, he found that individuals who ate a diet that was predominately low in animal protein (plant-based diet) had extraordinarily low levels of cancer, diabetes, and heart disease. Contrary to popular belief, people can get a sufficient amount of protein through eating fruits and vegetables, without the risk of high cholesterol and chemicals found in meat and dairy products (such as casein in cow's milk) that have been linked to health problems (heart disease and cancer). China and other Asian countries, where meat and dairy are consumed at levels that are considerably lower than in the US, generally have much lower incident rates of cancer, heart disease, and diabetes than the US. However, the meat and dairy industries in the US are powerful in terms of having the money (especially compared to many other agricultural groups) to lobby congress and government officials and to launch marketing campaigns to the public. The National Dairy Council, for example, typically has an annual budget of more than $165 million for dairy marketing campaigns, while the National Watermelon Promotion Board has to get by with $1.6 million (Campbell & Campbell, 2006). This might help to explain why you remember slogans like "milk does a body good," but don't remember anything about radishes. Exposure to such marketing campaigns over time has likely influenced our attitudes and beliefs about the health benefits of meat and dairy, despite evidence that they can cause disease (even when consumed in moderation).

Despite the statistical link between diet and disease, most Americans are reluctant to change their dietary habits. From a communication perspective, it appears that the mass media and advertising play an important role in terms of reinforcing the mainstream American diet in this country (Brownell & Horgen, 2004; Harris & Bargh, 2009). Since the food industry pays for advertising space on television and the radio, we are bombarded with advertisements for restaurants and food products that are not only meat and dairy heavy, but are typically high in sugar and fat as well. Obesity in the US has increased dramatically over the past 30 years (Ogden *et al.*, 2006), and this is a major contributor to major health problems. As consumers of the mass media, we learn about food choices at a surprisingly early age. Children who watch television learn that calorie-dense foods that are high in fat and sugar are delicious and rewarding to eat (Horgen, Choate, & Brownell, 2001). Food preferences develop early in the learning process (by the age of two or three), and they tend to predict food preferences later in life, and these preferences tend to be relatively stable (Birch, 1999; Skinner, Carruth, Bounds, & Ziegler, 2002). This may help to explain why health campaigns targeting dietary changes, such as eating more fruits and vegetables, have had limited success (Snyder & Hamilton, 2002).

For decades, fruits and vegetables have been highly regarded as cancer-fighting foods. In fact, the permeating 5 A Day message can be seen in produce aisles, magazine ads, and schools, and was supported in part by the National Cancer Institute. The campaign is little-by-little changing to Fruits and Veggies: More Matters (see Harvard School of Public Health, nd). According to the Harvard School of Public Health, the latest research suggests that the biggest payoff from eating fruits and vegetables is for the heart. See also CDC (nd).

Preferences for food appear to be solidified early in our lives, depending in large part on what we were exposed to in our early years. In other words, if you never liked broccoli as a kid, you will probably have a hard time learning to enjoy it as an adult. Harris & Bargh (2009) found that college students' unhealthy food preferences and diet were linked to prior television exposure. However, parental communication about diet was found to also influence food preferences and diet later in life, so this may be one potential way to offset the media's influence on our diet in future interventions.

International Health Communication Issues

Advances in technology, including communication technologies and globalization has led to a world that is more interconnected than at any other time in history. Environmental decisions that are made in China, such as government regulation of carbon emissions, or the decision to rely on factory farming in the US affect the entire planet (not just the countries individually). As we saw in Chapter 9, climate change, economic disruptions due to natural and human made disasters, and pandemics such as HIV and avian 'flu can affect people's health and well-being on a global level. With this global interdependency among nations, we see more and more international political debates regarding the best policies and practices individual countries should follow to prevent health risks and promote healthy behaviors. We can no longer afford to think of the US as an isolated nation in terms of our business practices, culture, and the individual behaviors we engage in since many of them have a wide-reaching effect on the health of the planet.

Climate change increases health hazards throughout the world by decreasing air quality, stimulating more extreme weather events, creating conditions that favor increases in food, water, and vector-borne infections, and enhancing heat stress conditions (Villagran, Weathers, O'Keefe, & Sparks, 2008). All of these conditions have great potential to negatively impact our health worldwide.

Although many people consider climate change as a threat to only wildlife and the environment, climate change also has significant implications for human health (Costello *et al.*, 2009; Maibach, Roser-Renouf, & Leiserowitz, 2008). Climate change literacy can make a huge difference as it is tied to individuals' existing relevant health issues. Patients experiencing climate change-related illness need more information and context about those health issues that result from environmental hazards (Villagran *et al.*, 2008). According to recent estimates by the World Health Organization, 24 percent of all illness in the world and 23 percent of deaths are due to adjustable environmental factors (Pruss-Ustun & Corvalan, 2006).

Healthcare providers are often influential leaders in the community, and, as such, could have a huge impact on increasing understanding, knowledge, efficacy, and subsequent behavior related to climate change (Villagran *et al.*, 2008).

Summary

Understanding the political underpinnings of health issues is important to the study of health communication, particularly in terms of how political beliefs are framed and disseminated by the media. In addition, it is important to understand how exposure to various political views through the media and everyday sources of communication influence people's existing attitudes and beliefs regarding health-related issues. In the new media environment, individuals have more choices than ever to obtain information from media sources that are consistent with their existing political beliefs. In addition, Web 2.0 technologies allow people to broadcast their political views and participate in political discussions at a mass level through blogs, Facebook, YouTube, and other channels. As we have seen, there are a variety of political issues surrounding health and healthcare. An understanding of the sources of political messages about health, characteristics of how these messages are framed, and the effects of these messages on audiences has become an important component of health communication research in recent years, and it will likely continue to spur additional research in the future.

References

Al-Bawaba, A. (2008). Medical tourism worth $100 billion by 2012. Retrieved July 14, 2008 from: http://www.albawaba.com/en/countries/UAE/226561.

Archer, R., Hoff, G. L., & Snook, W. D. (2009). Tobacco use and cessation among men who have sex with men. *American Journal of Public Health, 95*, 929.

BBC. (2011). Switzerland: Zurich votes to keep assisted suicide. Retrieved 19 July, 2012, from http://www.bbc.co.uk/news/world-europe-13405376.

Becker, G., & Newsom, E. (2003). Socioeconomic status and dissatisfaction with health care among chronically ill African Americans. *American Journal of Public Health, 93*, 742–748.

Bevan, J. L., Sparks, L., Ernst, J., Francies, J., & Santora, N. (in press). Information sources in relation to information quality, information-seeking, and uncertainty in the context of healthcare reform. In R. Ahmed & B. R. Bates (Eds), *Health Communication and Mass Media: Applying Research to Public Health Policy and Practice.* Farnham, UK: Gower Publishers.

Birch, L. L. (1999). Development of food preferences. *Annual Review of Nutrition, 19*, 41–62.

Block, G., & Keller, P. (1995). When to accentuate the negative: The effects of perceived efficacy and message framing on intentions to perform a health-related behavior. *Journal of Marketing Research, 32*, 192–203.

Brownell, K. D., & Horgen, K. B. (2004). *Food fight: The inside story of the food industry. America's obesity crisis, and what we can do about it.* New York: McGraw-Hill.

Centers for Disease Control (CDC). (2005). Health disparities experienced by racial/ethnic minority populations—United States. *Morbidity and Mortality Weekly Report; 54*, 1–3.

Centers for Disease Control (CDC). (nd). Fruits and vegetables. Retrieved July 22, 2012, from http://www.fruitsandveggiesmatter.gov/.

Costello, A., Abbas, M., Allen, A., Ball, S., Bell, S., & Bellamy, R. *et al.* (2009). Managing the health effects of climate change. *Lancet, 373*, 1693–1733.

Crowley, S. (2012). Health care reform and the Supreme Court (Affordable Care Act). *New York Times*, July 29. Retrieved August 1, 2012, from http://topics.nytimes.com/top/reference/timestopics/organizations/s/supreme_court/affordable_care_act/index.html.

Davis, T. C., Williams, M. V., Marin, E., Parker, R. M., & Glass, J. (2002). Health literacy and communication. *CA: A Cancer Journal for Clinicians, 52*, 134–149.

Doherty, R. (2010). The certitudes and uncertainties of health care reform. *Annals of Internal Medicine, 152*, 679–682.

Dutta-Bergman, M. J. (2004). Primary sources of health information: Comparisons in the domain of health attitudes, health cognitions, and health behaviors. *Health Communication, 16*, 273–288.

Entman, R. M. (1991). Framing: Towards clarification of a fractured paradigm. *Journal of Communication, 43*, 51–58.

Ford, A. L., & Yep, G. A. (2003). Working along the margins: Developing community-based strategies for communicating about health with marginalized groups. In T. L. Thompson, A. M. Dorsey, K. I. Miller, & R. Parrott (Eds), *Handbook of health communication* (pp. 241–262). Mahwah, NJ: Erlbaum.

Gamm, L., Castillo, G., & Pittman, S. (2003). Access to quality health services in rural areas—Primary care. In L. D. Gamm, L. L. Hutchison, B. J. Dabney, & A. Dorsey (Eds), *Rural healthy people 2010: A companion document to healthy people 2010* (Vol. 1., pp. 45–51). College Station, TX: The Texas A & M University System Health Science Center, School of Rural Public Health, Southwest Rural Health Research Center.

Gazmararian JA, Williams MV, Peel J, Baker, DW. (2003). Health literacy and knowledge of chronic disease. *Patient Education and Counseling, 51*, 267–275.

Gill, E. A., & Babrow, A. S. (2007). To hope or to know: Coping with uncertainty and ambivalence in women's magazine breast cancer articles. *Journal of Applied Communication Research, 35*, 133–155.

Gillotti, C. M., & Applegate, J. L. (1999). Explaining illness as bad news: Individual differences in explaining illness-related information. In B. B. Whaley (Ed.), *Explaining illness: Research, theory, and strategies* (pp. 101–120). Mahwah, NJ: Lawrence Erlbaum.

Go, P. (2008). Why is medical tourism so popular in America? Retrieved July 22, 2012, from http://ezinearticles.com/?Why-Is-Medical-Tourism-So-Popular-In-America&id=1170333.

Goodwin, L. (2011). Obama administration slams medical marijuana. Retrieved July 22, 2012, from http://news.yahoo.com/blogs/lookout/obama-administration-slams-medical-marijuana-194852453.html.

Greene, M. G., & Adelman, R. D. (2001). Building the physician-older patient relationship. In M. L. Hummert & J. F. Nussbaum (Eds), *Aging, communication, and health: Linking research and practice for successful aging* (pp. 101–120). Mahwah, NJ: Lawrence Erlbaum.

Hale, J. L., & Dillard, J. P. (1995). Fear appeals in health promotion campaigns: Too much talk, too little, or just right? In E. Maiback & R. L. Parrott (Eds), *Designing health messages: Approaches from communication theory and public health practice* (pp. 65–80). Thousand Oaks, CA: Sage.

Harris, J. L., & Bargh, J. A. (2009). Television viewing and unhealthy diet: Implications for children and media interventions. *Health Communication, 24*, 660–673.

Harvard School of Public Health. (nd). The nutrition source. Vegetables and fruits: Get plenty every day. Retrieved 22 July, 2012, from http://www.hsph.harvard.edu/nutritionsource/what-should-you-eat/vegetables-full-story/.

Horgen, K. B., Choate, M., & Brownell, K. D. (2001). Television food advertising: Targeting children in a toxic environment. In D. G. Singer and J. L. Singer (Eds), *Handbook of children and the media*. Sage: California. pp. 447–461.

Ickovics, J. R., Hamburger, M. E., Vlahov, D., Schoenbaum, E. E., Schuman, P., Boland, R. J. *et al.* (2001). Mortality, CD4 cell count decline, and depressive symptoms among HIV-seropositive women: Longitudinal analysis from the HIV Epidemiology Research Study. *Journal of the American Medical Association, 285*, 1460–1465.

Institute of Medicine (IOM). (2002). *Unequal treatment: Confronting racial and ethnic disparities in health care.* Washington, DC: National Academy of Sciences Press.

Kreps, G. L., & Sparks, L. (2008). Meeting the health literacy needs of vulnerable populations. *Patient Education and Counseling, 71*(3), 328–332.

Krieger, J. L., Moreland, J., & Sabo, J. (2010, November). Hillbilly or redneck? Linguistic stereotypes of rural Americans. Paper presented to the Intercultural Division at the annual meeting of the National Communication Association, November 15–19, San Francisco, CA.

Lesserman, J. (2003). HIV disease progress: Depression rates, stress, and possible mechanisms. *Biological Psychiatry, 54*, 295–306.

Levin, I. P., & Gaeth, G. L.(1988). Framing of attribute information before and after consuming the product. *Journal of Consumer Research, 15*, 374–378.

Maibach, E. W., Roser-Renouf, C., & Leiserowitz, A. (2008). Communication and marketing as climate change–intervention assets: A public health perspective. *American Journal of Preventive Medicine, 35*, 488–500.

Mason, A., & Wright, K. B. (2011). Framing medical tourism: An examination of appeal, risk, convalescence, accreditation, and interactivity in medical tourism websites. *Journal of Health Communication, 16*, 163–177.

McCarthy, G. M., Koval, J. J., & MacDonald, J. K. (1999). Factors associated with refusal to treat HIV-infected patients: The results of a national survey of dentists in Canada. *American Journal of Public Health, 89*, 541–545.

Merrill, R. M., & Allen, E. W. (2003). Racial and ethnic disparities in satisfaction with doctors and health problems in the United States. *Ethnicity & Disease, 13*, 492–498.

Merriman, B., Ades, T., & Seffrin, J. R. (2002). Health literacy in the information age: Communicating cancer information to patients and families. *CA: A Cancer Journal for Clinicians, 52*, 130–133.

Meyerowitz, B., & Chaiken, S. (1987). The effects of message framing on breast self-examination attitudes, intentions and behaviors. *Journal of Personality and Social Psychology, 52*, 500–510.

Netherlands Ministry of Justice. (1999). Fact sheet: Dutch drugs policy. Utrecht: Trimbos Institute, Netherlands Institute of Mental Health and Addiction. Retrieved 22 July 2012, from http://www.minjust.nl:8080/a_beleid/fact/cfact7.htm.

Neuhauser, L., & Kreps, G. L., (2003). Rethinking communication in the e-health era. *Journal of Health Psychology, 8*, 7–23.

Ndiaye, K., Krieger, J. L., Warren, J. R., & Hecht, M. L. (2011). Communication and health disparities. In T. L. Thompson, R. Parrott, & J. F. Nussbaum (Eds), *The Routledge handbook of health communication, 2nd ed.* (pp. 469–481.). New York: Routledge.

Ogden, C. L., Carroll, M. D., Curtin, L. R., McDowell, M. A., Tabak, C. J., & Flegal, R. M. (2006). Prevalence of overweight and obesity in the United States, 1999–2004. *JAMA, 295*, 1549–1555.

O'Hair, H. D., Kreps, G. L., & Sparks, L., (2007). Conceptualizing cancer care and communication. In H. D. O'Hair, G. L. Kreps & L. Sparks (Eds), *Handbook of communication and cancer care* (pp. 1-12). Cresskill, NJ: Hampton Press.

Pecchioni, L. L., & Sparks, L. (2007). Health information sources of individuals with cancer and their family members. *Health Communication, 21*(2), 143–151.

Price, V., & Tewksbury, D. (1997). News value and public opinion: A theoretical account of media priming and framing. In G. Barnett & F. J. Bosters (Eds), *Progress in communication sciences* (pp. 214–257). New York: Ablex.

Pruss-Ustun, A., & Corvalan, C. (2006). *Presenting disease through health environments.* Paris: World Health Organization (WHO).

Rothman, A. J., Martino, S. C., Bedell, B. T., Detweiler, J., & Salovey, P. (1999). The systematic influence of gain and loss-framed messages on interest in and use of different types of health behavior. *Personality and Social Psychology Bulletin, 25*, 1355–1369.

Rothman, A. J., Bartels, R. D., Wlaschin, J., & Salovey, P. (2006). The strategic use of gain- and loss-framed messages to promote health behavior: How theory can inform practice. *Journal of Communication, 56*, S202–S220.

Rusch, N., Angermeyer, M. C., & Corrigan, P. W. (2005). Mental illness stigma: Concepts, consequences, and initiatives to reduce stigma. *European Psychiatry, 20*, 529–539.

Saha, S., Arbelaez, J. J., & Cooper, L. A. (2003). Patient-physician relationships and racial disparities in the quality of health care. *American Journal of Public Health, 93*, 1713–1719.

Skinner, J. D., Carruth, B. R., Bounds, W., & Ziegler, P. J. (2002). Children's food preferences: A longitudinal analysis. *Journal of the American Dietetic Association, 102*, 1638–1647.

Smith, R. A. (2011). Stigma, communication, and health. In T. L. Thompson, R. Parrott, & J. F. Nussbaum (Eds), *The Routledge handbook of health communication, 2nd ed.* (pp. 455–468.). New York: Routledge

Snyder, L. B., & Hamilton, M. A. (2002). A meta-analysis of US health campaign effects on behavior: Emphasize enforcement, exposure, and new information, and beware the secular trend. In R. C. Hornik(Ed.), *Public health communication: Evidence for behavior change* (pp. 357–383.). Mahwah, NJ: Lawrence Erlbaum Associates.

Sparks, L. (in press). Health communication and caregiving research, policy, and practice. *Caregiving across the professions: A multi-disciplinary, coordinated perspective.* Springer.

Sparks, L. (Ed.). (2003a). Cancer communication and aging [Special issue]. *Health Communication, 15*(2).

Sparks, L. (2003b). An introduction to cancer communication and aging: Theoretical and research insights. *Health Communication, 15*, 123–132.

Sparks, L. (2011) Health messages and decision-making. TED talk on health message framing and decision-making at TEDx Orange Coast. Retrieved on 9 July, 2012, from http://www.youtube.com/watch?v=d4JNyyuonko.

Sparks, L., & Villagran, M. (2010). *Patient and provider interaction: A global health communication perspective.* Cambridge: Polity Press.

The Commonwealth Fund (2010). What will happen under health reform – and what's next? *Columbia Journalism Review*, 1–12. http://www.commonwealthfund.org/~/media/Files/Publications/Other/2010/2010_CJR_insert_What_Next_web_415.pdf

Villagran, M. M., Weathers, M. Keefe, B., & Sparks, L. (2010). Medical providers as global warming and climate change health educators: A health literacy approach. *Communication Education, 59*(3), 312–327.

Chapter 13

Epilogue: Looking Toward the Future of Health Communication Research

Throughout each chapter of this book, we have tried to highlight various research and theoretical trends within the various contexts of health communication research. As we have seen, these contexts range from provider–patient communication, caregiving, social support, organizational communication to the use of new technologies, mass communication, health communication campaigns, and political communication. While the highlighted research and theories in these areas will most likely continue to develop in the coming years, changes within society, healthcare, and communication technologies point to a number of emerging trends in health communication that will likely become important in the future.

This chapter briefly highlights a number of promising areas of health communication research that will likely be research trends in the future. Toward that end, the chapter will focus on a variety of topics, such as media convergence and self-care, mental health issues, emerging trends in intercultural health communication, research, developments in risk/crisis communication research. Moreover, the chapter will briefly discuss some of the limitations to current health communication research.

Emerging Trends and Challenges in Health and New Communication Technologies

As we continue into the second decade of the 21st century, various new communication technologies will continue to be developed and adopted by the public. The applications of these technologies will lead to further transformation of provider–patient interaction, social support, communication with healthcare organizations, health communication campaigns, and many other aspects of communication.

For example, as innovations in computer technology, wireless technology, biofeedback, software, applications, satellite technology, and many other areas take place,

Health Communication in the 21st Century, Second Edition. Kevin Bradley Wright, Lisa Sparks, and H. Dan O'Hair.
© 2013 John Wiley & Sons, Inc. Published 2013 by John Wiley & Sons, Inc.

these developments will likely lead to greater media convergence (or the combination of several technologies), which will likely lead to devices and applications that will provide greater convenience, efficiency, and in some cases, lower costs. For those of you who have iPhones or iPads, use social networking sites, smart phone applications, and so on, you probably have a good sense of how rapidly technology changes. As we have seen in this book, similar changes are occurring in the world of health as we speak, including the shift to electronic medical records, smart phone/computer applications for monitoring health status, increases in computer-mediated support for health issues, and computerized message tailoring in health campaigns. These innovations will likely be transformed as they are integrated with or replaced by even newer innovations.

These rapid changes in new communication technologies will present numerous challenges for health communication scholars in terms of research and theory development. As new technologies are adopted, this will add complexity to the study of how technologies are used and the effects that they have on health outcomes. New models and theories will likely need to be developed by health communication scholars to provide cogent explanations of their use and effects on the public.

In terms of implementing technologies in practical ways so that they will have the greatest impact on the health of those individuals who face the greatest healthcare needs, a number of barriers will likely provide challenges to health communication researchers and other scientists, government agencies, and healthcare providers. The barriers include limited access to new technologies due to limited financial resources, lower levels of education and literacy for certain populations as well as the costs to organizations, and other factors, such as the reluctance of researchers, administrators, and providers to adopt these technologies.

Emerging Trends and Challenges in Communication and Mental Health Issues

Healthcare consumers with mental health issues are often particularly vulnerable to health risks and have unique communication needs that have to be adequately addressed to provide them with the relevant health information they need to preserve their health. According to the Substance Abuse and Mental Health Services Administration, each year, nearly one in five US adults—which amounts to more than 45 million people—will experience some form of mental illness. In larger states like California, this means 7.4 million adults suffer from mental illness. Due to the stigma and embarrassment often associated with mental health problems, many of these people fail to receive the professional help they need.

Mental health messages in entertainment and news media have gained the attention of health communication researchers and non-profit organizations such as California Mental Health Services Authority (CalMHSA). Such organizations often work with the Entertainment Industries Council and dozens of related organizations to implement campaigns related to the responsible depiction of mental health issues in both entertainment and news media.

Some examples include: evaluating news stories reporting on suicide, TV shows depicting someone going through detox, if bipolar and schizophrenic symptoms are depicted accurately, looking at the accuracy of the science of prescription drugs such as abuse of painkillers, and many other representations of mental illness. The goal of this initiative is to ensure mental health issues are depicted responsibly in the news and entertainment media—print included—as well as reduction of stigma and discrimination associated with the invisible or less visible illnesses facing our society.

Emerging Trends and Challenges in Intercultural Health Communication

Campaigns to address intercultural health issues, ranging from the focus on health disparities among immigrants and other minority groups within the US to global health needs, are becoming increasingly important to understand from a health communication perspective. Such approaches involve transdisciplinary, multi-level integrated research to shed light on the complex interactions of the social and physical environment, behavioral factors, and biological pathways that determine health and disease in underserved populations, all of which can lead to understanding and reducing health disparities.

The need for effective communication about health risks and benefits is particularly acute, yet also tremendously complex, for reaching immigrant populations in the US, the most vulnerable healthcare consumer populations who are at greatest risk of suffering significantly higher levels of morbidity and mortality than other segments of the population. Often, these immigrant populations are among the poorest, lowest educated, and most disenfranchised members of modern society, and experience disparities in health outcomes, resulting in alarming levels of morbidity and mortality. Vulnerable populations often have significant health literacy difficulties, are challenged by intercultural communication barriers to accessing and making sense of relevant health information, and are often confused and misinformed about healthcare services, early detection guidelines, disease prevention practices, treatment strategies, and the correct use of prescription drugs, which can lead to serious errors and health problems.

Members of vulnerable immigrant populations who suffer significant health disparities are desperately in need of culturally relevant, accurate, and timely health information. Members of these vulnerable groups often include elderly, immigrant, socio-economically deprived, and minority healthcare consumers. Many vulnerable immigrant consumers in the US are non-native English speakers and encounter serious language barriers and health literacy challenges that necessitate adaptive, culturally sensitive communication strategies to provide them with needed health information.

Sometimes, healthcare providers may have trouble communicating in cross-cultural conversations due to language barriers. These instances can lead to what seem like confounding messages regarding causes of illness and appropriate treatment when cancer patients are from different cultures. Additionally, stereotypes can also inhibit openness among patients and providers when they view their patients' differing cultural beliefs or values about illness and treatments as inferior to their own. Due to this factor, researchers have found that people frequently seek out healthcare providers who share similar cultural backgrounds to their own, with the belief that they share the same values, or they may commonly rely on family members (who may or may not have medical knowledge) to provide care. This is a type of conversion strategy in which people seek out others who are similar to themselves. Culturally sensitive health communication is essential to providing vulnerable consumers with relevant information about health promotion and healthcare.

Emerging Trends and Challenges in Risk/Crisis Communication

Risk communication will continue to be a growing area of health communication research in the coming years. As we say in Chapter 9, risk communication deals with a wide range of issues involving health/risk information and preparation strategies to the public and key state and local government and non-government response partners before a tragic event occurs. Risk communication strategies for public health preparedness often concern agriculture, food, water issues; infectious disease and vaccines; mental health and general public health; as well as chemical, biological, nuclear, and radiological threats. Risk communication can be on a range of issues from frightening diseases such as cancer and AIDS to mental health to earthquakes and tsunamis (e.g. Japan) violence in schools (e.g. Virginia Tech University). Scientific uncertainty about diseases sometimes leads people to wonder about the possible ways in which they may have contracted them.

Through risk communication, the communicator hopes to provide the receiver with information about the expected type (good or bad) and magnitude (weak or strong) of an outcome from a behavior or exposure. Typically, it is a discussion about an adverse outcome and the probability of that outcome occurring. In some instances, risk communication has been employed to help an individual make a choice about whether or not to undergo a medical treatment, continue to live next to a nuclear power plant, pass on genetic risks, or elect to vaccinate a healthy baby against whooping cough. In some cases, risk communication is used to help individuals adjust to the knowledge that something that has already occurred, such as an exposure to harmful carcinogens, may put them at greater risk for a negative health outcome, such as cancer, in the future.

Advances in risk communication are more common than before. Federal agencies such as the CDC provide off-the-shelf communication programs than can be used by professionals seeking to formulate messages that have a greater chance of success with the public. The US Department of Homeland Security offers a Message Mapping program that provides step-by-step instructions for developing messages that resonate with particular audiences. As research continues to advance in risk communication, the chances will be greater that less harm and injury will be observed due to more effective warnings, reminders, and precautions. The investment in this research will be will spent to safeguard the public.

Ongoing Theoretical, Methodological, and Dissemination Issues Surrounding Health Communication Research

Conducting social science research in any context presents numerous challenges to researchers. Despite the best research ideas, methodological designs, and the research analysis skills of health communication scholars, every research study has limitations. These limitations can be things that were overlooked by the research, problems that stem from study participants, or the problems in terms of disseminating the research in a meaningful way so that it ultimately changes health behaviors or has an impact on the intended population.

Despite the immense contributions of scholars representing many disciplines to the body of health communication research, health communication is still a relatively young area of the communication discipline. As such, there is a need for new theory development and innovative approaches to studying health communication. As we have seen in this book, the health communication landscape is broad, and there are still many aspects of health communication that are poorly understood. In the future, more interdisciplinary work is needed that will bring together researchers from disciplines as varied as medicine, psychology, sociology, political science, communication, nursing, pharmacology, computer science, and public health. Such efforts are needed to refine and create new theories and research approaches that will better meet the needs of individuals facing health concerns.

For example, many health communication researchers rely on undergraduate student samples in experimental and survey research, and this limits the generalizability of study findings. To be fair, health communication scholars tend to be better than many other areas of the communication discipline in terms of conducting research on non-student populations, including cancer patients, minority groups facing health disparities, and older adults living with health problems. However, it can be difficult for researchers to gain access to these populations. Even when it is possible, finding suitable methods for researching these individuals can be challenging. There are a host of ethical and practical considerations when studying populations who are facing certain illnesses, discrimination, and low literacy. Moreover, all research methods have limitations. Surveys only allow us to draw certain conclusions about the relationships among variables measured in a questionnaire. Content analysis approaches do not always account for the massive amount of messages or information in contexts such as social networking sites or hospital websites. Naturalistic designs are limited to the experiences of a relatively small number of individuals. Experimental designs can be cumbersome, and researchers may have a difficult time attempting to study certain populations using tightly controlled experimental designs. In addition, experimental designs can lack realism and not accurately reflect what goes on in terms of health behaviors outside of the laboratory.

Finally, health communication researchers need to do a better job disseminating the results of empirically based research in a meaningful way to the populations who are most likely to benefit from the study findings. One barrier that contributes to this is the fact that most health communication researchers are highly educated individuals who possess an impressive array of research skills. Researchers are used to communicating their research findings to fellow scholars through journal articles, book chapters, and conference papers as opposed to individuals in the larger population who may have relatively little understanding of scientific research methods, theories, statistics, and academic jargon. Yet, this way of communicating research findings may have little impact on the members of populations who are in most need of understanding the implications of the research. In order for health communication research to be transformational, researchers, public health officials, and providers must find ways translate the research findings and their implications to specific easy-to-understand language. In addition, in order to find better ways to reach at-risk populations and provide members with the information they need, researchers, public health officials, and providers much do their part in terms of gaining a more comprehensive understanding of the needs, cultural norms, barriers, and characteristics of these populations.

Summary

Health communication will continue to be a vibrant area of research within communication and other disciplines. In the relatively short history of health communication research, scholars have made immeasurable contributions to our understanding of the nature of health and the key role that communication plays in a wide variety of health issues. Among these are key insights into patient–provider interaction, a deeper understanding of social support and health, recommendations to providers and health campaign designers about how to better reach and serve multicultural populations, and increased knowledge of how to better influence people to change risky behaviors that can damage health and maintain behaviors that are more likely to lead to lasting good health. However, as we have seen throughout the book and in this chapter, health communication scholars are faced with numerous challenges in terms of conducting research and translating that research into practical recommendations that will have the greatest effect on the public and the healthcare system.

Index

Health Communication in the 21st Century, Second Edition. Kevin Bradley Wright, Lisa Sparks,
and H. Dan O'Hair.
© 2013 John Wiley & Sons, Inc. Published 2013 by John Wiley & Sons, Inc.